集刊

集人文社科之思 刊专业学术之声

集 刊 名：水历史与水文明研究
主　　编：郑晓云
主办单位：水利部宣传教育中心
中国长江文化研究院
湖北大学历史文化学院
主编单位：湖北大学水历史与水文明研究所

WATER HISTORY AND WATER CIVILIZATION STUDIES (Vol.1)

第 1 辑

集刊序列号：PIJ-2019-377
中国集刊网：www.jikan.com.cn
集刊投约稿平台：www.iedol.cn

水历史与水文明研究

（第1辑）

郑晓云 主编

WATER HISTORY
AND WATER CIVILIZATION
STUDIES（Vol.1）

社会科学文献出版社
SOCIAL SCIENCES ACADEMIC PRESS (CHINA)

卷首语

水是生命赖以生存的基本物质，因此人类从生命开始的时候就必不可少地与水产生互动。在人类的长期生存发展过程中，水伴随着人类的足迹从远古走到今天，写就了一部人和水的历史。

在人类生存的自然环境中，不论是丰水地区还是干旱半干旱地区，亦不论河流流域还是湖泊畔、海洋边、崇山中，自然的水资源状况都不足以满足、适合人类的生存和发展，都必须要进行有效的水治理，营造一个适合居住和生计的环境，同时通过相应的技术手段和工具有效地利用水资源，满足生存和发展需要。因此自古以来，人类就通过治理河流、修筑堤坝来改善水供给、控制洪涝、营造良好的居住环境，同时通过各种方式收集利用雨水、获取地下水，引用泉水、河水等，满足生活和生产需要。因此，人类历史上出现了包括古代中国巨大的河流治理工程、古罗马时期宏大城市水利工程、中亚地区庞大的坎儿井工程、伊比利亚半岛上的埃塞克亚引水系统工程等在内的伟大的水利工程体系。

水利工程建设不仅改善了人们的居住环境和生产条件，而且促进了人类社会的发展。城市集中供水、远程调水等水利用系统形成于两三千年以前的古代社会，因水而形成的生活方式包括浴室沐浴、水冲厕所等至今仍然在人类社会中延续。世界各地的人们都拥有和水相关的生活方式。水的利用也构建了人类社会中的相关社会关系，人类也通过这些关系去维系水的公平有效利用。自古以来水也在人类的精神活动中扮演了重要的角色，水给人以启发和愉悦，人类依水而进行精神活动和创造。水不仅在人类最根本的生命维持过程中起到重要作用，同时在构建人类的精神世界、建设生存环境、获取生存资源、发展生产过程中也起到了重要作用。

水在人类文明的构建和发展过程中扮演了重要角色。古代埃及文明、中华文明、古希腊文明、罗马文明、古印度文明、玛雅文明等的兴盛都和水有直接的关系。与此同时，在跨越民族和国家的世界文明体系中，水同样是必不可少的构建要素，例如在基督教、伊斯兰教和佛教这三大宗教中，水的含义和使用都成为不可缺少的元素。在人类的历史发展过程中，不同的文明都形成了以水为核心的一种亚文明形态——水文明。水文明是基于水而构建起来的文明形态，有相应的理念、文化现象、制度、社会生活和物质建设作为支撑，这在人类历史上都可以获得广泛的印证。因此人类的发展史也是一部与水的互动史和水的人文史。不理解水在人类社会历史发展过程中的支撑作用和在人类文明发展过程中的构建作用，就不能真正认识人类的历史。

水是打开认识人类历史和人类文明之门的一把钥匙。我们今天仍然有必要去深入研究水和人类社会历史发展的关系，以及水对人类文明的支撑作用，这不仅仅是一种学术发展的需要，更是人类可持续发展的需要。通过对水历史的探究，从另一个角度去认识人类的社会历史发展，同时也总结历史经验教训，延续人类水文明的基因，夯实今天人类可持续发展的文化基础。历史的探究对保护水资源和环境、应对全球水危机、实现水的可持续利用有重要的价值。

水历史的研究和实践是近年来国际上备受关注的一个领域，也受到了联合国教科文组织的推动。联合国教科文组织曾经设立水历史项目，推动全球水历史的研究和开展学术活动。2001 年，在联合国教科文组织的推动下，正式成立了国际水历史学会，该机构成为全球水历史水科学活动的一个平台。联合国教科文组织也把“水与文明”这个主题放在重要位置，推动对水和文明相互关系的探索研究和水在可持续发展过程中的运用。很多有影响的国际科学组织也都把水历史作为重要的工作内容。近年来水历史研究交流活动在国际上十分活跃，每年都有很多相关的国际会议召开，取得了丰硕的成果。

《水历史与水文明研究》这本集刊的创办，正是在以上大背景下启动的。我们希望以此为平台，发表国内外学者的学术研究成果，开展相关的学术活动，促进学术交流。在未来的办刊中，我们将秉持以下几个方面的原则：一是坚持学术标准，发表有较高质量的研究文章。二是立足于中国丰厚的水历史研究资源，探讨水与中华文明形成和发展的关系，探讨中国博大精深的水历史与水生态文明建设的一脉传承。三是秉持国际化的理念，把这本集刊办成一份国际化的刊物，不仅关注中国的水历史和水文明研究，同时也关注海外的水历史和水文明研究。与此同时，不仅刊发中文的稿件，也将刊发一部分英文稿件，使之成为国际学术交流的一个平台。四是探讨通过历史研究服务于当代生态文明建设和应对水危机，普及水的人文科学知识，对公众水情教育做出贡献。

在即将付梓的这部首卷中，我们不仅编发了关于中国水利史研究的论文，也刊发了中国学者对海外水历史和水文明研究的成果。同时我们还刊发了海外学者的研究论文，向中国读者分享海外水历史和水文明的研究成果。本期重点刊发了关于希腊水历史的一组文章，研究探讨希腊这个古老文明中水的历史角色，相信读者会从中受到启迪。

本集刊在初创之期，要达到创办的目标不仅需要编者付出艰辛的努力，同样也需要专家学者和社会各界的鼎力支持，提出中肯的意见，赐予研究成果，关心支持这本集刊的成长。

编　者

2020 年 3 月

目　录

特　稿

特辑：古代希腊水历史

水与社会

海外水历史

水信仰

水情势

Content

Special Contribution

Special Issue: Water History of Ancient Greece

Water and Society

Overseas Water History

Water Belief

Current Water Situation

特　稿

中国古代水利的基本内容及主要特征

郭　涛*

摘　要： 本文概要叙述了中国古代水利及水利科学技术的产生和发展，以及防洪治河、农田水利、人工运河、城市水利四个基本组成部分形成发展的脉络，着重指出并分析了六个主要特征，即历史性与连续性、系统性与完备性、地域性与多样性、实践性与普及性、综合性与交叉性、经验性与局限性，为更好地了解和认识中国水利历史提供一个思考框架和参考背景。

关键词： 中国古代水利　农田水利　人工运河　城市水利

Abstract: This text briefly introduces the emergence and development of water conservancy and related science and technology as well as the development of its four basic components, namely flood control and river regulation, farmland water conservancy, artificial canals and urban water conservancy. Besides, more emphasis has been put on pointing out and analyzing six major features of the four components, including historicity & continuity, systematization & completeness, regional attribute & diversification, practice & popularization, comprehensiveness & intersection, and experience & limitation. This has provided a thinking framework and reference background for thc better understanding and recognition of the history of water conservancy in China.

Keywords: Water conservancy in ancient China; Farmland water conservancy; Artificial canals; Vrban water conservancy

人类文明史的第一页与洪水有关。只不过《圣经》中的传说是洪水毁

* 郭涛，中国建筑总公司。

灭了人类，只剩下诺亚方舟；而中国的传说则是大禹治水获得了成功，人类征服了洪水，此后大禹建立夏朝，开启中华民族国家的历史。这是一个值得思考的历史文化现象。从一定意义上可以说，中国的早期文明就是水利文明。

所以，研究中国的文明史必须研究中国的治水史，研究中国对水资源的开发、利用、保护的历史及其主要特征，因为这是中国文明的重要历史基础。

1 中国古代水利和水利科学技术在实践中产生与完善

中国古代水利的主要内容有四个基本组成部分，即防洪治河、农田水利（灌溉工程）、人工运河、城市水利。这既是古代水利事业的主要内容，也是古代水利科学技术的主要内容（见图1）。中国古代对水土保持不乏重要认识与实践，但内容相对单薄一些。这反映了古代对水土资源重开发而轻保护。水利机械在中国产生也很早，使用也很广泛，是古代水利的重要内容之一。但从科学技术分类讲，水土保持、水利机械更多属于机械工程学研究的内容，从参与对象和规模讲，无论是民间或政府都远不及其他四个组成部分。囿于篇幅，这两部分内容本文不作讨论。

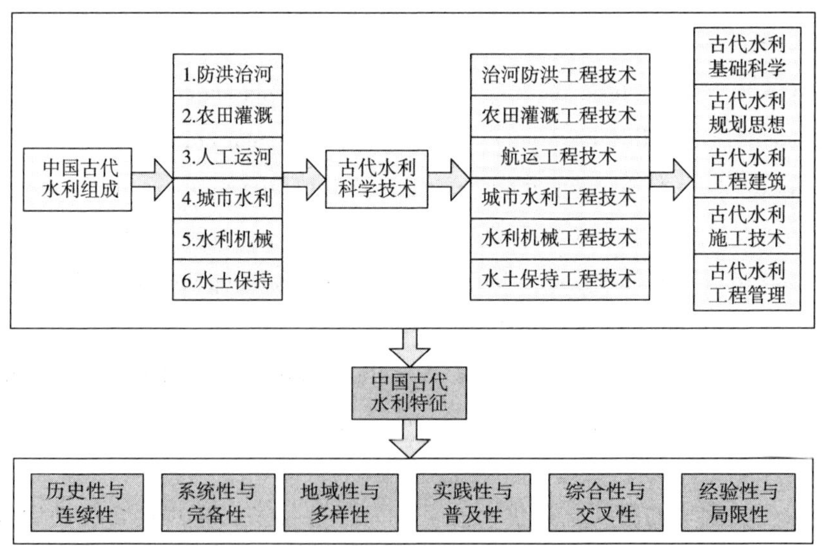

图1 中国古代水利基本组成与主要特征

远古时期，人类逐水草而居。进入农业社会，为了保护居民点和田地，需要防御洪水，排除积水，沿海地区还需要抵御潮水，这就产生了治河防洪工程。随着农业的发展，需要人工灌溉，这就需要开渠筑堰，于是产生了农田水利工程。商品交换和政治军事的需要出现后，人工运河工程应运而生。随着城镇的出现和发展，以城市防洪、居民生产生活用水、环境用水、城市供排水工程为主的城市水利问题随之产生。当今“水利”所包含的主要门类，几乎都可以在中国古代水利史中找到源流。

1.1 古代治河防洪工程的发展

大禹治水的传说反映了远古时期中国先民与洪水搏斗的艰苦卓绝历史。经过历代防御洪水、治理河道的无数次实践，逐渐产生了治河防洪工程门类和学科，这是中国古代水利古老而重要的组成部分。大禹是古代先民战胜洪水的智慧与力量化身，中华民族世世代代祭奠他。

在从共工到鲧到大禹治水的由失败到成功的漫长历程中，古代先民在理性上的主要收获是认识到“水性就下”的特点，应遵循“疏导”的基本治水方略，这是对水流运动规律的认识和运用。实践上的收获是堤防工程的产生与发展。

随着铁器的普及和使用，战国时期堤防工程如雨后春笋，局部堤防遍筑黄河下游两岸重要城镇附近河段。这是中国古代防洪工程，主要是堤防工程建设的第一个高潮。

但由于各诸侯国封建割据，这些堤防“以邻为壑，壅防百川，各以自利”。[①]

秦统一中国后，“决通川防，夷去险阻”。[②] 汉代继之，在黄河下游两岸逐步形成完整堤防系统。秦汉时期是中国历史上第二个堤防工程建设高潮。

黄河是世界上含沙量最高的河流。黄河的主要特点是水少沙多，迁徙不定。据研究统计，有史以来黄河至少发生过26次大改道。其中比较重要、历史记载比较清晰的有9次（见图2）。

秦汉时期对黄河水沙运行规律有了进一步的认识，治河方略争论热烈。随着堤防完善，河床相对稳定，河槽泥沙淤积加快，河患开始频繁，决口

---

① 《汉书·沟洫志》，转引自周魁一等《二十五史河渠志注释》，中国书店，1990，第30页。

② 《史记·秦始皇本纪》，转引自黄河水利委员会《黄河水利史述要》，水利出版社，1984，第43页。

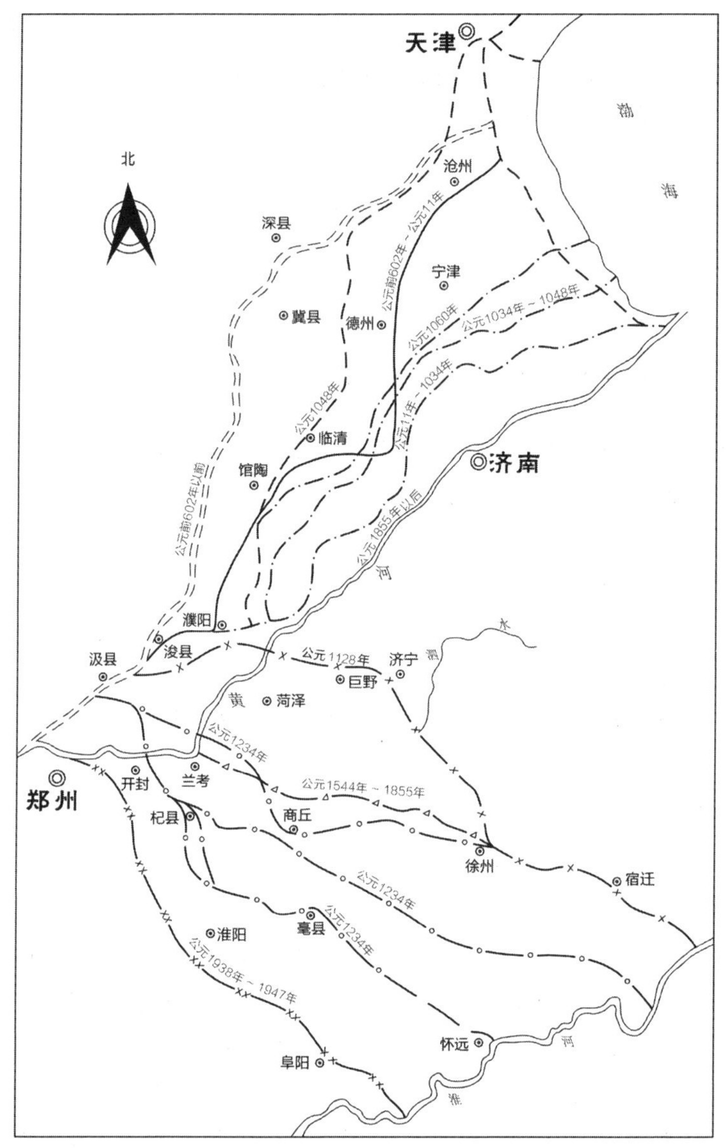

图 2　黄河下游河道变迁示意图

连年不断。东汉王景治河后，黄河相对安流。日益加剧的河患和大规模的治水实践，促进了防洪治河工程技术的进步。这一时期的治水理论成就，主要是出现了两种有代表性的治理黄河的主张。一是贾让的“治河三策”；二是张戎的“水力刷沙”说。实践成就也有两个，一是在黄河下游形成较完整的堤防工程；二是堤工技术有重大进步，典型代表就是王景治河的成功。

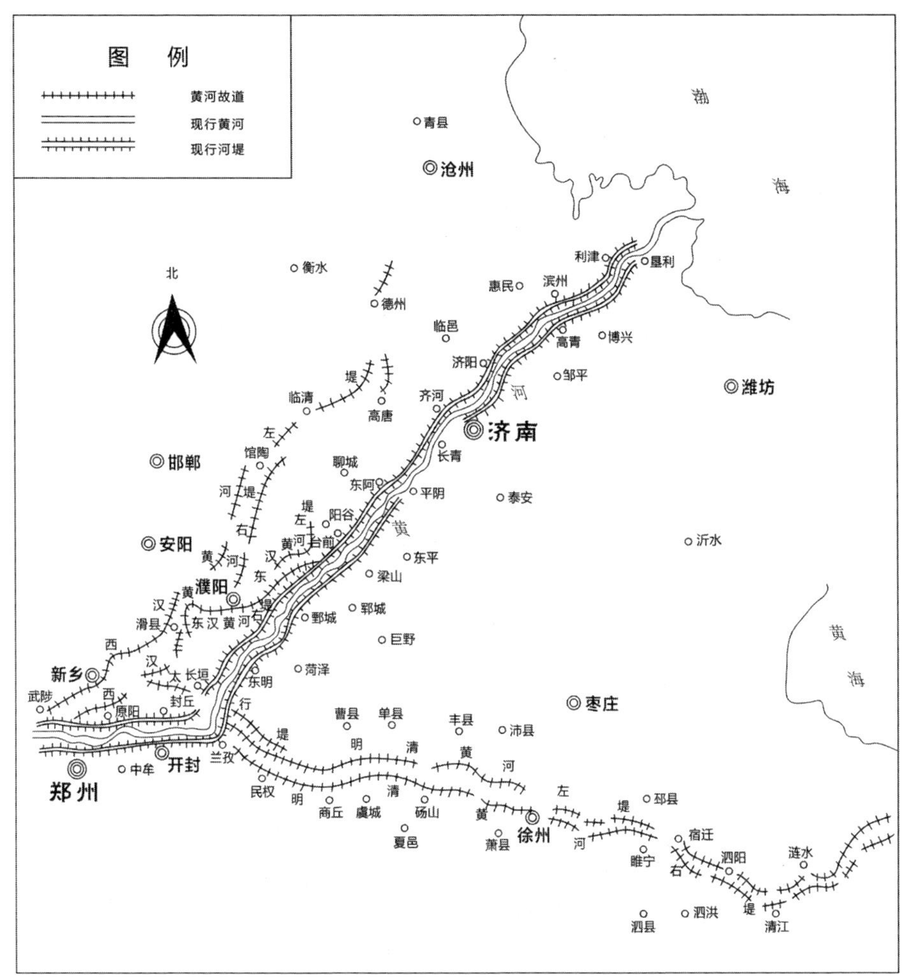

图 3　现存黄河下游古堤示意图

五代以后，防御海潮的海塘工程技术不断发展。

宋元时期，在河防施工技术、埽工（见图 4）和堵口技术方面取得了许多经验，对水沙运行规律已有较深入的观察分析。全面总结当时河工技术的专著也开始问世，如《梦溪笔谈》《河防通议》《至正河防记》等。宋元时期是中国古代堤防工程建设的第三个高潮（见图 5）。

明清时期是中国堤防工程建设和防洪治河工程发展的第四个高潮，传统的河防工程理论和技术更趋成熟。在治理多沙河流的经验和措施方面积累丰富。理论上的重要成就是“束水攻沙”论的成熟与完善。实践上的成就则是以双重堤防系统为代表的大规模堤工建设，实现了黄河下游河槽的

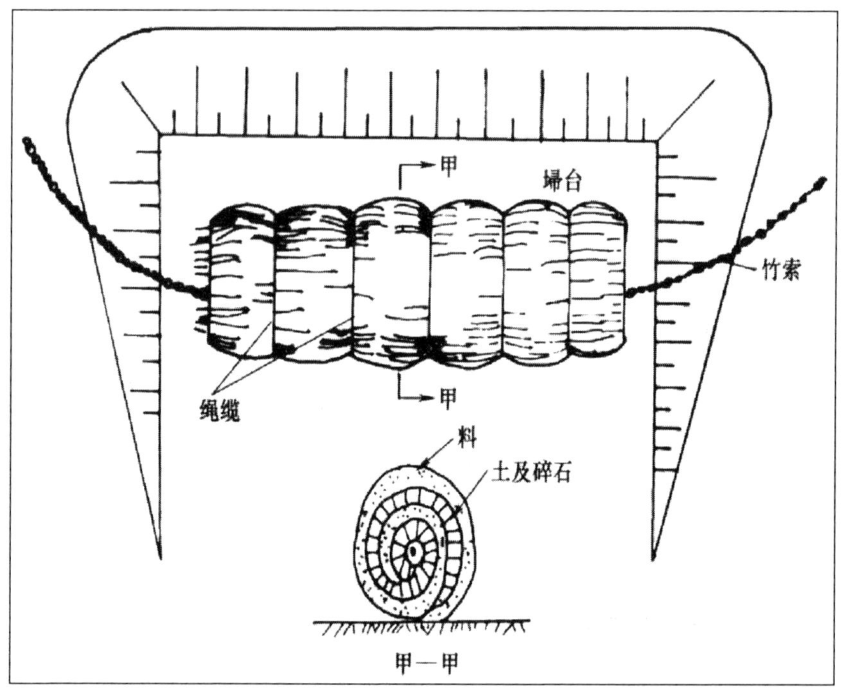

图4　宋代卷埽示意图

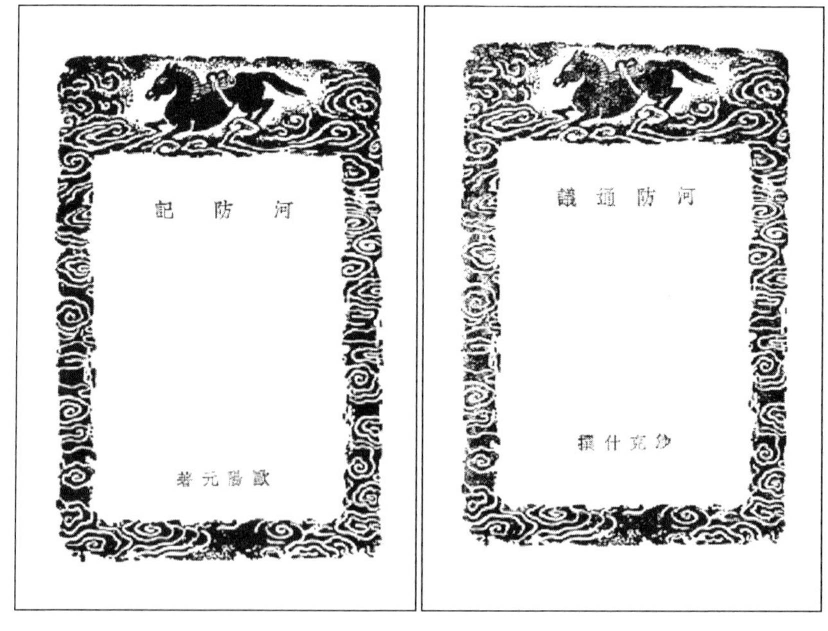

图5　《至正河防记》与《河防通议》

相对稳定，留下迄今可见的明清黄河故道。潘季驯、万恭、靳辅等倡导和身体力行的“束水攻沙”理论和实践就是代表（见图 6）。清代中期以后，治河防洪工程几无建树可言，主要忙于清口地区的堵口工程，直到黄河在 1855 年自河南铜瓦厢改道。其他江河的水灾也开始频繁发生。

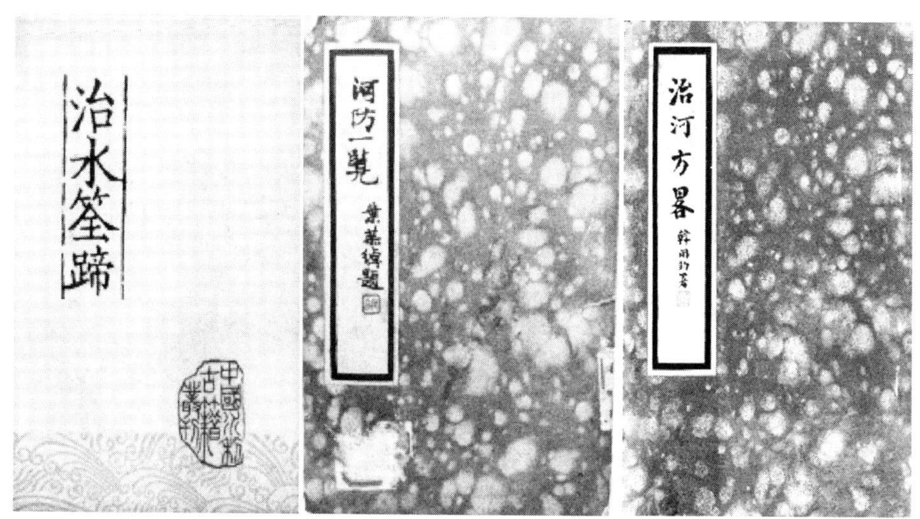

图 6　明万恭《治水筌蹄》、明潘季驯《河防一览》与清靳辅《治河方略》

1.2　古代农田灌溉工程的发展

灌溉工程及其理论和技术水平是中国古代水利科技水平的主要标志之一，其产生和发展反映了水利科学技术的演进历程。7000 多年前的河姆渡文化遗址已显示有水稻栽培的内容。

商代的甲骨文上已有井田制的记载。西周发展为沟洫灌排体系。春秋时期出现芍陂这样大型的蓄水灌溉工程。战国出现了低坝引水的漳水十二渠。秦代则建设了像都江堰、郑国渠那样的大规模引水、引浑淤灌工程。这些工程在取水枢纽、渠线规划方面已达到相当高的水平，在淤灌技术方面已有一定探讨总结。

汉唐农田水利工程进入全盛时期。农田水利工程在黄河、淮河流域和长江上游干支流地区普遍兴建，出现了关中地区、汉中地区、南阳地区、汝南地区、川西平原地区几个大型水利灌区。

在几千年来的农田水利实践中，逐渐形成了灌溉、排水、盐碱防治、拒咸蓄淡（见图 7）等多种农田水利理论和技术。这些理论和技术在历代河渠志、地理志、区域水利志、工程志中都有记录或总结阐述。特别是在王祯《农书》和徐光启《农政全书》中有比较系统的记载。

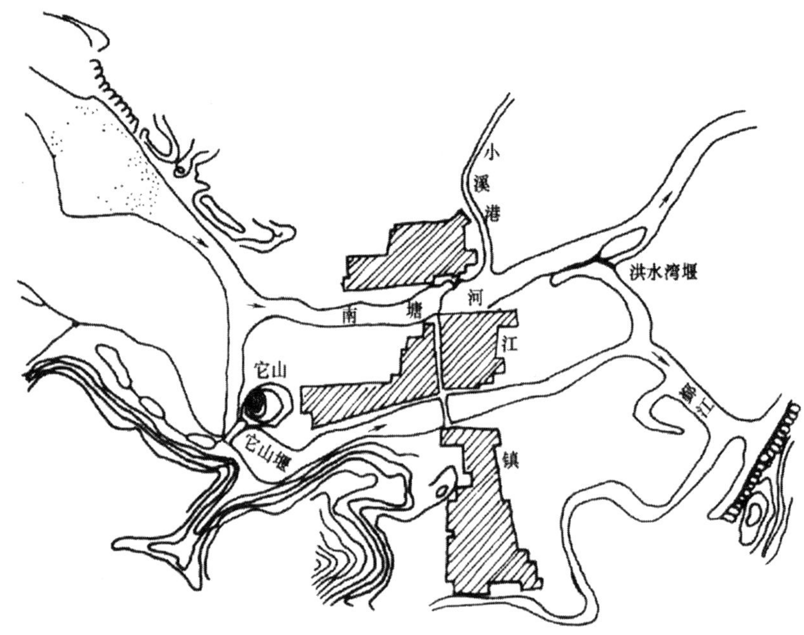

图 7　它山堰枢纽布置图

由于中国地形和气候的多样性，古代先民因地制宜创造了各具特色的灌溉工程形式。如丘陵地区的陂塘、平原地区的灌溉渠系、滨湖滨河地区的圩田（见图 8）、新疆地区的坎儿井等。这些工程形式和技术门类的形成、发展和不断完善，就产生了中国农田水利工程和农田水利学。

1.3　古代水运工程的发展

古代水利科学技术成就和水平的又一重要标志，是人工运河的出现和发展。春秋时期开凿的邗沟（前 486 年）沟通了淮河和长江水系。此后开凿的鸿沟（前 361 年）把黄河和淮河水系连接起来，不仅规模大，而且技术要求更高。因为此举沟通清水河流和多沙河流，黄河洪水风险和泥沙淤积问题随之产生。之后开凿的广西兴安灵渠（前 219 年）又沟通了长江水系和珠江水系，同时在渠线规划、枢纽布置、渠道底坡设计上都有许多创

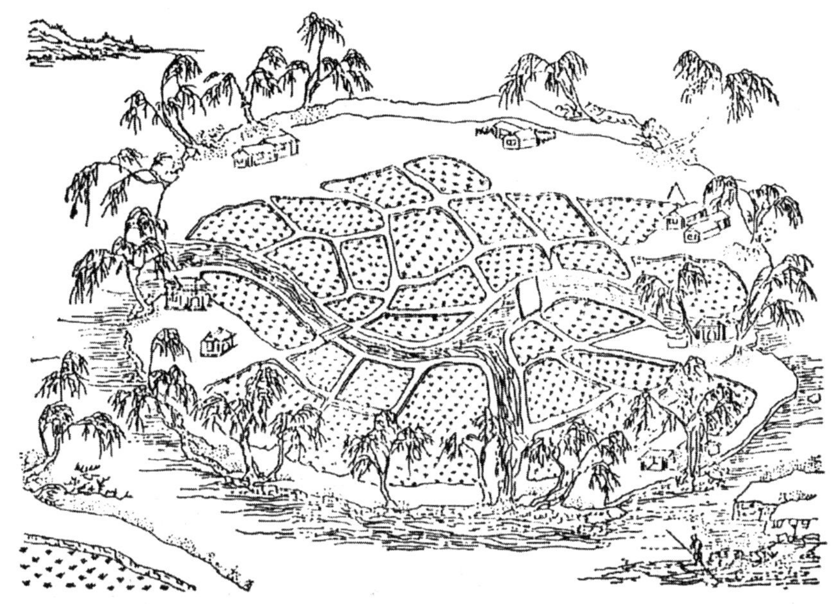

图 8　圩田工程示意图

造。曹魏时期（204 年），又开凿了白沟运河，把海河水系和黄河水系联系起来。至此，中国的长江、黄河、淮河、珠江、海河五大水系都被人工运河连通。隋代所开大运河，气魄更加宏大，以历代工程为基础，加以疏通连接，形成以洛阳为中心，东北通过永济渠抵涿郡（今北京），东南通过通济渠、山阳渎，从扬州过长江，经江南运河达杭州的隋唐大运河（见图 9）。宋代在人工运河船闸技术方面有重大发明创造，出现了复闸（984 年）和澳闸（1025 年），可调蓄局部河段水量和节约通航用水。复闸类似于现代船闸，比世界同类船闸早五六百年。澳闸节水原理与现代船闸的功能完全相同。

元代又进了一步，出现梯级船闸。船闸技术、水源工程和节水工程技术不断丰富发展，船队不仅可以通过水源枯竭的河段，而且可以翻山越岭，从北京直达杭州，建成世界最长的人工运河。明清时期对运河渠线、水源工程、防洪安全工程进一步优化、完善，最后形成今日京杭运河。这是中国古代水利科学技术的集成和重要标志，也是世界人工运河史上的灿烂篇章。1855 年黄河在河南铜瓦厢决口，从此改道北流。洪水在山东张秋把京杭运河拦腰冲断，大运河损毁极为严重。但是，大运河至今仍保持了绝大部分的区间运行功能。

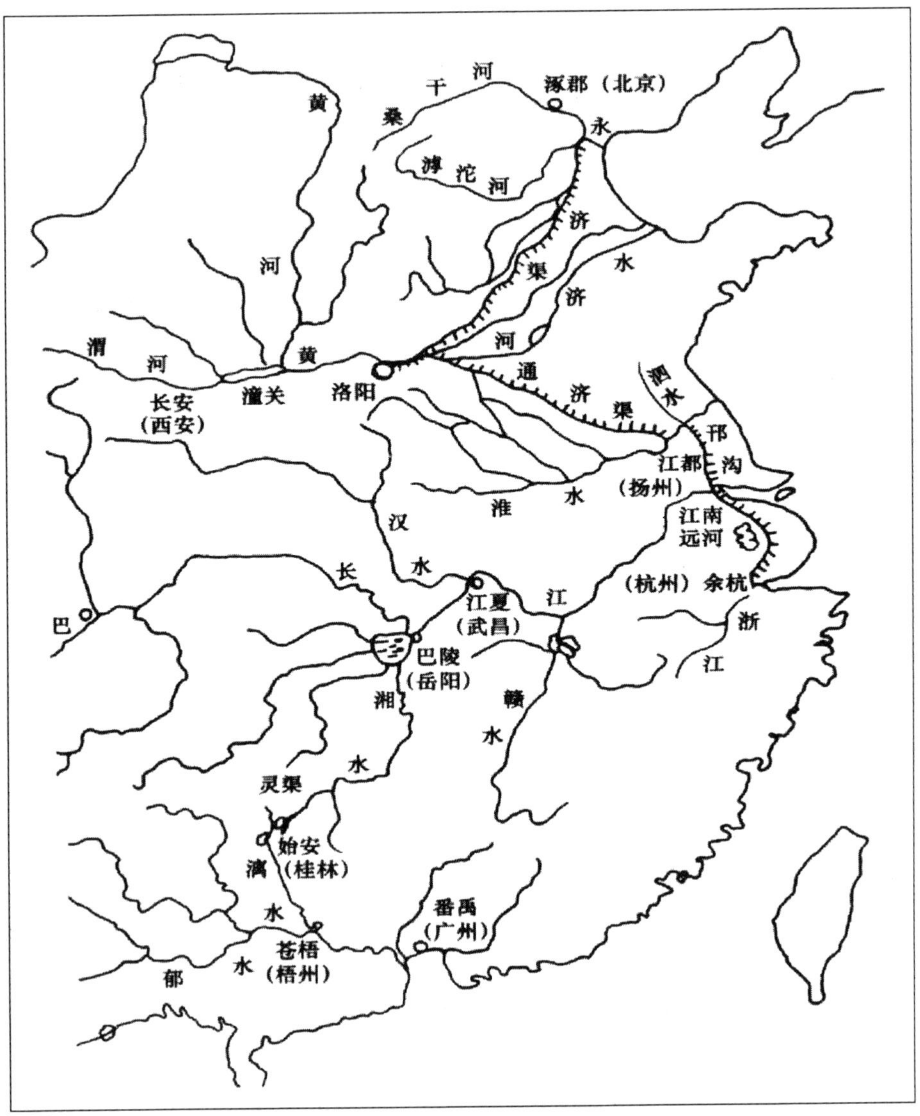

图 9　隋唐时期全国运河干线示意图

1.4　古代城市水利的发展

没有水就没有城市。中国早期的文献中常有“市井”的字样。1000 多年前的唐代人张守节这样解释“市”与“井”的关系：“古人未有市及井，若朝聚井汲水，便将货物于井边货卖，故言‘市井’。”这就是“因井为市”“处商必就市井”的道理。这一解释清楚地说明了水与城市起源的关系。随着城市的发展，城市水利内容日益丰富，地位更加重要。中国古代城市水利的内容主要包括城市供排水、城市防洪、城市交通和近郊灌溉、城市环境美化几个方面。

（1）古代城市建设的水利四原则

中国古代在城市发展过程中，围绕解决城市水利的几项主要任务在实践中总结出建城的水利原则，成为古代城市规划建设的重要理论。这些原则在《管子》一书中阐述得最为集中和系统，主要有四条。

第一，选择城址应高程适当，以便取水之利、避水之害。《管子·乘马》篇说："凡立国都，非于大山之下，必于广川之上。高毋近旱，而水用足；下毋近水，而沟防省。因天材，就地利，故城廓不必中规矩，道路不必中准绳。"这就明确指出了选择城址的基本条件是既要防洪，又要防旱，且要因地制宜，不必统一照搬某一模式。

第二，选择城址应在土地肥沃又便于布置水利工程的地方。《管子·度地》篇说："故圣人之处国者，必于不倾之地，而择地形之肥饶者。乡山左右，经水若泽，内为落渠之泻，因大川而注焉。"[①] 这就是说，城市所在地应当水脉畅通，既便于取水，又能够排水，水道相连，直注大川。

第三，城址选好后，应建城墙，城外再建廓，廓外还有土堤。地势高则应挖渠引水，地势低则应修筑堤防挡水。这就是《管子·度地》篇说的："归地于利，内为之城，城外为之廓，廓外为之土阆。地高则沟之，下则堤之，命之曰金城。"

第四，城市防洪、引水、排水是十分重大的事，有关规定君王都应亲自过问。《管子·问》篇中说："若夫城之厚薄，沟壑之浅深，门闾之尊卑，宜修而不修者，上必几之。"[②]

从上述原则可以知道，在2000多年前，中国在城市规划建设中，城市水利问题已经列为重要的指导原则。说明在先秦时期，中国已有丰富的城市建设实践，并从这些实践中总结出规律性认识，而城市水利问题则是其中最重要的内容之一。这些原则此后影响了中国2000多年的城市规划与建

① 《管子·度地》，转引自中国水利水电科学研究院《中国水利史稿（下册）》，中国水利电力出版社，1989，第222页。

② 《管子·问》，转引自中国水利水电科学研究院《中国水利史稿（下册）》，中国水利电力出版社，1989，第223页。

设实践，有些原则至今还具有积极的影响。

（2）古代典型的城市水利实践

围绕解决城市水利中的防洪、供水、排水及水源、城市水运及交通问题，中国古代有许多各具特色的优秀城市。列其典型者，古老的城市防洪工程中做得好的如西周时期的淹城（在今江苏常州市南）；城市供排水、水运和综合用水做得突出者，如西汉时的长安（见图 10）、东汉时的洛阳、唐宋时期的杭州、元明清时期的北京（见图 11）；城市水运工程做得突出者，如北宋时期的开封（见图 12）、仪征；解决城市供水水源问题措施突出者，如四川成都、山东济南、江西宜春等城市。

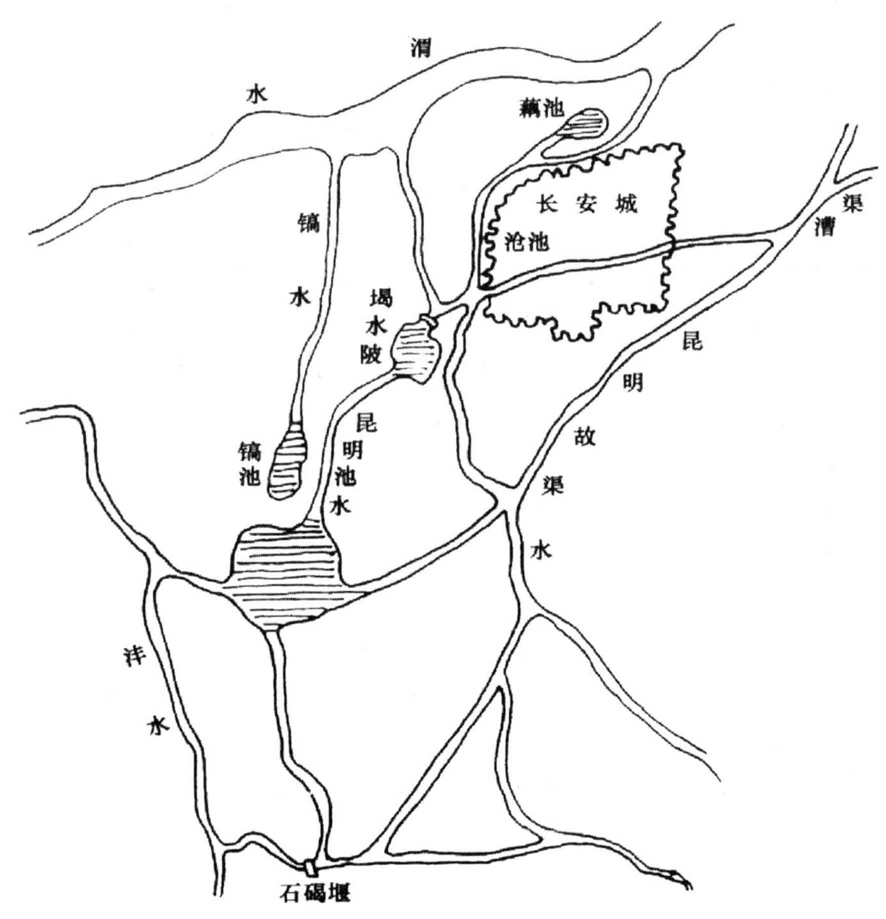

图 10　西汉长安城市水利示意图

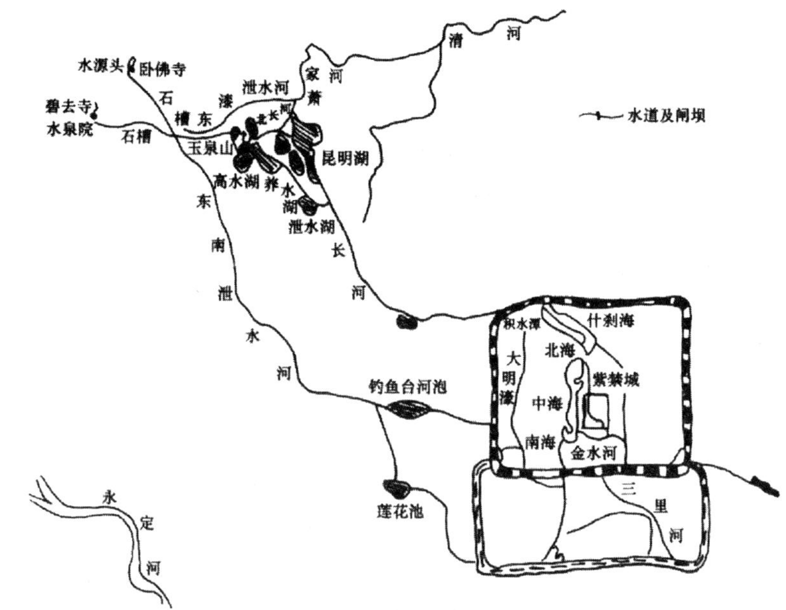

图 11　清代北京昆明湖水源工程示意图

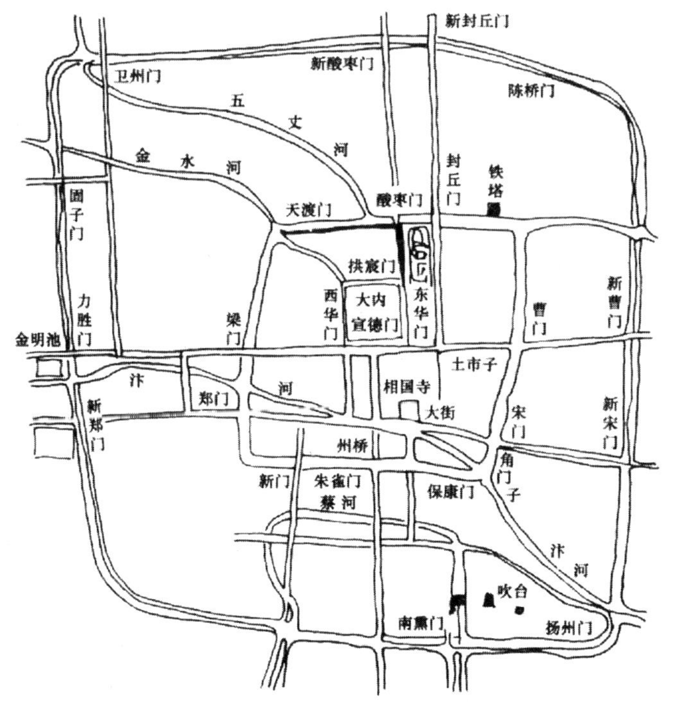

图 12　北宋开封水运工程示意图

2　中国古代水利科学技术的主要特征

前文概述了中国古代水利及其科学技术的四大基本组成部分。总结其发展脉络，可以看出以下主要特征。

2.1　历史性与连续性

中国古代水利科学技术的起源与发展，具有突出的历史性与连续性。所谓历史性，是指中国古代水利科学技术从整体上看起源悠久。所谓连续性，是指中国古代水利科学技术的发展变化随治水实践而不断进步，一脉相承，从未中断，且史料完整，遗址丰富。其发展路径、脉络、阶段都十分清晰，没有文化断层和发展断裂。这得益于中国很早就形成大一统的国家，虽几经战乱分合，但还是维护了大一统的疆域。而且自古以来，无论是官书正史、方志，还是民间野史杂著，对重大治水活动、水利事件都有详细记载。不仅保留了大量著名水利工程遗址，而且还保留了大量记载历代治水活动的水利文献，还有不少古代水利工程历经千百年而效益不衰，沿用至今，使后人可以充分地对中国古代水利科学技术的产生、发展及其规律、成就、经验、教训进行系统研究。这是世界任何其他国家都无法比拟的优势。

从西汉司马迁《史记·河渠书》开始，中国历朝历代的正史中都有每个历史时期的重大治水活动、重大水灾的专门记载。

先秦文献中的水利史料，以《尚书·禹贡》最为著名。《管子·度地》则是先秦时期水利科学技术的全面总结。《尔雅·释水》是先秦时期专门解释水体、水态的著作。

水利专著则是古代水利史料最集中的文献。如跨水系的综合类资料书《行水金鉴》《续行水金鉴》《再续行水金鉴》《淮系年表》等。按水系编纂的江河专志，集中了所述水系的重要史料，包括决溢水灾、河道演变、工程沿革、河漕管理等。

还有区域水利志书、水利工程志书、水利论著、古农书中的水利专篇等。还有各种地理著作、各种类书、丛书中的水利史料等。

据粗略估计，中国古代水利专著不下数百种、数千万字。这浩如烟海的水利史文献是中国水利历史及其科学技术的历史性与连续性的见证。

2.2 系统性与完备性

中国古代水利科学技术，从学科门类到专业技术领域都体现了系统性与完备性，而不是单个的、分散的、零碎的。它涵盖了防洪工程、灌溉工程、水运工程、城市水利工程以及水利机械工程和水土保持工程等。除了19世纪后期才出现的水力发电外，中国古代水利工程的内容几乎包括了现代水利工程的所有门类，不仅涉及水文科学技术、水利规划技术、水工建筑技术、水利工程施工技术、水利机械技术，而且包括水利工程管理的丰富内容。有些发明创造居世界领先地位，如双重堤防、溢流堰、船闸、澳闸等。现代水利科学技术的主要门类，几乎都可以从中找到源流。这得益于中国几千年来持续不断、规模浩大、内容丰富的水利工程实践。像中国古代水利科技这样门类齐全、形成体系，在世界范围都是少有的。

2.3 地域性与多样性

中国地域的辽阔和地理自然条件的多样性、复杂性，水资源时空分布的不均衡性，决定和造就水资源开发利用类型的多样性和水利工程特点的多样化。如长江中下游湖区的圩垸水利、丘陵地区的“长藤结瓜”水库群灌溉、江河上游地区的无坝引水灌溉、北方多沙河流的浑水灌溉、沿海地区的拒咸蓄淡工程等，呈现千姿百态的格局。地域和水资源条件的多样性催生了中国古代水利类型的丰富多样性，并使中国古代水利科技成就璀璨夺目。

2.4 实践性与普及性

中国古代水利科学技术是实践性很强的科学技术。无论是原理、技术和方法，都直接接受治水兴利活动千百万次的全方位检验，接受自然和历史的检验。实践不断验证其科学性和有效性。如四川都江堰，其枢纽布置、鱼嘴的位置几经变动。目前的状况是清代光绪年间形成的。实践证明现在的位置是比较合适的。由于实践性强，许多看似简单却很实用的施工技术，如土石方开挖技术、土方填筑技术、干石砌筑技术、桩基工程技术等，不仅造就了历史上许多宏伟的水利工程，而且非常适合普通民众掌握使用和普及传播。这也是历史上大规模水利实践活动的群众技术基础。有些传统技术还长期在农村和偏远山区小型水利工程中使用。

2.5 综合性与交叉性

水利科学技术的发展进步，不仅取决于水文学、水力学、水利工程学、农田水利学等水科学，而且与地理学、地质学、数学、物理学、农学等自然科学甚至经济科学、环境科学紧密相关，与一定时期的社会、政治、经济状况和整体科技水平相关，并以它们为支撑和前提。因此，中国古代水利科学技术是一门综合性、边缘性、交叉性很强的科学技术。

2.6 经验性与局限性

中国古代水利科学技术是经验性很强的科学技术，这也是由其实践性决定的，千万次的水利实践积累了丰富的治水经验。实践产生经验，又验证经验，然后上升为规律性认识，这就是科学。但是，任何经验都有局限性，其成功具有相对性。中国古代自然科学领域重实证分析、定性分析，欠缺抽象思维、逻辑思维和定量分析。所以，对丰富的治水经验和工程技术的总结往往停留在前科学的定性阶段，而弱于定量的描述和更本质层面的抽象规律性表述。如水文科学，中国很早就有水文、气象记录，雨情、水情的基本数据很多，但就是没有用数学对浩繁的基础数据进行梳理归纳研究，没有产生现代的水文统计科学，没有产生像阿基米德那样的科学家。这是中国古代水利科学技术的局限，也可能是中国古代传统科学技术的共性弱点。近代以来，随着中国社会的变革和中外科技交流的加强，中国传统水利科技也发生了深刻变革，开始向着现代水利科技迈进。

特辑：古代希腊水历史

Hydro-technologies in Greece During the Minoan Era (ca. 3200 – 1100 BC)

A. N. Angelakis

米诺斯时代（约公元前3200～公元前1100年）希腊的水利技术

A. N. 安吉拉克斯

Abstract: Significant characteristics of the Minoan civilization are: (a) Their peaceful living with environment and neighbors; although the Minoans were dominating in the Mediterranean for almost two millennia, in none of the numerous wars and/or conflicts that occurred in the region, they were directly or indirectly involved; (b) A special democratic regime was prevailed, in which women were equal to men and free; And (c) Minoans were focused in culture and technology. The Minoan technological developments are unprecedented in the world's history, as shown by the numerous paradigms on water resources technologies used and water, wastewater, and stormwater management. These paradigms are relevant to water supply, fountains, cisterns used to store rainwater or spring water, aqueducts, dams, wells, water treatment systems, baths and toilets, sewerage and drainage systems, irrigation and drainage of agricultural land practices, and water use for recreation. Significant hydrologic and hydraulic achievements in Minoan Crete, Greece are considered and discussed. Research priorities based on past hydro – technologies, which have the potential to advance the sustainable management of water resources will be identified. Minoan hydro – technologies could be updated by considering today's apparatus and knowledge and looking for their possible applicability particularly in regions under water shortage.

Keywords: characteristics of the Minoan; water supply; sewerage and drainage systems; irrigation; water use for recreation

摘　要：米诺斯文明的显著特征是：（1）与自然环境及邻居的和平相处。尽管米诺斯统治地中海近两千年，但在该地区发生的众多战争冲突中，他们没有直接或间接参与其中；（2）实行了男女平等和自由的特别民主制度；（3）米诺斯人注重文化和技术。米诺斯的技术发展成就在世界历史上是前所未有的，这可以从其使用的水资源技术以及水、废水和雨水管理的众多范例中看出。这些范例与供水、喷泉、用于储存雨水或泉水的蓄水池、渡槽、水坝、井、水处理系统、浴室和厕所、污水和排水系统、农业土地的灌溉和排水以及娱乐用水有关。由于在米洛斯克里特岛上的这些至关重要的水文和水利成就，希腊才会被经常提及和讨论。本文确定的优先内容是基于过去的水利技术，这些技术有可能促进水资源的可持续管理。米诺斯的水利技术可以升级更新，特别是在缺水地区，因为综合考虑了今天的装备和知识，并寻找它们可能的适用性。

关键词：米诺斯特征　供水　水处理系统　污水和排水系统　灌溉　娱乐用水

1　Introduction

The Minoan civilization, the first known European civilization, developed mainly on and ruled the island of Crete, τηε Aegean islands and the eastern coastal areas of today Turkey during the Bronze Age (from about 3200 BC to 1100 BC). Surprisingly little is known about it, although it flourished for nearly two millennia, not even the name used for this "nation" at that time (Angelakis *et al.*, 2014). The term Minoan is a modern one, firstly used by A. Evans (1921 – 1935) who discovered the palace of Knossos and derives from the legendary King Minos, first King of Crete, (son of Zeus and Europa) who, according to Greek mythology, ruled the island of Crete (Fig. 1). An ancient civilization rich in trade of all kinds of goods, with access to amenities, such as plumbing, paved roads, and well-planned towns, that would not be seen again for several centuries, the Minoans had little need of weapons, and life revolved around grand palace complexes.

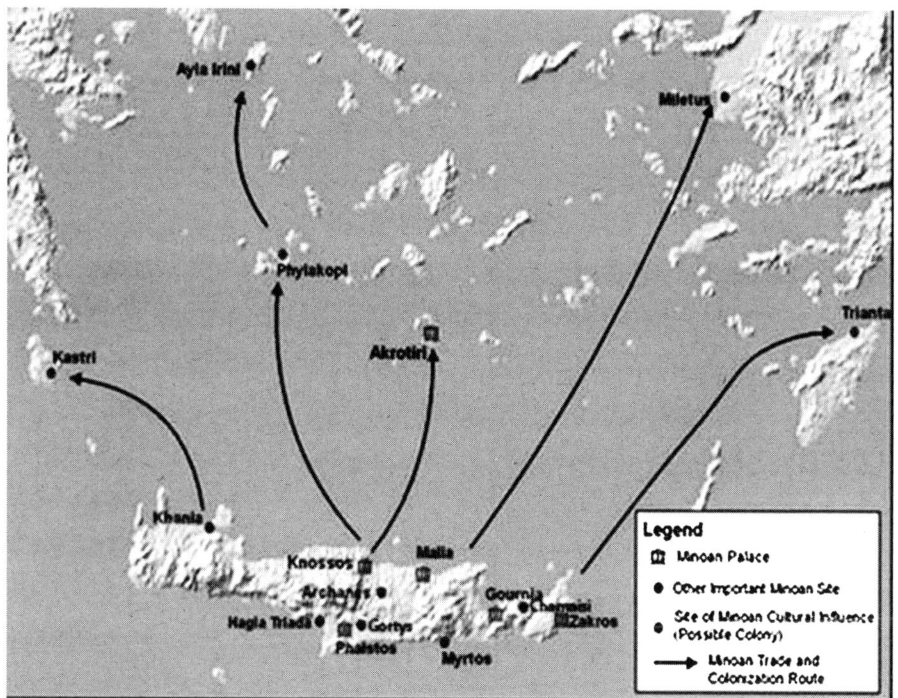

Figure 1 Map of some important Minoans archaeological sites.

Major Minoan center were the eastern Crete (e. g. Knossos, Malia, Phaistos and Zacros, Santorini (Akrotiri) and Miletus. The Historian Ephorus (*ca.* 400 - 430 BC) says: Miletus was first founded and fortified above the sea by Cretans, where the Miletus of olden times is now situated (Strabo, Book 14, Section 1.6). It was a Minoan commercial center.

During the Minoan era a number of water scientific fields on water resources management had been developed, including hydrogeology, aqueducts and water impounds, water and wastewater mains, runoff management, agricultural irrigation, as well as the use of water for recreation purposes (Angelakis, 2017a; Angelakis *et al.*, 2005; Koutsoyiannis *et al.*, 2008). These are suggesting that water resources "engineers" of the Minoan times had a good degree of understanding of the basic water sciences principles, water management techniques and sustainable water concepts, well before the scientific approach of our times (Angelakis and Spyridakis, 2013; Angelakis and Vavoula, 2012; Gorokhovich *et al.*, 2011).

The major archaeological sites in the inland of Crete are the "palaces" of Knossos, Malia, Phaistos and Zakros and Akrotiri (Santorini) (Angelakis and Spyridakis, 1996). Views of that at Knossos and Phaistos "palaces" are shown in Figure 2.

(a)

(b)

Figure 2 Views of the palaces at (a) Knossos and (b) Phaistos (photos A. N. Angelakis).

Beginning in 1420 BC, the Minoan civilization begun to decline due the severe drought and was overrun by the Mycenean civilization from the mainland Greece (Angelakis, 2017a). Thus, the advanced Minoan water technologies were expanded to the Greek mainland. Thereafter, during the Archaic, Classical and Hellenistic periods (*ca.* 650 – 67 BC) it did not stand in the cultural foreground during this time, nor did it play an influential role in international politics. In comparison of the water infrastructures used later on in Classical urban areas (e. g. in Athens) to those elaborated in in Minaon Era (e. g. Knossos), a couple of millennia BC, Wilson's (2000) conclusion is justified, that the individual elements of the water supply and drainage systems appear relatively early and remain largely unmodified until the Middle Ages.

The scope of this paper is to present a review of the main achievements in hydrological and hydraulic works in Minoan Greece during the Minoan Era (ca. 3200 - 1100 BC). The great achievements and their importance are presented and discussed including their influence not only on the following civilizations but also on present times. Water resources management practices and examples of hydro - technologies in Minoan Era are as follows.

2 Climate

In eastern Mediterranean area, and especially in the island of Crete, fluctuations show increasing and decreasing cycles of climatic conditions alternating chronologically, lasting from a few decades to over centuries. The climatic and hydrologic conditions in Crete have been characterized by high variability both spatially and temporally through the long history of the island (Markonis *et al.*, 2016). They summed up all the available sources and presented a picture of the climatic variability in Crete during the last ten thousand years, which showed alternations of warm/cold and moist/dry periods, lasting from a few centuries to some millennia (Fig. 3). This picture demostrates clearly the instability of climatic conditions of the whole region (Markonis, 2016).

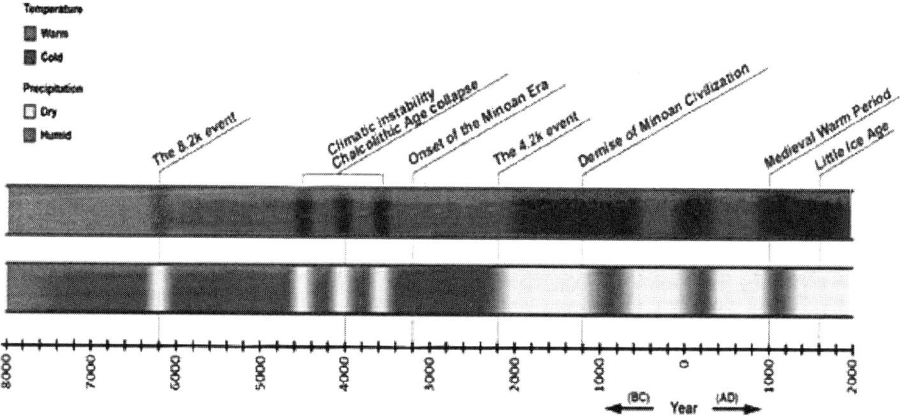

Figure 3 Climate reconstruction of Crete for the last 10000 years based on proxy and historical data (with permission of Markonis, 2016).

3 Water Supply Networks

The Minoans had developed a special water pipe technology. They used terracotta pipes, approximately 70 – 75 cm long with a conical geometry (Fig. 4). In Knossos palace, closed teraccota were used (Angelakis *et al.*, 2007). It seems that the geometry of the pipes was not based on hydraulic principles, but on manufacturing and assembly (Dialynas *et al.*, 2006). The possible reasons for the conical shape of Minoan pipes could be: (a) The construction of such pipes was easier than that of cylindrical ones; (b) The conical shape serves better connection; (c) The pressure could be controlled more easily on rough terrain; (d) The design of the network was easier in the case of curved walkways; And (e) The pricipitation and deposition of sediments on the walls of the pipes, particularly in the case of water with high pH, could be avoided (Angelakis *et al.*, 2012).

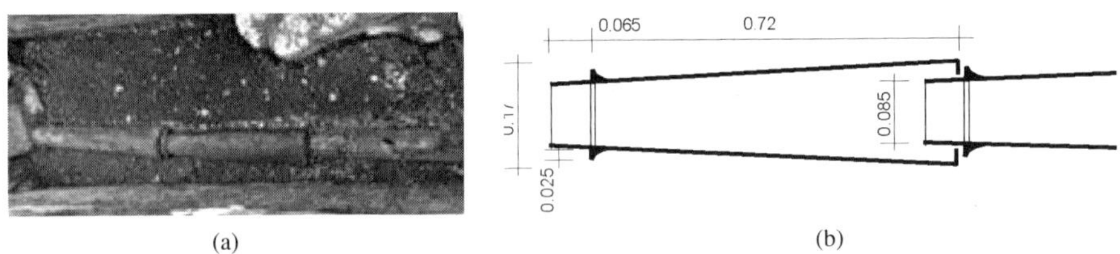

(a) (b)

Figure 4 Water supply terracotta pipes: (a) a real network segment and (b) pipe dimensions (Koutsoyiannis et al., 2008) (photo by A. N. Angelakis).

In addition to the terracotta pipes used for water supply similar pipes of rectangular cross sections were used for the collection and storage of rainwater (Fig. 5). Such pipes were used in the Pyrgos – Korifi, in southeastern Crete, where no other water source was available (Cadogan, 2007).

4 Fountains

The most typical examples are the fountains known as *tyktes* (new). They referred to a type of fountain of late – Classical and/or early – Hellenistic period

(a) (b)

Figure 5 Harvesting and storage rainwater in Pyrgos – Korifi, Myrtos, in southeastern Crete: (a) Terracotta pipes used for collection of rainwater (From the Vila Ariadne, Iraklion, Crete), and (b) Cistern of 66 m^3 capacity in which the rainwater was storage (photos A. N. Angelakis).

known as *ayrkrene* (from the Greek word *avrokrene*). The facilities at the Caravanserai, located opposite the main entrance of the palace of Knossos are characteristic. There was always water available from the aqueduct of Knossos for washing the visitors. It was the so – called sacred fountain (Pendlebury, 1950). Such fountain in the *Caravanserai* of Knossos, consisted of a rectangular basin with dimensions 2.00 m × 1.60 m (Fig. 6a). The basin was accessible by three steps and the water came directly from a source located in the floor of the house (Evans, 1921 – 1935).

Another characteristic *tykti* fountain was found in the southwest corner of the room of the palace of Zakros (Fig. 6b). An opening led into a small chamber where the water was collected and lifted under the floor at the base of a square underground fountain (Angelakis, 2015). Its dimensions were 3.00 m × 4.00 m and dated to the Late Minoan period (*ca.* 1500 BC).

5 Cisterns

The Minoan cisterns were basically cylindrical. The total volume of each Minoan cistern ranged from 5 m^3 to 100 m^3. The most well-known were presented by Angelakis (2016). In terms of form, cisterns were holes with irregular shapes dug out of sand and loose rock and lined with waterproof plaster (stucco), resulting in

(a)

(b)

Figure 6 Minoan fountains: (a) in Caravanserai Knossos and (b) in the central square of the "palace" of Zakros (photos by A. N. Angelakis).

sophisticated structures (Gorokhovich *et al.*, 2011). Two basic types are distinguished. (a) Those used for collecting and storing rainwater. One of the earliest Minoan cisterns was found in the centre of a house complex at Chamaizi (Fig. 7a) dated from the third to the second millennium BC (Davaras, 1976). (b) Those storing water, which is transferred from spring sources or other surface sources through aqueducts dated to the late Minoan period (Fig. 7b) (Antoniou *et al.*, 2006; Mays *et al.*, 2013).

(a)

(b)

Figure 7 Typical Minoan cisterns: (a) in Chamezi Minoan village and (b) in Tylissos houses (photos by A. N. Angelakis).

6 Aqueducts

As already mentioned, in areas with water springs water was transported to palaces and other habitable spaces, mainly by open stone – made conduits, un-

(a)

(b)

Figure 8 Parts of the Tylissos aqueduct: (a) Part of the central conduit located at the entrance of the three Vilas, and (b) secondary conduit and a small lithic cistern used for removal of suspended solids of water before its storage to the main cistern (photos by A. N. Angelakis).

like closed conduits used during the Classical Roman, and later during the Venetian and Ottoman period. A typical example is the aqueduct Tylissos of a total length of 1.40 km in an open conduit (Fig. 8), unlike the aqueduct of Knossos, where the water was transferred originally from the *Mavrokolymbos* spring and later from neighboring springs, by a combination of open conduits and terracotta pipes (Angelakis *et al.*, 2007; Nikolaou *et al.*, 2017). Later on during the Neopalatial period the water supply of Knossos was transferred from springs located in the Jiouchtas area, 10 km southern of palace. More evidence of Minoan aqueducts can be found in Angelakis *et al.* (2007) and De Feo *et al.* (2013).

7 Wells

As mentioned before, in Minoan Era the water supply conditions of palaces and other residential areas, were differentiated not only according to time periods, but also being dependent on the hydrological conditions of each region (Koutsoyiannis and Angelakis, 2003; Koutsoyiannis *et al.*, 2008; Angelakis *et al.*, 2016). In areas with underground aquifers, and limited available surface water sources, such as in the "palace" of Zakros, the Komos port, and the town of Palaikastro in southeastern Crete, digging and lifting technologies of underground water were well developed（Εικ. 9）. The depth of Minoan wells was less than 20 m, usually 12 – 15 m and their diameter less than 5 m, usally 1. 5 m（Floods, 2012; Mays *et al.* 2007）. The practice used to lift the water was remarkable. Yannopoulos *et al.*（2015）reported that there were evidences that the Minoans were using the device known as *shadoof*（in Greek *κηλώνειονήγεράνι*）. Another example of Minoan well is that in Komos port shown in Figure 9b. More on groundwater utilization in Minoan Era were given in Angelakis and Voudouris（2014）and Angelakis *et al.*（2016）.

(a) (b)

Figure 9 Minoan wells:（a）in the Palaikastro town in eastern Crete and（b）in Komos port in the south Crete（photos A. N. Angelakis）.

8 Dams

Dams were constructed in various parts of the world, since the Bronze Age（Khan *et al.*, 2019）. In Minoan era, the best known are those found in the rocky little valley of Choiromandres, located on the eastern end of Crete, with strong slope extending from east to west（Tsatsanifos, 2015）. In *ca.* 2nd millennium BC, Minoans attempted to regulate the flow of the stream through a system of two dams, in order to protect arable land from erosion after heavy rainfall, and also to irrigate their fields（Fig. 10 top）. It seems that the construction started in the Palaiopalatial period (*ca.* 1900 – 1700 BC), whereas the dams rescued today were constructed of megalithic materials during the Neopalatial period (*ca.* 1700 – 1450 BC). Today its length is 27 m and height 3.10 m, whilst the thickness of the base is greater than that of the crest (HYDRIA Project, 2011).

(a) (b)

Figure 10 Water flow regulation through a system of dams in Choiromandres (HYDRIA Project, 2011) (top) and Minoan dams: (a) Remnants of the main dam in the valley of Choiromandres (Angelakis, 2017a) and (b) part of the dam in Pseira, Mochlos (Bctancourt, 2012) (bottom).

Similar hydraulic structures were found in the island Pseira (Mochlos), located in the gulf of Mirabello in northeastern Crete (Betancourt, 2012) (Fig. 10b). The Minoans in order to ensure water for irrigation of agricultural crops and livestock on the island, built two water management systems: (a) small dams to intercept runoff waters in the seasonal streams and (b) larger dam for storing water (Tsatsanifos, 2015).

9 Water Supply Treatment Systems

Next to the water storage cisterns, well protected sandy filters were used for treatment of surface water before storage (Angelakis and Koutsoyiannis, 2003). Such facilities were found in Phaistos, where the water supply of the palace was dependent on rainwater harvesting (Fig. 11a). Also, Defner (1921) described clay - made oblong structures (hydraulic filters) with small holes in one end, possibly used as small filters at the outputs of the water from the water reservoirs (cisterns) (Fig. 11b). In such a filter, the turbulent water flow created relatively small pressures in the external perforated walls due to the high flow rate. Thus, the outflow released suspended and maybe some dissolved solids (Spanakis, 1981).

Also Minoans used sedimentation tanks for removing suspended solids from potable water (Fig. 11b). In addition to the terracotta filters, in some case cisterns were associated with small canals collecting water from rainfall and from mountain streams (Viollet, 2007).

10 Drainage and Sewerage Systems

In a part of the central government house of the palace of Minos, rainwater of large capacity was collected in underground stone-made drains, which passed down the corridor that led to the north entrance (Angelakis and Spyridakis, 2013; Angelakis *et al.*, 2014). Sewage was also collected in the same drains. Gutters collected water from the roofs of buildings and probably sent it to the toilets of the last floor. Generally, drains and sewers were built of dressed stones and were large enough to make it possible to clean and maintain (Angelakis, 2016).

The sewerage and drainage systems were built of stone blocks lined with cement and measured about 79 by 38 cm per section. Probably the upper system was open. The sewers and drains, then, were large enough to permit men to enter

(a)

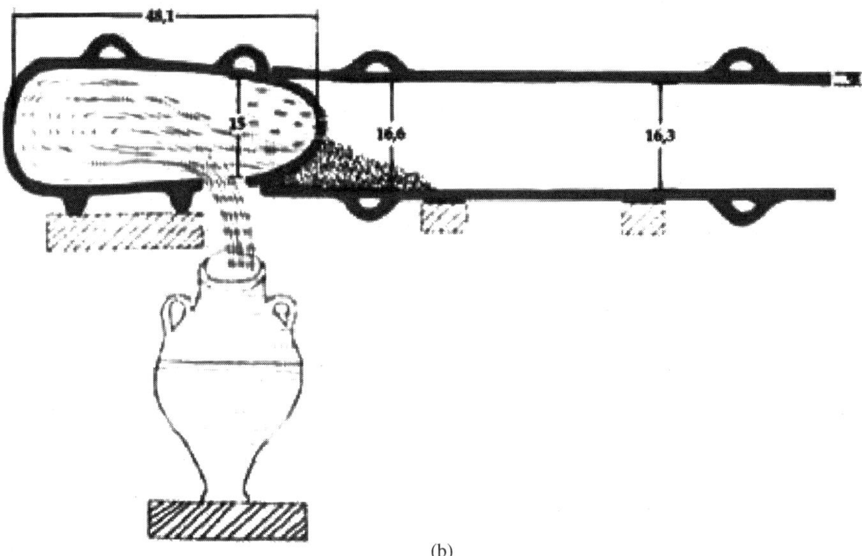

(b)

Figure 11 Minoan water supply treatment system: (a) sand filter next to a water storage cistern in palace of Phaistos and (b) water filter (photo by A. N. Angelakis).

them for cleaning and/or maintenance; in fact, manholes were provided for that purpose in the parts that were covered. Airshafts at intervals also helped to ventilate sewers (Graham, 1987). Finally, the drainage and sewerage systems of the palace, running underneath most of the palace, with baffles and overflows was slowing down the runoff and prevented flooding. A plan of a part of sewerage and drainage system about 100 m under the "Queen's Megaron" at Knossos is illustrated in Figure 12.

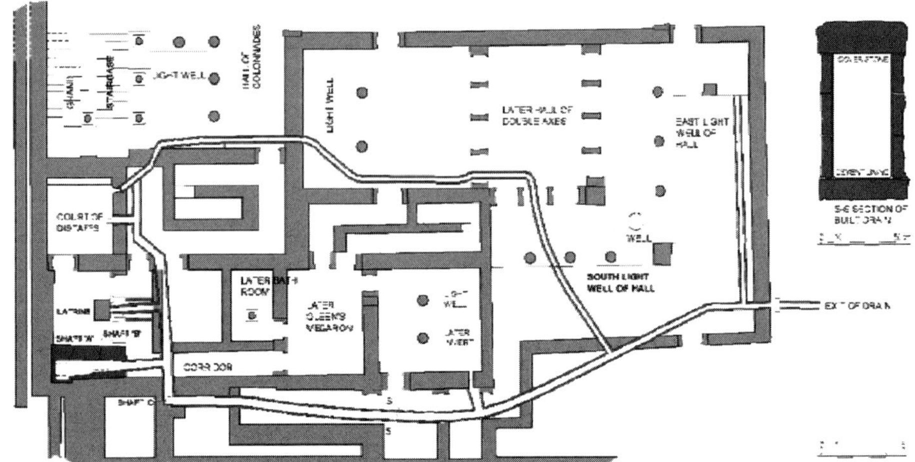

Figure 12　Part of the sewerage and drainage system in the palace of Knossos beneath the Domestic Quarter（modified from Antoniou and Angelakis, 2015）.

The central drainage and sewerage system of the palace of Phaistos（Fig. 13a）is similar to that of Knossos. The most advanced ancient Minoan drainage and sewerage system seems to be that in the Vila of Hagia Triada（Fig. 13b）. This system was admired by several visitors, including the Italian writer A. Mosso（1907）, who visited the area in the early 20th century. During a heavy rain, he noticed that the drains/sewers functioned perfectly and he recorded the incident saying: *I doubt if there is other case of stormwater drainage system that works 4000 years after its construction.* Also, the American H. F. Gray（1940）, said: *you can enable us to doubt whether the modern sewerage and drainage systems will operate at even a thousand years.* Therefore, the Minoan plumbers planned and constructed projects that functioned for centuries, unlike today, when if a project operates well for 40 – 50 years is considered satisfactory（Koutsoyiannis *et al.*, 2008）.

11　Baths and Other Purgatory Infrastructure

11.1　Baths

The basic type of Minoan bathrooms is that found next to the dining room of

(a)

(b)

Figure 13 Minoan sewerage and drainage systems: (a) The output of the central system in the Phaistos palace and (b) part of the central sewerage system in Hagia Triada Vila (photos by A. N. Angelakis).

Queen. This type of bath is basically similar to those found in Phaistos and Malia Da house (Fig. 14a & b). However, in Knossos palace its floor was not at the lower level. Portions of clay pipes were found just outside the room's door. Obviously water was passed through a small canal on the floor, outside the door of the bathroom (Angelakis, 2017b).

(a) (b)

Figure 14 Minoan baths: (a) royal bathroom in the palace of Phaistos and (b) Minoan bathroom in house known as Da in the palace at Malia (photos by A. N. Angelakis).

11.2 Lustral chambers or basins

It should be noted that at that time, in addition to drains/sewers, bathrooms were not considered necessary, merely convenient, and most palaces did not have them. Although the function of Minoan rooms is difficult to define, Evans (1921 -

1935), who discovered the palace of Knossos, identified three rooms as bathrooms. The main type, which resembles the bathrooms discovered at Phaistos and Malia, is that found near the Queen's Megaron in the palace. However, there is a difference in the level of the floor and the consequent absence of steps. Evans (1921 - 1935) referred to these rooms as "*lustral chambers or basins*". Also, Graham (1984) assumed that a room which started out as a lustral chamber or basin later became an ordinary bathroom. In fact, investigations by Platon (1990) led to assume that this also happened twice in the houses at Tylissos; and a careful study could show the same to be true for the bathroom of the Queen's Hall in the palace of Minos (Graham, 1984). Thus, it could be supported that Minoans in their latter days began putting cleanliness before godliness (Mays and Angelakis, 2012). Lustral basins at palaces in Kato Zakros and in Malia are shown in Figure 15.

(a) (b)

Figure 15 Lustral basins: (a) at the palace in Kato Zakros and (b) at the palace in Malia (photos by A. N. Angelakis).

11.3 Toilets

One of the most interesting rooms in the ground floor in the residential quarter of the Knossos palace was identified as a toilet. The toilet consisted of a wooden seat about 57 cm from the ground with an earthenware "pan" and a rooftop reservoir as a source of water (Antoniou *et al.*, 2016). The toilet could thus be flushed even during a rainless summer, either by an attendant outside the lavatory or by the user (Angelakis *et al.*, 2005). The toilet in the residential quarter of the Palace of Minos in Knossos is probably the earliest flush lavatory in history toilets (Fig. 16). Toilets similar to those of Knossos were found in Phaistos, in Malia, and in other settlements (Graham, 1987). A house in the area of the Palace of Malia called Da has toilet seat in almost perfect condition, built of solid stone, on the contrary of that in the toilet in the residential quarter at the Palace of Knossos. The toilet could be purified even during dry summer, by somebody else or by the user himself.

12 Water for Recreational and Environmental Use

The first indications for use of water for recreation are reported for the Minoan Era. The Minoan "hydraulic engineers" seem to have had enough knowledge and had developed water use technologies even for recreational and environmental improvements. Various findings suggest the existence in the "palaces", such as the "jet d'eau" (jets or jet of water) at the Knossos, fish farms, aquaria and other related facilities. The first serious indication in the ancient Greece of water use for recreation is one type of "jet d'eau" discovered in the House of Frescoes at Knossos palace (Fig. 17a), found in the Archaeological Museum of Iraklion (Angelakis and Spyridakis 1996).

Another indication of such water use is the underground cistern, with a diameter of 7 m, which was discovered in the central part along the so-called royal apartments of the palace of Zakros (Fig. 17b). The room is called Tank Room (Platon, 1990). For the use of this pool several theories and opinions have been reported, such as use for swimming, as an aquarium, and for religious ceremonies (Alexiou, 1964).

13 Minoan Theaters

A certain example of this period is the north western opened area of the palace at Knossos (Fig. 18a), called the "theatre" by Evans (1921 – 1935). A such similar place exists in the palace of Phaistos (Fig. 18b). These reconciliation /

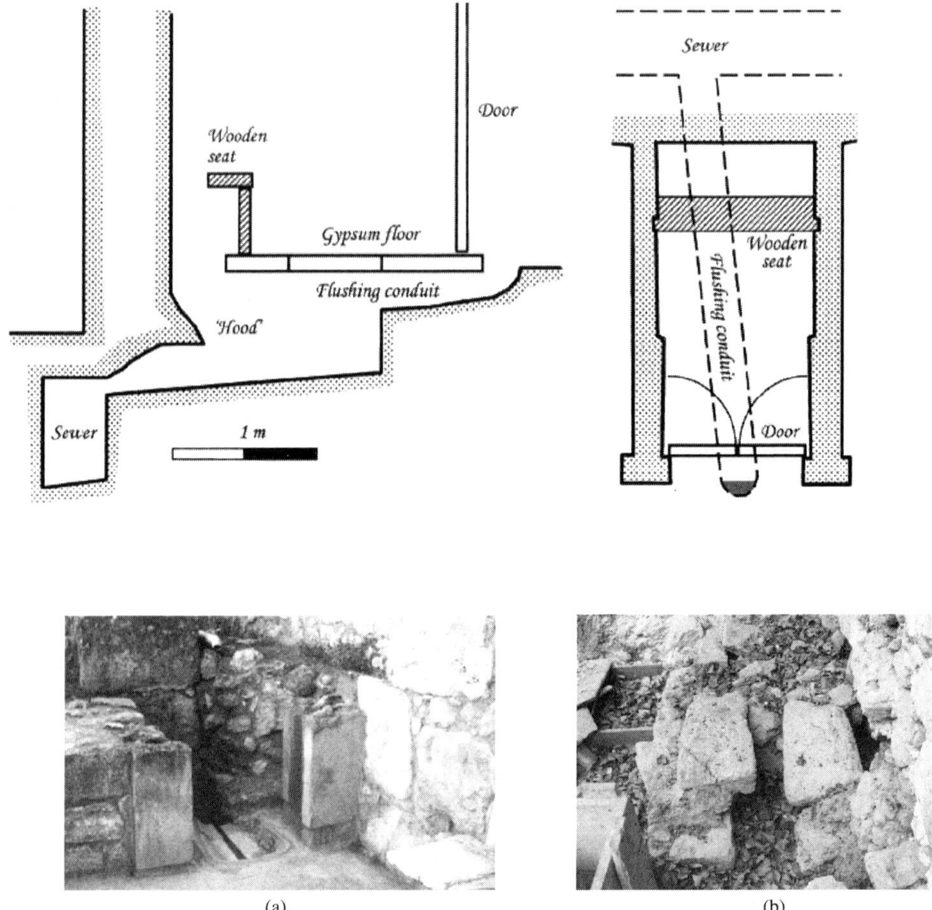

Figure 16　Minoan toilet in the residential quarter of palace of Knossos:（a）section and plan of ground-floor toilet（top）and general views of toilets:（a）at Knossos and（b）at Da house in Malia（bottom）(adapted from Antoniou et al.，2016).

congregation places，are considered as precursor theaters of those developed later on in Classical，Hellenistic and Roman times. It is a platform with rows and steps formed as an angle-shaped opened area. At the bottom of the steps begins a narrow raised road that divides a paved court. Evans（1921 – 1935）believed that the court was used for ceremonies，watched by standing viewers（Kollyropoulos *et al.*，2015）. At the palace of Knossos the raised paved road，known as the "Royal road"，continues in the opposite direction. In all these places efficiently operating drainage systems were in use (Kollyropoulos *et al.*, 2015).

(a) (b)

Figure 17 Projects used for recreation water: (a) fresco representing a type of diffusers at Knossos, and (b) circular tank in a central square of the palace of Zakros (photos by A. N. Angelakis).

(a) (b)

Figure 18 The Minoan theatres: (a) at Knossos and (b) at Phaistos (photos by A. N. Angelakis).

14 Roads

Paved roads connected the palaces and towns of Crete through the interior of the island. The first paved road network was constructed in the middle Minoan period (*ca.* 1700 – 1450 BC) and reached impressive density during the late Minoan period (after *ca*. 1450 BC). While ancient paved roads are difficult to identify today in the countryside, several well preserved examples appear in the Minoan ruins of Gournia and other Minoan palaces (Driessen and Schoep, 1994).

Most streets in Minoan settlements date to Middle Minoan period; later ruins follow earlier alignments, beneath the pavings, and some middle Minoan houses were actually constructed on top of the earlier streets. This is the case at Gournia, Malia, and Palaikastro, where the street system probably dates to Middle Minoan period but was subsequently repaired. Likewise, at Komos in the southern area of Iraklion, a fine paved road preceded the construction of Building T. A good paradigm is the ancient road in Knossos known as "Royal road", which is considered the "oldest road in Europe" (Fig. 19a). The Royal Road appears to be a Late Minoan reconstruction of an earlier pavement (Driessen and Schoep, 1994). Several grandstands were made in middle Minoan times along the Royal Road, with only part being rebuilt at the very end of late Minoan times. It connects the palace (Theatre area), the House of Frescos, and the Little palace. It is very well paved with stone slabs and on either side, there are cement wings and drains (Pendlebury, 1950).

(a)

(b)

Figure 19 Drainage system in central roads: (a) the "Royal road" known as the "oldest road in Europe" in the palace of Knossos and (b) at Palaikastro town (photos by A. N. Angelakis).

In addition, a similar situation is observed in the town of Palaikastro in the eastern Crete where the central road of the town is well designed and constructed by considering the drainage of the rainwater shown in the left side of the road (Fig. 19b). All the central sewers were beneath the streets (e. g. Knossos and Phaistos), were drainage systems were on both sides of the streets and stairs.

15 Flood Protection of "Minoan Viaduct"

The "Minoan Viaduct" is one of the most impressive structures discovered so far in the archaeological site of Knossos palace and the bulkier technical work of Minoan Crete. According to the excavator A. Evans (1921 – 1935), about half of its height was saved. It consists of four columns (width 3. 2 – 4. 60 m), made of carved limestone alternating with stepped openings, probably for the free passage of stormwater flowing from the steep hillside (Angelakis *et al.*, 2014). The stepped openings (width 2. 30 – 3. 10 m) are from three to four tiers. In the opinion of Evans, it was arched and was made with ekforic system in order to be very well protected (Fig. 20).

Figure 20 Part of the original wall of the "Minoan Viaduct" with the stepped openings in the Caravanserai at Knossos palace (photo by A. N. Angelakis).

16 Epilogue

It should be noticed that Minoans lived in harmony with nature and their environment; those that did not, failed. The multicolored wall – paintings in Minoan Palaces depict a life full of creativity, good taste and in complete harmony with the natural environment (Evans, 1921 - 1935). Local water supply sources were first used by the people during the Minoan Era. When these were exhausted, local and temporal transfers were instituted and the necessary hydraulic structures built such as water cisterns (Angelakis, 2016).

Archaeological and other evidence suggest that during the Middle Minoan period mainly a cultural explosion, unprecedented in the history of ancient civilizations, was held in Minoan society. This is demonstrated by the advanced techniques applied to water, wastewater, and storm water management. These techniques include various disciplines of water resources, water networks, especially those in urban areas, recovery and use of surface resources, construction of baths and other sanitary and purification structures, drainage and disposal of wastewater and rainwater systems, rehabilitation projects and farmland irrigation and drainage and finally water use for recreation (Angelakis, 2017a).

One of the most prominent features of the Minoan civilization was the hydraulic architecture, construction and operation of water supply systems and those for collection and disposal of waste and rain waters in the palaces and other settlements. In most Minoan palaces and towns nothing was more remarkable than the complex and highly functional water supply, drainage and sewerage systems (Evans, 1921 - 1935). Moreover, the use of wastewater for irrigation of agricultural lands is also indicated. The design philosophy of Minoan hydro-technologies has to be further considered in light of its success. Thus, the development of effective water supply management projects, in short - water areas should also include historical knowledge. This rich inheritance of Minoan, hydraulic works should not be restricted only to its cultural value, but also, and more importantly, viewed as an example for sustainable water hydro-technologies (Markonis *et al.*, 2016).

From these and other reports on technologies related to water resources and wastewater in the Minoan Era, we could conclude that:

(a) The Minoans lived in harmony with the environment.

(b) No fundamental differences are noticed in design and construction of water projects since then. The main differences concern the scale, and the available equipment.

(c) The development of technology was preceded of the development of the science.

(d) The hydraulic technology developed originally during the Bronze Age (e. g. in Minoan Greece and Indus Valley), improved further in ancient Ionia during the Archaic times (e. g. Thales Miletus) and took of in Classical Athens (e. g. Anaxagoras and Aristotle).

(e) It has two basic characteristics: safety in extraordinary conditions (e. g. wars) and long-term durability. In many cases, these constructions operated efficiently for millennia.

(f) There was integrated management of water resources, with provision for matching demand and supply and possible future increased needs.

(g) Looking back to the long past of human inhabitance at the Minoan places one can clearly outline some principles on which past hydro-technologies were based; notably they are the very same that are used in many applications of the present.

Lessons learned should be summarized as follows. (a) The meaning of sustainability in modern times should be reevaluated in light of ancient public works and management practices. Technological developments based on sound engineering principles can have extended life span. (b) Security, with respect to water and wastewater, is of critical importance in the sustainability of a population.

Finally, Gray (1940) gives clearly the great interest of the Minoans in sanitation as follows: "*We often hear to talk about the "modern" hygiene as it was something that developed recently and there seems to be a prevailing idea that urban sanitation is something very modern established somewhere in the middle of the last* 19*th century. Perhaps these ideas are trying to strengthen a somewhat problematic idea in the modern culture* [...], *but when examined in the light of history that is anything but new or recent. Indeed, in the light of history, it is surprising, if not bitterness, that man has gone so poorly, if at all, about four thousand years* [...]. *Archaeological evidences shows that people* [*Minoans*] *had to proceed very comfortable and healthy living, with a considerable degree of beauty and luxury* [...]. *This was done about four thousand years ago.*"

17 Recommendations

Research priorities based on past hydro-technologies, which have the potential to advance the sustainable management of water resources should be identified. To put in perspective the ancient water management principles and practices discussed in this paper, it is important to investigate the Minoan hydro-technologies in terms of their:

(a) Evolution. An important question to be considered is whether all Minoan technologies were entirely developed by Minoans or some of them did exist during the Neolithic times. Same holds for the technologies later on used in Archaic and Classical Greece. We cannot assure whether or not the Minoans' knowledge on water resources survived after its collapse about 1100 BC (Angelakis *et al.* 2013).

(b) Technological advances. To some extent, the differences between Minoan and modern times hydro-technologies are mostly found in the apparatus and the scale of applications with practically no differences in the fundamental principles used. For example, flushing toilets equipped with seats resembling present – day toilets and drained by sewers existed from Minoan times.

(c) Design and construction principles. Naturally, it is difficult to estimate the design and construction principles of Minoan "engineers" . but it is notable that several ancient works have operated for very long periods, some until recent times. For example, waste and storm-water drainage systems were functioning for millennia. On the other hand, engineers in our times typically design constructions for functioning about 40 to 50 years, as dictated by economic considerations. Thus, the sustainability and durability of Minoan water technologies should be further studied.

(d) Today's applicability. Minoan hydro-technologies could be updated by considering today's apparatus and knowledge and looking for possible applicability particularly in regions under water shortage. Resent report of WHO (2018) indicate that: (i) 2.6 billion people do not have adequate hygiene conditions, (ii) 2 billion people drink polluted water, and (iii) 1.8 million people/yr die from related diseases. Probably the study and exploitation of knowledge from Minoan hydro - technologies, combined with the current available knowledge and technologies, could improve the current situation, especially in the developing world, with environmentally friendly, low cost and high-performance technologies.

References

Alexiou, S. (1964). *Minoan Civilization*. S. Alexiou and Sons, Iraklion, Greece (in Greek).

Angelakis, A. N. (2015). The History of Fountains and Relevant Structures in Crete, Hellas. *Journal for Global Environmental Issues*, 14 (3/4): 200 - 215, DOI: http://dx. doi. org/10. 1504/IJGENVI. 2015. 071865.

Angelakis, A. N. (2016). Evolution of Rainwater Harvesting and Use in Crete, Hellas through the Millennia. *Water Sci. and Techn.: Water Supply*, 16 (6): 1624 - 1638, DOI: 10. 2166/ws. 2016. 084.

Angelakis, A. N. (2017a). Hydro - technologies in Minoan Era. *Water Sci. and Techn.: Water Supply*, 17 (4), 1106 - 1120; DOI: 10. 2166/ws. 2017. 006.

Angelakis, A. N. (2017b). Urban waste - and storm - water management in Greece: Past, Present and Future. *Water Sci. and Techn.: Water Supply*, 17 (5): 1386 - 1399; DOI: 10. 2166/ws. 2017. 042.

Angelakis, A. N. and Spyridakis, S. V. (1996) The status of water resources in Minoan times - A preliminary study. In: *Diachronic Climatic Impacts on Water Resources with Emphasis on Mediterranean Region* (A. Angelakis and A. Issar, Eds.). Springer - Verlag, Heidelberg, Germany, pp. 161 - 191.

Angelakis, A. N. and Koutsoyiannis, D. (2003). Urban Water Resources Management in Ancient Greek Times. *The Encycl. of Water Sci.*, Markel Dekker Inc., (B. A. Stewart and T. Howell, Eds.), Madison Ave. New York, N. Y., USA, pp. 999 - 1007.

Angelakis, A. N. and Vavoula, G. (2012). Evolution of Urban Hydro - technologies in Crete, Hellas Through the Centuries. In: *Protection and Restoration of the Environment* XI, CD Proceedings and Book of Abstracts, 3 - 6 July, 2012, Thessaloniki, Hellas, pp. 323 - 345.

Angelakis, A. N. and Spyridakis, S. V. (2013). Major Urban Water and Wastewater Systems in Minoan Crete, Hellas. *Water Sci. and Techn.: Water Supply*, 13 (3): 564 - 573.

Angelakis, A. N. and Voudouris, K. (2014). Evolution of Geohydrology theough the centuries with emphasis on the Hellenic civilizations. In: *Proc. of the 10th Hydrogeology Confer-*

ence, Thessaloniki, Greece, 8 – 10 October, 2014, pp. 71 – 96.

Angelakis, A. N., Koutsoyiannis, D. and Tchobanoglous, G. (2005). Urban wastewater and stormwater technologies in ancient Greece. *Water Research*, 39, 210 – 220.

Angelakis, A. N., Savvakis, Y. M., and Charalampakis, G. (2007). Aqueducts During the Minoan Era. *Water Sci. and Techn.*: *Water Supply*, 7 (1): 95 – 102.

Angelakis, A. N., Dialynas, M. G., and Despotakis, V., (2012). Evolution of Water Supply Technologies in Crete, Hellas Through the Centuries. In: *Evolution of Water Supply Throughout Millennia* (A. Angelakis *et al.*, Eds). IWA Publishing, London, UK, Ch. 9: 227 – 258.

Angelakis, A. N., Kavoulaki, E., and Dialynas, M. G. (2014). Sanitation and Stormwater and Wastewater Technologies in Minoan Era. In: *Evolution of Sanitation and Wastewater Management through the Centuries* (A. Angelakis and J. Rose, Eds). IWA Publishing, London, UK, Ch. 1: 1 – 24.

Angelakis, A. N., Voudouris, K., and Mariolakos, I. (2016). Groundwater Utilization through the Centuries with Emphasis on Hellenic Civilizations. *Hydrogeology J.*, 24: 1311 – 1324, DOI 10. 1007/s10040 – 016 – 1392 – 0.

Angelakis, A. N., De Feo, G., Laureano, P., and A. Zourou, A. (2013). Minoan and Etruscan Hydro – technologies. *Water*, 5: 972 – 987.

Antoniou, G. and Angelakis, A. N. (2015). Latrines and wastewater sanitation technologies in ancient Greece. In: *Sanitation, Latrines and Intestinal Parasites in Past Populations* (P. D. Mitchell, Ed.). Taylor & Francis Ltd, Imprint: Ashgate publishing limited, Farnham, UK, Ch. 4: 41 – 68, ISBN 978 – 1 – 4724 – 4907 – 8.

Antoniou, G., Xarchakou, R., and Angelakis, A. N. (2006). Water Cistern Systems in Hellas from Minoan to Hellenistic Period. In: *Proc. of 1st IWA International Symposium on Water and Wastewater Technologies in Ancient Civilizations*, 28 – 30 October 2006, Iraklion, Hellas, pp. 457 – 462.

Antoniou, G., De Feo, G., Fardin, F., Tamburrino Tavantzis, A., Khan, S., Fie, T., Ieva Reklaityte, I., Kanetaki, E., Zheng, X. Y., Mays, L., and Angelakis, A. N. (2016). Evolution of Toilets Worldwide Through the Millennia. *Sustainability*, 8 (8), 779; doi: 10. 3390/su8080779.

Cadogan, G. (2007). Water Management in Minoan Crete, Greece: The two cisterns of one Middle Bronze Age settlement. Water Sci. and Techn., *Water Supply*, 7 (1): 103 – 112.

Betancourt, P. P. (2012). *The Dams and water*: *Management systems of Minoan Pseira*, INSTAP Accademy Press: Philadelphi, Pennsylvania, USA.

Defner, M. (1921). *ΔιϋλιστήριοΥστερομινωϊκήςΕποχής*. ΑρχαιολογικήΕφημερίδα,

78, Iraklion, Greece (in Greek).

Dialynas, M. G., Lyritztis, A. G., and Angelakis, A. N. (2006). Historical Development of Water Supply of the City of Iraklio, Greece. In: *Proc. of 1st IWA International Symposium on Water and Wastewater Technologies in Ancient Civilizations*, 28 - 30 October 2006, Iraklio, Greece, pp. 671 - 676.

Davaras, C. (1976). *Guide to Cretan Antiquities.* Noyes Press, Noyes Building, Park Ridge, New Jersey, USA.

Driessen, J. and Schoep, I. (1994). The architect and the scribe: Political implications of architectural and administrative changes on MM 11 - LM IIIA Crete. In: *Proceedings of the 5th International Aegean Conference/*5e Rencontre égéenne internationale. University of Heidelberg, Archäologisches Institut, 10 - 13 April 1994, edited by Robert Laffineur and Wolf - Dietrich Niemeier, Vol. 2: 649 - 664.

Evans, S. A., (1921 - 1935). The palace of Minos at Knossos: A comparative account of the successive stages of the early Cretan civilization as illustrated by the discoveries. Vols. I - IV, Macmillan and Co., London, UK (Reprinted by Biblo and Tannen, New York, USA).

Gorokhovich, Y. Mays, L., and Ullmann, L. (2011). A Survey of Water Technologies of the Ancient Minoans and Traditional Knowledge. *Water Sci. and Tech.: Water Supply*, 11 (4): 388 - 399.

Graham, J. W. (1987) *The Palaces of Crete.* Revised Ed. Princeton University Press, Princeton, New Jersey, USA

Gray, H. F. (1940). Sewerage in Ancient and Medieval Times. *Sewage Works Journal*, 12 (5): 939 - 946.

HYDRIA Project (2011). Water Management in Prehistoric Crete: The case of Choiromandres, Zakros. HYDRIA Project Collection, Storage & Distribution of Water in Antiquity Linking Ancient Wisdom to Modern Needs (http://www.hydriaproject.net/en/greece - crete-water - management - in - zakros - area/importance3/), 2011.

Khan, S., Dialynas, E. G., Kasaraneni, V. K., and Angelakis, A. N. (2019). Similarities of Minoan and Indus Valley Prehistoric Hydro - technologies. *Water Supply* (accepted).

Kollyropoulos, K., Antoniou, G., Kalavrouziotis, I., Krasilnikoff, J., Koutsoyiannis, D., and Angelakis, A. N. (2015). Hydraulic Characteristics of the Drainage Systems of Ancient Hellenic Theatres: Case Study of the Theatre of Dionysus and Its Implications. *ASCE*, J. Irrig. Drain Eng., 141 (11), pp. 04015018 - 1 - 9 (doi: 10.1061/(ASCE) IR.1943 - 4774.0000906).

Koutsoyiannis, D. and Angelakis, A. N. (2003). Hydrologic and Hydraulic Sciences and Technologies in Ancient Greek Times. *The Encycl. of Water Sci.*, Markel Dekker Inc., (B. A. Stewart and T. Howell, Eds.), Madison Ave. New York, N. Y., USA, pp. 415 – 417.

Koutsoyiannis, D., Zarkadoulas, N., Angelakis, A. N. and Tchobanoglous, G. (2008) Urban water management in ancient Greece: Legacies and lessons. *Journal of Water Resources Planning and Management*, 134, pp. 45 – 54.

Markonis, Y., A. N. Angelakis, A. N., Christy, J., and Koutsoyiannis, D. (2016) Climatic variability and the evolution of water technologies in Crete, Hellas, *Water History*, 8 (2), 137 – 157, doi: 10. 1007/s12685 – 016 – 0159 – 9.

Mays, L. W. and Angelakis, A. N. (2012). Gods and Goddesses of Water. In: *Evolution of Water Supply Throughout Millennia.* IWA Publishing, London, UK, Ch. 1: 1 – 18.

Mosso, A. (1907). Escursioni nel Mediterraneo e gli scavi di Creta, Treves, Milano, Italy.

Nikolaou, T. G., Christodoulakos, I., Peperides, P., and Angelakis, A. N. (2017). Evolution of Cretan (Greece) Aqueducts and their Potential for Hydroelectric Exploitation. *Water*, 9 (1), 31; DOI: 10. 3390/w9010031.

Pendlebury, J. D. S. (1950). *Οδηγός τηςΚνωσού*. ΜετάφρασηαπόΝ. Πλάτων, Iraklion, Greece.

Platon, M. (1990). New indications for the problems of purgatory cisterns and bathrooms in Minoan World. In: *Proceedings of the 6th International Cretologic Congress.* Literary Association Chrysostomos, Chania, Hellas, A2, 141 – 155 (in Greek).

Spanakis, S. (1981). *The Water Supply of Iraklion*, 828 – 1939. The Technical Chamber of Hellas, Iraklion, Greece (in Greek).

Tsatsafinos, Ch. (2015). Ancient Greek dams. Common Conference of HHA, HWA, and HCoMWR, Athens, 10 – 12 December 2015, II: 997 – 1004 (in Greek).

Viollet, P. – L. (2007). Water Engineering in Ancient Civilizations 5000 Years of History. *In*: Assoc. of Hydraulic Research (IAHR). Originally in French, L'Hydraulique dans les Civilisations Anciennes. Tailor & Francies Group, CRC Press. Translated into English by Forrest M. Holly, Jr. IAHR, Madrid, Spain.

Wilson, A. (2000). Drainage and Sanitation, In: *Handbook of Ancient Water Technology*, (Ö. Wikander, Ed.), Brill, Leiden, The Netherlands, pp. 151 – 179.

WHO (World Heald Organization) (2018). Drinking – water. WHO Press, CH – 1211 Geneva 27, Switzerland, https: //www. who. int/en/news – room/fact – sheets/detail/drinking – water.

Management and Groundwater Exploitation in Ancient Greece Through the Centuries

Konstantinos S. Voudouris *

几个世纪以来古希腊地下水的开采和管理

康斯坦丁诺斯·S. 沃道里斯

Abstract: Utilizationof groundwater is recorded since the prehistoric period in ancient Greece. Springs were the first source for water supply in first Greek settlements. The construction of wells is known since the Minoan and Mycenaean civilization. Later, in historical times many ancient wells is recorded around the Athens Agora. The construction of wells is based on local conditions, e. g. geology, hydrogeology, topography, climatology, as well as to the local tradition. In addition, rainwater collection systems from the roofs (harvesting) were used for domestic use. Finally, the construction of Eupalinos tunnel in Samos island (2500 years ago), based on qanat technique, represents the peak of ancient Greek hydrotechnology.

Keywords: Eupalinos tunnel; Hellenic civilizations; qanats; springs; wells

摘　要: 地下水的利用在古希腊史前时期就有记录。在最初的希腊定居点，泉水是供水的第一来源。水井的建造自米诺斯和迈锡尼文明就开始

* Lab. of Engineering Geology & Hydrogeology, Dept. of Geology, Aristotle University of Thessaloniki (AUTh) Greece, GR 54124, E-mail: kvoudour@ geo. auth. gr.

UNESCO Center for Integrated and Multidisciplinary Water Resources Management, AUTh.

为人所知。后来，在历史长河中，许多古老水井都被记录在雅典的基石周围。水井要根据当地的地质、水文、地形、气候等情况以及当地的传统来建设。此外，屋顶的雨水收集系统被家庭使用。最后，基于坎儿井的技术，2500年前在萨摩斯岛建造的欧帕利诺斯隧道代表了古希腊水利技术的巅峰。

关键词： 欧帕利诺斯隧道　古希腊文明　坎儿井　泉水　水井

... the principle all of the things is the water…

Thales of Miletus (624 - 546 BC)

Water was one of the most critical issues for the survival of mankind and played an important role in the creation of the settlements. Nomadic man needed water for drinking and used water environment for fishing and hunting. Later, in ancient civilizations humans created water mills to grind wheat, developed drainage, built canals, aqueducts, anti flooding works, cisterns and dams for water storage, and pipes for water transport.

About 7,000 years ago the general climatic conditions in the Eastern Mediterranean became similar to the present day (Voudouris, 2012). This period is characterized by the development and spread of agriculture and increased water demands and people started to harvest and store water in cisterns that were used mainly for drinking purposes. In the early prehistoric times, the daily consumption of water for drinking and cooking purposes is 3 - 5 L/person (Mays et al., 2012), whereas in Classical city of Miletus it was 18 L/person (Kramer, 2002).

After the agriculture development humans constructed wells, irrigated land and built dykes (levees) for floods protection. The ancient civilizations were dependent upon sophisticated systems of water supply (dams, cisterns, galleries, tunnels, etc). These works required a well-organized society (Angelakis & Spiridakis, 2010; Koutsoyiannis et al., 2008).

Human effort was first made to utilize surface waters and springs and therefore the settlements were close to them (Tigris, Euphrates, Nile, Indus, Yellow). People also started to develop drinking water transport systems, which took place through simple channels. Later on one also started using hollow tubes. Egypt used hollow palm trees and China and Japan used bamboo trunks. Eventually one started using clay, wood and even metal (Zheng & Angelakis, 2018). Groundwater has also been a source of water supply since the dawn of human history and agricultural activity.

The ancient Greeks, as opposed to other people, avoided living near rivers, probably for protection from floods and water related diseases, e. g. malaria. The first settlement of many of their towns was on a hill and the water demands were met by springs. The earliest known permanent settlement, which can be classified as urban, is Jericho from 8000 – 7000 BC, located near water sources. In Europe the Neolithic settlement of Sesklo located in the northeaster Thessaly (central Greece) is considered as one of the earliest known Neolithic settlement of Europe. It covered an area of approximately 20 ha (1 ha = 10, 000 m^2) during its peak period at ca. 5000 BC and comprised about 500 to 800 houses with a population estimated potentially, to be as large as 5, 000 people. It is located near springs and other bodies of water. At the same time the first evidence of the purposeful construction of the water supply and drainage and sewerage systems including water treatment devices in Europe comes from Minoan Crete. Advanced hydraulic technology, including small dams, channels, cisterns etc. was developed in the Aegean islands during the Cycladic period (3100 – 1600 BC), as well as on mainland Greece during the Mycenaean period (1600 – 1100 BC). Also the first primitive water supply treatment systems developed (Antoniou et al., 2014; Angelakis & Zheng, 2015).

When the water demands were increased in connection with irrigated agriculture, the groundwater exploitation was expanded with the construction of qanats and dug wells. Rainwater harvesting systems were expanded in areas under low water availability including sedimentation and/or filtration devices, e. g. Aegina Island (Fig. 1). Rainwater collected from the roofs and stored in cisterns was used for domestic use (washing) and water from springs and groundwater was used for drinking purposes.

In Historical times (ca. 650 BC – 330 AD) the advancement of water technology and management is demonstrated with aphythora of hydraulic works in several archaeological sites (e. g. Athens, Pella, Miletus, Naxos, Delos, Crete,

 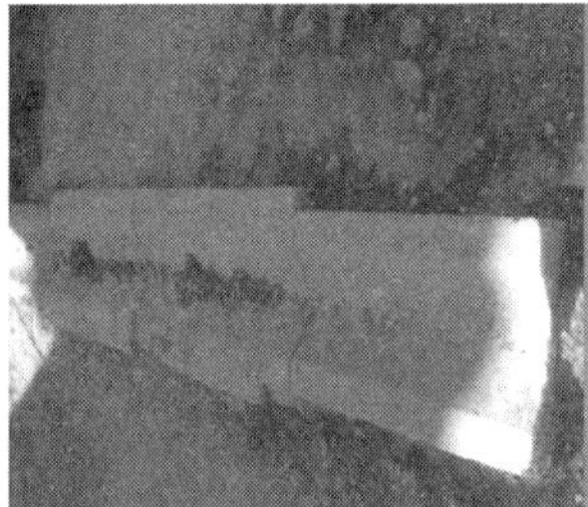 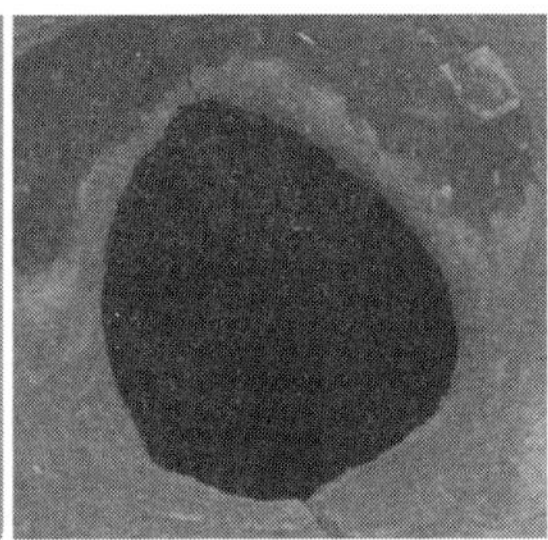

Figure 1 Harvesting system of temple of Afaia in Aegina Island (Photos by K. Voudouris).

and Samos). During the Hellenistic and Roman period the water supply of cities relied on the springs and rivers. In the case of extended dry periods, the water supply was assisted by the exploitation of groundwater from shallow aquifers. The Romans had constructed water supply systems to transfer water for domestic use in the cities, as well as for irrigation purposes. The aqueducts that carried water to the Roman cities from a long distance (100 Km) are admirable; the surviving remains of many aqueducts demonstrate their strong technique (Kaiafa, 2008).

In the Byzantine period, the construction of aqueducts was abandoned and emphasis was put on the construction of tanks or cisterns. The tanks and cisterns were constructed in order to collect rainwater.

Groundwater development dates from ancient times. There is evidence that, during the Minoan period (3500 – 1200 BC) in the island of Crete, wells (with a depth of 10 – 20 m and diameter less than 5 m) and springs were used for water supply (Fig. 2).

During the archaeological excavation of the ancient Athenian agora (marketplace and civic center where ancient Greek democracy first was born) over 400 wells, both public and private were found (Chiotis & Chioti, 2012, Fig. 3). Digging wells was a standard practice all over of Athens, due to the lack of surface waters (rivers).

The material used in the walls of wells are (Angelakis & Voudouris, 2014): 1) wells with blanks walls, 2) wells with stone walls, 3) wells coated with clay walls, 4) wells wit brick wells, 5) molded wall wells and 6) wells with rings of terracotta.

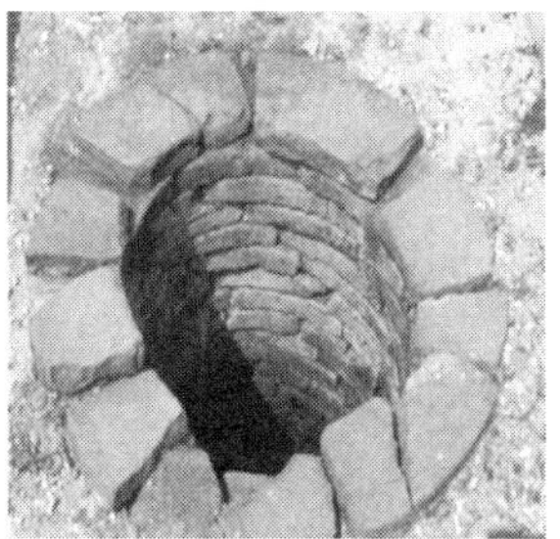

Figure 2 (Left): Stone Age well from Palaikastro town in eastern Crete Island (Greece) and (Right): Roman brick built well from Dion (North Greece).

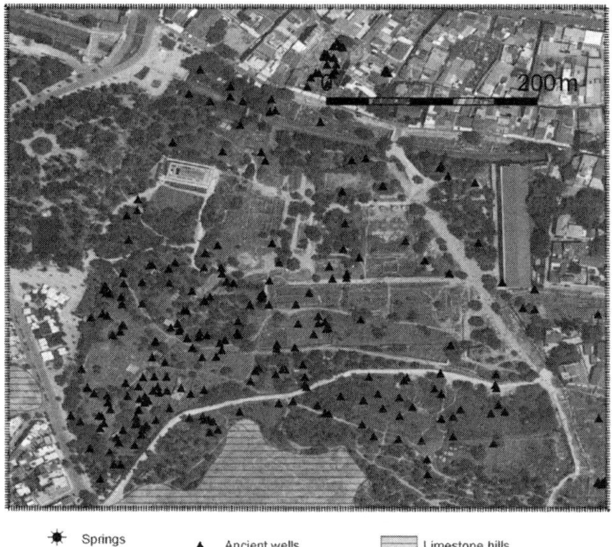

Figure 3 Distribution of ancient wells around the Agora of Athens (Chiotis & Chioti, 2012).

Well construction in the Near East was accomplished by man and animal and was aided by hoists and primitive hand tools. Egyptians had developed drilling systems in rocks as early as 3000 BC. Ancient Chinese also developed a drilling tool for water wells, which is similar to modern machines. Based on the C – 14 dating of the well wood, it was concluded that the oldest well in China was built in 3710 ± 125 BC (Voudouris et al., 2019).

The greatest achievement in groundwater exploitation by ancient peoples was in the construction of long galleries or qanats, which collected water from alluvial deposits and soft sedimentary rocks. Qanats or kariz, which means chain of wells, use remarkable technology of water supply. They are gently sloping, artificially constructed underground galleries, which bring groundwater from the mountainous area to the lowlands where water is needed, sometimes many kilometers away. Many qanats are still in use stretching from China in the east to Morocco in the west.

At the highest point of the mountain the initial (mother) well is constructed in order to ascertain the presence of groundwater. A windlass is set up at the ground surface and the excavated soil is hauled up in buckets. Every 10 – 30 m, vertical wells (shafts) are dug for the removal of soil and ventilation of the tunnel (Fig. 4). Furthermore, the shafts enable access for repair – works. Then, a tunnel is constructed downstream with a height of 1.2 – 2 m and a width of 0.8 – 1.5 m. Qanat tunnels were hand-dug, just large enough to fit the person doing the digging. The water moves along the bottom of the tunnel. The maximum length is approximately 40 – 50 Km. The first qanats were constructed in Persia (ancient Iran) and then spread towards Arabian Peninsula and Egypt (Voudouris et al., 2013). East of Iran the qanats expanded towards Pakistan, Afghanistan and along the oases of Silk Road to China. The longest qanat near Zarand (Iran) is 29 Km long with a mother well depth of 96 m and with 966 shafts along its length. The expansion of Islam led to diffusion of qanats in Mediterranean countries (Spain, Italy, Cyprus, etc).

The technique of tunneling had been used during the prehistoric period in ancient Greece. In the Kopais basin (Viotia, Greece), a tunnel of length 2.2 Km with 16 vertical wells was discovered. This tunnel was constructed in order to drain the basin, which would flood during wet periods. The largest tunnel of Greece is the tunnel of Samos (1 Km), but the largest in total length (tunnel and transfer conduit) is that of Chortiati, Thessaloniki (20 Km) with a water discharge of 80 m^3/h.

The oldest aqueduct in Greece is the tunnel of Samos, which is one of the greatest engineering achievements of ancient times. This tunnel was constructed by-Eupalinos during the sixth century BC (*ca.* 2500 years ago), based on qanat

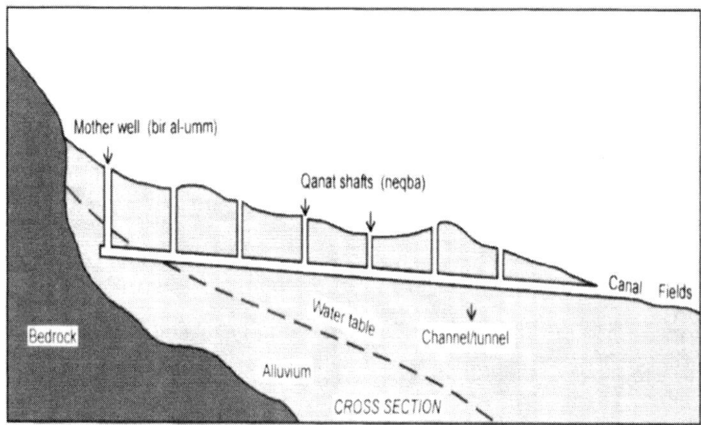

Figure 4 Typical cross-section of a qanat (Lightfoot, 2000).

technology (Apostol, 2004; Voudouris et al., 2013). The goal was to transfer water into the town from a spring that existed at a village, Agiades, northwest from the city. The tunnel that was built for this purpose was dug through limestone by two separate teams advancing in a straight line from both sides of the mountain (Fig. 5).

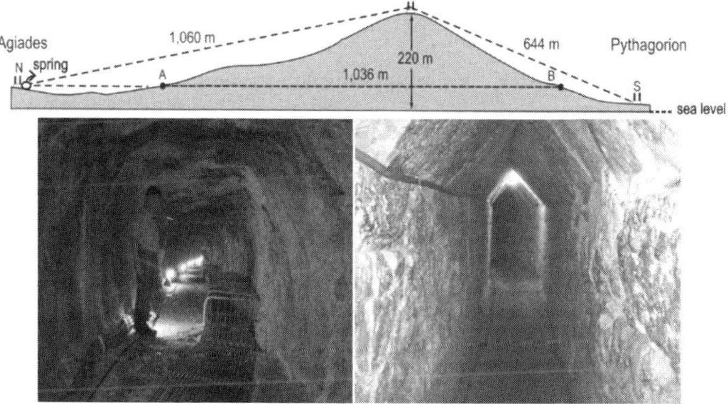

Figure 5 Eupalinos tunnel in Samos Island (Voudouris, 2012).

During the Renaissance of the Middle Ages the basic principles of hydraulics were developed and many hydraulic structures were created by using new materials. In contemporary times (1900 AD – present) the modern water technology of building of dams and reservoirs, drilling deep boreholes, hydroelectric power plants, irrigation and drainage systems was developed.

The methods of drilling for water have improved rapidly during the past 150 years. It is pointed out that the deepest boreholes of Greece have been drilled in Crete Island at a depth of 650 m below ground surface (Angelakis et al., 2016). The perfection of the borehole turbine pump during the period 1910 – 1930 added a further stimulus to the drilling technology (Davis & DeWiest, 1966).

The concluding remarks can be drawn as follows.

– Springs were the first source for water supply in ancient Greece.

– The water technology is characterized by durability and sustainability.

– Water management was related to the geology, geomorphology, topography and the local hydrological and climatic conditions.

– The link of technology with science and philosophy in ancient Greece was an important progress. Rational approach, (based on correct reasoning or ορθόςλόγος in Greek), in decision making was the most important achievement in ancient Greek civilization.

– Ancient peoples used mainly horizontal works for water supply (tunnel, galleries, aqueduct, and qanats) as opposed to using modern vertical works (deep boreholes).

– The Eupalinos tunnel, an outstanding engineering achievement representing the peak of ancient hydraulic technology, which was built 2500 years ago, has been preserved through time.

The ancient technologies and water management practices are a useful tool for current-day engineers. The works demonstrate that the ancient people in Mediterranean countries had an outstanding engineering knowledge of water supply. The study of these works will help solve the current water problem in many areas. The horizontal works (tunnels, galleries, and qanats) have the advantage of avoiding seawater intrusion problems in coastal areas. Furthermore, these water supply works have the advantages of saving energy (no pumping water) and reducing water losses from evaporation. Finally, these works are effective for water harvesting in semi-arid areas.

References

Angelakis, A. N. andSpyridakis, D. S. (2010). Water supply and wastewater management aspects in ancient Hellas. *Water Science and Technology*, *Water Supply* 10 (4), 618 – 628.

Angelakis, A. N. andVoudouris, K. (2014). Evolution of hydrogeology and groundwater utilization through the centuries with emphasis on the Greek civilizations. Proc. of the 10th International Hydrogeological Conference, Thessaloniki, Greece, 8 – 10 October 2014, pp. 71 – 96.

Angelakis, A. N. and Zheng, X. Y. (2015). Evolution of water supply, sanitation, wastewater and stormwater technologies globally. *Water* 7: 455 – 463.

Angelakis, A. N., Voudouris, K., Mariolakos, I. (2016). Groundwater utilization through the centuries with emphasis on Hellenic civilizations. *Hydrogeology Journal* 24, 1311 – 1324.

Antoniou, G. P., Lyberatos, G., Kanetaki, E. I., Kaiafa, A., Voudouris, K., Angelakis, A. N. (2014). History of urban wastewater and stormwater sanitation technologies in Hellas. In *Evolution of Sanitation and Wastewater Technologies Through the Centuries* (Eds Angelakis, A. N. & Rose, J. B.), Chapter 6: 101 – 148.

Apostol, T. M. (2004). The tunnel of Samos. *Engineering and Science*, No 1, 30 – 40.

Chiotis, E. D. and Chioti, E. D. (2012). Water supply of Athens city, Greece in Antiquity. In *Evolution of Water Supply Through the Centuries*, (Eds A. N. Angelakis, L. W. Mays, D. Koutsoyiannis& N. Mamassis,). IWA Publishing, London, UK, Ch. 16, 407 – 442.

Davis, S. N., DeWiest, R. (1966). *Hydrogeology*. John Wiley & Sons, p. 463.

Kaiafa, A. (2008). Urban water supply and drainage systems in Hellenistic and Roman Macedonia. Doctoral dissertation, Dept. of Architecture, Aristotle University, Thessaloniki, Greece (in Greek).

Kramer, M. (2002). Water supply in ancient Greece. http://www.geo.tu – freiberg.de/oberseminar/os03_04/manuela_kramer.pdf.

Mays, L. W., Sklivaniotis, M. and Angelakis, A. N. (2012). Water for human consumption through the history. In *Evolution of Water Supply Through the Millennia* (Eds Angelakis, A. N. et al.). IWA Publishing, London, UK, Chapter 2: 19 – 42.

Koutsoyiannis, D., Zarkadoulas, N., Angelakis, A. N., Tchobanoglous, G. (2008). Urban water management in Ancient Greece: Legacies and Lessons. *Journal of Water Resources Planning and Management* 134, 45 – 54.

Lightfood Dale, R. (2000). The origin and diffusion of qanats in Arabia; new evidence from the northern and southern Peninsula. *The Geographical Journal*, Vol. 166, Part 3, 215 - 226.

Voudouris, K. (2012). Diachronic evolution of water supply in eastern Mediterranean, In *E-volution of Water Supply Through the Millennia*, (A. N. Angelakis, L. W. Mays, D. Koutsoyiannis& N. Mamassis, Eds). IWA - publishing, London, UK, Chapter 4, pp. 77 - 89.

Voudouris, K., Christodoulakos, Y., Stiakakis, M., Angelakis, A. N. (2013). Hydrogeological characteristics of Hellenic aqueducts - like Qanats. *Water* 5, 1326 - 1345.

Voudouris, K., Valipour, M., Kaiafa, A., Zheng, X. Y., Kumar, R., Zanier, K., Kolokytha, E., Angelakis, A. (2019) . Evolution of water wells focusing on Balkan and Asian civilizations. *Water Supply* 19, Issue 2, 347 - 364, IWA Publishing.

Zheng, X. Y. and Angelakis, A. N. (2018). Chinese and Greek ancient urban hydrotech-nologies: similarities and differences. *Water Science and Technology*, *Water Supply*, 18 (2).

References of Herodotus to Hydrology, Hydraulics and Hydraulic works

K. L. Katsifarakis and I. Avgoloupis

希罗多德关于水文、水力学和水利工程文献的研究

K. L. 卡西法拉克和 I. 阿夫戈卢比

Abstract: This paper includes a short presentation of the references to hydrology, hydraulics and hydraulic works, contained in the work *Histories* of Herodotus, which was written during the fifth century B. C. Two of them, regarding: a) the floods and the sources of Nile and b) the artificial expansion of a lake and the diversions of Euphrates River by Nitocris, Queen of Babylon, are further discussed and critically evaluated. Our conclusion is that the work of Herodotus can be generally considered as a valuable source on technical issues.

Keywords: Herodotus; Nile floods; Nile sources; Babylon; hydraulic works

摘　要：本文简要介绍了公元前5世纪希罗多德的著作《历史》中有关水文学、水力学和水力工程的参考文献：(1) 洪水和尼罗河之源；(2) 对巴比伦女王尼托克利斯 (Nitocris) 人工扩张湖泊并改变幼发拉底河河道的问题进行了进一步的讨论和批判性评价。我们的结论是，希罗多德的工作可以被视为技术问题上的一个有价值的来源。

关键词：希罗多德；尼罗河洪水；尼罗河源头；巴比伦；水利工程

1 Introduction

During the recent decades there is a growing interest in the evolution of scientific knowledge in general and in the history of hydraulics and hydraulic works, in particular. This is not surprising, since development of human civilization has been based on man's ability to handle energy and water resources. This interest is testified by the large number of relevant books and papers that are already available (e. g. Angelakis et al, 2012; Aristodemou and Tassios, 2018; Biswas, 1972; De Feo et al, 2013; Mays et al, 2007).

One of the important sources on different uses of water in antiquity is the work of Herodotus *Histories*. In this paper we try to investigate its validity, since it has been questioned by certain subsequent authors. Our research has been based on the Oxford edition of the ancient text (Herodoti Historiae, Oxford University Press, 1975) and the edition of Godley, appearing at: http://www.perseus.tufts.edu/hopper/text?doc=Perseus:text:1999.01.0126.

2 Herodotus and His Work

There are many and easily accessible sources regarding the life of Herodotus, e. g. De Romilly, 1995; https://thegreatthinkers.org/herodotus/biography/. Nevertheless, many details of his life are only approximately known. It is generally believed that he was born in 485/484 B. C. in Halicarnassus, a Greek city of the Asia Minor coast, present day Turkey, shown in the map of Fig. 1. Presumably, his family was rich, and he had access to very good education. As a freedom-lover, he participated in failed attempt against the pro-persian tyrant of his home town, and he was exiled to the island of Samos. Later on, though, he returned to Halicarnassus and expelled the tyrant. During his life, he spent some time in Athens and he travelled a lot around the then known world. These travels helped him a lot in authoring his only (and unique) work, namely the *Histories*. Herodotus died in the Greek colony Thurii, Southern Italy, sometime between 429 and 413

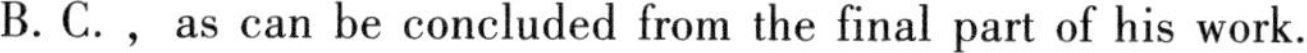

B. C. , as can be concluded from the final part of his work.

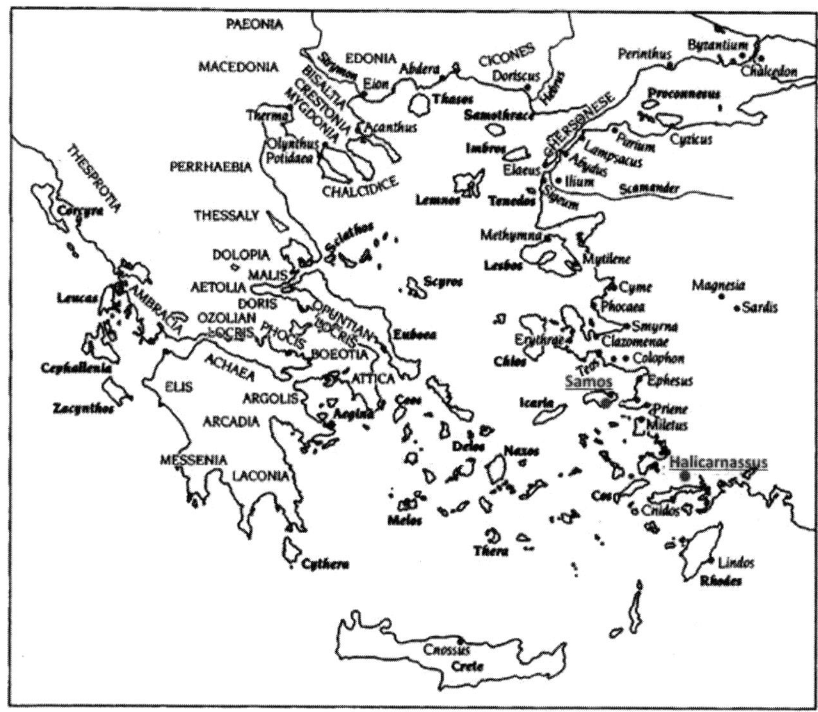

Fig. 1 Map of Asia Minor, Greece and the Aegean Sea.

Source: https://erenow.net/ancient/historiesherodotus/29.php (reworked by the authors).

The main axis of Herodotus work, which is divided into 9 books, is the rise of the Persian Empire and its conflagration with Greek city-states, during the 5th century B. C. ; but it also includes rich and diverse information on many peoples and places. What differentiates Herodotus from earlier authors is the conscious search for the reasons behind facts. He tries to gather material form inscriptions and works of others, he discusses and asks the opinion of priests, civil servants and eyewitnesses. He travels long distances to check things with his own eyes. He tries to evaluate the information that gathers, and when he has doubts he makes it clear. Nevertheless, some of the details that he presents and some of his evaluations are not accurate. For this reason, some ancient authors, like Plutarch, questioned the validity of his work, while others, like Cicero, who named Herodotus "Father of History", admired it. This dispute has continued until our times. Some recent scientific findings, though, such as the discovery of a shipwreck in Nile that fits perfectly to the Herodotean description of unusual river boats, have added to the credibility of Herodotus. Finally, it should be mentioned that new and positive light has been recently shed on the work of Herodotus by scientists of different disciplines, such as political science (e. g. Schlosser, 2014; Thompson, 1996).

3 References to Hydrology, Hydraulics and Hydraulic Works

The main references to hydrology, hydraulics and hydraulic works, that we have spotted in the work of Herodotus (Avgoloupis and Katsifarakis, 2009), appear in the following list, classified by geographical area, namely: a) Egypt, b) Mesopotamia, c) the part of Asia west of Mesopotamia and d) Europe (mainly Greece). The respective extracts of the ancient text appear in parentheses. Descriptions of bridging rivers and the Hellespont are not included.

a) Egypt (map of. Fig. 2)

The floods and the sources of Nile (II. 19 – II. 34).

The works of Pharaoh Min in Memfis, including a dyke to change the route of Nile and the construction of an artificial lake (II. 99).

The canal between Nile and the Red Sea, a substitute to modern Suez Canal. Herodotus states that Pharaoh Necos failed to construct it, but Darius, king of Persia was successful (II. 158).

The irrigation and water supply channel network, constructed by Pharaoh Sesostris, in order to feed areas away from the Nile (II. 108, II. 137).

The impressive Moeris Lake, considered as artificial by Herodotus (II. 101, II. 149, II. 150).

The channels bringing water from Nile and surrounding the Pyramids of Kheops and Khephren, who are described as wicked rulers (II. 124, II. 127).

The canals surrounding the Bubastis Temple, which carried water from Nile (II. 138).

Fig. 2 Map of Egypt and the western part of Asia.

Source: https://erenow.net/ancient/historiesherodotus/29.php (reworked by the authors).

The "secret" conduit used byNitocris, Queen of Egypt for murderous purposes (II. 100).

b) Mesopotamia (map of Fig. 3)

The artificial expansion of a lake and the diversions of Euphrates River by Nitocris, Queen of Babylon (I. 185).

The flood – protecting levees, built by Semiramis and Nitocris, Queens of Babylon (I. 184).

Lining of the banks of Euphrates in the city of Babylon (I. 186).

Network of irrigation channels in Mesopotamia, to which the land fertility was due (I. 193).

Diversion of Euphrates River by Cyrus, king of Persia, in order to facilitate his attack to Babylon through the river route (I. 191).

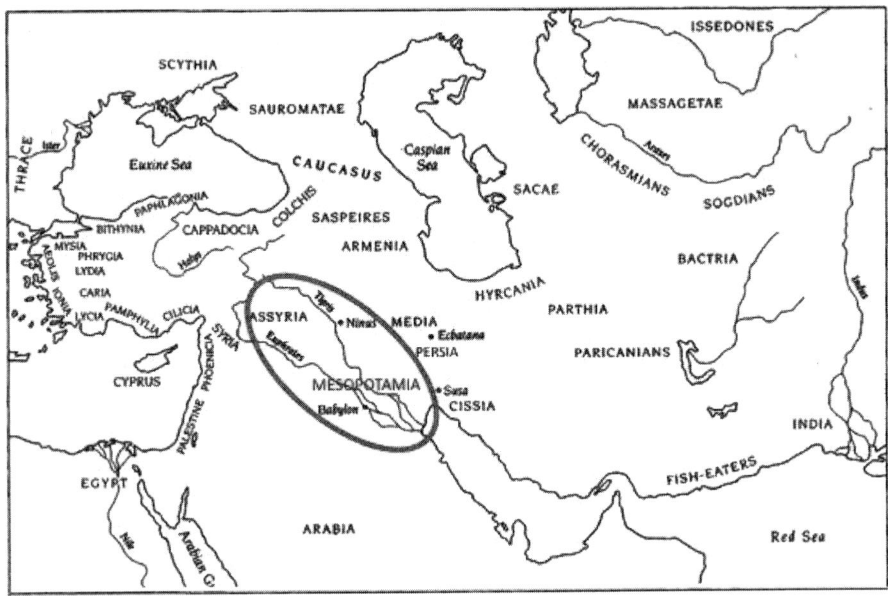

Fig. 3 Mesopotamia, in the Persian Empire.

Source: https://erenow.net/ancient/historiesherodotus/29.php (reworked by the authors).

c) The western part of Asia

The diversion of Halys River in Asia Minor by Croesus, king of Lydia, in order to facilitate its crossing by his army (I. 75).

The 180 canals, constructed by Cyrus, king of Persia, in order to divert Gyndes, tributary of Tigris River (I. 189).

The attempt to trench the Isthmus of Cnidos at the Asian Minor coast, as defense measure (I. 174).

The dams constructed by Darius, king of Persia, in northern Persia, and used to extort local people in need of water (III. 117).

The pumping of tar and oil (VI. 119).

The water supply of the Persian army by the Arabs during the campaign of the Persian king Cambyses against Egypt (III. 9).

d) Europe (mainly Greece)

Rivers running dry during the Xerxes campaign against Greece (VII. 43, VII. 58, VII. 108 - 109, VII. 124 - 127, VII. 129, VII. 196).

The water supply tunnel of Eupalinos in Samos Island, Greece (III. 60).

The breakwater of the Samos port (III. 60).

The Athos peninsula canal, in Macedonia, Greece, to allow for safe passage of the Persian fleet (VII. 22 - 24, VII. 37, VII. 116 - 117, VII. 122).

The plan of Xerxes to flood the Thessaly plain, Greece, by constructing a dam on the only river that drains it (VII. 128 - 130).

Use of hot water for ground erosion, as a defensive measure against cavalry attack (VII. 176).

4 Discussion of Selected References

In this paper we discuss in more detail the following:

- The floods and the sources of Nile.
- The artificial expansion of a lake by Nitocris, Queen of Babylon.

4.1 The floods and the sources of River Nile (II. 19 - II. 34)

Herodotus describes the course of River Nile through Egypt and discusses the importance of its deposits for the country in the first section of the second book. He starts discussing its flood explicitly in II. 19, where he states that its flow is low in winter and high during summer, unlike all other rivers. Then he investigates the causes of this unique behavior. First, he asks the Egyptians, whose wisdom he respects, but he gets no answer. Then he presents the theoretical opinions of three-

Greeks (without naming them) in a rather derogatory way and dismisses all of them.

According to the first, the floods of the Nile are due to the etesian winds (namely the NW winds that blow in Eastern Mediterranean during summer), which inhibit the outflow of its waters to the sea. Herodotus refutes this theory, using two very good arguments: a) In certain years no etesian winds have blown, but Nile exhibited the same flood patter, and b) The etesian winds should have the same effect on other rivers, flowing in direction opposite to them. He adds, remarkably, that this effect should be even more pronounced in rivers with currents less strong than that of the Nile.

The second theory holds that the water of Nile come directly from the Ocean, which flows around the whole Earth. Herodotus (in II. 20) correctly calls it even less scientific than the first one and refutes it, stating that he considers the existence of River Ocean a myth, introduced in poetry by Homer or some other older poet (II. 23).

The third theory (attributed by subsequent Greek authors to Anaxagoras) states the Nile is fed from melting snow. Herodotus calls it even more erroneous, although more rational than the others, since the Nile flows from hottest areas to cooler ones. He adds the following arguments to support his claim: a) The winds blowing from these areas are hot; b) The whole area is snowless, since it is rainless; and c) Local people are black, because of the heat. Ironically, in this case, the approach of Herodotus is reasonable but wrong, since it is based on erroneous data. He was not aware of the climatic conditions at the area of the Great African Lakes, where the sources of the Nile are found.

After refuting existing theories, Herodotus states that he should present his own. According to it, the sun during winter is closer to Africa; moreover, the sky there is clear and the land warm, so the sun "pulls" a lot of water from Nile towards him and doing that he "pushes" it upwards. Then, the winds catch, scatter and dissolve it. For this reason, winds blowing from that country are the most rainy. During summer, though, the sun returns to the middle of the sky, and pulls water from all rivers alike. Moreover, all rivers except for the Nile are fed by rain during winter time. The above explanation is wrong; nevertheless, it shows that Herodotus understands the basic notions of the hydrologic cycle, like evaporation and water vapor transfer by the winds.

Herodotus then presents an example of scientific curiosity and research, namely his quest for the sources of Nile (II. 28 – II. 34). As he cannot find reliable information, he travels up to the city of Elephantine, around 1000 km from the mouth of Nile. There, he hears that an additional part of Nile is known, which someone needs four months to travel, partly by ship and partly on foot. Moreover, the direction of its flow there is from West towards East. From then on, the river course is unknown. Herodotus, then presents his theory that the Nile flows in the middle of Africa from west to east, the same way that Ister transverses Europe in the same direction, and that the course of the two rivers is equal. He bases his theory upon: a) An information that certain Nasamones (people living along the north coast of Africa), after crossing part of the African desert, had arrived at a large river, flowing from west towards east, where they spotted crocodiles; b) Some similarities that he finds between Nile and Ister; and c) His belief about symmetry of the world. While his theory is completely erroneous, we should give Herodotus credit for the following: a) His thirst for knowledge, and b) his scientific approach. In his own words, he draws conclusions for the unknowns from what is known (II. 33). Again, it is not the reasoning, but the missing data that betray him.

By the way, Herodotus refutes, quite correctly, the information, offered to him by an educated Egyptian, that the spring of Nile is bottomless. This claim was based on measurements conducted by Pharaoh Psammetichus, who had let a very long rope down to the spring, but it never reached its bottom. Herodotus, in good faith, does not exclude the possibility that the measurements took place, but he refutes the conclusion. His explanation is that river currents have prevented the rope from reaching the spring bottom.

4.2 The artificial expansion of a lake and the diversions of Euphrates River by Nitocris, Queen of Babylon (I. 185).

Herodotus, in I. 185, describes a huge hydraulic engineering project, undertaken for defense purposes. He attributes it to Nitocris, Queen of Babylon. As a reason, he mentions the aggressivity of Medes, who had already conquered many cities, including Ninus. The whole project consisted of two parts: The first aimed to avoid a surprise attack by enemies using Euphrates, which flowed through Babylon. To achieve this goal, she turned the course of the river form straight to crooked, at a selected site upstream of the city, in order to increase its length and to slow down water velocity. The respective text of Herodotus is quite clear and has raised no doubts. But the text which describes the second part of the project, and refers to a lake, has puzzled scholars. For instance, How and Wells (1975) find it "most obscure", while Asheri (2007) states that "Herodotus seems not to have understood the function of the lake".

Hopefully we have arrived at its correct interpretation in a previous work of ours (Katsifarakis and Avgoloupis, 2013), having the reasonable initial attitude that Herodotus is accurate, unless proven otherwise. We based our conclusions, both on engineering and philological considerations. Regarding the philological arguments, we have interpreted literally the key-phrase "*ὤρυσσεἔλυτρονλίμνῃ*". The word "*ὤρυσσε*" means dug and the word "*λίμνῃ*" means lake (in the Dative case). Finally, the word "*ἔλυτρον*", accordingto the dictionary of H. G. Liddell – R. Scott, generally means case (from a bow-case to cases of bodies of water, namely reservoirs). From the engineering (and practical) point of view we took into account that the purpose of the lake was to serve as a defense barrier and that the work had to be constructed in very short time. So, we have arrived at the following interpretation: The Babylonian ruler, called by Herodotus Nitocris, did not construct a new artificial lake, but laterally extended a pre-existing one, that was situated close to the river portion, that she changed from straight to crooked. Then, the respective text should be interpreted in the following way (Katsifarakis and Avgoloupis, 2013):

"Then a long way upstream of Babylon she dug a perimetric extension to a lake a little aside from the river, always digging down to the water level, and making its circumference equal to 420 furlongs; and she used all that was dug out of this hole, disposing it along the edges of the river. And when she had it all dug, she brought stones and made a coping all around the lake. She did both of these, namely the river to wind and the dug area to be a marsh, so that the current would be slower, its force broken by the large number of windings, and that the passages to Babylon would be crooked, and that the way around the lake coming next to them would be long. "

5 Concluding Remarks

Herodotus is a valuable source of information on hydraulic works constructed during and before the 5th century BC by different people, and on the respective scientific knowledge. He has got an inquiring mind, ceaseless thirst for knowledge and he tries to follow a scientific approach. His conclusions are not always correct, since sometimes they are based on erroneous or insufficient data. Nevertheless, if we approach his work positively, namely believing that it is accurate, unless proven otherwise, we may reach better and more accurate interpretations.

References

Angelakis A., Mays N. W., Koutsoyiannis D., Mamassis N. (2012). *Evolution of Water Consumption Through the Millennia*, IWA Publishing, London.

Asheri D. "Book I", in O. Murray and A. Moreno (eds.) *A Commentary on Herodotus Books I – IV*, 57 – 218, Oxford, 2007.

Aristodemou G. A. and Tassios Th. P. (eds). (2018). *Great Waterworks in Roman Greece: Aqueducts and Monumental Fountain Structures*, Archaeopress Publishing Ltd. Oxford.

Avgoloupis I. and Katsifarakis K. L., (2009). "References to hydraulics and hydrology in the work of Herodotus", *Hydrotechnika*, 18 – 19, 21 – 34, 2009 (in Greek).

Biswas A. K. (1972). *History of Hydrology*, North Holland Publ. Company, Amsterdam – London.

De FeoG., Angelakis A. N., Antoniou G. P., etc. (2013). Historical and technical notes on aqueducts from prehistoric to medieval times. *Water* 5 (4): 1996 – 2025.

De Romilly J. (1995). *A Short History of Greek Literature*, Chicago: University of Chicago Press.

Godley A. D. （Ed.）（1999）. Herodotus, *The Histories*

http：//www. perseus. tufts. edu/hopper/text? doc = Perseus：text：1999. 01. 0126.

Herodoti Historiae, Oxford University Press, 1975.

How W. W. and Wells J. （1975）. *A Commentary on Herodotus*, 144 – 45, Oxford.

Katsifarakis K. L. andAvgoloupis I. （2013）. "A new approach to the description of a Babylonian hydraulic work by Herodotus", *Classical Quarterly*, 63（2）: 888 – 891.

Mays L. W. , Koutsoyiannis D. and Angelakis A. N. （2007）. "A brief history of water supply in antiquity", *Water Science and Technology*: *Water Supply*, 7（1）: 1 – 12.

Schlosser J. A. （2014）. "Herodotean Realism", *Political Theory*, 42 – 3: 239 – 61.

Thompson N. （1996）. *Herodotus and the Origins of the Political Community*, New Haven: Yale University Press.

The Online Liddell – Scott – Jones Greek – English Lexicon:

http：//stephanus. tlg. uci. edu/lsj/#eid = 34972&context = lsj&action = hw – list – click.

https：//thegreatthinkers. org/herodotus/biography/.

https：//erenow. net/ancient/historiesherodotus/29. php.

水与社会

围垦活动中的水域产权纠纷、宗族与跨宗族联合

——以民国湖北樊湖水域为例

徐　斌*

摘　要：本文以湖北省档案馆所藏的四宗民国湖案为例，讨论了光绪年间樊口闸坝之争事件后樊湖水域的社会状况。1925年（民国十四年）樊口大堤修成后，水面淤生出大量的农田，刺激着水域上灌溉用水权、湖地种植权与湖草收益权等产权形态的发展，这些产权大多是通过湖规的逐渐形成、买卖，乃至于打官司等方式，衍生自明初以来便扎根于湖区的渔户宗族手中之湖业。由于水域在物理上的不可分割性，在湖区已经形成了“宗族—同业甲宗族联合—全湖宗族联合”的社会群体序列，虽然内部多有矛盾，但对外部而言，水域社会仍是一个相对封闭的世界。水面淤生成田，原本的社会运行规则依然得以延续，这一状况导致外来者若非实力雄厚则很难为业已成形的湖区社会所认可。因而，樊口闸坝之争事件应当理解为一个相对封闭的湖区群体对外来者的排斥，而不是渔农等产业间的矛盾。

关键词：樊口　水域产权　宗族　水域社会　围垦

Abstract: During the reign of Guangxu, the Fan - kou Dam dispute ended with the imperial court ordering the construction of the dam. After the construction of Fan - kou dike in 1925, a large number of farmland was deposited from the lakes, which stimulated the development of water rights, lake land planting rights and lake grass revenue rights. There are two ways to establish these rights:

* 徐斌，武汉大学历史学院副教授。

first, property transaction; second, the "lake regulation" formed through negotiation or lawsuit. They derived from the fishing rightsownedbythe fishermen familieswho lived there since the early Ming Dynasty. Since the water area is not easy to be divided, the lake area has formed a social group sequence of "clan – Yejia clans – the whole lake clans" . Although there are many internal contradictions, to the outside, the water area society is still a relatively closed world. The original rules of social operation are still being continued. This situation makes it difficult for outsiders to be recognized by the formed lake society unless they are strong. Therefore, the dispute between Fan – kou Dam should be understood as the exclusion of outsiders from a relatively closed group in the lake region, rather than the contradiction between fishing, farming and other industries.

Keywords: Fan – kou; Water rights; Clan; Water region society; Reclaim land from lake

一 问题的提出

产权是中国经济史研究的核心问题，然而，以往的研究大多聚焦于农耕文明之根本的土地，对河湖水域的产权形态则往往语焉不详，间有涉及者，亦多从王朝国家与土地的角度予以解说，仅视之为土地的附庸或是延伸。[①] 近些年来，随着民间文献等史料的发掘，学者们开始从水域自身的角度讨论产权与社会组合方式、秩序的形成与发展等话题，由于内陆地区的大型水域主要集中在长江中下游地区，因而相关的讨论也以这些地区为主，其中又以长江中游地区的讨论更为深入。[②] 可以说，这些研究较为深刻地揭

① 参见徐斌《以水为本位：对“土地史观”的反思与“新水域史”的提出》，《武汉大学学报·人文科学版》2017年第1期。

② 例如张小也依据湖区宗族的家谱，讨论了湖北汈汊湖数姓对“湖分”的争夺，力图从“当时人们的观念世界”出发，在区域社会的结构与发展脉络中理解民事法秩序（张小也：《明清时期区域社会中的民事法秩序——以湖北汉川汈汊黄氏的〈湖案〉为中心》，《中国社会科学》2005年第6期）；梁洪生、刘诗古利用在鄱阳湖区发现的湖册、渔业契约、家谱等文献，敏锐地从湖区水域的“水无硬界”等特性出发，指出该水域的业权存在“季节性模糊”，及其对于水面权交易的影响；此外，针对所使用的这些民间文献，梁洪生还指出它们有着一个不断“生产”和更新的过程，应作“短时段”划分；刘诗古则进一步讨论了鄱阳湖渔民社群有关水面产权观念的变化，从而推动着湖区渔业捕捞秩序的（转下页注）

示了内陆地区的河湖水域有别于土地的产权形态，并使得我们能够在一定程度上站在水上看水，这不仅是对以往站在土地上看水的单一向度进行了补充，更呈现出一种新的研究视阈。

另外，研究视阈的转换同样带来了更深层次的思考，即仅仅关注水域本身的变化是否就能展示出完整的水域世界？质言之，是否仍然需要将土地与水域联系起来进行综合考察？进一步的问题则是如何将二者有机结合起来。毫无疑问，正如荀子所云："泽人足乎木，山人足乎鱼。"[①] 水域世界从来都只是相对独立地存在，自形成伊始便与周围世界存在着广泛的物质交换。清代江汉－洞庭等湖区的民众对此的回答，则揭示出二者间除经济交往以外更为直接的关联。清代江汉平原流传着"鱼贵米贱""鱼贱米贵"的民谚，[②] 说明了土地与水域二者之间不可割裂的联系性。由于围垦水域而形成的垸田肥沃异常，平年收获颇丰，当水灾来临时，种植农业遭受打击，与之相反的是渔业则会获得丰收。很显然，水域在这里被视为是潜在的土地，而水域与土地间的联系性主要是源自土地对水域的侵入。这是一个自宋代已然开始的历史过程，背后则是王朝国家力量对于水域世界的介入并逐渐加强控制。传统王朝国家以土地为依托，以种植农业为根本，形成了灿烂的农耕文明，但却并不意味着国家就放弃了对水域世界的控制，在国家控制渐趋加强的历史过程中所形成的诸如家谱、水面契约、湖册等民间文献，正是王朝国家作为制度性力量在水面出现之后，"泽人"与之进行博

(接上页注②)形成与发展（梁洪生：《捕捞权的争夺："私业"、"官河"与"习惯"——对鄱阳湖区渔民历史文书的解读》，《清华大学学报·哲学社会科学版》2008年第5期；《从"四林外"到大房：鄱阳湖区张氏谱系的建构及其"渔民化"结局——兼论民国地方史料的有效性及"短时段"分析问题》，《近代史研究》2010年第2期；刘诗古：《明末以降鄱阳湖地区"水面权"之分化与转让——以"卖湖契"和"租湖字"为中心》，《清史研究》2015年第3期；《清代内陆水域渔业捕捞秩序的建立及其演变——以江西鄱阳湖区为中心》，《近代史研究》2018年第3期）；对于有着江汉、洞庭湖群的两湖地区，笔者亦曾使用赤历、家谱、契约以及各类官方文献，从整体上梳理了明清时期这些水域产权形态的演变状况，指出在明初河泊所制度、明中期开始大规模围垦水面的活动，以及明清商品经济的发展，导致了水域产权分化为捕捞权、湖水灌溉权、湖草收益权、湖地种植权等多种形态（徐斌：《明清两湖水域产权形态的变迁》，《中国经济史研究》2017年第2期）。

① 《荀子·王制》，辽宁教育出版社，1997，第35页。

② 光绪《江陵县志》卷二十一《风土·风俗》（《中国地方志集成·湖北府县志辑》第31册，江苏古籍出版社，2001，第66页）载："荆州旧为鱼米之乡，方言云鱼贵则米贱，米贵则鱼贱。"

弈的产物或衍生物，这才是湖区民间文献的根本属性。可以说，当王朝国家力量进入水域世界之后，水域与土地间产生了更为紧密的联系，且主要表现为土地以及以土地为根本的王朝国家对于水域的侵入，因此，对此之后的水域世界的考察，理所当然地必须要与土地相结合，也必须关注到湖区民间文献产生与使用、流传的制度性背景。

历代王朝在水域上推行的各种制度中，明代的河泊所制度非常关键。明初朱元璋广设河泊所，编排渔户，对统治区域内的水域征收鱼课，可以说这是统一的中央王朝首次大规模地介入水域世界之中。各地区中位于长江中游的湖北地区河泊所设置最早、数量最多，在这一地区，由于国家将渔户与办课水域联系在一起，以利于鱼课的落实，此项措施的实施在明以后逐渐带来的结果是，一方面国家既满足了税收的需要，又加强了对水域世界的控制；另一方面，渔户则逐渐控制了办课水域，形成了产权观念。可见，这种产权观念乃在国家与“泽人”的互动过程中形成。互动之中，国家的力量基本打乱了原有的水域秩序，进而促使了一种新秩序的渐次形成，即造就了一个湖主与捕捞者相分离的分层与多元的水域世界，从而使“产权”在该世界中居于核心地位。[①] 因而，产权既是一把解开水域世界密码的钥匙，同时也只有在具体的水域世界中，将土地与水域二者有机结合起来，才能更为清晰准确地了解这把钥匙。这正是研究河湖水域产权形态的意义之所在。然而，水域毕竟不同于土地，各种异于土地的自然特性，造成水域上形成的产权形态与土地有着较大的区别，进而又导致了水域“新秩序”呈现出有别于土地的社会形态。其中，最主要的方面当为“水无硬界”，[②] 因为水域在物理上不便如田地那样分割成小块、各归田户，在此状况下，只能由若干渔户共同拥有一片水域，从事渔业生产，河湖便逐渐形成为同甲业户之“同业”。[③]因此，“同业”遂成为理解水域社会的关键之处。

那么，在以土地为依托的王朝国家不断侵入的情况下，除了将水域变

① 徐斌：《明清两湖水域产权形态的变迁》，《中国经济史研究》2017 年第 2 期；“同业”者，乃是渔户自己的说法，黄冈《刘氏宗谱》卷首一《业甲序》［民国丙戌年（1946），藜照堂刊本］云：“业甲者，业渔以供国赋也。甲有八，我居其一，八家同业。”

② 湖北省档案馆藏 LS7－2－779：《湖北省高等法院审理天门严少陵、刘玉善等确认取鱼权利案（1948）》，附《大栎萧氏家乘全书》卷二十四《建设志》。

③ 徐斌：《明清两湖水域产权形态的变迁》，《中国经济史研究》2017 年第 2 期。

为土地这一最为直接的后果，明代以后的水域与土地究竟还产生了哪些关联，这些关联又是怎样产生与发展的呢？另外，水域变成土地之后，对湖区的社会形态造成了什么样的影响，又呈现出怎样的社会场景呢？在湖北境内的河湖水域上，各种产权形态的出现有先有后，历史演进至民国时期，各种产权形态的发育则趋于成熟，使得我们可以在民国这个具体的时间节点上，对这些水域产权形态进行综合考察。基于此，本文将民国时期以樊口为入江口的樊湖水域作为主要研究对象，意图对上述问题有所回答。

二　樊口闸坝之争与民国湖案

樊口自古闻名，所产武昌鱼盛誉在外，由樊口入江的樊湖水域面积较大，直至今天仍是湖北地区最大的湖泊群之一。顾炎武在《肇域志》中称："樊溪，在樊山西南，控县南湖泽凡九十九，东为樊口，入于江，一名樊港。"[①] 所谓"湖泽凡九十九"，即"此港九十里内港汊分歧，旁通各湖，如蔓系瓜。其右有洋湖、鱼湖、月山湖、泾头湖、鸭儿湖、江夏湖、鲊洲湖等湖共十二湖，其左有枨洲湖、夏兴湖、三山湖、保安湖等湖共六湖"，[②] 各湖皆通过"九十里"樊溪，经樊口入于长江。晚清时期，水域涵盖"江夏以南，通山以北，咸宁以东，武昌、大冶以西，群山环之，平衍八百余里"，[③] 各湖中最大者为梁子湖，这些河湖在当地统称为樊湖水域。

光绪年间，樊湖水域上发生了一件震惊朝野的大事件。光绪三年（1877年）十一月初七日，湖广总督李瀚章派兵掘毁了当地士绅在樊口所修的大坝。此大坝的兴修是在当地士绅多次向省府请愿未获批准之后私自建筑的，被掘毁之后，士绅们开始动用各种资源，尤其是湖北籍京官等人脉

① （清）顾炎武：《肇域志》卷三《湖广·武昌府》，上海古籍出版社，2004。

② 光绪《武昌县志》卷二《水利·附樊口建闸奏议·巡阅长江水师前兵部侍郎臣彭玉麟跪奏，为遵旨查明樊口地方江水入湖之处，必应修补老堤，建筑新闸，以卫民田，恭折仰祈圣鉴事》，页十三下至页二十二上，光绪十一年重修本，武汉大学图书馆藏。

③ 光绪《武昌县志》卷二《水利·附樊口建闸奏议·侍讲张之洞樊口闸坝私议》，页十三下至页二十二上，光绪十一年重修本，武汉大学图书馆藏。

关系，使得此事受到了慈禧太后的高度重视。光绪四年（1878 年）八月初七日，时任兵部侍郎的彭玉麟奉旨孤身前往樊口秘密进行踏勘调查，勘后，即以主张筑堤建坝复旨。由此，清朝统治阶级内部逐渐形成了分别以李瀚章与彭玉麟为中心的“掘堤派”与“建堤派”两个派别集团，展开了针锋相对的争辩。最终，建堤派的主张得到了慈禧的基本认可，命在樊口建立闸坝，该事件得以暂时告一段落。

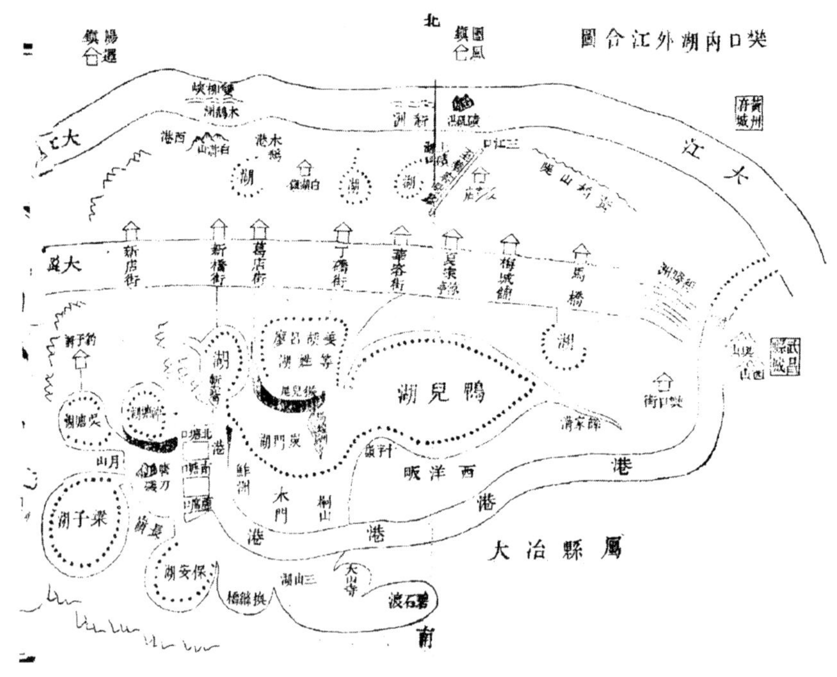

图 1　樊口内湖外江合图

资料来源：（清）范鸣龢：《淡灾蠡述》，光绪五年刻本。

两派的主张中，掘堤派的主要着眼点在于整个长江中下游流域内更为长期的水利安全，即沿江诸湖与长江本来就是自然界中不可分割的一个整体，湖泊起到了洪水期调节江湖水位的水柜作用，若是强行将之阻隔开，只是部分的地方受益，却极易造成更大规模的水患。[①] 作为建堤派的代表，

① 光绪《武昌县志》卷二《水利・附樊口建闸奏议・头品顶戴湖广总督臣李瀚章、湖北巡抚臣潘蔚跪奏，为樊口创建石闸关系民间利病，遵旨查明具奏，一面饬议举行，并将历办情形恭折缕陈，仰祈圣鉴事》，页十三下至页二十二上，光绪十一年重修本，武汉大学图书馆藏。

彭玉麟声称："查梁子湖各港汊两岸皆平畴沃野，农民赖以安业，滨湖各州县所属田亩，惟武昌县十居其五，各县又分居其五。"滨湖田地可岁收"六百余万石"之谷，殊属可观，而且"国多惟正之供"，[①] 正由于此，在他的眼中，樊口的筑坝建闸，可以有效地巩固这些湖田。

事实上，明清以来两湖地区作为著名的粮食产地，都得益于类似的对水面的围垦，围湖造田创造出了一种新的田土形式，即垸田，这正是明中期"湖广熟，天下足"谚语产生的背景。[②] 垸田不断地被开垦出来以至于过度的开发，在清嘉道以后则带来了水旱灾害频发等严重的环境后果。[③] 很显然，上述樊口闸坝事件的爆发以及由此引发的朝中政策之争，正是这个长时期的结构性变化在积累到相当程度之后的短期剧烈反应，可以说，樊口大闸的建立标志着土地对该水域的侵入达到了一个高峰。不过，因樊湖水域属岗边构造湖，并不易完全围垦成田，因而，樊湖水域提供了一个可将水域与土地综合起来考察的典型个案。

不仅如此，光绪年间朝廷中的政策之争，显示出统治阶级只是将水域当作土地的附庸之本质。对于两派各自的主张，张之洞曾评价道："余从邸抄中得彭李两疏，读之，彭疏质实，为樊口以内农民计，李疏闳通，为滨江全局计。"[④] 该论看似公允，不过且先不论建堤派的出发点是为了保护围垦成田的土地，即使是掘堤派对过度围垦水域的警惕，仍旧是侧重于围垸的发展使得江湖关系发生演变，造成洪涝灾害频发，以至于危及岸上居民生命安全，并破坏了农业生产。二者都是站在土地的立场上看水，并未过多考虑依水为生的渔民等水上活动人群的利益，甚而，彭玉麟还不无讽刺

---

① 光绪《武昌县志》卷二《水利·附樊口建闸奏议·巡阅长江水师前兵部侍郎臣彭玉麟跪奏，为遵旨查明樊口地方江水入湖之处，必应修补老堤，建筑新闸，以卫民田，恭折仰祈圣鉴事》，页十三下至页二十二上，光绪十一年重修本，武汉大学图书馆藏。

② 参见张建民《"湖广熟，天下足"论述》，《中国农史》1987年第4期；张国雄：《"湖广熟天下足"的内外条件分析》，《中国农史》1994年第3期；张家炎：《明清长江三角洲地区与两湖平原农村经济结构演变探异——从"苏湖熟，天下足"到"湖广熟，天下足"》，《中国农史》1996年第3期。

③ 参见张建民《清代湖北洪涝灾害论略》，《江汉论坛》1984年第10期；《围湖造田的历史考察》，《农业考古》1987年第1期；《清代江汉—洞庭湖平原堤垸农业研究》，《中国农史》1987年第2期；《清代两湖堤垸经营研究》，《中国经济史研究》1990年第4期。张国雄：《清代江汉平原水旱灾害的变化与垸田生产的关系》，《中国农史》1990年3期。

④ 光绪《武昌县志》卷二《水利·附樊口建闸奏议·侍讲张之洞樊口闸坝私议》，页十三下至页二十二上，光绪十一年重修本，武汉大学图书馆藏。

地称："农民恒弱、渔户恒强，农民恒愚、渔户恒黠。"[①] 故此，对该水域的考察又提供了一个反思以往站在国家与土地的立场上看水之局限的契机。

长时期的变化不会因为一起事件的爆发就戛然而止，然而，经历了光绪年间的樊口闸坝之争事件后，这一地区便游离于人们的视线之外了。事实上，樊口闸坝的正式建成时间是在1925年（民国十四年），此后，许多变化更具体或者更为明显地展现。因而，对于光绪年间闸坝之争更为深入的理解，理应去观察闸坝修成后该水域到底发生了什么样的事情。

湖北省档案馆藏有四宗有关樊湖水域的产权纠纷案件，分别是案例（1）《湖北省高等法院黄冈分院和鄂城司法处对邵炳林、刘道华恢复水道纠纷案的判决（1948）》；[②] 案例（2）《湖北省高等法院黄冈分院和鄂城司法处对吴仁山、姜法廷湖草分割纠纷案的判决（1948）》；[③] 案例（3）《湖北省高等法院审理鄂城县钟芳敦、刘发祥等确认湖汊所有权案（1937）》；[④] 案例（4）《湖北省高等法院黄冈分院和大冶县司法处对程选东、刘正宏等湖产所有权纠纷上诉案的判决（1948）》。[⑤] 这些案例为人们了解民国时期樊湖水域的具体状况提供了殊为难得的材料。其中，案例（2）（3）（4）均是有关水域本身的产权纠纷案。案例（2）是对于湖草收益权的争夺，案例（3）是关于湖地的莲藕种植权的纠纷，案例（4）是由于湖产本身的买卖而导致的纠纷。案例（1）则是水域变成土地之后所发生的水利纠纷。可见，此数个湖案不仅直接展现了水域向土地转换过程中以及转变之后的具体情形，

---

① 光绪《武昌县志》卷二《水利·附樊口建闸奏议·巡阅长江水师前兵部侍郎臣彭玉麟跪奏，为遵旨查明樊口地方江水入湖之处，必应修补老堤，建筑新闸，以卫民田，恭折仰祈圣鉴事》，页十三下至页二十二上，光绪十一年重修本，武汉大学图书馆藏。该起事件也引起了学者们的兴趣，其中美国学者罗威廉关注于樊口建坝之争事件本身，他注意到了事件背后所展示出的清政府决策的程序问题，并从地方与中央政府之间关系的角度指出："清朝的政体在很大程度上表现为各种利益集团相互影响的多元体制。"（〔美〕罗威廉：《治水与清政府决策程序——樊口大坝之争》，王先亭节译，欧阳跃峰校，《安徽史学》1996年第3期）；杨国安则从产业结构的角度，认为该起事件是由于水资源综合利用而引起的农业、商业、航运、渔业等各经济领域间的冲突（杨国安：《樊口闸坝之争：晚清水利工程中的利益纷争与地方秩序》，《中国农史》2011年第3期）。

② 卷宗号LS7－2－336。

③ 卷宗号LS7－2－366。

④ 卷宗号LS7－2－753。

⑤ 卷宗号LS7－2－558。

同时也显示了这一转换过程对于水域本身在产权形态等方面所产生的影响。

卷宗所反映的内容当然远不止这些，在庭讯以及反复的上诉与答辩中，原被告双方以及证人们都详细地报告了各自的家庭状况、产权的由来、纠纷的缘故等，透露出纠纷参与双方的社会背景、湖区的社会组织形态、湖业如何管理等多重信息。另外，湖北省大冶市档案馆还藏有一批有关樊湖水域的湖册，这些资料不仅使我们可以窥见在樊口大闸建立之后发生于该水域上的纠纷中各种具体而微的细节，更可深入湖区的日常，探究湖区的内在运行规则。下面对此四宗湖案分述之。

三　土地、湖草与湖地：内涵不一的水域产权纠纷

1. 变成土地后的水利纠纷与灌溉权益

与土地直接相关的案件是案例（1）中 1947 ~ 1948 年鄂城县邵氏与刘氏关于恢复水道的纠纷。1947 年五六月间，“旱魃为灾”，邵氏宗族的邱三塆、樊家垅、王家垅、邱家嘴、鬣马嘴等处数百亩田地需要灌溉用水，但一向用水的门首学堂大堰被刘氏私围小堰十余口，以至于阻塞了原有的灌救水道，于是邵氏向鄂城县司法处提起上诉。不久后，被告刘氏则以该堰为刘氏绍九公祖在乾隆十二年价买自他人的私有坝垱相辩护，并提出反诉，希望确认坝垱所有权。[①] 从表面上看，这是一起普遍存在于乡村的关于田地用水权之纠纷，不过，原告邵氏所提出的桭洲湖湖契等证据以及庭讯中各方的供词等，则透露出这件纠纷案的与众不同。

据邵氏称：桭洲湖汊，在樊口堤未建筑以前，与长江通泛，水位极高，初无所谓坝垱枧沟，自樊口堤于民国十四年建成之后，水位低落，汊内多现淤牛，近地农人始有坝垱之设，以便蓄鱼栽藕，图谋私利，枧沟之修，以便灌救田禾、通行船只。[②]

原来，此桭洲湖乃是梁子湖中的一个湖汊，该水域 1925 年（民国十四年）建成樊口堤闸，造成湖区水位下降，使得更多的土地淤生而出，其中，

① 湖北省档案馆藏 LS7－2－336：《湖北省高等法院黄冈分院和鄂城司法处对邵炳林、刘道华恢复水道纠纷案的判决（1948）》，《湖北鄂城县司法处民事判决卅六年度诉字第四三号》。

② 湖北省档案馆藏 LS7－2－336：《湖北省高等法院黄冈分院和鄂城司法处对邵炳林、刘道华恢复水道纠纷案的判决（1948）》，《民国三十七年四月十日邵炳林民事上诉》。

振洲湖便大部变为土地。

樊湖水域是一种“敞水湖”，主要来水是从长江倒灌，兼以少量的周围山泉及降雨。对于大堤建筑之前的水域情形，邵氏称道：“窃民乡地区辽阔，位于外江内湖之间，地势高下不一，自逊清以来，每于雨水较多，外江水泛年分，内地悉成泽国，居民恒以捕鱼为业，如遇雨量稀少，外江水浅年分，而湖内水位亦每每退至湖心，地方居民悉赖湖汊旧有车沟水道，灌溉高地多数田亩，以为生存，从古相沿，世守无异。”[①] 闸坝建成后，主要的水源被阻隔，使得水域范围大为缩小。可见，从光绪年间樊口拟建大闸，至民国十四年大堤与大闸陆续修成，樊湖水域也由原本的江湖相通，转而江与湖逐渐分隔，彻底改变了江湖格局，樊湖水域范围内的湖田得到了巩固并进一步发展。民国时期樊口堤闸的修成，也意味着民国政府仍然延续了清廷的政策主张，体现出历代政府对于土地的一贯追求，在这里，历史依旧沿着数百年来的变化轨迹进一步发展。

因水位的退却，湖区内的这些淤生土地便面临着一个用水灌溉的问题，此乃邵、刘两族爆发矛盾的缘起，双方矛盾的焦点则在于邵氏认为灌溉坝垱以及所开之水道为原有湖主公共所有，其中邵氏占有股份，刘氏所围的坝垱“强占共有物，霸为刘家私有”；刘氏却并不认可这种说法，认为自己价买自他人的坝垱，理应有围成小坝的处置权。[②]

邵氏指出：振洲湖，分为上下两湖，共名为六笊湖，即六笊众姓公有，共载银正十一两一钱三分一厘七毫，为各湖主每年分别完纳，此外又有黄土湖相与毗连……所谓六笊众姓者，即邻地田、鲁、朱、杨、王、李、张、赵等二十余姓，均有振洲湖份，各完银粮，惟邵姓（即上诉人）则占全湖六分之三（有上诉人买契二纸可证），初审以各邻证认为系争之处均属共有物，按共有湖汊为少数份子侵占，开凿私堰，不顾公共利益，其为不法，已可显见。[③]

① 湖北省档案馆藏LS7－2－336：《湖北省高等法院黄冈分院和鄂城司法处对邵炳林、刘道华恢复水道纠纷案的判决（1948）》，《民国三十七年七月九日邵炳林民事上诉》。

② 湖北省档案馆藏LS7－2－336：《湖北省高等法院黄冈分院和鄂城司法处对邵炳林、刘道华恢复水道纠纷案的判决（1948）》，《民国三十七年三月十九日湖北省高等法院黄冈分院民事判决（三十六年度上字第三九五号）》。

③ 湖北省档案馆藏LS7－2－336：《湖北省高等法院黄冈分院和鄂城司法处对邵炳林、刘道华恢复水道纠纷案的判决（1948）》，《民国三十七年四月十九日邵炳林民事上诉》。

由上可知，邵氏的逻辑是因为振洲湖原本属众姓公有，由该湖淤生而成的土地当然应归众姓公有。在这里，邵氏的逻辑可以分为两层，其一是关于“众姓公有”。显然，这种“同业”的思维在一定程度上体现了基于水域自身特性的水域逻辑。邵氏逻辑的第二层含义是湖主名下的水面开垦成土地之后，仍归其所有。这也是清代以来湖北地区河湖水域上相沿已久的惯例，如康熙朝名臣于成龙在黄州府知府任上进行土地清丈时，即称：“又有阳逻等处湖套，清水曰湖，止水曰汊，载蘚铁干鱼正供，长江流水业甲纳府钞正供，江水崩淤不常，凡有新淤水套，应归长江业甲。”[①] 至民国时期，大部分的湖主因名下的部分水面被渐次围垦，从而同时具有了湖主与地主的双重身份，据樊湖水域《民国三十七年三山河泾湖吴氏粮册》记载，该族在本县粮册上立有多个粮户户头，其中“老名吴伍，今的名吴福伍”负责完纳鸟求穴等子池的湖稞，以及占有蒿儿洲等草场；其他分立的吴玠陞等户头则分顶本甲水域淤生湖田的钱粮，可见，吴氏宗族分立数户的做法，实质上是以原有的渔户户头主要来应纳湖课，而用其他的户头去控制新淤出来的湖田。[②] 光绪年间樊口闸坝之争中，彭玉麟曾谓渔业与农业间的冲突，导致农民支持建筑堤坝以固湖田，渔民支持毁堤以利渔业。[③] 但吴氏等族的情况却说明了该水域的渔户同时拥有土地与水面，这就很难让人相信彭玉麟的说法能够成立，因而，对于光绪年间樊口建闸事件不能仅从渔农等产业间的矛盾等表面现象进行解释，而且要结合产业背后的人群来加以理解。

对于在这些淤生而成的土地上所留存下来的用以灌溉的坝挡以及水道，邵氏强调它们仍是由原有湖泊演变而来，与水域所淤生出的土地无异，因而，理因由原来的湖主作为共有物予以继承。可见，邵氏的主张整体上遵循的是在水陆转换之中“水域”的那部分运行逻辑，质言之，他们是将淤生土地视为原先水域的延伸，而不是将之作为完全新生的事物。

作为纠纷的另一方，刘氏显然明白对于湖分是没有办法去争的，他们

---

① （清）于成龙：《筹江淤地亩认粮议》，乾隆《黄冈县志》卷十四《艺文志·古文上·议》，《中国地方志集成·湖北府县志辑》第16册，江苏古籍出版社，2001，第384～385页。

② 大冶市档案馆藏珍贵档案2：《乾隆三十六年河泾湖界至湖课清册及华家湖课名册》，《民国三十七年三山河泾湖吴氏粮册》。

③ 光绪《武昌县志》卷二《水利·附樊口建闸奏议·巡阅长江水师前兵部侍郎臣彭玉麟跪奏，为遵旨查明樊口地方江水入湖之处，必应修补老堤，建筑新闸，以卫民田，恭折仰祈圣鉴事》，页十三下至页二十二上，光绪十一年重修本，武汉大学图书馆藏。

反复声明的是“我们的坝垱是祖传的”“我们是争坝垱，不是争湖”，[①] 所提供的核心证据即为乾隆十二年的一纸契约。

> 立大卖坝垱约人孟汝霖有祖遗关内大坝一口，坐落石山堡黄土湖南边邵家塆下，上顶杨人坝堤为界，下齐湖脚为界，西至周人湖地坑下刘人草场为界，东至刘人草场为界，四界明白，凭中说合，情愿出卖与刘绍九兄弟名下子孙永远为业，当得时值纹九价银八两整，比日亲领讫，自卖之后，听从买主管业完粮，孟门亲疏人等不得生端异说，恐后无凭，立此大卖文约永远为证。
>
> 本坝载秋米三升，在贤二孟永太户内完纳，米听刘人推收过户，孟人不得阻滞。
>
> 凭中　孟汝时　郭义远
>
> 　　　杨明卿　刘东旭
>
> 乾隆十二年腊月十二日立　亲笔[②]

以此契约，刘氏希望确认他们的坝垱所有权。很显然，他们采取的策略是就坝垱而论坝垱，并不指明这个坝垱曾经淹没于水面之下，乃属水域的一部分，试图将官府的思维带入传统乡村中对于土地灌溉用水的争夺逻辑之中，在这种逻辑中，“水”是从属于土地的，为土地服务而体现价值。可见，刘氏试图强调的是在水陆转换之中“土地”的那部分运行逻辑，双方矛盾的背后所涉及的其实是水域垦成土地之后水域与土地两种逻辑思维的冲突。

邵、刘两族人口较多，均为湖区的大族，原本都在振洲湖内拥有股分，只是邵姓所持股份更多。在庭讯中，邵、刘两族各执一词，邵氏指刘氏乾隆年间的契约系属伪造，他们的私堰围于民国二十八年，事实上邵氏也于民国二十九年私围了坝垱。[③] 这一案件显示了在土地向水域侵入的情况之

① 湖北省档案馆藏 LS7－2－336：《湖北省高等法院黄冈分院和鄂城司法处对邵炳林、刘道华恢复水道纠纷案的判决（1948）》，《民国三十六年十二月五日湖北高等法院第六分院民事言词辩论笔录》。

② 湖北省档案馆藏 LS7－2－336：《湖北省高等法院黄冈分院和鄂城司法处对邵炳林、刘道华恢复水道纠纷案的判决（1948）》，附录证据《乾隆十二年孟汝霖卖坝约》。

③ 湖北省档案馆藏 LS7－2－336：《湖北省高等法院黄冈分院和鄂城司法处对邵炳林、刘道华恢复水道纠纷案的判决（1948）》，《民国三十六年十二月五日湖北高等法院第六分院民事言词辩论笔录》。

下，不仅水面可以直接转变为土地，还会加剧湖区内各宗族间的矛盾，并在此矛盾中刺激了灌溉用水权的出现。

2. 为土地服务的湖草收益权之争

民国《蒲圻乡土志》云："春来万物丛生，树枝木叶，何一非培壅之料？然要不若湖草之茁壮而秀嫩也。采取既易，腐化亦速，信原肥之要素。"湖草因汲取水中的氮而成为一种很好的肥料，也引发了人们的争夺，"故（蒲圻）西北乡一带，多争湖之讼，非争水也、鱼也，争草而已"。[①]不止蒲圻县湖区如此，包括樊湖水域在内的许多平原湖区因为土地开垦的加速，对肥料的需求量加大，也使得湖草本身的价值越来越大，其收益权便逐渐脱颖而出，可见，湖草收益权亦是在土地的刺激下从水域中衍生出的一种产权形态。案例（2）中 1947 ~ 1948 年鄂城县蒲团吴氏与姜氏的纠纷，所争者便是关于黄土塘的湖草。

黄土塘为梁子湖的一个湖汊，"周围姓杂"，该湖汊的股权也较为复杂，"全湖共十六股，吴姓有十六股之一，十六年中有一年当年值管，姜姓十六年中有九年半当管，杨姓十六年中有四年当管，其余各湖友共有一年当管"。[②]其中，姜姓的股权来自于 1945 年以祖遗申天澥湖股份与胡公茂所有之黄土塘"亥""卯""未"年份管理与股份调换，以及买自季姓的湖份而来。[③]所谓"当年值管"，"乃管理全湖取鱼办赋及管理按股分草等事务耳，非轮至十六年，始有权利行使之谓也"。[④]

1947 年春，湖主吴氏与姜氏就分草事宜而发生纠纷，其中，吴氏认为：缘民祖遗粮湖一口，坐落本村背后，叫名黄土塘，全湖股份，历代取得有十六股之一之股权。每轮至民村当管之年份，当然有收取全湖天然孳息权利，其他各湖友逐年搅草肥田，必须备酒备款，向民村承拌，轮至其他湖友当管年份，对于全湖鱼苗蒿草，均取得使用收益之权，足征非当年湖友

---

① 民国《蒲圻乡土志》第四篇《人文》第二十二章《农业》第二节《稻》，第 57 页，民国十二年永盛印书馆出版。

② 湖北省档案馆藏 LS7 - 2 - 366：《湖北省高等法院黄冈分院和鄂城司法处对吴仁山、姜法廷湖草分割纠纷案的判决（1948）》，《民国三十六年三月十九日职员吴汉文报告》。

③ 湖北省档案馆藏 LS7 - 2 - 366：《湖北省高等法院黄冈分院和鄂城司法处对吴仁山、姜法廷湖草分割纠纷案的判决（1948）》，《民国三十六年四月姜步洲具状》。

④ 湖北省档案馆藏 LS7 - 2 - 366：《湖北省高等法院黄冈分院和鄂城司法处对吴仁山、姜法廷湖草分割纠纷案的判决（1948）》，《民国三十七年二月二十三日吴仁山等民事上诉》。

承拌，约期取草。其手续相沿不革者如此，其行使权利、绝无侵害者又如彼，历年各守湖规，互不侵犯，昭昭在人耳目。[①] 简言之，吴氏认为该族所有的水域股份理所当然地包含了湖草的收益权，只不过除了当管之年外，其余时间的取草需要“备酒备款”，以获得其允许。

对于这一点，冲突的另一方姜氏倒是没有异议，只是他们认为“过去吴姓多年未曾在黄土塘取草，独今年就要取草，诚为不解”，[②] 并且在姜姓尚未成为黄土塘湖主之前，他们则是通过支付一定费用的方式，从该湖湖主手中获取湖草，据称：“春季搅取水草，以作肥田之用，迭年搅草，均向季姓湖主备款备酒，判搅手续。”[③] 可知在这一过程中，湖草的收益权逐渐成为水域上一项新的产权形态。对于这项产权，据另一位拥有股份的“湖友何仁和”在庭讯中称：“他（指吴氏）判草我不知道，湖内也没有一定的规矩，但是判草也要得。”[④] 可见，该项湖草的收益权到底由谁来具体落实，则处于一种不稳定的状态。看起来，湖区的习惯是由当年值管的湖主主持搅草与分草事宜，全湖湖主可“备酒备款”向当值者要求按股份判草，这里的“备酒备款”当视为各湖主向当值者支付的管理费用，因而，收益权的主体应当为全体湖主。但是，由于当值者实际主持该项权利，以至于他们在事实上获得了湖草的收益权，甚而，某些并非湖主之人也可以从其手中分到湖草。

或许，有关湖草的收益权在樊口大堤尚未修建以前便已出现在樊湖水域之上，不过，这一案件中吴姓在多年未曾取草之后，开始向值年湖主提起分草，显示了湖主希望对收益权的主体进一步加以明确的趋势。这应当与樊口大堤的修筑不无关联，似乎可以这么说，大堤修成后促使了更多的土地淤生而出，为这些农田服务的湖草便更具价值，从而促使湖主们更为

① 湖北省档案馆藏 LS7－2－366：《湖北省高等法院黄冈分院和鄂城司法处对吴仁山、姜法廷湖草分割纠纷案的判决（1948）》，《民国三十六年三月二十日吴仁山等呈由》。

② 湖北省档案馆藏 LS7－2－366：《湖北省高等法院黄冈分院和鄂城司法处对吴仁山、姜法廷湖草分割纠纷案的判决（1948）》，《民国三十六年三月十九日职员吴汉文报告》。

③ 湖北省档案馆藏 LS7－2－366：《湖北省高等法院黄冈分院和鄂城司法处对吴仁山、姜法廷湖草分割纠纷案的判决（1948）》，《民国三十六年三月廿六日姜步洲等呈由》。

④ 湖北省档案馆藏 LS7－2－366：《湖北省高等法院黄冈分院和鄂城司法处对吴仁山、姜法廷湖草分割纠纷案的判决（1948）》，《民国三十六年三月廿六日鄂城县政府军法庭讯问笔录》。

认真地对待这一权益形态。无疑，民国十四年樊口闸坝的建成，是该水域围垦造田活动的一个高峰，同时也是两湖乃至长江中游地区长期以来持续不断的围垦水面活动之体现，在这里，樊口大堤化身成一个爆点，激发出一些新的矛盾（如灌溉权之争），进而又将原本业已存在的，诸如湖草收益权之争等矛盾更为明白地展现在人们的视野之中。此外，参与纠纷的吴姓以及“湖友”的说法中，说明了通常情况下水域中有关湖草的收益权等新的权益形态，是通过“湖里的规矩”而加以确定的，亦可知这些新的权益形态是从湖水这个整体之中衍生而来。

3. 种植湖地之争

众所周知，包括樊湖水域在内的长江中游的河湖因受季风的影响，都存在着雨季水泛、旱季水涸的现象，湖泊的形态并不固定，水与陆的界线呈季节性变化，这种变化便使得某一部分的湖区会在水与陆之间不断转换。针对这一特性，在湖北地区的某些湖区还出现了这种季节性涸出的湖地与湖水所有权的分离。据民国十二年编成的《中国民事习惯大全》称：

> 湖地湖水所有权之分合（湖北郧县、汉阳两县习惯）
>
> 郧县习惯，有湖地始有湖水，有湖水即有湖地，其所有权无有分而为二者。汉阳习惯，湖水湖地之所有权各别，均属所有人各照契据所载管业，系契据上分而为二，非习惯上分而为二，大都有湖地权者，多系栽种水藕，以备水涨时，仍可享其权利。有湖水权者，多系捕取鱼虾，无论水退水涨，均可享受湖水内之权利，界限天然，无待划分，其所以有纠葛者，系因水涨湖满，有湖地权者，欲藉其湖地，以侵湖水权（如捕鱼虾、刈水草之类），而有湖水权者，亦欲藉其湖水权，以侵越湖地权（如采莲挖藕之类），彼此冲突，乃致发生争执。①

该段记载显示，首先，该书的编辑是民国政府为制定民商法而进行的民事习惯调查，这一信息表明，从明初开始，在经历了数百年的发展之后，经由王朝国家的介入所形成的产权意识已经完全内化为民间的习惯。

其次，“郧县习惯，有湖地始有湖水，有湖水即有湖地，其所有权无有

① 施沛生编《中国民事习惯大全》（民国十二年九月）第二编《物权》第四类《地上权之习惯》，上海书店出版社，2002 年影印本，第 351 页。

分而为二者”，可知在位于秦巴山区的郧县，湖水与湖地二者的关系是湖水从属于湖地，并且二者并未分离，显示出山区中土地占据了主导地位。与之相反，在汉阳等平原湖区，二者的关系则表现为湖地从属于湖水，因之可见，山区与湖区遵循的是两种不同的运行逻辑。前者乃是多数以土地为主要谋生资源的乡村社会常见之习惯，至于后者，平原湖区大多习惯相通，与汉阳隔江相望的樊湖水域，湖地同样是作为湖水的附庸而出现，并且在莲藕等经济作物种植的促进下，湖地的重要性愈发凸显，湖地的所有权也就逐渐地从湖水所有权中独立出来。案例（3）中鄂城县钟氏与刘氏于 1937 年关于梁子湖的某一处湖汊所有权纠纷案，便说明了樊湖水域的人们将湖地视为水域的延伸，并从水域的角度看待这些湖地。

1937 年 5 月 27 日，刘氏向鄂城县司法处提交讼状称：“祸因邻恶钟芳金、钟联少、钟芳敦等垂涎莲业利益，倚滥棍主谋，狼狈相依，陡起觊觎，胆于古历三月十二日结合党羽，各持器械，竟在庙塆、五房塆两处插标栽莲，恶意占领。”①

随即，钟氏于 6 月 1 日提交了民事辩诉称：近年内湖莲业发达，强邻刘发祥等垂涎是塆之水势平浅，泥土肥沃，颇合植莲之用，屡次向民等租借，坚辞未允，致拂其意，乃散布流言，非以武力占领不可……民等恐成事实，难于抵制。比于三月，按照世守之业固有范围之内，播种莲秧，而该刘发祥等果然出其野蛮手段，统带数十余人，竟将民等所植莲藕抢去八九石。②

据此，可知双方对于湖地的争夺，源自“近年内湖莲业发达”之故。莲藕属经济作物，与商品经济的发展有着密切的联系，莲藕的种植需要在“水势平浅，泥土肥沃”之处，此即为湖地。这种湖地与成熟的田地不可同日而语，是一种介于水域与土地间的中间状态，如果要将之作为“土地”而用以“种植”的话，所有者大多只能以其地种藕植莲。可以说，这种湖地产权的孕育及湖地与湖水所有权的分离，既是商品经济发展的产物，更是人们从“种植”的角度对湖区加大利用的结果。

---

① 湖北省档案馆藏 LS7 - 2 - 753：《湖北省高等法院审理鄂城县钟芳敦、刘发祥等确认湖汊所有权案（1937）》，《民国二十六年五月二十七日刘发祥等民事上诉书》。

② 湖北省档案馆藏 LS7 - 2 - 753：《湖北省高等法院审理鄂城县钟芳敦、刘发祥等确认湖汊所有权案（1937）》，《民国二十六年六月一日钟芳敦等民事辩诉书》。

为证明其所有权，原告刘氏指出：缘民等共有祖遗子池四处，土名庙塆（坐落北野祠门首，以庙取名，故名庙塆）、五房塆（坐落五房村门口，故名五房塆）、油榨塆、秀才澥。该地坐落均在茅圻塘内，西以湖东券公水毗连，东南北俱以抵岸为界，每岁在刘贵保户完纳粿银五两八钱三分六厘，并有官册、粮券、示谕、判词各项证据，临审呈验。自前清乾隆三十六年分湖编册之后，各姓子池，各管各业，水涨则拦栈取鱼，水涸则打草割茭，附近淤生易滏为岸，有水有陆，历管无异。①

钟氏则指刘氏"欲以派沙抵水、夺岭移山之鬼蜮伎俩，越境飞占民等世守之湖场，以为恶等兴利之渊薮"，并称"民等所管之榴松沟内钟家塆四界昭然，既不与恶等湖地接壤，尤不与恶等山水毗连，一在天之南，一在地之北，总之，风马牛不相及，岂容有混争之点"。②

撇开双方互诉中其他丰富信息勿论，单就湖地的所有权方面来说，上述双方的争论焦点主要在于，湖场到底是刘氏所谓的茅圻塘，还是钟氏所称之"榴松沟之钟家塆"，至于两族在诉辩中所展示的逻辑倒是完全一致，即子池湖水由该族占有，他们也就顺理成章拥有了湖地。可见，樊湖水域的湖地的所有权乃是衍生自湖水，该湖区民众从水域的角度看待湖地。

以上三宗民国时期湖案，显示了在"土地"的不断侵入之下，水域与土地之间所发生的关联。各种关联之中，首先也是最重要的是水域可以直接变成田地；其次，土地的淤生又促使水域自身发生新的变化，体现在产权形态方面，即不仅是因这些淤生土地需要灌溉而出现了用水的灌溉权，水域上的湖草也因为可用于肥田，其收益权也在为土地服务的需求下逐渐明晰，至于处于水陆过渡的湖地，则在"种植"思维以及商品经济的刺激下，用以种藕植莲，从而湖地之产权便愈发凸显。无疑，这是湖北乃至长江中游地区长期以来持续不断围垦水面活动的体现，民国十四年樊口闸坝的建成，则在一个"侵入"达到高潮的聚光灯下，激发出一些新的矛盾（如灌溉权之争），进而又将原本已经存在的某些矛盾（如湖地种植权与湖草收益权之争）更为明白地展现在人们的视野之中。

---

① 湖北省档案馆藏 LS7－2－753：《湖北省高等法院审理鄂城县钟芳敦、刘发祥等确认湖汊所有权案（1937）》，《民国二十六年五月二十七日刘发祥等民事上诉书》。

② 湖北省档案馆藏 LS7－2－753：《湖北省高等法院审理鄂城县钟芳敦、刘发祥等确认湖汊所有权案（1937）》，《民国二十六年六月一日钟芳敦等民事辩诉书》。

矛盾促使新的产权形态出现。上述湖案显示，各项产权形态均是衍生自湖主所有的水域之上，无论是用水灌溉，还是湖地种植，抑或收益湖草，均是源自原本业已形成的湖主对水域的整体占有，而且这些新的产权形态大多是通过湖规的逐渐形成，甚至是打官司等方式而得以凸显。那么，这些湖主到底是怎样的一群人呢？他们所组成的水域世界是怎样的？当水域变成土地之后，对湖主们又造成了何种影响，呈现出怎样的社会场景呢？以上产权纠纷的主体均为宗族，无疑指向了理解水域产权之关键乃在于湖区的宗族。

四　宗族与跨宗族：湖主的水域世界

一般而言，湖北地区的湖主们大多为明初所编立的渔户演变而来，他们自明代以来通过缴纳鱼课，逐渐取得了办课水域的所有权。[①] 樊湖水域亦不例外。乾隆年间大冶知县便称，“看得本湖（即河泾湖）、张（即张家湰）华（即华家湖）两湖业甲祖代相承，各办各稞”，[②] 此“业甲”者既是明初对渔户进行的类似于里甲的征课编组，同时也用以指称渔户本身，也正是由于业甲的“祖代相承”，在渔户逐渐演变成宗族之后，宗族既作为赋役单元而存在，也由此成为水域产权的所有者。然而，并不是说产权所有者都是宗族，虽然宗族作为一个整体参与纠纷案中，但湖业不见得就是该宗族的公产，某些时候族人也会持有私人的股份。案例（1）中邵氏提供了一份有关桭洲湖买卖的契约，在该件契约中，湖业股份的持有者有大量的个人，有“明高公份下”的宗族房支，以及“杨泗会”这种以水神信仰为纽带的族人小群体，邵氏族内的私人股份来自于“祖置分关项下及自置”，然后又卖与族内的一个房支“邵德轩公名下后裔”，[③] 可知湖业的股份通过继承、分家及买卖在族内颇为频繁地流转。

契约中以“湖笊”指称湖股，是指该湖是以“笊”来分配股份。“笊”

① 徐斌：《明清两湖水域产权形态的变迁》，《中国经济史研究》2017年第2期。

② 大冶市档案馆藏珍贵档案2：《乾隆三十六年河泾湖界至湖课清册及华家湖课名册》，《河泾湖册（未注年份）》。

③ 湖北省档案馆藏LS7－2－336：《湖北省高等法院黄冈分院和鄂城司法处对邵炳林、刘道华恢复水道纠纷案的判决（1948）》，附录邵氏证据《民国二十五年邵南沚等卖桭洲湖契》。

本身是渔户用来下栈圈围子池的一种工具，一般按长度计算。大概由于需要花费一定的材料及人工成本用以制造“笊”，以及安放下栈，这些成本便是按照各自应享利益的比例进行摊分，因而成为标识股份的代名词。桭洲湖又称为“六笊湖”，属田、鲁、朱、杨、王、李、张、赵等20余姓公有，其中“六笊”即“六丈”，民国时期邵姓有该湖股份“湖笊二笊五，即二丈五尺”，因而拥有全湖约41.7%的股份。[①] 在这里，诸如桭洲湖之类的湖业以“笊”的方式分配股份，根源正是水域在物理上的不便分割性。水域的不可分割性使得湖业的持有者难以完全自顾自家，并且，前引《民国三十七年三山河泾湖吴氏粮册》等文书显示了明清以来“渔户”一直是承办鱼课的赋役单位，二者相结合便造就了在湖业部分为族人私人持有的情况下，邵氏仍以宗族的整体面貌打官司的局面，于是，宗族对外起到了整体族人的保护伞作用，对内则由于宗族管理阶层的存在而对族人具有约束力，这种形势下，宗族成为湖区社会组织中较为稳定的一环。

水域的不可分割性，还使得明初通常会在同一片办课水域上编立数名渔户，如黄冈《刘氏宗谱》所云：“业甲者，业渔以供国赋也。甲有八，我居其一，八家同业”，[②] 可知业甲之谓，正因甲内各渔户存在“同业”关系而来。这种同业的关系，更进一步在渔户宗族层面之上，以同甲为基础而形成了各个渔户宗族进行联合的群体形态。起初，以同一业甲为单位的宗族联合组织还只是在办纳鱼课的时候起作用，较为单纯地承担赋役之责，随着时间的推移，便因共同的利益而逐渐演变成湖区中跨宗族的社会群体。因位于梁子湖西边而得名的西梁湖上有“杨俊卿、邓李毕、聂何龙、吴任毛、张陈何、姚王李、汤曾徐、王钦宋、何汤甫等，祖充江夏县金口埫业甲”，[③] 其中“邓李毕”“吴任毛”等数姓联名的业甲即反映出此类跨宗族社会群体的存在，以“汤曾徐”为例，由汤资、曾申、徐良山等渔户组成，[④] 民国三十七年，其中一户与余姓争夺甲内的东港池、七里湖、三角湖

① 湖北省档案馆藏LS7-2-336：《湖北省高等法院黄冈分院和鄂城司法处对邵炳林、刘道华恢复水道纠纷案的判决（1948）》，《民国三十七年四月十日邵炳林民事上诉状》。

② 黄冈《刘氏宗谱》卷首一《业甲序》，民国丙戌年（1946），藜照堂刊本。

③ 湖北省档案馆藏LS7-2-302：《湖北省高等法院对蒲圻县民王明新、余新祥等湖地共有权纠纷案的判决（1948）》，附录《万历二十七年八月初九日给金东西水稞全册》。

④ 湖北省档案馆藏LS7-2-302：《湖北省高等法院对蒲圻县民王明新、余新祥等湖地共有权纠纷案的判决（1948）》。

等子池的业权时，其他各户便施予援手。[1]

联合起同甲各宗族的基础是共同占有水面，不过，在私利的诱惑下跨宗族的联合亦常常面临着挑战。对此，跨宗族群体通常的处理方法是将共有的湖业进一步细分，如案例（2）所示，其中一种做法是各族以股份的方式划分各自的湖业，然后又以轮年的方式“当年值管”，主持湖产的分配等公共事务的管理。在这里，宗族间的联合类似于宗族与族人在湖业中的关系，各姓在多以股份的方式实现了私有的情形下，由于仍需要协同作业之故，同一片水面上的各宗族与其他湖主相比，还是更具亲切感。如在上述各纠纷案中，经常出现“湖友”与“湖邻”这种湖主们对于同甲与不同甲关系的自称，其中以“湖友”指称同业之上的其他宗族，“湖邻”用指非同业的其他湖主，显示了人们在意识层面对所属群体的划分。[2] 所不同的是，跨宗族的联合与宗族相比，缺乏血缘联系纽带以及能够起到实际约束作用的族中管理阶层，因而并不如宗族稳固。隐藏在案例（3）的背后，便是这样的故事。

案例（3）中刘氏曾云“乾隆三十六年分湖编册之后，各姓子池，各管各业”，是指该年武昌知府姚棻奉新任湖广总督富明安之命查知“调查该县（大冶县）征收湖稞旧册，子池各有业户，因年代久远，地名人名多与现在更换不同，又未载有毗连界址，以致积年争讼”，[3] 从而重新编订湖册，以绝讼端之事。应当说，不仅是湖邻间有矛盾，湖友间的矛盾同样无处不在，樊湖水域乾隆年间已然分湖一次，却不是唯一，只要还存在共有的现象，就无法杜绝矛盾的出现，从而导致还会进一步的细分湖业。

茅圻塘原为同甲的“谈、刘、张”三姓共有，案卷中附录了一份三姓于咸丰年间的分湖契约，云：“奈三姓人心不古，每于各姓门口湾汊违众私取，数起争端，爰酌请湖邻一干，将该湖湾汊近各姓门口者，分与各姓自取鱼鲜茭草”。[4]

---

① 湖北省档案馆藏 LS7－2－302：《湖北省高等法院对蒲圻县民王明新、余新祥等湖地共有权纠纷案的判决（1948）》。

② 在樊湖湖区的田野考察中，笔者非常深切地感受到人们对于“湖友”与“湖邻”的区分，“湖友”这种同一业甲内各宗族间具有相当的亲近感，他们经常会将业甲内数姓连在一起来说明一件事情。

③ 大冶市档案馆藏珍贵档案 2：《乾隆三十六年河泾湖界至湖课清册及华家湖课名册》，《河泾湖界址底册（民国五年）》。

④ 湖北省档案馆藏 LS7－2－753：《湖北省高等法院审理鄂城县钟芳敦、刘发祥等确认湖汊所有权案（1937）》，《本案附录证据》。

在此案中刘姓为已经划至该族名下的湖业与钟姓构讼时，谈、张二姓虽然在庭讯中出面，但经常以“我还不晓得”等语应答，并未作有利于刘姓的证词，[①] 由此可以推测谈、张二姓与刘姓之间应当素有积怨。不过，谈、张、刘三姓的分湖是就某一处大湖汊中的小湖汊，辅以下栈的方式划至各姓名下，但对于小湖汊以外的较大水面却不太容易进一步区分，而是仍以三姓公有的形式留存下来。[②] 这也是湖区较为通行的做法。[③] 在多数情况下，正是由于存在着这种“公业”，同一业甲的各渔户宗族的联合仍可称为具有一定凝聚力的社会群体。

将小湖汊划归各姓，留下不易区分的水面作为共有部分，从这一点来看，整个湖泊又可视为一个扩大版的业甲。一般来说，全湖的湖水有“官水”与“子池”之分，据乾隆三十六年时任武昌知府姚棻称：所谓官水者，每当春夏水涨之时，湖内捕鱼船只，不分界限，概以水底湖岸而止，为官水，其完稞银分别船只大小及在船所用磨网、摄网、方网名目，三五七钱至四五钱不等。统计十甲官水取鱼船只业民岁纳额稞一半。所谓子池者，秋冬水落之际，于沿湖港湾汊处所栏栈取鱼，栈内名为子池，外仍属官水，向以栏栈所围子池之大小，各别稞银之多寡，自数分数钱至两六七钱不等。[④]

据此可知樊湖水域的官水为全体渔户在春夏水涨时公共所有，湖主们掌握的只是秋冬季节“沿湖港湾处所”的子池产权。全湖所有湖主的子池产权事实上都是季节性的业权，进一步亦可知湖主对于水面的围垦实际上

---

① 湖北省档案馆藏 LS7－2－753：《湖北省高等法院审理鄂城县钟芳敦、刘发祥等确认湖汊所有权案（1937）》，《鄂城县司法处审讯笔录（民国廿六年六月十七日）》。

② 湖北省档案馆藏 LS7－2－753：《湖北省高等法院审理鄂城县钟芳敦、刘发祥等确认湖汊所有权案（1937）》，《鄂城县司法处审讯笔录（民国廿六年六月十七日）》。

③ 如前引黄冈《刘氏宗谱》（民国丙戌年，藜照堂刊本）卷首一《业甲序》云：业甲者，业渔以供国赋也。甲有八，我居其一，八家同业，是业私以营生，公以裕国。其濟泥湖，坐落霍家圃中，周围湖岸田地，计四担有零，每年承谷稞三担有零。八甲轮流催收，周而复始。又轮车河一段，抵过牛埠，下抵竹叶湾，计二十余里。轮流管绍，与濟泥湖同。然此八业之公所也。至我甲之私管绍业以供国赋者，则有三店上之圩渠垱、赤土坡之铁杆湫、郏城北城北之旧洲湖、团湖西之白湖、许家庙上之五似嘴、黄家畈之锁碁塘、过贤埠之龙家潭、三汊港之猪婆垱，以及近地小河大垱、长沟短泊，无非上以供国赋之有常，下以垂子孙之永远，而不敢舍业以嬉云。（道光十六年）可知此处同一业甲的湖业就包括了“公所”与刘氏的私业。

④ 大冶市档案馆藏珍贵档案 2：《乾隆三十六年河泾湖界至湖课清册及华家湖课名册》，《河泾湖册（未注年份）》。

将某些季节性占有的水面变成了自己的永久性土地产权。

据笔者收集的一份嘉庆二十四年文书称：

> 特授大冶县正堂加五级纪录五次阮，为禀恳示禁等事。据徐际云、刘钦居、尹发龙、龙万九、万依振、李瑞德呈称：缘身等河泾前湖立有五总，纳粮百十余两，半出子池，半出业户。内有邹公塘官水，坐落横山堡，听众取鱼办赋，不過支舡小业，安静无事。近有造用雷网又名霸网，其网巨大且长，一网下去，拦湖半边，小业丝罾之类稍失回护，包入其内，每致彼此争闹，酿成大事。身等属在邹公塘五总之家，不求迷禁，祸福眉睫，用是公恳赏准示禁，照常取鱼，庶免酿成巨祸等情。据此，除词批示外，合行出示严禁，为此示仰河泾湖五总渔业人等知悉，嗣后尔等在湖在塘取鱼办赋，只许照常各用小舡小网，毋许造用雷网霸网拦湖截取，致滋事端。自示之后，如有抗违不遵，仍蹈前辙，许五总并该地保甲人等据实赴县指禀，以凭拿究，如敢徇隐不举，察出一并治罪，决不口宽。各宜凛遵毋违，特示。嘉庆廿四年（1819）五月廿七日示。

可见，湖总对官水负有管理之责，且得到官府的支持。此“湖总”者类似于土地上的里长户，据《河泾湖册》称，“向例湖分十甲，每甲各设湖总一名”,① 知其为甲内各渔户宗族的联名牵头者，于是，在以业甲为单位形成的跨宗族社会群体的基础上，又出现了一个全湖范围的湖总联合体。

由此可见，在民国之前的湖区已然形成了“宗族—业甲宗族联合体—全湖联合体”的社会组织序列，从宗族到跨宗族再至整个湖区，以宗族为基础而形成了层级不同的社会群体，并且随着层级的升高，联系性愈加弱化，有关产权的矛盾就愈容易爆发。从前述水域上各种权益形态均是衍生自整个湖水这一状况来看，在水域转化为土地之后，仍然在延伸着湖区的思维方式，这种状况不仅出现在产权方面，更加体现于湖区的社会组合方式之上，可以说，“土地”向“水域”的侵入，虽然暴露出许多的矛盾，促使了新的权益形态的出现，却并没有完全改变湖区的社会组合方式。

---

① 大冶市档案馆藏珍贵档案 2：《乾隆三十六年河泾湖界至湖课清册及华家湖课名册》，《河泾湖册（未注年份）》。

按乾隆年间大冶知县的说法，樊湖水域的湖业“或传自祖遗，或得自契买”，[①] 依靠买卖获得湖业，从而成为进入湖区社会的一种重要方式。从湖业买卖的主体来看，湖业的买卖可以分为两种，一类是湖主之间的买卖，另一类是原本没有湖业之人买入湖业。前者发生在湖主家族的内部，或者是湖友间、湖邻间的湖业流转，通常情况下随着不同层级的社会群体凝聚力的逐渐减弱，矛盾也呈现出更易爆发的趋势。至于后者，如果说从明初以来一直生活于湖区的渔户宗族之间尚且能够形成一定的湖规，以至于在全湖范围内形成一个相对封闭的世界，那么，当湖区以外之人通过买卖进入到水域世界之后，面临的困难更可想而知。作为原本非湖区世界之人，他们虽然取得了合法的湖业产权，但是否能够为原本的水域世界所接纳就只能另当别论。案例（4）中 1946～1948 年大冶县垱下湾程氏与刘氏关于湖产所有权的纠纷，便说明了如果自身实力不够的话，即使是买了湖业，仍然会在水域世界中举步维艰。

垱下湾乃樊湖水域中河泾湖之湖汊，刘氏称，有琏、有爵二公于嘉庆八年凭中价买程光炽兄弟所有“二十二股内折卖一半之产权”，但刘氏后裔“户小丁零”，屡屡遭到程氏“禁止民姓吃水、洗衣、车水”等欺凌，民国三十五年四月二十二日，“刘正炎在堰内车水灌田，讵知程希周等统率全村数十人，竟将我村水车毁碎，堤埂掘挖，妨害交通，又把上堰垦田为独有”，刘氏的怨气终于爆发，于民国三十六年二月提起民事告诉。[②] 程氏则指刘氏买湖的契约系属“过契”，早就失效，“此次系刘正华恃其毕业高中，与大冶县（即原审）司法官之子盟订兄弟，交游宽广，手眼庞大，故将此过契寻出，作为侵占张本，任人皆知”。[③]

其实程、刘两姓孰对孰错，多次参与调解与庭讯的地方士绅及法官心里都十分清楚。刘姓本为“与王、方两姓看守坟山”之“佃人”，[④] 作为一

① 大冶市档案馆藏珍贵档案 2：《乾隆三十六年河泾湖界至湖课清册及华家湖课名册》，《河泾湖界址底册（民国五年）》。

② 湖北省档案馆藏 LS7－2－558：《湖北省高等法院黄冈分院和大冶县司法处对程选东、刘正宏等湖产所有权纠纷上诉案的判决（1948）》，《垱下湾刘家村全村家长为争垱下湾湖所有产权，召开全村会议，推举当事人出庭申诉纪录（民国三十六年二月十九日）》。

③ 湖北省档案馆藏 LS7－2－558：《湖北省高等法院黄冈分院和大冶县司法处对程选东、刘正宏等湖产所有权纠纷上诉案的判决（1948）》，《程选东民事上诉（民国卅七年一月十三日）》。

④ 湖北省档案馆藏 LS7－2－558：《湖北省高等法院黄冈分院和大冶县司法处对程选东、刘正宏等湖产所有权纠纷案的判决（1948）》，《程选东等民事具呈（民国三十五年五月六日）》。

位湖区的后来者，刘氏在嘉庆八年通过价买的方式进入水域世界之后，虽历一定之时日，然在民国年间刘氏后裔亦只有6户30余口，不如由渔户发展而来的程氏族大人众，[①] 在1940年代6户中好不容易出了个高中生，因而才生出一些底气去与程氏相抗。至于刘氏反抗的结果，在鄂城县司法处的审判中，刘氏应占理而获胜，程氏却并未就此收敛。在接下来省高等法院的庭讯中，法官对刘姓说："据你说原有十一股，在十一股内作让出四股吧。如听本院的话，后来免得生祸患，你想想吧。"[②] 最终，此事还是在刘姓的退让下以法官的建议而暂时获得解决。

另外，此案还显示了民国十四年樊口大堤筑成后，水陆变迁对程、刘两姓间的矛盾起到了推波助澜的作用。全湖的水位退却后，垱下湾于民国二十四年间程、刘两姓公共"将此湖高埠两堰筑堤蓄藕"，筑堤围出了一百石田的面积，之后，两姓开始在堤内陆续开出田地。[③] 与只是打草捕捞的渔业利益相比，这一新出现的巨大利益导致了程氏心理的失衡，他们无法容忍户小丁零的后来者刘氏与之平起平坐，以至于拒不承认刘氏的股权，为此，程氏还伪造了多份光绪年间族人将湖股卖与宗族的契约，使得有关契约真伪的辩论成为该案的一个核心话题。[④] 由此看来，刘氏真可谓是一入"江湖"身不由己，"江湖"果然是一个弱肉强食的险恶世界。

五 结论

明清以来两湖地区作为著名的粮食产地，得益于对水面的围垦，围湖造田创造出了一种新的田土形式垸田。垸田不断地开垦以至于过度的开发，

---

① 程氏为河泾湖一甲湖总"程秀七、八"之后裔，参见大冶市档案馆藏珍贵档案2：《乾隆三十六年河泾湖界至湖课清册及华家湖课名册》，《河泾湖册（未注年份）》。

② 湖北省档案馆藏LS7－2－558：《湖北省高等法院黄冈分院和大冶县司法处对程选东、刘正宏等湖产所有权纠纷案的判决（1948）》，《湖北高等法院第六分院民事言词辩论笔录（民国三十六年八月四日）》。

③ 湖北省档案馆藏LS7－2－558：《湖北省高等法院黄冈分院和大冶县司法处对程选东、刘正宏等湖产所有权纠纷案的判决（1948）》，《湖北高等法院第六分院民事言词辩论笔录（民国三十六年八月四日）》。

④ 曾为联保主任的喻先保等证人的说法，证实了程氏伪造契约之事，湖北省档案馆藏LS7－2－558：《湖北省高等法院黄冈分院和大冶县司法处对程选东、刘正宏等湖产所有权纠纷案的判决（1948）》，《湖北高等法院第六分院民事言词辩论笔录（民国三十六年八月四日）》。

在清代嘉、道以后带来了水旱灾害频发等严重的环境后果。作为长时期结构性变化积累到相当程度之后的短期剧烈反应，光绪年间樊口闸坝事件的爆发，标志着土地对该水域的侵入达到了一个高峰。民国十四年樊口堤闸的修成，使得长江与樊湖水域的关系从原本江湖相通变为江湖分隔的格局，既激发出新的矛盾，亦将原本或隐或现存在的矛盾在人们的面前展露无遗。新的矛盾促使了诸如灌溉权等新的产权形态的出现，也使得湖草收益权、湖地种植权等已经存在的权益得以彰显。而且，各项产权形态均是衍生自湖主所有的水域之上，大多是通过湖规的逐渐形成，甚至是打官司等方式，从业已形成的湖主对水域的整体占有中分离出来。这种情况既说明了湖区中将土地视为水域的延伸这一逻辑，同时显示了在水域转换成土地之后，湖主所构筑的水域世界在某种程度上得以延续。

因为水域具有不可分割的特性，民国之前的樊湖水域上，以"同业"为基础而逐渐形成了"宗族—同业甲宗族联合—全湖宗族联合"的社会群体序列。这是一个从明初编立渔户之后逐渐形成的湖主世界，在整个湖区形成了一个相对封闭的水域世界，虽然通过湖业的买卖，湖区之外的人可以进入湖区，使得这个湖主的水域世界具有一定的流动性，但并不见得就一定能为原先的水域世界所接纳，如果自身实力不够的话，即使是买了湖业，依旧会在水域世界中举步维艰。

在光绪年间樊口闸坝之争中，彭玉麟曾谓渔业、商业等与农业间的冲突，导致农民支持建筑堤坝以固湖田，渔民支持毁堤以利渔业，[①] 论者亦多从其说，看起来这种观点只看到了表面现象，更深层次的原因则是先来者与后来者之间的冲突，即一个自明初以来逐渐形成的相对封闭的湖区群体对外来者的排斥。彭玉麟曾称："农民恒弱、渔户恒强，农民恒愚、渔户恒黠。"[②] 在某种意义上这种说法是成立的，作为水域世界的既得利益者，由于拥有子池的所有权，渔户宗族本身就是围垦这些子池水面的急先锋，兼具着湖主与地主双重身份，在水陆变迁之后，他们仍旧掌握着湖区的话语

---

① 光绪《武昌县志》卷二《水利・附樊口建闸奏议・巡阅长江水师前兵部侍郎臣彭玉麟跪奏，为遵旨查明樊口地方江水入湖之处，必应修补老堤，建筑新闸，以卫民田，恭折仰祈圣鉴事》，页十三下至页二十二上，光绪十一年重修本，武汉大学图书馆藏。

② 光绪《武昌县志》卷二《水利・附樊口建闸奏议・巡阅长江水师前兵部侍郎臣彭玉麟跪奏，为遵旨查明樊口地方江水入湖之处，必应修补老堤，建筑新闸，以卫民田，恭折仰祈圣鉴事》，页十三下至页二十二上，光绪十一年重修本，武汉大学图书馆藏。

权。这一现象提示我们，在明清以来长江中游地区围垦水面的洪流中，即使围垦成田，原先的水域社会运行规则依然得到了相当的延续。因此，在对围垦水面而形成的新型田土进行考察时，就不能不关注到围垦之前的那个水域世界。我们不仅是要“站在水上看水”，还要进一步“站在水上看土地”。

渠碾争水，耕牛被劳

——论汉唐关中的漕运建设与农业灌溉用水之争

祝昊天*

摘　要：在传统社会中，水利之于农业生产往往有着至关重要的影响。汉唐时期的关中地区，为解决粮食供给，配置有大量的水利工程建设。一方面，借以沟渠引水推行灌溉，充分挖掘本地区的农业生产潜力；另一方面，则是开渠通漕，征调关东地区的钱粮西运补给。但问题是，关中地处西北内陆，水源毕竟有限，要满足农田灌溉、漕渠运输、粮食加工等多种使用，难免存在分配不均的情况。更何况，私人竞逐水利，纷纷选择在上游拦堤筑坝，进一步加剧了用水上的矛盾纠纷。针对这些情况，王朝统治者们虽尝试过干预，却很难令行禁止。唐代后期，私修水利泛滥导致渭河下游漕运缺水不济，长安几度面临断粮，反倒是要征用大批耕牛运粮救急，结果“陆运牛死众多”，使关中农业生产陷入困局，加快了李唐王朝的整体衰落。

关键词：汉唐时期　关中　水利建设　农业灌溉　用水之争

Abstract: In the production process of traditional Chinese society, water conservancy construction often has a crucial influence on agricultural development. Taking the guanzhong area in the Han and Tang dynasties as an example, a large number of water conservancy engineering facilities were built to solve the problem of food supply. On the other hand, the government digging channel to transport grain to the west to provide “blood transfusion” . But for a long, along the wei river water often require diversion for irrigation, transportation, water pro-

* 祝昊天，武汉大学历史学院博士研究生。

cessing, and all kinds of private water conservancy crisscross overlap, have built weir intercepting, further aggravated the contradiction of water allocation disputes. In this regard, although dynastic rulers tried to intervene, but it was difficult to do so, so they had to pass on the burden in the form of tax reform; As a result, the canal transport water shortage make chang 'an almost grain, but to requisition a large number of cattle transport grain emergency; In view of the fact that "many cattle died in land transportation", the agricultural production in guanzhong inevitably fell into a dilemma.

Keywords: Han and Tang Dynasties; Guanzhong; Water conservancy construction; Agricultural irrigation; Water use struggle

众所周知，在传统社会的生产模式下，水利之效往往有着十分特殊的意义，不仅为土地增产、粮食加工所使用，亦可以通渠行漕，使大宗货物的运输变得更加便捷。特别是在气候条件较干旱的西北内陆，这些用途尤为显著。作为汉唐时期的京畿之地，关中地区很早就有大规模的水利建设，并且形成了高度发达的人工渠系网络，改造了区域内的水环境。因此，素有学者围绕水环境与水利工程建设的选题展开论述，[①] 但就这一时期用水分配的问题却还少见讨论。在水资源相对有限的前提下，过度开发水利并不一定都有助于农业生产发展。相反，还会牵扯到社会的方方面面，在特殊的历史背景下延伸出许多新的矛盾和纠纷。

一　汉唐关中农田水利建设的基本概况

在华夏文明起源的过程中，关中地区很早就出现了种植活动，农业开发的历史十分悠久。鉴于黄土疏松的自然特性，稍经引水灌溉，即可改造

① 有关关中水利的研究，可参见郑肇经《中国水利史话》，商务印书馆，1939；史念海《河山集》（第一册），三联书店，1963；戴应新《关中水利史话》，陕西人民出版社，1977；黄耀能《中国古代农业水利史研究——中国经济史研究之一》，台北：六国出版社，1978；武汉水利电力学院、水利水电科学研究院《中国水利史稿》编写组《中国水利史稿》（上册），水利水电出版社，1979；周魁一《农田水利史略》，水利水电出版社，1987；叶遇春主编《泾惠渠志》，三秦出版社，1991；李令福《关中水利开发与环境》，人民出版社，2004。

成肥沃的土壤，故使这一地区的统治者历来都很重视水利建设。其间，尤以“汉唐两代，关中水利全面发展，形成了以自流灌溉为特征的网络系统”,[①] 既促进农业的繁荣，也奠定了王朝盛世的物质基础。

值得一提的是，渭河北岸能够利用地势落差引泾灌排，变碱卤之地为沃野，构成了关中平原上面积最大的灌区，亦为整个农业生产的核心区域。可以说，引泾灌区的创建过程就是中国早期水利史的一个缩影。战国以降，随着铁制工具推广、普及，使先民的生产技术得到大幅提升，加之实践经验积累，大型水利工程开始出现。秦王政采纳了水工郑国的提议，“令凿泾水自中山西邸瓠口为渠，并北山东注洛三百余里，欲以溉田”，不久，“渠就，用注填阏之水，溉泽卤之地四万余顷，收皆亩一钟”“于是关中为沃野，无凶年，秦以富强，卒并诸侯，因命曰郑国渠”,[②] 这标志着引泾灌渠建设的开始。在此基础上，西汉时人沿郑国渠北侧另开六辅诸渠，借以“益溉郑国渠傍高仰之田”，扩大灌溉面积。至太始二年（前 95 年），“赵中大夫白公复奏穿渠”，又计划“引泾水，首起谷口，尾入栎阳，注渭中，袤二百里，溉田四千五百余顷”，称之曰“白渠”，连同郑国渠形成了南北并行灌溉的格局。得此水利之饶，引泾灌区已初成规模，正如民谣所说：“田于何所？池阳谷口。郑国在前，白渠起后。举锸为云，决渠为雨。泾水一石，其泥数斗，且溉且粪，长我禾黍，衣食京师，亿万之口。”[③]

此外，关中东部建有引洛淤灌而“未得其饶”的龙首渠，西部还有灵轵渠、成国渠和蒙茏渠等建设，一并做引水灌溉使用。[④] 同时，考虑到关中本土的产粮仍有不足，汉武帝时又在渭河南岸新开凿了一条并渭漕渠，运输关东漕粮。按照大司农郑当时所说，如以“关东漕粟”由河入渭，走天然河道不仅路途绕远，且还多有困难险阻，这才想到要“引渭穿渠起长安，并南山下，至河三百余里”，另辟一条人工运粮专线。但在具体开凿渠道的过程中，仍兼顾“渠下民田万余顷，又可得以溉田”，及至水到渠成，“其后漕稍多，而漕下之民颇得以溉田矣”,[⑤] 也算取得了预期效果。

---

① 王双怀：《关中平原水利建设的历史审视》，《陕西师范大学学报（哲学社会科学版）》2015 年第 1 期。

② 《史记》卷 29《河渠书》，中华书局，1959，第 1408 页。

③ 《汉书》卷 29《沟洫志》，中华书局，1962，第 1685 页。

④ 参见《关中水利开发与环境》，第 103 ~ 111 页。

⑤ 《史记》卷 29《河渠书》，第 1409 ~ 1410 页。

由此可见，秦汉时期大批量的工程建设奠定了关中农田水利开发的基础。特别是以人工渠道的纵横连接，构建渠系发达的灌溉网络（见图1），确立了日后关中地区灌溉农业的生产条件。

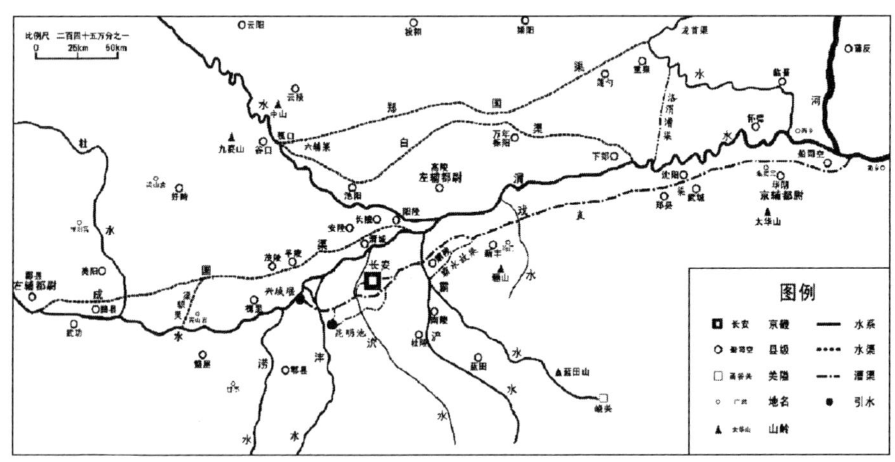

图1　西汉关中水利分布示意图

随后，王朝频繁更迭，关中更是久经丧乱，必须要到隋唐王朝重构国家统一，才有条件进入全新的建设发展时期。根据现有材料整理所见，“唐朝水利建设没有像汉代那样有一个汉武帝时代的兴修高峰，而是持续发展，对汉代旧有渠道实行定期维修”。引泾灌渠的两次改造就很说明问题。鉴于泾河河床下切的现象过于严重，唐时已经很难再像前朝那样直接做围堰横绝，这导致了郑国渠的旧渠断水废弃，而沿线的支渠渠道只得纷纷从上游冶、清、浊、漆、沮诸水引流，逐步与引泾工程脱离，分化成相互独立的灌溉渠系。而原有的南线诸渠则继续引泾灌溉，白渠渠道在经过数次修复、改建之后，一分为三，形成了南、北、中三条干渠，并且新添三限闸、彭城堰等分水设施，辅之以干、支、斗渠使用，改以“三白渠”相称。① 另外，为了解决粮食供给不足的问题，隋、唐两朝皆有重疏汉代漕渠的故道，添设转运仓储，以调拨更多的关东漕粮补给京师。②

总体而论，相较于秦汉时期轰轰烈烈的水利建设，唐代更多是以继承、

① 参见《关中水利开发与环境》，第173～193页。

② 关于隋唐时期关中漕渠的研究，参见祝昊天《隋唐时期关中漕渠新考》，《唐史论丛》第28辑，三秦出版社，2019，第107～122页。

改造为主，尤其是以“三白渠”为核心的灌溉渠系重建，在很大程度上改变了原来的灌区格局，亦使得白渠沿线的灌溉效益得以最大化发挥。

但与以往情况不同的是，除国家主导的水利工程外，唐代关中地区还有大量的私修水利出现。事实上，类似的问题早在西汉中后期就已显现，按《史记·河渠书》的说法：始自昭宣以来，“用事者争言水利”，时常以“关中辅渠、灵轵引堵水……皆穿渠为溉田，各万余顷”，乃至“佗小渠披山通道者，不可胜言”。[①] 循此趋势发展，等到西汉末年王莽召开治河会议以前，就已经是“今西方诸郡，以至京师东行，民皆引河、渭、山川水溉田”。也正因如此，受上游私渠分水引流的影响，才导致下游出现缺水、断流，致使漕渠淤废。而为了争抢更多的水源，河道沿线纷纷逐级设堰拦水，相当于“肢解”了一条条自然的河流，让河流自身的调蓄能力大幅下降，开始暴涨暴落，结果“春夏干燥，少水时也，故使河流迟，贮淤而稍浅”，而“雨多水暴至，则溢决”，[②] 甚至严重影响黄河水患的防治。

应该说，唐代私修水利的情况还要更复杂一些，除私渠引水溉田之外，还有大量的私修碾硙占水存在。关于碾硙一物，日本学者西嶋定生有过详细论述，在他看来，“碾硙是水平运动的磨，主要用来制造小麦粉”，原本是一种传统的加工设备，却由于水力的应用，使“它从南北朝以后，特别是在唐代，急速地发达起来，成为营利投资的对象”。这其中，“大部分是庄园附属制粉加工厂的主要工具”。[③] 国内学者亦认为，中国人对于碾硙、水磨的运用始见于北朝记载，后来几经发展，延续到隋唐时期才得以形成一个具有相当经济意义的产业。[④] 考虑到碾硙的机械运作必须要借助水力驱动，一样需要拦河设堰、蓄水充能。特别是在引泾灌区一带，利用现有的渠系可以直接就近架设碾硙，进行加工，从而免去运输之劳，使粮食生产加工形成一条完整的产业链。所以，富商巨户纷纷效法，私修碾硙，竞相

---

① 《史记》卷 29《河渠书》，第 1414 页。

② 《汉书》卷 29《沟洫志》，第 1697 页。

③ 刘俊文主编《日本学者研究中国史论著选议》，夏日新、韩昇、黄正建等译，中华书局，1992，第 362 页。

④ 参见王利华《古代华北水力加工兴衰的水环境背景》，《中国经济史研究》2005 年第 1 期；方万鹏《“相地作磨”：明清以来河北井陉的水力加工业——基于环境史视角的考察》，《中国农史》2014 年第 3 期；方万鹏《张舜民〈水磨赋〉与王祯“水轮三事”设计之关系再探》，《文物》2015 年第 8 期。

逐利，以致私碾设置逐渐呈泛滥之势，而“碾硙占水”的现象也愈来愈多，甚至严重影响到正常的农耕生产，引发水权纠纷，构成了关中地区一个较为严重的社会问题。

二 唐朝统治者的应对措施

一个不容忽视的问题是，关中居处西北内陆之地，虽有水利之饶，却并没有太多的富裕水源。更何况，农田灌溉、漕粮运输、碾硙加工各个方面都要用水，如果完全放任私碾抢占水源，不仅那些势单力薄的自耕农会无水灌溉，就连维系长安供给的漕渠用水亦不得保证，这将直接影响到整个唐朝统治的稳定。故此，为尽可能地平衡水源分配，唐朝统治不惜以政令的形式严禁私碾，并且多次主导拆除灌渠沿线私碾的活动。

依据文献记载，可知唐朝至少组织过四次强拆私碾的行动。起先，偷设私碾只是一种富商牟利的投机行为，但已引起了唐朝统治集团的注意。永徽六年（655年），雍州长史长孙祥向高宗进奏：“往日郑、白渠溉田四万余顷，今为富商大贾竞造碾硙，堰遏费水，渠流梗涩，止溉一万许顷。”特请重修二渠，借以改善灌溉条件。高宗原本以为只要疏渠引流即可，却被长孙无忌提醒：“比为碾硙用水，洩渠水随入滑，加以壅遏耗竭，所以得利遂少。”这下才意识到了问题的严重程度，“于是遣祥等分检渠上碾硙，皆毁之”。[①] 但“未几，所毁皆复”，[②] 可以想见，第一次拆撤行动并不怎么彻底。

随后，在利益的驱使下，就连王公贵戚、寺院僧侣也都纷纷加入其中，竞相添设私碾，一时间蔚然成风。为遏制住寺院经济的迅猛扩张，唐睿宗在《诫励风俗敕》中明确指出：“寺观广占田地，及水碾硙侵损百姓，宜令本州长官检括，依令式以外，及官人百姓，将庄田宅舍布施者，在京并令司农即收，外州给贫下课户。”[③] 但事与愿违，诸如“太平公主与僧寺争碾硙”的事件发生，标志着权贵势力开始借机抢夺私碾。结果，来自民间的富商、僧侣相继被排挤，“诸王公权要之家”却逐步垄断了私碾经营，形成

① （唐）杜佑：《通典》卷2《食货》，中华书局，1988，第39页。
② （唐）李吉甫：《元和郡县图志》，卷1《关内道》，中华书局，1983，第11页。
③ （北宋）宋敏求：《唐大诏令集》，中华书局，1959，第570～571页。

了一种特殊权利。这些权贵“缘渠立硙”，为保证自家用水，纷纷从上游筑堰开渠、截水蓄流，直接使下游水源干涸、“以害水田”，给灌区生产带来了严重影响。及至开元九年（721 年），“所历咸有声绩”的李元纮被擢升为京兆尹，他奏请唐玄宗下令疏决三辅诸渠，并将那些占据水源的私碾拆除，让利于民，[①] 总算勉强控制住了这种发展势头。同时，出于加强监管措施的需要，在开元年间编纂成文的《唐六典》中还有专门制定用水细则，强调“凡水有溉灌者，碾硙不得与争其利”，为优先保障农业生产的灌溉用水，“自季夏及于仲春，皆闭斗门，有余乃得听用之”。此外，严令禁止官员以权谋私，明确要求“凡官人不得于部内请射田地及造碾硙，与人争利”，借以提升执法的权威性。[②]

但好景不长，这样的局面并没能持续多久，随着安史之乱的爆发，唐朝深陷于内忧外患之中，根本就无暇顾及监管。在这一段时间里，“豪戚壅上游取硙利”，遍布于灌渠沿线，“且百所，夺农用十七”，[③] 影响的程度远甚于从前。广德二年（764 年），丧乱初定，农业生产亟须恢复，工部侍郎李栖筠“复陈其弊”，重提拆撤私碾一事，引起朝廷重视。权衡再三，唐代宗“敕工部侍郎李栖筠、京兆少尹崔沔拆公主水碾硙十所”，并明确要求“通白渠支渠，溉公私田”，经过一番努力，灌溉得以恢复，而“岁收稻二百万斛，京城赖之”，成效显著。[④] 据文献记载统计，这次行动总共“拆去私碾硙七十余所”，可见执行情况比较彻底。但仅仅过去一年多时间，“先臣（李栖筠）出牧常州，私制如初”，等同枉费。据此而论，唐朝此时既无力再行禁止，亦不能控制私碾架设，整个事态发展也逐渐失去了控制。

长此以往，“私碾占水”愈多，而灌溉用水愈少，不仅粮食产出减少，引泾灌区的田地面积持续下降，及“至大历中，利所及才六千二百余顷”，[⑤] 相较之于永徽六年“止溉一万许顷”的规模，萎缩了不少，显现“私碾占水”这一问题的严重性。到大历十二年（777 年）末，由于私碾泛滥，占水过多，“畿内百姓连状，陈泾水为碾硙拥隔，不得溉田”，事态已经很难

① 《旧唐书》卷 98《李元纮传》，中华书局，1975，第 3073～3074 页。

② （唐）李林甫：《唐六典》卷 7《尚书·工部》，中华书局，1992，第 226 页；卷 30《三府督护州县官吏》，第 749 页。

③ 《新唐书》卷 146《李栖筠传》，中华书局，1975，第 4736 页。

④ （北宋）王谠：《唐语林》，中华书局，1987，第 59 页。

⑤ 《元和郡县图志》，卷 1《关内道》，第 11 页。

再维持下去。迫于民怨沸腾所带来的种种压力，应京兆尹黎干所请，唐代宗“乃诏发使简覆，不许碾硙妨农”，[①] 还特别强调要“撤硙以水与民”，[②] 保护生产。但与以往情况较不同的是，此次拆撤私碾的诏令尚未执行，便遭到了权贵势力的百般阻挠，《旧唐书·郭子仪传》载：“（郭）暖，子仪第六子。年十余岁，尚代宗第四女升平公主……大历中，恩宠冠于戚里，岁时锡赉珍玩不可胜纪。大历十三年，有诏毁除白渠水支流碾硙，以妨民溉田。升平有脂粉硙两轮，郭子仪私硙两轮，所司未敢毁彻。公主见代宗诉之，帝谓公主曰：吾行此诏，盖为苍生，尔岂不识我意耶？可为众率先。公主即日命毁。由是，势门碾硙八十余所皆毁之。”[③] 不难想见，鉴于前几次拆碾行动都未有结果，唐代宗本人还是下定决心想要大力整治一番的，他要求升平公主、郭子仪等显贵“为众率先”，拆除各家私碾。只不过，参照历次拆碾的结果来看，私碾虽可拆，但暴利难禁，这最后一次的拆碾行动也很难从根本上解决问题。

综上所述，四次拆碾行动均有取得一定的效果，但大都未能长期坚持下来。应该说，仅凭借强干官吏的个人表现，不足以解决问题。特别是在唐朝国势日渐衰落的情况下，朝廷方面已经很难再行有效监管，亦不能制止私碾偷设。故此，私碾屡拆不撤、屡禁不止，而用水之争却愈演愈烈。最终，可怜农户只能眼睁睁地看着灌溉水源不断缩减，陷入窘境。

三　以税制改革为代表的政策转变

私碾成泛滥之势，主要还是因为潜在的利益所驱动。值得注意的是，按照唐代前期的租庸调制，碾硙经营并不属于税收之列，故使其产出完全可以划归个人所有，无须向官府缴纳税款。税制上的“漏洞”存在，往往会造成暴利产生，进而吸引大批的逐利者参与，推动私碾数量的快速增长。

那么，“私碾占水”的问题又是缘何产生？仅从水文条件上来看，南山诸流短促湍急，水势强劲，似乎应该更早得到开发，但大多数碾硙的选址

① （北宋）王钦若等编撰，周勋初等校订《册府元龟》卷497《河渠二》，凤凰出版社，2006，第5647页。

② 《新唐书》卷83《诸帝公主传》，第3663页。

③ 《旧唐书》卷120《郭子仪传》，第3470页。

依然还选择在渭河北岸沿引泾灌渠一线集中分布，形成了“壅隔上流，置私碾百余所，以收末利”的景象。[①] 论及个中缘由，其实另有原因。一方面，引泾灌渠的“渠水发源本高，向下枝分极众”，[②] 且还存在着一定的高程落差，可供渠堰引水顺势导流，带动碾硙水轮的机械运作。另一方面，引泾灌区作为关中农业的主产地，临近长安，交通区位优势十分明显，若建址于此，既可以在原产地直接进行加工、脱粒入仓，又能够就近转运、节省不必要的运输损耗。也正因如此，鉴于经济效益的考量，最初的建造者才执意选择把碾硙架设在灌渠附近，而后继者纷纷效法，形成集聚之势。如此一来，农田、碾硙皆要用水，而私碾却想方设法地抢占水源，不给灌渠放水，经年日久，势必引发水权纠纷。

值得一提的是，在大历十三年这次的拆碾行动中，统治者虽态度坚决，却仍然留有一些余地。依据《册府元龟》所述：“帝思致理之本，务于养人以田，农者生民之原，苦于不足，碾硙者兴利之业，主于并兼，遂发使行其损益之由，佥以为正渠无害，支渠有损，乃命府县凡支渠硙一切罢之……以是年有诏，毁除白渠水支流碾硙，以妨民溉田。”[③] 这说明，拆撤的八十余所私碾都只是那些架设在灌渠支流上的设施，并未涉及主渠之列。事实上，这种看似自相矛盾的做法并非没有道理，彼时长安城中存在有相当数量的消费群体，如不保留一定数量的碾硙维持粮食加工，势必引发供应上的短缺，这无疑是统治者所不愿意看到的结果。

由此分析，唐朝拆碾的动机也不一定都是为了保护农本。因为“私碾占水”的问题存在导致灌溉水源减少，这将在很大程度上影响到朝廷在引泾灌区的税粮征收，而私碾主却可以抢占公家灌溉水源，用作自家经营牟利。故此，在统治者看来，私碾经营其实是一种变相的“损公济私”行为，必须严令禁止。但在实际执行的过程中，却很难做到真正落实，彻底根治。实际上稍有监管不力，就有“死灰复燃”的现象发生。结果，私碾只会越拆越多，形成泛滥之势。所以在最后一次拆撤过后，唐朝官方再未组织任何行动，事实上已选择放弃。

不久，新继位的德宗采纳了宰相杨炎的提议，诏令废止一切苛捐杂税，

① 《册府元龟》卷497《河渠二》，第5647页。

② 《通典》卷2《食货》，第39页。

③ 《册府元龟》卷497《河渠二》，第5647页。

定于建中元年（780 年）颁行两税新法。自此，改变了自战国以来以人丁为主的赋税制度，而“唯以资产为宗，不以丁身为本”,[①] 使赋税制度由“舍地税人”向“舍人税地”方向发展，“反映出过去由封建国家在不同程度上控制土地私有的原则变为不干预或少干预的原则”。[②] 这样一来，改变以计资而税的方法，就可以将碾硙等不动资产一并纳入课税范畴，等同于官方间接承认了私碾经营的“合法化”。同时，这也暗示唐朝统治者在该问题的处理态度上发生转变，因为在税制改革之后，唐朝政府完全可以通过资产税的征收来弥补由粮食减产所造成的损失，自然也就无心再去强拆碾硙，更不可能会去抑制私人经营。

唐朝官方的政策转变其实并未解决关键问题，只不过是把沉重的负担间接转嫁到自耕农身上。以牺牲引泾灌区的粮食产出为代价，虽暂时缓解了社会矛盾，但“私碾占水”的问题依然存在，水源分配不均，致使基层群体的用水之争仍旧无法得到解决。

四 陆上转运的耕牛

随着灌溉水源的减少，粮食产量也随之减少，要保证关中地区数以百万计的人口消费，唯有通过漕运从关东地区征调更多粮食入关，这使得黄河、渭河一线的运输压力陡然增加。

但问题在于，渭河原本就是“一条靠雨水补给的多沙性河流”，其下游河道多曲折蜿蜒，水浅沙深，[③] 并不利于开展大规模的运输活动，遂有汉时另行开辟漕渠，借以增加漕运运量。事实上，唐代所面临的情况依旧如此，唐朝初年限于隋末战乱的破坏，一直迟迟未能恢复东西之间的漕运往来，迫不得已，只好改用“八递”牛车经崤函古道辗转运粮。但陆运粮食的运量毕竟有限，不能满足关中地区庞大的消费需求。稍遇灾荒年景，统治者就要往返于长安、洛阳两京之间，或如高宗、武后，直接常住洛阳，反倒省却了漕运西行的必要。直到李唐重建，还都长安，恢复漕运一事才被重新提及。开元二十一年（733 年），按京兆尹裴耀卿重提“节级便取”的运

---

① （唐）陆贽：《陆贽集》，中华书局，2006，第 722 ~ 723 页。

② 陈明光：《20 世纪唐代两税法研究评述》，《中国史研究动态》2000 年第 10 期，第 2 ~ 11 页。

③ 中国科学院地理研究所渭河研究组：《渭河下游河流地貌》，科学出版社，1983，第 5 页。

输方法，遂有恢复漕粮输入，“凡三岁，漕七百万石，省陆运佣钱三十万缗”，暂缓缺粮状况。[①] 随后，“陕郡太守李齐物凿砥柱为门以通漕”，打通黄河航道，使漕运得以“辟三门巅，逾岩险之地，俾负索引舰，升于安流”，[②] 运粮至永丰仓。继以韦坚“治汉、隋运渠，起关门，抵长安，通山东租赋”，不仅重新疏通了漕渠，还在浐灞交汇处新开了广运潭作为物资集散的码头。至此，河、渭漕运再度兴盛，随着关东漕粮源源不断地输入，“及安禄山反于范阳，两京仓库盈溢而不可名”，[③] 关中地区再没有出现过大规模的饥荒。然而，安史之乱的爆发打破了局面，当“是时淮、河阻兵，飞挽路绝”，加之漕渠渠道也因为缺水淤废，从关东输入关中的漕运线路几乎全部断绝。及至平叛战争结束后，唐朝才起用刘晏等人准备恢复漕运，“晏始以盐利为漕佣”，吸引民间商贾加入，“复江淮转运之制，岁入米数十万斛以济关中”，虽暂解燃眉之急，却已不复盛唐时期的景象。其后，随着唐朝国势的整体衰落，就连维持住现有规模也变得日趋艰难，诸如大中五年（851 年）“漕米岁四十万斛，其能至渭仓者，十不三四”的情况更是频频发生。[④]

至此，漕运发展逐渐式微，而唐朝政府也已无力再行恢复之举，要弥补漕运减少的损失，只得让更多漕粮改换陆运入关。值得注意的是，在陆运漕粮的过程中，因为是以牛车运输为主，经常还有征调民间耕牛参与运粮的记录。

如《旧唐书·韦嗣立传》记载：景龙三年（709 年），“时中宗崇饰寺观，又滥食封邑者众，国用虚竭”，针对这一情况，韦嗣立上述谏言，“臣窃见比者营造寺观，其数极多……转运木石，人牛不停，废人功，害农务”，并强调“事既非急，时多怨咨”，借以规劝唐中宗不要骄奢淫逸。[⑤] 为满足统治者个人的穷奢极欲，征调大批的耕牛用来转运木石，以致影响到了正常的农务。《资治通鉴》中亦有详细记述：“是岁，关中饥，米斗百钱。运山东、江、淮谷输京师，牛死什八九。群臣多请车驾复幸东都……上怒

---

① 何汝泉：《唐代转运使初探》，西南师范大学出版社，1987，第 10 页。

② 《旧唐书》卷 49《食货志下》，第 2116 页。

③ 《旧唐书》卷 48《食货志上》，第 2087 页。

④ 《旧唐书》卷 49《食货志下》，第 2119～2120，2122 页。

⑤ 《旧唐书》卷 86《韦嗣立传》，第 2870 页。

曰：‘岂有逐粮天子邪！’乃止。”该年的关中地区确有发生大规模的粮食歉收，而为运粮赈济故，导致“牛死什八九”在路上。

有此前车之鉴，唐睿宗复辟以后即着手漕运建设，并专门在崤函古道间开辟出了一条名为“八递”转运的线路，史称“自景云中，陆运北路分八递，雇民车牛以载”，通过大量征用民间牛畜，借以施行接力运输，至“开元初，河南尹李杰为水陆运使，运米岁二百五十万石，而八递用车千八百乘”。[①] 随后，唐玄宗又采纳了裴耀卿的建议，本着“水通则随近运转，不通即且纳在仓”的原则，充分利用沿途漕仓衔接水陆转运，推广“节级便取”的运输方法，使漕粮“自太原仓浮于渭，以实关中”。[②] 这样一来，运输效率确实得到了大幅提高，但高强度的运输工作又造成了新的问题。及至天宝十年（751 年）时，河南尹裴迥以“八递伤牛”故，不得不申请线路调整，“乃为交场两递，滨水处为宿场，分官总之”，[③] 是为分漕省牛之策，借以增加中途休息，来减少畜力的损耗，避免“伤牛”。针对这一现象，唐玄宗在《量减祭祀应用牛牲诏》中也有提及：“牛之为畜，人实有赖，既功施播种，亦力被车舆，自此余牲，尤可矜悯。”[④] 强调保护耕牛的重要性。在关中漕渠尚未疏通的情况下，漕粮输送完全依赖陆运车转，势必要大量征调民间耕牛。如以“八递”为例，途经崤函山地两百余里运程，按“八递用车千八百乘”进行推算，则往返替换的常备牛畜应该不少于两千之数，其间损伤、劳累致死数只会更多。所以，正如李白诗云“吴牛喘月时，拖船一何苦”，[⑤] 生动地描绘了人畜劳苦、疲于运输的事实。而大量的耕牛、畜力被征作运粮，必然会影响到漕运沿线的正常生产。

对此，唐人不是没有清楚认识，“君所恃在民，民所恃在食，食所资在耕，耕所资在牛，牛废则耕废，耕废则食去，食去则民亡”[⑥] “农功所切，实在耕牛”。[⑦] 但在具体执行的过程中，却很少有真正爱惜牛畜的行为表现。正如《新唐书·食货志》所载：“贞元初，关辅宿兵，米斗千钱。”长安城

---

① 《新唐书》卷 53《食货志三》，第 1367 页。

② 《旧唐书》卷 49《食货志下》，第 2116 页。

③ 《新唐书》卷 53《食货志三》，第 1368 页。

④ （清）董浩：《全唐文》，中华书局，1982，第 358 页。

⑤ （清）曹寅、彭定求等编撰《全唐诗》，中华书局，2017，第 266 页。

⑥ 《新唐书》卷 118《张廷珪传》，第 4262 页。

⑦ 《旧唐书》卷 17《敬宗本纪》，第 511 页。

内一度出现粮荒，以致使“太仓供天子六宫之膳不及十日，禁中不能酿酒”。为此，饥饿的禁军几乎哗变，幸得韩滉及时运送三万斛米西行至陕州，消息传来，这才暂时稳定住了人心。为将这批粮食尽快运送到长安城，唐朝政府甚至不惜“以飞龙驼负永丰仓米给禁军”，尽数征调长安周边的各类牲畜运粮救急，结果又导致“陆运牛死殆尽”,[①] 实属无奈之举。

五　漕粮与耕牛之间的抉择

事实上，经过贞元二年（786 年）这次紧急运粮，关中地区的耕牛数量锐减，谁知贞元七年（791 年）又有“关辅牛疫死，十亡五六”，再次折损大半。受此影响，农业生产已不能维持，“上遣中使以诸道两税钱买牛，散给畿民无牛者”。[②] 由此可见，关中地区的耕牛资源已经匮乏到了何等程度。其后，“诸军讨淮西，四年不克，馈运疲弊，民至有以驴耕者”，究其缘由，还是因“牛弊于运转，民至无以耕”所致。[③] 显然，农民以驴代牛进行耕作，也从一个侧面反映出中晚唐耕牛缺失的客观事实。

耕牛短缺的问题一度超过了漕运的重要性，成为统治者优先考虑的头等要务。就在唐德宗“以诸道两税钱买牛”的次年，初任宰相的陆贽随即就向唐德宗谏言“减漕省牛”，并提出了一套整改方案。《资治通鉴》述道：“旧制以关中用度之多，岁运东方租米，至有斗钱运斗米之言。习闻见而不达时宜者，则曰：国之大事，不计费损，虽知劳烦，不可废也。……顷者每年自江、湖、淮、浙运米百一十万斛，至河阴留四十万斛，贮河阴仓，至陕州又留三十万斛，贮太原仓，馀四十万斛输东渭桥。今河阴、太原仓见米犹有三百二十馀万斛，京兆诸县斗米不过直钱七十，请令来年江、淮止运三十万斛至河阴，河阴、陕州以次运至东渭桥，其江、淮所停运米八十万斛，委转运使每斗取八十钱于水灾州县粜之，以救贫乏，计得钱六十四万缗，减僦直六十九万缗。”[④]

应该说，此时的河、渭水运并不通畅，漕粮完全依赖于牛车陆运。为

---

① 《新唐书》卷 53《食货志三》，第 1369 页。
② 《旧唐书》卷 13《德宗本纪》，第 371 页。
③ 《资治通鉴》卷 240，第 7737 页。
④ 《资治通鉴》卷 234，第 7536 页。

尽量地节省运费开支和畜力损耗，在粮储相对充足的前提下，唐朝政府开始有计划地削减漕运数额，改以短距离的调仓补粮。但这样一来，随着漕运规模的持续萎缩，漕运运道的建设、维护也会式微，加之“堰遏费水”的问题愈演愈烈，引泾灌渠尚且无水可用，更何况漕渠一线总长三百余里的渠道。结果，按照《旧唐书·敬宗本纪》载，宝历二年（826 年）已有将“太仓广运潭复赐司农寺”,[①] 可以想见，此时的关中漕渠年久失修，已废弃许久。值此情况下，关中地区的漕运又全部转回牛车陆运，即便运粮数额或有减少，但仍然要征用大量的耕牛运输，反倒有些事与愿违。

再后，关中漕运的衰落使统治者又切身感到了漕运不通所带来的困扰。此时，面对渭河行漕“岁旱河涸，掊沙而进，米多耗，抵死甚众”的艰难局面，长安城因引泾灌区粮食减产而供给不济，漕粮运输的难题再一次摆到了统治者眼前。

为此，咸阳令韩辽奏请重开兴成渠旧漕，意欲恢复漕渠运输，却在朝堂之上引发了一番激烈争论。当时，右相李固言考虑到国家的实际情况，“以为非时”，并不赞同重疏漕渠的提议。可是，唐文宗却直言“苟利于人，阴阳拘忌，非朕所顾也”,[②] 不顾朝臣的反对，执意想要落实。究其原因，当如中书侍郎李石所述“此漕若成，自咸阳抵潼关，三百里内无车挽之勤，则辕下牛尽得归耕，永利秦中矣”。[③] 如是，唐文宗之所以坚持要重疏漕渠，就是为了节省陆运占用的牛畜，进而降低运粮成本，以保障关中本地的农业生产。但就实际情况所见，这只不过是唐文宗个人一厢情愿的想法，因为“结合唐后期两税法施行后很难大规模征调力役和地方财政拮据的情况”，唐朝政府根本无力再去重疏漕渠，甚至有学者怀疑韩辽是否有过疏凿漕渠一事。[④]

由此可见，唐代后期，即便统治者已经清楚认识到了漕粮运输对于耕牛占用所带来的影响，想去“减漕省牛”，却也限于国力衰落，不能打破现行模式，从而无法在耕牛资源的分配、使用上做出任何实质性的改变。

---

① 《旧唐书》卷 17《敬宗本纪》，第 520 页。

② 《新唐书》卷 53《食货志三》，第 1371 页。

③ 《旧唐书》卷 172《李石传》，第 4485 页。

④ 郭声波：《韩辽是否疏凿了漕渠?》，《中国历史地理论丛》1988 年第 2 辑。

六　结论

围绕京师长安粮食供给这一核心问题，汉唐时期皆通过兴修农田水利、扩大漕粮输入加以解决，前者为挖掘关中本土的农业生产，后者则是国家统筹的物资调配，两种途径一并构成了关中地区最主要的粮食来源。但事物的发展都有其限度，特别是在河流水源相对有限的前提下，关中地区存在大量过度开发水利的现象，反倒严重影响了社会生产的长远发展。尤其唐代农田灌溉、漕渠运输、碾硙加工多个方面皆要用水，水源分配本就难以均匀，而各类私修水利又竞相逐利，交错重叠，争夺水源，更是进一步加剧了用水分配上的矛盾纠纷，私碾屡拆不禁，“堰遏费水”。唐朝统治者很难从根本上解决私修水利的利益驱动，只得通过税制改革的方式转嫁社会负担，但这一切都是以牺牲关中本土的粮食生产为代价。受此影响，唐代后期只能更依赖关外漕粮的输入，然而漕渠渠道缺水淤废，运输不畅，朝廷只得大量征调民间耕牛陆上运粮，结果却是“陆运牛死殆尽”，反过来又影响了漕运沿线正常的农业生产。对此，唐朝统治者虽尝试过调整，却不能达到平衡，终于形成了一个恶性循环。最后，长安城失去了持续稳定的粮食供给，军心动摇，根本无力再去压制地方的反叛势力，在客观上加速了李唐王朝统治的衰败。

清代河西走廊水案中的官绅关系*

潘春辉**

摘　要：在清代河西走廊水案调处中，官绅之间存在着依附与对抗的双重关系。一方面，官府依靠士绅等调处民户之间的小型日常水利纠纷。另一方面，士绅也要依赖官府权威，维护自身的社会地位与权益，尤其在面对一些长期无法有效解决的顽固性水利纠纷中，士绅尤其仰赖官府的支持。二者之间的对抗同样明显。在既得利益面前，士绅有时会成为官府实现地区水利公平的障碍，为此河西官府会采取相应措施管控士绅。而士绅亦会利用其在乡村社会的影响力，反制官府。以水案为切入点，可揭示官绅之间的复杂关系，这是清代西北水利社会史研究的新视角。

关键词：清代　河西走廊　水案　官绅关系

Abstract: In the water case mediation of the Hexi corridor in the Qing dynasty, there was a dual relationship between the gentry and the government. On the one hand, the government relied on the gentry to mediate small daily water disputes between households. On the other hand, the gentry also depended on the government to maintain their social status and rights and interests, especially in the face of some stubborn water conservancy disputes that could not be effectively solved for a long time, the gentry especially depended on the government's support. The rivalry between the two was equally obvious. In the face of vested interests, the gentry would sometimes become an obstacle for the government to a-

* 本文为作者主持的国家社会科学基金项目《明清以来祁连山地区的用水机制与地方秩序研究》（19BZS095）的阶段性成果。

** 潘春辉，女，汉族，山东即墨人，西北师范大学历史文化学院教授，历史学博士，主要从事西北史地研究。

chieve regional water justice, so the government in Hexi would take corresponding measures to control the gentry. The gentry also used their influence in the rural society to oppose the government. Water case as a breakthrough point, can reveal the complex relationship between the gentry and the government.

Keywords: Qing Dynasty; Hexi Corridor; Water case; Relationship between the entry and government

清代河西走廊水资源匮乏，水利管理历来是该区社会治理的核心议题，各种水利纠纷的调处则是社会治理中的重头戏。史称该区“年年均水起喧嚣”[①]“从古到今，这里每县的人民，一致认为血可流，水不可失，持刀荷锄，互争水流，断折臂足，无一退让，死者、伤者一年之内，不知多少”。[②] 在水案调处中，往往需要官府与士绅等地方精英的合作方可顺利完成。另外，为保水利的既得利益，官绅之间的争斗亦同时存在。透过水案的处理，可清楚地看到官绅之间既合作又对抗的双重关系。有关官府、管水吏役在水利纠纷处理中的意义，笔者已作了一些探讨。[③] 在此，就清代河西走廊水案调处中的官绅关系再作进一步讨论，以为西北水利社会史的深入研究提供新的观察视角。

一　合作与依靠

清代河西走廊的水利纠纷大致可分为两类，一类为上下游、各县之间的争水，此类水案须由官府出面主导处理，地方士绅等为辅。另一类为同渠、同村户民日常之间的争水，此类小型水利纠纷一般由乡村士绅与管水吏役等主导处理，官府仅起督率作用。在各种类型水案的处理中，官府与士绅之间的相互依附及合作关系普遍存在。清代河西走廊官绅之间的合作与依靠主要表现为两个方面，一方面，官府需要依靠士绅解决民间的小型水案，在大型水利纠纷的调处中士绅亦可辅助官府；另一方面，清代河西地区的士绅也时时处处要依靠官府权威，维护自身的社会地位与权益。

---

① （民国）赵仁卿：《金塔县志》，第一〇卷。

② （民国）江戎疆：《河西水系与水利建设》，第八卷。

③ 潘春辉：《水官与清代河西走廊基层社会治理》，《社会科学战线》2014 年第 1 期；潘春辉：《水事纠纷与政府应对——以清代河西走廊为中心》，《西北师大学报》2015 年第 2 期。

首先，官府仰赖士绅解决民户的日常水利纠纷，大型水案的调处中双方亦存有较紧密的合作关系。清代河西走廊因水源匮乏而致水利纠纷不断，民间小型水案层出不穷，政府往往无力亦无暇处理，因而官府一般会将小型水案的调处权统归于管水吏役与乡绅。在清代河西走廊，管水吏役与士绅往往本身就合二为一，即担任管水吏役者多为士绅。据史料记载，河西水规中对渠长等管水吏役的选举资格进行了限定，如敦煌县规定：

> 渠正非具有下列资格之一者不得公举。一、应在上下渠分轮流之列者。二、曾任渠长、排水者。三、曾任地方水利监察会会员者。四、办理乡区公益三年以上著有声望者。第二十五条，渠长非具下列资格者不得被选。一、充当排水一年以上者。第二十六条，排水非具有下列资格之一者不得充任。一、家道殷实者。二、在本渠有田地半户以上者。三、本渠坊会首、乡望素孚者。①

这样的规定，使得出任水官者多来自乡村上层的士绅地主等。士绅通过制定水规、兴建水渠等方式担负起了河西地区日常水案的处理工作。

在清代河西走廊的水规议定中士绅是不可或缺的成员。据敦煌县《普利渠渠规》，敦煌普利渠渠规遭恶人破坏后水利纠纷频发，为此，在乡绅龚翰文的召集与倡导下，“合渠绅衿、农约、坊甲人等公到会所议定章程”，②新的《普利渠渠规》因之诞生。以新渠规为依据，有效地调解了各争水势力之间的争斗。再如，光绪十二年酒泉下四闸公议水规，绅耆、农约、士庶代表则是水规议定的既定三方势力。③ 除参与渠规制定外，士绅还通过兴建水渠、修治渠坝的方式解决水利纠纷。如清光绪年间，甘州草湖、二坝共用弱水浇灌，后因弱水微细，加之未能及时修筑渠坝，致使河堤崩跌，无水可灌，水案乍起。为此，二坝士绅于兴门认为如果能够导引山丹河水引灌即可解决问题，然而却遭到上下坝民的反对。在多次兴讼之后，二坝胜诉。在于兴门的带领下，疏渠导引山丹河水，开渠使水。④ 我们看到士绅

① （民国）吕钟：《重修敦煌县志》。

② （民国）吕钟：《重修敦煌县志》。

③ （民国）《甘肃河西荒地区域调查报告（酒泉、张掖、武威）》第六章《水利》第二节《灌溉方法》。

④ （民国）《甘州水利溯源》。

在调处各日常水利纠纷中尚能秉公持正。如，山丹县士绅马良宝担任暖泉渠水官，为人公正不阿，秉公处理水案，“河西四闸强梁，夜馈盘金劝退步，良宝责以大义，馈者惭去，于是按粮均定除侵水奸弊，渠民感德”。士绅毛柏龄亦是山丹暖泉渠水官，“秉公剖析，人称铁面公”。[①] 清光绪十九年高如先被举为临泽二坝下渠长，“秉公持正，水利均沾”。[②] 这些士绅能够较公正地处理水利纠纷，成为河西官府调处乡村日常水利纷争的臂膀。

士绅除了在上述小型水案的调处中扮演关键角色外，在大型水案的调节中亦能较好地辅助官府开展工作。清代河西走廊涉及多县及上下游的大型水案须由官府出面调停，而官府在调解水利纠纷时，士绅亦往往能够与官府合作，帮助官府调处水案。如乾隆二十七年酒泉县茹公渠水案中，酒泉、金塔二县争水，肃州州判与金塔县府在处理该案时，根据金塔士绅等人对案情的呈奏，判定金塔坝得水七分，茹公渠得水三分。[③] 再如安西、玉门两地争水案中，因皇渠年久失修，无水浇灌，田苗悉枯。玉门、安西两处为此争讼不休。为此，安西县长曹馥“会商诸绅”，在与士绅商议的基础上成立了皇渠会。皇渠会通过各个士绅捐资积累资金以资助皇渠的修治，“积资生息岁作工食”，从此“庶几于渠无抛荒之忧，于年有丰登之兆也”。[④] 得到了士绅的支持，皇渠会因而成立，水渠修治得到保障，水利纠纷亦从而解决。从上述大型水案调处中士绅的参与可以看到，士绅的支持能辅佐官府更好地解决水案。

其次，士绅阶层须依靠官府权威以维护自身的权益，尤其在面对一些长期无法有效解决的顽固性水利纠纷中，士绅尤其仰赖官府的支持，方能获得水利公平。清代河西走廊一些水利纠纷往往持续时间很长，少则三五年，多则数十年，双方矛盾累积多年而得不到有效解决。处于纠纷弱势的一方士绅往往会带领民众上控官府，以求得官府支持从而获得水利公平。

清代河西地方士绅为民请命、依靠官府的代表性人物，还要数镇夷堡的阎如岳。康熙年间，甘州府高台县与镇夷堡共同使用黑河水灌溉，然而高台、临泽等县地处黑河上游，每年春季需水时节，地处上游的高台各渠

---

① （清）黄璟、朱逊志等：《山丹县志》。

② （民国）《创修临泽县志》卷一二《耆旧志·高如先传》。

③ （民国）赵仁卿：《金塔县志》，第三卷。

④ （民国）曹馥：《安西县采访录》《叙·安西皇渠会叙》。

拦河阻坝，造成下游镇夷堡无水可浇，两地民众因争水几至打伤人命。下游民众在镇夷堡绅耆阎如岳的带领下数次兴讼，“如岳倡率里老居民，申诉制府绰公，求定水规。辄收押，乃甘州、高台民众力强，贿嘱看役，肆凌虐，备尝艰苦，如岳百折不回”。[①] 康熙五十四年，阎如岳[②]带领民众“等遮道哭诉背呈受苦情由”，得到官府支持后，得以重订分水章程。然而，“孰知定案之后高民又有乱法之人，阳奉阴违或闭四五日不等仍复不遵”。康熙六十一年，恰逢年羹尧前往甘肃，阎如岳率领士民等“报辕苦陈受苦苦情”，为此年羹尧下令将两地合为一县，但仍然无法实现水利公平，“亦有刁民乱法先开渠口者仍复不少，镇五堡仍复受害”。雍正四年年羹尧再次途经肃州，镇夷五堡士民阎如岳等“携拽家属百事哭诉苦情”。[③] 年羹尧采取强力措施，将地方官员革职查办，由安肃道派毛目水利县丞巡河，封闭甘、肃、高台渠口，并派夫丁严密看守渠口以防上游乱开渠口，至此该水案方得以解决，镇夷堡水利方有保证。后人为此修建阎公祠堂以彰显阎公事迹，“于芒种前十日祝如岳并年羹尧，至今不替”,[④] 为民争水的阎公在地方上拥有很高声望。可见，面对上游强行违规，处于弱势的下游地区往往由乡村士绅带领民众控诉争竞，获得官府支持后方能保证应有的水权。阎如岳成为地方绅耆带领民众争取水利权力的典型，同时也清晰反映出士绅对官府权威的仰赖。另据民国档案记载，金塔酒泉争水中，金塔县士绅赵积寿负责金塔水务，该绅多次为金塔民众申请水源，民国二十五年时为金塔讨要讨赖河水，却遭到酒泉民众的控诉。酒泉民众多次上控官府认为赵积寿扰害酒泉水利，要求惩处赵积寿，甚至一度上告至省政府。对此省府对赵积寿的处理意见为“对赵积寿未免言过其实”[⑤]并告诫民众以后不得如此中伤赵积寿。从此记载中我们可以看到，官府往往保护为地方事务服务的士绅，官绅之间的契合一直存在。

总体而言，清代河西走廊官绅之间的合作与依靠是双向的。一方面，

---

① （民国）徐家瑞：《新纂高台县志》，《人物·善行》。

② “阎如岳”在有些史志中将其书写为“闫如岳”。此处以“阎如岳”为准。

③ （民国）张应麒修、蔡廷孝：《鼎新县志》，《水利·附录镇夷闫如岳控定镇夷五堡并毛双二屯芒种分水案》。

④ （民国）徐家瑞：《新纂高台县志》，《人物·善行》。

⑤ 《甘肃省政府关于仰查酒泉金塔民众因均水互控事给七区专员的训令》，张景平等主编《河西走廊水利史文献类编》，科学出版社，2016。

官府依赖士绅为其解决日常的民间争水，在大型水案中士绅也可起到辅助作用。另一方面，从为民请命可清晰地体现出在水利不公面前士绅阶层对官府的依赖。

二 对抗与管控

在清代河西走廊实际的水事纠纷调处中，官绅之间也同时存在着对抗与冲突。士绅有时会因利益而成为基层水利不公的制造者，并因此站到官方的对立面，进而抗拒官府。为此，要实现地方良好的用水秩序及正常的官绅关系，河西地方政府会有一些相应的管控措施来约束士绅。

清代河西走廊士绅与官府的对抗主要源于个别士绅对乡村水利的危害。事实上，清代河西地区因士绅强霸水利而产生的水利不公并不在少数，在既得利益面前，士绅与官府产生的对抗亦并不少见。据河西地方史料记载，所谓"刁生劣监"等地方头面人物有时会成为扰害地方水利的领导者与怂恿者，如安西县三道沟昌马水口案，安西、玉门争水，乾隆四十七、四十八、四十九年间，玉门农约相继为奸，强堵水口，并蒙骗官府，致使官府作出错误的判断，"以致玉县奸民得计，而安西良民受害"。[①] 虽然此后安西直隶州重新作出批示，然而玉门民众在地方头面人物的支持下仍"逞刁不服"。[②] 士绅阶层公然带头对抗官府，造成水利不公以及两地长期的争水与纠纷。民国时期，有学者总结河西走廊水利纠纷产生的原因时曾言：

> 故各地争案之起还是在于：1. 分水之法失尽善。2. 交界处之土劣士绅籍势抢夺，不按规定。3. 一方人民之偷挖水渠，致使另一方的愤怒。4. 贪官污吏之籍私偏袒，甚至怂恿民众，行暴豪夺。[③]

河西走廊争水的原因中"交界处之土劣士绅籍势抢夺，不按规定"占重要一条，一些士绅不遵水规造成地区水利争执与不公。士绅在水利管理中的负面作用，已与官府期望的官绅合作以实现水利平稳的目的相背。为

---

① （民国）曹馥：《安西县采访录·安西义田碑记》。
② （民国）曹馥：《安西县采访录·民政·水利》。
③ （民国）江戎疆：《河西水系与水利建设》，第八卷。

此，清代河西官府对士绅采取相应管控措施。

清代河西官府对士绅的管控可从以下几个方面谈起。

首先，官府会对破坏基层水利的士绅进行打压与震慑，以保证地方水利秩序的平稳。清宣统元年，金塔坝、王子坝争水，其间所谓“刁生劣监”多次翻控。为此，王子庄州同在水利碑刻之末刻明“如再有刁生劣监，无知愚民胆敢藉端生事者，定行按律严惩”，[①] 以震慑不服管理的绅民。又如清代末年，敦煌下永丰、庄浪二渠因浇水顺序不当，上流豪绅强占水源，致使二渠未能按期浇灌，“屡因夺水滋事”。为此，地方官察知其弊，“抑强扶弱”“勒令二渠与八渠同归一律，由下浇上”，方得利益均沾。[②] 再如，乾隆年间，山丹河浇灌山丹、张掖及东乐县丞所属共十八坝地亩，浇灌按照纳粮多寡分配水额。然上坝认为本坝纳粮多而水额少，因此士绅王瑞怀带领六轮闸口民众共同上控官府。甘州府细查后认为，“惊蛰时冰冻初开为时尚冷，先从下坝以次通浇而及于上坝，其时渐融，于地较近，通盘折算已无偏枯”。[③] 因此，王瑞怀等“始各恍然悔悟”，亦不再争控，原先跟随他上控的六轮闸口民众亦改口自称“实系牵捏混告”。对此，甘州府认为“王瑞怀等并不细查原委妄希占利，屡次滋讼殊属不合”，将王瑞怀等“拟以戒责以示惩儆”。[④] 官府通过惩戒带头控官之士绅，以平息各方争执。在上述案件中，因为利益的不同，在官府看来，个别士绅已成为扰动基层水利平稳的带头人。而官府对士绅的惩儆以及士绅的败诉则体现出，在多数情况下，官绅对抗中官府多能占据上风。

其次，对于与官府交好的士绅，官府打压的步伐与效果则会相应减缓。一般情况下，清代河西官府对所谓乡村“豪右逞强、奸民侵略”之事，都会出面“治之”。[⑤] 但如若官绅交好，那么官府则可能姑息不良士绅的作为。据陈世镕《古浪水利记》所记，古浪四坝、五坝共用一水，五坝在四坝之左，地稍高，稍有不均则五坝受旱。而四坝之豪绅胡国玺强占水利，在四坝之口开一汊港，“谓之副河，必灌满其正河，次灌满其副河，而五坝乃得

---

① （民国）赵仁卿：《金塔县志》，第三卷。

② （民国）《敦煌县乡土志》，第二卷。

③ （民国）徐传钧、张著常等：《东乐县志》。

④ （民国）徐传钧、张著常等：《东乐县志》。

⑤ （清）南济汉：《永昌县志》，第三卷。

自灌其河。古浪疆域四百里，其爪牙布满三百里。五坝之民饮泣吞声，莫敢谁何也。他坝岁纳数千金，以为治河之费，其徵收视两税尤急。用是一牧羊儿而家资累万”。[①] 而胡国玺能如此胆大妄为，其重要原因即为“结交县令尹”，与官府交好，并以此挟制官府，“其假之权，不知自谁始，而为所挟制者已数任矣”。[②] 胡国玺扰害地方水利多年，受害民众诉讼不止，而几任县府对其劣迹管控不力，因而造成了严重的水利不公。因此，随着新任官员的到任，对胡国玺的惩治也就随之而来。

> 余至，五坝之民呈诉。余往勘验，实以其一坝而占两坝之水，藉以科派取利。即令毁其副河，以地之多寡为得水之分数。详请立案，胡国玺照扰害地方例惩办，而讼以息。特记之以诏后之令斯土者，尚无为地方奸民所挟制也。[③]

古浪县府立案详查，将胡国玺以扰害地方罪惩办。此案结案后，特告诫下任官员不要为地方奸民所挟制。从此案中我们可以看到士绅们通过交好县府官员，可缓和官府对其打压的力度与进程。

再次，除以国家权威对士绅进行打压外，清代河西官府还以各种手段对士绅进行笼络，并赋予士绅一定的特权，促使其更好地为官府服务。如乾隆七年十二月甘肃巡抚黄廷桂奏：甘、凉、西、肃等处渠工应照宁夏之例，无论绅衿士庶按田亩之分数，一例备料勷办，其绅衿不便力作者许雇募代役。[④] 即士绅可不必放下身段参与修治水渠等苦差，可通过雇募代役的方式保持体面。再如据《酒泉县洪水坝四闸水规》所记，洪水坝四闸绅耆农约士庶人等，每年为争当渠长兴讼不休。而士绅们争当渠长的一个重要原因，是可获得诸如多浇水时的特权：“旧渠长春祭龙神应占水四分，渠长各占水二十八分，农约每人应占水一分，字识应占水四分。”[⑤] 可见，官府赋予士绅各种特权，一方面可使士绅阶层能够更好地为官府服务，另一方

---

① （清）陈世镕：《古浪水利记》，《皇朝经世文续编》，第一一八卷。
② （清）陈世镕：《古浪水利记》，《皇朝经世文续编》，第一一八卷。
③ （清）陈世镕：《古浪水利记》，《皇朝经世文续编》，第一一八卷。
④ （清）《大清高宗纯皇帝实录》，第一八一卷。
⑤ （民国）《甘肃河西荒地区域调查报告（酒泉、张掖、武威）》第六章《水利》第二节《灌溉方法》。

面，士绅也可利用这些特权提升自身在基层水利社会中的地位。

最后，面对政府的管控，清代河西士绅也在适时地做出反抗与调试，有时官府并不能完全如意。如清乾隆年间，镇番县县令文楠在查勘该县水道的基础上，认为水道弯曲易淤，准备将“东河西改”，因此“议诸绅衿”。县令在与县里士绅商议以后，并未得到士绅们的支持，反而造成了“县人大哗，訾言纷纭”的局面，并最终致使该县令辞职。[①] 可知，士绅利用他们在基层社会中的深厚影响力，有时可在官绅权力博弈中占据上风。

可见，在多数情况下官府能够实施对士绅的管控。但其中也存在着特例，如士绅可通过交结官府从而减轻及逃避打压，士绅也可动用其在乡村社会中的影响力而使官府的管控失效，甚至反制官府。透过水案的调处，可以洞见清代河西官绅之间复杂的权力博弈。

三 余论

借助士绅等地方精英来完成国家对乡村水利事务的管理是清代基层政治的重要特点。在水利纠纷频仍的河西走廊地区，政府将乡村水利纠纷调处权利更多地下放给士绅等基层精英，官绅之间的互动与交集就显得更为繁复，而双方的关系会随着利益的变动而有所不同。一般而言，对于日常的小型水利纷争，官府会全权委托士绅、水官等地方头面人物处理。即在乡村日常水案的处理中，官府仰赖士绅。在大型的水事纠纷处理中，士绅也能够起到重要的辅助作用，协助官府完成水案的处理工作。与此同时，在一些上下游或多县的大型水利之争中，本身处于受害者与弱势地位的士绅则需要依靠官府的支持方能获得水利公平。官绅之间的依靠与合作在清代的河西走廊普遍展开。

需要说明的是，清代国家将基层日常水案调处权归于地方精英，一方面可借助地方头面人物的力量加强基层水务的治理，而另一方面却助长了这些人物在水利事务中的权势，清代河西走廊一些水利不公的产生本身就是源于士绅等的贪腐，如《民勤县水利规则》记载，“民勤水利规则创于清初康雍以还，……一百余年来河夫会首操纵水权，习弊相仍”。[②] 官府放权

① （民国）谢树森、谢广恩等编撰，李玉寿校订《镇番遗事历鉴》。

② （民国）《民勤县水利规则·敬告全县父老昆弟切实奉行民勤县水利规则》。

给士绅管理基层水务，也确实带来了一些负面影响。同时，若士绅与官府水利利益相悖之时，双方的冲突与对抗就不可避免。因此，清代河西官府采取相应的措施对士绅进行管控。

多数情况下官府会在与士绅的抗衡中获胜，但也并不尽然，士绅有时会倚靠其在乡村水利社会中的地位与影响而占据上风。因此，清代河西走廊的士绅与官府之间的关系会随着利益的变化而呈现疏密不同。冲突应是官绅各自展示其在乡村水利社会地位的一种方式，官府需强调其绝对权威，而士绅也需要不时地表现其在基层社会中的影响力。正如兰欣所指出的："精英们在（清）王朝结束之前总的来说并没有视国家权力为威胁……精英们依然从与国家的纽带中获取特权；与官员的冲突更可能的是在政府内部创造一个增强接触的期待，而不是培养一个分离的政治权力的集体性要求。"[①] 官绅之间的合作与冲突，都是在可控及可接受的范围内。也正因为如此，虽然清代河西走廊的水利纠纷数量多而繁复，但总体都能够得到平复。

"河西讼案之大者莫过于水利"，[②] 以水案为切入点，可清晰地透见清代河西走廊水利社会中士绅与官府的微妙关系。二者既有合作倚靠，又有对抗与龃龉，但合作应是其主流。河西走廊水案中的官绅关系可为水利社会史的研究提供一个新的观察视角。

---

① Mary Backus Rankin, *Elite Activism and Political Transformation in China*, p. 28.

② （清）张玿美修，曾钧等：《古浪县志》，《地理志·水利碑文说》。

史前河南水环境与农业文明的产生*

贾兵强**

摘　要： 水是生命之源，生产之要，生态之基。地处黄河中下游的河南水环境变化剧烈。因此，防止洪涝灾害成为中原先民最主要的水事活动之一。史前时期，人类治水活动构成华夏文明之源，其内容不仅包括筑堤建坝、修筑城池、疏浚河道、堆筑高台等防御水患的实践，而且还包括凿井、挖池、修渠以利取水、蓄水、排灌等开发利用水资源的活动，从而出现人类农业文明的曙光。史前时期河南优越的水环境孕育中华农业文明，水利技术、水井和农田耕作工具是农业文明产生的重要条件。

关键词： 史前河南　水环境　农业文明

Abstract: Water is the source of life, the key to productionand the foundation of ecology too. The water environment of Henan, which is located in the middle and lower reaches of the Yellow River, changes greatly. Therefore, the people had the most important water activities of preventing the flood disastersin the Central Plains. During the prehistoric period, the water control activities of human constituted the source of Chinese civilization. Its contents not only included the construction of dams, city, dredging, piling up high walls and other flood prevention practices, but also included sinking Wells, digging ponds, building for water, storage, drainage and irrigationWater storage, irrigation and drainage, and other development and utilization of water resources activities. The dawn of human agricultural civilization was the product of water control activities. Research

---

* 本文为河南省高校科技创新人才（人文社科类）支持计划（2016CX022）阶段性研究成果。

** 贾兵强，博士后，华北水利水电大学副教授、硕士生导师，研究方向为水文化、农业史。

suggests that superior water environment in Henan gave birth to the Chinese agricultural civilization. The important conditions for agricultural civilization were the wells and farming tools of Henan in prehistoric period.

Keywords: Henan in prehistoric period; Water environment; Agricultural civilization

水环境是人类社会赖以生存和发展的重要因素之一。在史前的水事活动中，中原人民逐渐形成了识水、治水、用水、护水的思想、理念、行为、风俗、习惯等，诸如大禹治水的传说、汤阴白营水井、平粮台古城遗址都代表了史前时期中原水环境变迁与农耕文化。中原先民在史前水事活动中，积累了丰富的水利技术，对中华民族的农耕文明产生了深远的影响。

一　水环境与水资源

水环境主要包括河流、湖泊、沼泽、湿地等自然水体及运河、陂塘、沟渠等人工水体等水资源以及地理位置、气候概况、植被等地理环境和人文环境。中原地区河流众多，有着较为丰富的径流资源和地下水资源。其中地表径流总量主要蕴藏在江、淮、黄、卫四大水系中。流域面积在100平方千米以上的河流在整个地区有460多条，各个区域的河流分布较为均匀。除了本区内自产流352.82亿立方米外，还有从中原地区之外流入境内的年径流量64.55亿立方米。因此，中原地区地表径流的毛总量约为869.07亿立方米。但由于年际变化大，年内分配不均，黄河过境流量因上游利用情况变化而不稳定，所以要全部利用这些地表水资源是不可能的。就本区径流的地表水资源而言，山区径流约208.9亿立方米，平原地区有年径流量143.92亿立方米。[①]

河南境内的水资源主要有河系水道和淮系水道。河系水道是指中原地区境内北部以黄河为主的河流体系，具体又可分为两支：一是黄河水系，其支流有济水、沁水、丹水、洛水、伊水、汜水等。二是河北的卫河水系，其支流有漳河、安阳河、汤河、淇河等。淮系水道是以中原地区南部的淮河为主体的河流体系，具体也可分为两支：一是淮河水系，支流有洪河、

① 马雪芹：《明清河南农业地理》，洪叶文化事业有限公司，1997，第38页。

沙河、汝水、颍河、史河、白露河等。二是汉江水系，主要支流有唐河、白河。唐河支流有泌河和毗河，白河支流有湍河、万河、潦河等。两大水系共有河道近20条，为本区的水利灌溉事业提供了良好的条件。

史前时期，河南曾经分布着大量的湖沼，唐代还增加了许多新的湖泊和沼泽。但是随着宋金之际黄河南泛，中原地区的湖泊、沼泽出现了变化，它们或淤浅，或被开垦为农田。从史前时代一直到周代以前，中原地区正处在气候温暖时期。从孢粉所反映植被类型来看，当时中原地区的气候明显要比现代温暖而湿润，这个基本的特征得到平原内及相邻地区众多的孢粉分析的证实，因此这个时期通常也被称为全新世高温期。在距今8000～3000年，中原地区的植被类型要比现代要多。[①]而从安阳殷墟考古发掘中发现大量的动物骨骼，包括了29种动物，除了猪、牛、羊、犬等家畜外，还有一些野生动物，它们的来源无疑是商王田猎时的收获。商代田猎区大约在今河南沁阳一带。因此这些动物基本上可反映中原地区北部的动物群，以及这些动物群所对应的自然环境。在这些动物中有中、小型的猿和竹鼠，它们目前只分布在长江流域。大型的犀牛和象等动物目前仅存在于热带地区，考古发现证明距今8000～3000年时期它们活动的地域要比现代宽，但其成群活动一般不超过亚热带北界。这些动物的存在表明，在公元前14～11世纪时，中原地区气候比现在温暖。

水利事业是人类对自然环境的应对、利用和改造，是对自然灾害的抵御和自然资源的开发利用，特别是对水旱灾害的防御和对水资源的开发和利用，从本质上讲属于人与自然关系的一部分。因此，水利事业离不开具体的生态环境和自然资源，特别是水环境和水资源。同时，水利事业的主体是人，人是社会化的动物，因此，水利事业也与社会环境，包括政治、经济、文化等相关联。各个时期的水利也受到当时经济社会状况的制约。总之，水利事业的发展在客观上取决于地形、水资源等自然条件，更取决于一个稳定的社会环境。

二　农业文明的产生条件

钱穆先生认为农业文明程度的高低是与各水系的灌溉水准相依归的，

---

① 王星光：《生态环境变迁与夏代的兴起探索》，科学出版社，2004，第57页。

他对水系等级也进行了分类，“如黄河、长江为第一级，汉水、淮水、济水、辽河等可为第二级，渭水、泾水、洛水、汾水、漳水等则为第三级，此下还有第四级、第五级等诸水系。……此外还有涑水、淇水、濮水、伊水、澧水等小水系”。[①] 黄河则为华夏文明的发展提供了丰厚的养分，使农耕文明在这片丰饶的东方古陆产生、发达，并最终成为主导中国社会进步的力量。

河南位于黄河中游的下段和黄河下游的中段，东有辽阔无垠的豫东冲积平原，西依巍峨连绵的伏牛、熊耳山脉；南有蜿蜒起伏的桐柏、大别山脉、南阳盆地；北有太行山脉、华北平原；奔腾澎湃的黄河浩浩荡荡从中间穿过。优越的地理位置和丰富的自然资源，使河南自远古起就成为黄河流域古老文化的一颗明珠。黄河被称为中华民族的母亲河，是因为在黄河中下游产生了高度发达的古代文明。同时，河南境内的淮河、伊洛河、漳河等沿河的台地和平原，土层深厚，土质肥沃，气候温和，雨量充沛，既有适合狩猎采果、种植五谷的地方，又有能躲避水灾的地方，为古代人类提供了良好的生存环境。[②]

史前时期，中原地区优越的生态环境，吸引了人类先祖在这里繁衍生息。《孟子·滕文公上》：“草木畅茂，禽兽繁殖，兽蹄鸟迹之道交于中国。”旧石器时代，中原气候温暖，雨量充沛，河流纵横，湖泊密布，森林连绵，动植物繁盛。适宜的生存环境，为中原农耕文化产生奠定了基础。在全新世中期，中国大地出现了温暖湿润的气候环境。[③]在新石器时代，中原气候依然温暖湿润，年平均气温比现在高 3～5℃，降水量也明显多于现在，更适合各种动植物生长和繁殖。竺可桢在《中国近五千年来气候变迁的初步研究》一文指出：“仰韶时代气候温和，年平均温度高于当代 2℃。”[④] 当时中原地区自然植被茂密，遍布郁郁葱葱的森林和草原，其中生长着众多种类的亚热带植物和动物。河流纵横交错，再加上河南境内的土壤主要是黄土，含有大量的氮、磷、钾等营养元素，具有一定的天然肥力，不需要进

---

① 钱穆：《中国文化史导论》，商务印书馆，1994，第 712 页。

② 赵保佑：《中原文化及其现代价值》，《中州今古》2001 年第 5 期。

③ 曹伯勋：《中国第四纪气候研究及对我国未来气候与环境变化的探讨》，《中国区域地质》1990 年第 2 期。

④ 竺可桢：《中国近五千年来气候变迁的初步研究》，《考古学报》1972 年第 1 期。

一步分化即可生长植物，只需用木、石等简单的工具就可耕作，加之土层深厚，便于保墒蓄水，在当时的生产力条件下，中原地区最适宜人类获取生活资料和发展生产，故而在这里最先发展起了原始农业。伊洛河盆地以及太行山前土层深厚，疏松肥沃，便于耕种，成为我国最早的农业开发区。

生产力的发展，生产工具的不断改进，也是中原农耕文化兴起的原因之一。考古证明，旧石器时代河南已经发现采集野生谷物的生产工具。如河南安阳小南海洞穴遗址和许昌灵井遗址中出土的弧背长刮器，主要用途是收获野生谷穗，其形制已与新石器时代的石刀和石镰相当接近。[①] 在新石器时代，中原地区发现了可以说是整个黄河流域迄今发现最早也最有代表性的农耕文化遗址，即距今八九千年的河南裴李岗文化。[②] 到仰韶文化时期，随着人口的增加，居住地域的扩大，生产技术的提高，开辟荒地以垦耕的石铲、中耕用的石锄、收割用的镰刀及加工谷物的石磨盘等都已十分精致、耐用，标志着农业进入了锄耕（或耜耕）阶段。在龙山文化时期，随着人口的增加，居住地域的扩大，生产技术的提高，我国的原始农业已进入了发达阶段。[③]

三 治水与农业文明的起源

农耕文明是我国古代农业文明的主要载体，是中华文明的重要组成部分。而水是生态之要，生产之基。“缘水而居，不耕不稼”，[④]不仅形象地展示了原始社会人类与水的关系，而且也说明水与农耕的渊源。史前人类治水活动不仅包括筑堤建坝、修筑城池、疏浚河道、堆筑高台等防御水患的实践，还包括凿井、挖池、修渠以利取水、蓄水、排灌等开发利用水资源的活动，[⑤]由此构成中华农业文明之源。

水利是农业的命脉。面对滔天洪水，中华民族依靠自己的智慧、力量和百折不挠的精神，与洪水进行顽强抗争，并最终战胜了洪水，广为传诵

① 安志敏：《河南安阳小南海旧石器时代洞穴的试掘》，《考古学报》1965年第1期。

② 开封地区文管会、新郑县文管会：《河南新郑裴李岗新石器时代遗址》，《考古》1978年第2期。

③ 王星光：《试论中国耕犁的本土起源》，《郑州大学学报（哲学社会科学版）》1987年第1期。

④ 《列子集释·汤问篇》。

⑤ 张应桥：《我国史前人类治水的考古学证明》，《中原文物》2005年第3期。

的“大禹治水”的故事即反映了这一点。大禹采用疏导的办法治水，推进了我国水利事业的发展，也促进了数学、测绘、交通等相关技术的进步。《孟子》说：“当尧之时，天下犹未平。洪水横流，泛滥于天下。……尧独忧之，举舜而敷治焉。”由此可见，尧舜时期“洪水横流，泛滥于天下”，[①]致使茫茫大地，一片汪洋。为了制止洪水泛滥，保护农业生产，禹总结父亲的治水经验，改鲧“围堵障”为“疏顺导滞”的方法，利用水自高向低流的自然趋势，顺地形把壅塞的川流疏通。大禹把洪水引入疏通的河道、洼地或湖泊，然后合通四海，从而平息了水患，使百姓得以从高地迁回平川居住和从事农业生产。[②]治水成功后，大禹“身执耒锸，以为民先……尽力乎沟洫”，[③] 兴建水利灌溉工程，开垦土地，植谷种粮，栽桑养蚕，发展农业生产。特别是利用低洼积水之地“予众庶稻”，禹率领群众引水灌田，种植水稻。考古发现，在登封王城岗遗址出土的磨制石器有铲、斧、凿、刀、镰、镞等，炭化农作物有粟、黍、稻、大豆，说明当时农业工具得到改良和进步，耜耕得到大力推广。[④]另外，通过对“九州”的土壤普查，分清了土壤的品质优劣，在了解各地不同物产的同时，可以根据不同的土壤性状，因地制宜种植不同的农作物，促使旱作和稻作都得到了较快发展。沟洫农业的兴起是大禹“卑宫室而尽力乎沟洫”[⑤] 的继续和发展，标志着先民在改造自然的道路上向前更进了一步。[⑥]

在新石器时代，中原地区就开始了农耕实践。中原地区发现了可以说是整个黄河流域迄今发现最早也最有代表性的农耕文化遗址，即距今八九千年的河南裴李岗文化。[⑦]黄河流域土壤肥沃，具有良好的保水和供水性能，是原始农业生产的适宜土壤。因而，处于黄河流域的裴李岗时期成为我国古代农业的重要起源地。[⑧]在裴李岗文化中，不仅出现了粟类和稻类的农作

---

① 《孟子·滕文公上》。

② 贾兵强：《大禹治水精神及其现实意义》，《华北水利水电学院学报（社会科学版）》2011年第4期。

③ 《韩非子集解·五蠹》。

④ 安金槐、李京华：《登封王城岗遗址的发掘》，《文物》1983年第3期。

⑤ 林定川：《孔子语录》，浙江工商大学出版社，2015，第270页。

⑥ 王克林：《略论我国沟洫的起源和用途》，《农业考古》1983年第2期。

⑦ 开封地区文管会 新郑县文管会：《河南新郑裴李岗新石器时代遗址》，《考古》1978年第2期。

⑧ 贾兵强、朱晓鸿：《图说治水与中华文明》，中国水利水电出版社，2015，第3页。

物，还出土了与之相对应的农业生产工具和粮食加工工具，诸如石斧、石铲、石刀、石镰、石磨盘和石磨棒等。据对裴李岗、沙窝李、莪沟、铁生沟、马良沟 5 处遗址的统计，发现有石镰 37 件，石刀 4 件，石磨盘 80 件，石磨棒 42 件。[①]裴李岗文化中出土数量众多的石磨盘和磨棒是谷物加工工具，证明当时已有丰富的谷物需要加工。在裴李岗文化中，发现的收割和加工工具制作精细，数量较多，说明这些农业工具是在长期采集、狩猎经济的制造、使用中发展而来。正是由于采集和谷物加工工具的进步和使用，人们从事采集活动收获量不断增大，谷物加工技术的进步，使植物籽粒更适于人们的胃口，这使得先民们越发看重栽培这些植物对自己谋生的重要性。[②]

裴李岗文化出土的农业工具种类之全，数量之多，制作之精，也反映出当时的农业生产已具有一定的水平。工具种类之完备，说明当时的农业生产已经有一定的基础，尤其是铲和锄的出现，说明当时的农业已进入锄耕农业阶段，而且是粟作与稻作兼有的原始农业生产。[③]

通过对裴李岗文化的研究，我们发现裴李岗文化遗址的分布具有以下三个特点：第一，遗址坐落在靠近河床的阶地上，或在两河的交汇处，一般高出河床 10～20 米，这类遗址具有较好的生存环境和生存空间。第二，遗址坐落在靠近河流附近的丘陵地带，遗址的位置本身较高，距河床较远。这类遗址既临河，又有大片可供农耕的土地，也是人类生息活动的好场所。第三，遗址坐落在海拔较低并且邻近河流的平原地带，这类遗址一般距河床较低，所以，周围环境多为平坦的沃田。[④] 如许昌丁村遗址为平原地带，位于老溴河南岸，比河床高出 3 米，距裴李岗 50 千米。新郑裴李岗遗址位于裴李岗村西北的一块高出河床 25 米的岗地上，双洎河河水自遗址西边流过，然后紧靠遗址的南部折向东流，遗址就在这一河弯上。由此可知，裴李岗文化是的中华古代农业文明的重要源头之一，与治水活动密切相关。

四　水井与定居农业的产生

水井的出现，改变了人类生活的进程，人们由渔猎为生到从事农业生

---

① 王吉怀：《从裴李岗文化的生产工具看中原地区早期农业》，《农业考古》1985 年第 2 期。

② 王星光：《工具与中国农业的起源》，《农业考古》1995 年第 1 期。

③ 贾兵强：《裴李岗文化时期农作物与农耕文明》，《农业考古》2010 年第 1 期。

④ 王吉怀：《论黄河流域前期新石器文化的特征与时代特征》，《东南文化》1999 年第 4 期。

产，饲养家畜、纺织与制陶，从而出现人类农业文明的曙光。对于水井与文明的关系，苏秉琦先生认为水井与文明起源有高度相关性。[①]定居农业的一个重要标志是凿井技术的发明和运用。凿井技术的逐步成熟是台地农业向平原农业过渡的重要反映。[②]根据考古资料，我国北方迄今发现年代最早的水井遗迹在中原地区。其中，在伊、洛河三角平原龙山文化矬李遗址的水井和汤阴龙山文化白营遗址的木构架支护深水井，印证了“伯益作井”等文献记载。[③]

传说远古时代中原地区就已经有水井。泌阳盘古山，就是当年盘古开天辟地、繁衍人类、造化万物的地方。盘古山顶峰的北坡，山势陡峭，松林葱郁，顶峰以下约50米处，有一口盘古井。自上至下有重叠“之”字形山径可到井旁。井周芳草葱茏，外围马尾松环立。井口为椭圆形，直径近1米，由天然岩石形成，水面如同明镜，汲水饮之，水质清澈，甘甜爽冽，沁人心脾。传说盘古兄妹便用此水生活。[④]

根据目前考古资料，我国迄今发现年代最早的水井遗迹是河姆渡遗址二层发掘的一座浅水井。到了距今6000年的马家浜文化时期和距今5000年左右的良渚文化时期，已经出现了农田灌溉用井。[⑤]在河南的舞阳、汤阴、临汝、鹿邑、洛阳、平顶山、禹县、郾城、偃师、驻马店和辉县等地区已经发现水井遗迹。根据目前考古发现，中原地区龙山文化时期已经发现有两口水井，一口在汤阴白营遗址，一口在洛阳锉李遗址。其中，汤阴白营遗址水井是中原地区发现最早的水井。汤阴水井的井壁是用木棍以井字形结构方式自下而上层层垒成，井深11米，叠压的井字形木架共有46层。河南汤阴水井是中原地区迄今发现的结构最复杂的水井，为研究中国水井的起源和构筑技术提供了宝贵资料。[⑥]从汤阴水井井底出土大量的汲水陶器来看，汤阴水井主要是汲水井，兼具苗圃用水。

另外，在河南洛阳矬李遗址发现一口水井，还发现一条仰韶文化时期

① 苏秉琦：《中国通史》（第二卷），上海人民出版社，1994，第323页。

② 吴存浩：《中国农业史》，警官教育出版社，1996，第139页。

③ 李先登：《夏商周青铜文明探研》，科学出版社，2001，第18页。

④ 张正、王瑜廷：《盘古神话》，中州古籍出版社，2006，第100页。

⑤ 贾兵强：《夏商时期我国水井文化初探》，《华北水利水电学院学报（社会科学版）》2010年第3期。

⑥ 安阳地区文物管理委员会：《河南汤阴白营龙山文化遗址》，《考古》1980年第3期。

宽4米、深0.4米、内填白色细砂土的古渠道。[①]在洛阳锉李遗址同时还发现一段水渠，宽2～3米、深1米。[②]上述在矬李遗址发现的水井和水渠遗迹，可以说明当时农业上已经出现灌溉水利技术了。凿井溉田，可以利用地下水提高劳动自然生产率，进而提高整个农业劳动生产率，增加农作物单位面积产量。所以，井灌对农业文明社会发展有重要的作用。在辉县孟庄遗址中南部发现龙山文化水井4口。[③] 井内出土大量深腹罐、盆、豆、甑等陶片，井底还出土9件完整高领瓮及大量高领瓮碎片。在此发现的高领瓮，可以视为当时的灌溉汲水器具。

在中原地区龙山文化时期，除了发现汤阴白营水井和洛阳锉李水井与农业有关系外，在驻马店杨庄遗址也发现水井。[④]根据在驻马店杨庄遗址的标本层位中采集到大量水稻植硅石，[⑤] 我们可以知道，杨庄水稻种植已成规模。杨庄遗址位于杨庄村西，紧靠练江河北岸，为高于周围地表1～2米的漫坡状高地，在河岸的台地发现水井和稻作物，可以说明龙山文化时期杨庄已经具备原始农业灌溉体系。

在龙山文化时期，中原地区农业生产工具种类和数量都在增加，除石斧、石铲、石刀等外，还普遍使用了蚌制的刀镰和铲等。2006年6月至2008年1月，山东大学考古系在博爱西金城遗址发现龙山时期水井3口。[⑥]井内出土很多生产工具，以铲、刀、镰数量最多，这表明西金城遗址龙山文化农耕技术的发达。尤其是2004年秋季，郑州大学历史学院和郑州市文物考古研究所在登封南洼遗址发现二里头文化水井3口。[⑦] 在南洼水井中出土大量的石器、骨角器、蚌器、陶器和少量铜器的生产工具，其中农业生

---

① 洛阳博物馆：《洛阳矬李遗址试掘简报》，《考古》1978年第1期。

② 方酉生、赵连生：《试论中原地区文明的起源》，《史学月刊》1989年第2期。

③ 河南省文物考古研究所：《河南辉县市孟庄龙山文化遗址发掘简报》，《考古》2000年第3期。

④ 宋豫秦、李亚东：《驻马店市杨庄龙山时期与二里头文化遗址》，载中国考古学年鉴编辑委员会《中国考古学年鉴（1993）》，文物出版社，1995，第126页。

⑤ 邹逸麟：《历史时期黄河流域水稻生产的地域分布和环境制约》，《复旦大学学报》1985年第3期。

⑥ 河南省文物管理局南水北调文物保护办公室、山东大学考古系：《河南博爱县西金城龙山文化城址发掘简报》，《考古》2010年第6期。

⑦ 郑州大学历史学院考古系、郑州市文物考古研究院：《登封南洼2004～2006年二里头文化聚落发掘简报》，《中原文物》2011年第6期。

产工具有石器铲、斧锛和镰。标本 05H15：76 石镰，砂岩，灰色，磨制精细，弧背平刃，单面刃较锋利，尾部较短，长 14 厘米，宽 5 厘米，厚 1 厘米。（见图 1）标本 04H97：1 石镰，砂岩，浅棕色，磨制精细，器短小，尾部宽长，短刃内曲，前端较细，残长 13.8 厘米，宽 4.5 厘米，厚 0.9 厘米。（见图 1）。

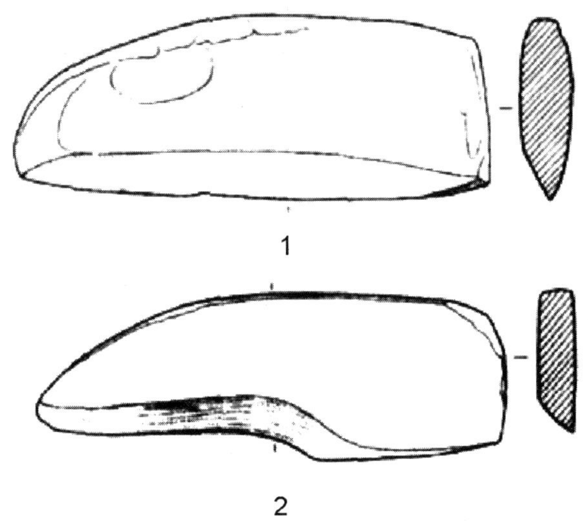

图 1　登封南洼石镰

资料来源：《登封南洼 2004～2006 年二里头文化聚落发掘简报》，《中原文物》2011 年第 6 期。

《吕氏春秋·勿躬篇》载："伯益作井"。《经典释文》卷二《井卦》下引："世本云：'化益作井'。宋衷云：'化益伯益也，尧臣'"。因此，伯益作井是一种较为普遍的说法，较为可信，这与河南龙山文化晚期所发现的临汝煤山龙山文化遗址中发现的两口水井时间大致相符合。[①]《世本·作篇》有"田头作井以灌田"的明确记载，这不仅说明水井的发明与文明的起源有着密切的关系，而且通过文献与实物相印证，证明在四千多年前中原地区已经比较普遍用人工凿井来取水了。

总之，水井的发明，是生产力发展的一种标志。水井发明以后，大大方便了中原先民的生产和生活，人们不仅可以离开河旁、湖畔，深入广阔的平原上去开发土地、定居生活，而且还可以扩大耕种面积，可以灌溉浇

---

① 中国社会科学院考古研究所河南二队：《河南临汝中山寨遗址发掘报告》，《考古学报》1982 年第 4 期。

地，可以抗御干旱，增加农作物的收成，发展农业生产。[①]

五　结语

综上所述，河南优越的水环境和丰富的水资源，对史前时期中原地区农业社会产生了深刻的影响，不仅有利于兴建农田水利工程、发展农业生产以及进行粮食加工等，而且有利于众多鱼类水产的栖息繁育，为渔业的发展提供了可靠的生态自然资源。从某种意义上说，史前河南水环境促进了中原原始农业文明的发展，在古代中原农业社会文明变迁中起着重要作用。

① 贾兵强：《中国先秦水井文化研究》，中国水利水电出版社，2018，第 63 页。

Local Knowledge on Exploitation and Rational Use of Water Resources of Tai Ethnic in Tuong Duong Distric, Nghe An Province, Vietnam

Nguyen Hong Anh

越南义安省襄阳县泰族水资源开发与合理利用的地方性知识研究

阮宏安

Abstract: Tuong Duong is a charming land, but the natural conditions are extremely harsh, the terrain is complicated, called "Indochina oven" cause of hot weather, and is also one of 62 poorest districts of Vietnam. Tuong Duong is the settlement of 6 ethnic groups (Tai, Khmu, Tay Pong, Tho, O Du, Hmong), in which Tai has densest population and resides in the large area of the Western Nghe An region.

Long-term settlement on this difficult land, Tai people always adapt to harsh natural conditions, accumulate experience to create a system of knowledge on exploitation and use of natural resources (water) in daily life and production. One of the special knowledge is to use the traditional irrigation system "muong, phai, lai, lin" (ditches, dam) and water wheel (pat), with many other knowledge on environmental protection.

Although, many traditional knowledge on water has changed, but basic of traditional knowledge on exploitation and rational use of water resources in daily life and production still exist in Tai's community here, still imbued with water cultural identity through their awareness, understanding, practice, and belief.

Keywords: local knowledge; Tai ethnic; Exploitations and rational use of water; Tuong Duong; Nghe An; Vietnam

摘 要：襄阳县是一片迷人的地区，但自然条件极其恶劣，地形复杂，有被称为“中南半岛烤箱”的炎热天气，是越南62个最贫困地区之一。沱江是6个民族（泰族、克木族、泰邦族、措族、敖都族、苗族）的聚居地，其中泰族人口最为密集，居住在Nghean西部地区的大片区域。

长期定居在这片艰苦的土地上，泰人始终积极适应恶劣的自然条件并积累相关经验，在日常生活和生产中创造了一套自然资源（水）开发利用的知识体系。其中一个特别的知识是使用传统的灌溉系统“muong，phai，lai，lin”（沟渠、水坝）和水轮（pat），以及许多其他的环保知识。

虽然许多传统的水知识已经发生了变化，但是在日常生活和生产中开发和合理利用水资源传统知识的基础仍然存在于泰人的社区中，他们的意识、理解、实践和信仰仍然浸透着水文化认同。

关键词：地方性知识　泰族　水资源的开发和合理利用　襄阳　义安　越南

Tai people always said: "where there is a water, there is a Mueang, so where there is a Mueang[①], there is a chiefdom (feudal lord)" or "where a water is, there is the paddy field, and there is rice"...

The Tai settlements were built along streams and rivers, so many village or places in Tuong Duong are named by the water source: Nam (water), Huoi (stream), Xop/Vang (brook/hole), such as: Nam Xan village, Xop Nam village, Vang Mon village, Huoi Co village... Although today many name of villages are renamed by Viet names, but the old names remains in the minds of the elderly.

Tuong Duong is a beautiful mountain district of Nghe An province, home of 6

① Mueang consists several villages.

ethnic groups of Tai, Khmu, Tay Pong, Tho, O Du, and Hmong, to approximately 467 thousand people, in which Tai ethnic has densest population (about 324 thousand) and resides in the large area of the Western Nghe An. Although located on an average altitude of 800 – 1000 m above sea level, with steepest terrain and fold and fault-block mountains, and on the confluence of Nam Non and Nam Mo rivers, where begins Lam river (Tai people called Nam Pao), belongs the Ca river basin, where there are many streams, waterfalls, rapids and springs that make great landscapes, bring about potential for tourism with travel routes on river for exploration, commerce and recreation, but the climate is severely, called "Indochina oven", make travel difficult, dangerous.

Moreover, because of complex terrain with the system of cracks by geological features, so ability to store the water in underground pockets of water is low and short, and water storage in hydropower reservoirs and irrigation is also difficult, causing drought in the dry season. Conversely, rainwater converges highly, and overflows is fast when falling high amount of rain that makes flash floods and flooding (Pham Van Hung, 2014). This causes difficulties in production and daily life, so Tuong Duong is one of 62 national poverty districts, and most difficult mountain district of Nghe An. In addition, with the increasing frequency of Elnino, the vaporization is highly to make the climate here become more severely. There is a long drought period from May to July and a heavy rain period from September to October, causing many flash floods or flooding and affecting use of water during the year.

The meteorological and hydrological monitoring data of the Division of Meteorology and Hydrology at Tuong Duong station shows that the average annual amount of rainfall is from 1300 – 1400 mm, and according to the calculation results of the research team, the volume of the surface water resource is more than 3 billion m^3/year. Nevertheless, the amount of water is unevenly distributed between seasons and between areas, leading to frequent floods and droughts. Although the river and stream network is quite dense, it lacks regular flow due to low water table in dry season here. Beyond four wide hydropower reservoirs there are nearly a dozen small hydroelectric reservoirs constructed that have greatly affected the flow (river, stream) – a natural water supply source for residents here.

So, the water is more and more important in daily life and for the production of the ethnic community here. In science, water resource is a concept that consists of surface, rain and underground. When the goal of Sustainable Development was issued, the water quality has been set as an indicator of development, according to which, the water purification and accessibility are one of the evaluating sustainable development standards at national or global level. But in folk opinion, water is in river, stream and rain only. And Tai ethnic in Tuong Duong have got a treasure of excellent knowledge on the exploitation and rational use of water resources. The experience and knowledge on use of water has made a part of cultural value with their ethnic identity.

Local knowledge (LK) is a "rounds out the knowledge – practice – belief complex that describes traditional knowledge" (Berkes Fikret, 2012: 16 – 18) integrated with scientific knowledges, that has transfered and acquired through livelihoods and becomes "recognition" of the community (Pham Quang Hoan, 2003; Nguyen Thi Phuong Loan, 2012), in which traditional /folk knowledge is the base and core of local knowledge, always adapting to environmental changes.

Local knowledge (LK), though, is the experience that the community accumulates in the life, but has got a very high scientific value. There are many resemblance between the local knowledge and the science of rationality in the exploitation and use of natural resources generally, and water particularly.

Firstly, local knowledge is the awareness and understanding of the community about living space with the rational division of this areas: residence zone, cultivating zone, grazing zone, fishing zone, hunting and gathering zone, sacred zone (sacred foresst, mountain, well-spring) ...closely conected with natural resources (water). Local knowledge is similar to science on territorial organization. Scientists show that rational and scientific territorial organization will ensure a balance between the ability to supply natural water and the human water accessibility in daily life and production (Pham Hoang Hai et al., 1998; Tissen R. et al., 2008; Xauskin Yu. G., 1981). These points are related to land use, organization and conversion of reserves of natural ecosystem into agricultural ecosystems to suit the conditions for accessibility and using water.

Secondly, local knowledge is the cultural practice system of the community, adapting to natural conditions, including irrigation techniques (ditches, dam, water wheels), storing water, cultivation, aquaculture, synchronizing techniques of exploitation and use of land with organic agricultural production, selecting varieties of plant related to use of water and increasing coverage of plants to protect aquatic resources. This point has suited for science. The scientists have proved that to exploitation and rational use of natural resources (water), needs civilization harmonized with natural conditions (Vu Tu Lap, 2004; Perier Kh. X et al., 1977; Pierre Gourou, 2003) that includes environmentally friendly techniques of exploitation and use of water; water storage; managing water, sanitation and hygiene. Along with that is the synchronous implementation of issues related to aquatic resources with water consumption effectively.

Thirdly, local knowledge is beliefs (spirituality, sacred), together with rules and regulations of customary laws that have conducted activities of community on the exploitting and using natural resources (water), protecting the environment, thenceforth, forming an environmental culture and ecological ethic of individuals and communities. At the same time, relationships of individuals and community in the possession of natural resources are an objective basis to create rationality and sustainability in expoitation and use of natural resources (water). Scientists have assumed that the basis of exploitation and rational use of resources (water) are an environmental culture and ecological ethic, in the context of which ownership rights of natural resources is certificated (Ha Huy Thanh, 2001).

Fourthly, the exploitation and rational use of natural resources should be carried out based on creating an added-value capital of resources (Hoang Hung, 2005; Vu Tan Phuong, 2006). Also through increasing coverage of vegetation and development index of forest, the water resources are creating and increasing both volume and quality. This is considered creating an added-value of water. Accordingly, to create an added-value of resources (water), first of all, we need to base on the community and set up livelihoods for community. Specifically, it is forest production livelihoods to changing vegetation system, which will also increase an added-value of water in both volume and quality. In another way, creating forest an added-value is the basis of exploitation and rational use of water. "Based on community" is understood to give them right to manage resource (ownership rights), together with use of the their native experience (local knowledge). Through the livelihood, scientic knowledge will be transfered and acquired, and become "cognition" of the people and the community, enriching the local knowledge system.

The ultimate goal has to achieve: (1) Exploitation and use of a variety of water sources for daily life and production; (2) Maintenance and increase in volume and quality of water to ensure a balance between the supplementary ability of nature and human accessibility; (3) Ensuring clean water sources for daily life and production.

Local traditional knowledge on water of Tai people in development context

In Tai's ethnic language, except "nam" (water) is a general term for all variety of water: "huoi nam" (stream) is a big flow of water, "huoi noi" (brook) refers to a small flow of water, or "huoi top" (large stream) means river. The flows from underground sprays up or the water emerges from a fissure in the rock is called a "bo nam" (water mine/well – spring). "Nam pun" refers to underground water; "nam phon" is rain water; "nam buoc" is a stagnant water; "nam noong" is water pond; "vang" refers to water hole. "Headwater" area place, where sacred forests are always located in, where spirits exist, and where public worship of the village is...

First of all, river and stream (surface) or rain are sources supplying water to life. In the remote villages, everyday the Tai's women always go getting the water from well-springs. At the well-springs, they have stacked stones around like as small dam for flow prevention forming water storage, and then they have installed a long bamboo pipes across the dam as mouth outlet. Below in the base of dam they have arranged the big stones as a bench, making foothold and limiting erosion. To prevent leaves into the flows, the women have put bamboo fences in the flow above about 5 – 6 m away the water storage. The villagers usually have to clean well-spring, because here sometimes still worship of village is performed. They used plastic bottles of 0.5 – 1.5 litres or biger instead of bamboo bottles to store water. They prefer plastic bottles. They said that the weight of plastic bottle is lighter than bamboo, and plastic bottle can store more water. They have assumed that water in plastic bottles is cleaner, because plastic bottle is not mouldy as bamboo and with top cover of bottle, and water should be not "dropped out" and keep dean for a long time.

In Hoa Binh town and some villages near to the town or in some villages of central communes, authorities make reservoirs and pump the water to town and villages. Households use water that is supplied by Water Company of district, and have to pay according to consumption that is counted by water meters. In oder to exploit water from well-spring, Water Company has constructed concret wall like dam as flow prevention and big concrete water storage tanks as water supplying station here. They have installed some metal pipes as mouth outlet leading water to the big filteration tanks, then into the storage tanks. The water is pumped from big water storage tanks into the public tanks of village, or into the home of each household for use through flexible plastic pipes system, instead of previous bamboo pipe system. Instead of bamboo wattles (fences), wire mesh is put on for leaves prevention. In 2018, over 80% of households have clean water at home. Luong Thi Sam's family (Yen Na comune) are very pleased, althought they are at the end of the village, far from the water source. They now have accessed clean water from the public tanks. And now, They have bought a stainless steel tank, and harevst clean water from public tank by flexible plastic pipes into stainless steel tank at home. In summer, they don't worry about clean water..

In several other communes, which are located in high mountains, where has severe climate with hot weather, drought or flood, such as in Nga My, Xieng My, people use well water. In each village, the wells are dug or drilled by development projects or authorities since year 2000. In the year 2018, 100% of villages has got well and 80% of households are supplied clean water. More and more households like to use well water, because they feel that water in well is cleaner. However they only know how to use them, although they have not yet got techniques and experiences to drill or dig wells.

Due to lack of waters in the hot (dry) season, and the dirtier water in the rain season by flood, they have to harvest and store rainwater. They have also learned how to harvest rainwater from Viet people in rainy season. They use square plastic canvas, then tie 4 corners to 4 bamboo trees, cuta hole in the middle of canvas and install big plastic pipes in this hole as mouth of outlet. Finally after tying mouth of outlet they put it into the ground tank to harvest water.

The concept of "Clean water", "Storage of water", "Saving water", "Sanitation", "Hygiene", "Lack of water", "Climate change" is familiar and has entered the perception of the people to change the way of exploitation and use of water, and even becomes their practice now in their life.

(1) The clean water is now understood by the people that the water has passed by the filtration of sand and gravel. At Tuong Duong, the authorities and UNICEF, OXFAM, PAM have constructed public concrete water tank systems that include a filtration tank and storage tank. Water from spring is led to filtration tank, then through a filtration system into a storage tank. In 2017, 100% of the village had public tank system and 92% of households in the central villages of communes were able to use filtered water by this method. Ms Vi Thi Cai said that before, when the rainy season came back, the water was dirty, and they had to wait till water settled for a few days. Now, her grandchildren know how to clean the water. Any woman or man between the ages of 20 and 60 is proficient in how to clean cooking water in rain and flooding season. They know how to use alum to settle water, and then use chloramine B to disinfect water. In the past, the Tai people used to directly drink without boiling or filtering water from well-spring or rain water. Today's residential well and spring water systems go through so many levels of filtration, and 100% of the households have changed this habit, 45% of household use bottled water to drink. Especially, since the hydroelectric plant Ban Ve was operating, 17% of households have equipped electric water purifier RO with boiling.

(2) Previously, they only have stored water in bamboo bottles several days, and each household has got dozens of bamboo pipes at home. Now, they have got

many kind storing waters that are made by new material as plastic bottles, buckets, pots, stainless steel tanks... instead of bamboo. Now in Tuong Duong, 100% of villages have built a public storage tanks system (each village has on average 5 – 10 tanks). Some households have built concrete tanks themselves or bought stainless steel tanks (up to 38%). Several well-to-do households (18%) have got two separate tanks (filtration and storage) and stainless steel tanks. The filtration and storage tanks are constructed underground to limit evaporation in summer. The stainless steel tank stores water after filtration, which is placed on the roof or on a mountainsides. Water is pumped from a below pump in underground tank into the stainless steel tank and then into the home for use by a flexible plastic pipe system.

They use upstream water to cook, midstream to wash, and downstream to graze their animals. Before 1980s, streams are places where everyday children had a bath and played, Tai women had bath, washing, getting water and talking together. They were places of community activities. Tai have utilized the flows to install a water powered rice-pounding mortar. This is a familiar poetic image expressing community cohesion. But now 95% of households use their own bathroom, tanks or public bathroom beside the public tanks. And most activities of village are transferred to places of public tanks. Hydropower and irrigation reservoirs, and the rural water program also have an impact on the change of this. People said that in the past, flows here were very clean and clear, able to look clearly at water weeds, pebbles and gravels in the spring bed, and water weeds are a favorite food of Tai people. Now the water is muddy, the flows is slow, and they cannot use water weeds as food as before. The stream is only a place of grazing animals, fishing, or performing worship of the village.

Also many years ago, well-spring water is a place where community have performed worship, but now it seems to be forgotten. Around the well-spring it is quite dirty, because for a long time it is not cleared. Well-spring is only cleared when the village has got a worship, except for several remote villages that are located at High Mountain are a so far from town, in Vietnam Laos frontier zone.

In the years of 1990s, Tai had learned how to utilize the flows to install small –

capacity of 0. 5 to 1 – 1. 5 kW generators until the hydropower plant Ban Ve began to operate. Currently, still a few households use this generator to light in upland fields. When the Ban Ve hydropower plant was operating, many households bought electric pumps to get water from wells.

Tai people also use water of river and streams to cultivate wet-rice fields, graze animal and fish. It can be said that the Tai's system of irrigation such as ditches, dam, water wheels is not only one of the material cultural elements, reflecting the folk experiences that have been summarized in exploitation and use of surface water for wet – rice production, but also shows their cultural identity and characteristics of use of water: (i) they are the earliest ethnic minority having wise irrigation techniques; (ii) driving water into the most complex terrain; (iii) Adapting to natural conditions for the exploitation and labour saving.

Currently, in the mountain commune far from town, such as Yen Na, Yen Hoa, Yen Tinh, where the impact of development is still low, and where the terrain is complex, the method of traditional water supply for wet-rice still exists. Now farmers still use water wheels, and several youngsters here have learned techniques making water wheels from elders. Not only that, making water wheels has also created an income for their household, because they have sold and installed water wheels in Laos.

Mr Luong Van Thuong said that, to make the water wheel, they had to spend 5 – 7 days, and used 120 bamboo trees to make wheels. To bring water to the fields, they need more and more bamboo. They have to split long bamboo trees to make water troughs, and then they make foots system holding troughs. Their work is difficult and hard, especially when the fields are far from water source and high above, and they usually have to repair because of animals or rain. However, now flexible plastic pipes systems leading water take the place of bamboo pipes. He explains that using new materials: (i) makes installing easier, because flexible plastic pipe is possible putting free on ground with different and difficult terrain, because of free length; (ii) flexible plastic pipes are more durable than the bamboo, so is not indestructible by animals as bamboo pipe and easy to repair; (iii) they can buy it anywhere and more cheaper than bamboo pipe; (iv) especially, the cost is lower.

Currently, hydropower Ban Ve is operating with that, and many irrigation (reservoirs, concrete canal system, pump station) is constructed. Therefore, villages, commune and town around the hydropower Ban Ve are supplied with cultivation water by the district hydropower plant Ban Ve and District Division of Agriculture, instead of the traditional system of irrigation (ditches, dam, water wheels) and traditional water management. In order to use water efficiently and economically, Tai people have been using some new seed of high-yield commodity paddy with short growth time that is adapted to climate change instead of indigenous plants. The crop is conducted by agricultural branches in accordance to the water supply of hydropower plants. However, according to the analysis of agricultural experts, some current new seed of high-yield commodity paddies are being used. they need much more water, fertilizers and pesticides to ensure productivity. These new methods of cultivation are replacing traditional ways, leading to irrational exploitation and use of natural resources (water), and polluting soil and water sources. A study that compared the need of water of the two methods of cultivation, have given the below results:

Table 1 Water need of demonstration of cultivation (Native and new high-yield seeds)

Items	Traditional method		New method	
	Summer – Autumn Paddy	Winter – Spring Paddy	Summer – Autumn Paddy	Winter – Spring Paddy
Volume of water (m^3/ha/crop)	4. 7597	4. 4100	5. 1657	4. 9550
Total (m^3/ha/year)	9. 1697		10. 1207	

Source: *Doan Doan Tuan và other* (2012).

In addition to irrigation, Tai people also have been using water for livestock (grazing animal and poultry downstream). They have wrapped around by bamboo wattles (fence) beside downstream to breeding ducks. Especially, in aquatic farming they often have dug a small lake in garden to fish farming. The wisdom is in that the stream water is circulated in small lake through the system inlet and outlet pipe, which is blocked by small bamboo wattles, so fish is not drift off.

Furthermore, Tai people also have farmed fish in wet-rice fields. The fish crop in wet-rice fields is their custom. They have fed fishes aquatic creatures, and fish has increased oxygen in water. Therefore, paddy has been well growing, and they have harvested paddy and fishes at the same time. Not only that, Tai people also have fished by environmentally friendly methods. Mr Luong Van Phuong in Bon village has stacked stones in a section of small stream as a dam at a height of 30 centimeters (called a "ly" in Tai language), and then he has opened a small exit outlet, where he put "tang xon" (bamboo trapfish) with bait, so fishes will be catched when going to look for food. After stacking stones in the section of small stream, Mr Hang in Xieng My used eggs of ant into bait. While fishes are baiting, he will throw there a kind of pounded wild leaves, making fish dormant, and finally, he can harvest fish by hand, In deeper and wider section of streams, Tai people have caught fish by nets... With such farming and fishing methods, the water source is not polluted, the landscape and environment are not destroyed. It is also one of the ways to rationally use water resources of the Tai people in villages far from town. Conversely, in some villages near to the town, where there is largest area of wet-rice farrming in Tuong Duong, people have abused fertilizer, chemicals, especially herbicides. Tai people do not have the habit of manuring even compost in previous traditional cultivation, so certainly that can not farm fish in the wet-rice field.

In the past, except the only way to Tuong Duong, people used to travel on river by wooden boats, which is small and long to cross rapids easilier, and can not be toppled. Since hydroelectric plant Ban Ve is operated, fishing and aquaculture were being farmed in the reservoir and became new livelihood of several households living beside the reservoir. The scientific knowledges on the fishery in reservoir is updated instead of fishing knowledge on the river that has increased household income. Although, the "professional" in fishery has been enhanced, and environmental pollution has decreased. But exploitting fishes thoroughly for the restaurants has caused aquatic resources to be exhausted rapidly after 4 years since hydroelectric power plant Ban Ve began to operate, which forecast a irrational exploitation of resources. According to the report of the District People's Committee, curently, in the Tuong Duong district there are 156 models of aquatic farming of Tai's household that are approved and implemented in the reservoir area. The rationality of the exploitation and use of water resources in new livelihoods is: (i) to conserve native species that possibly will become extinct; (ii) to create an added-value capital of aquatic resources, (iii) to create new livelihood model that is ecotourism based on added-value capital of resources, (iv) to minimize loss of existing resources. In addition, their experience to travel on river previously help them in new livelihood. Some Tai's households have fitted motor into the wooden boats instead of rowing, and some other well-to-do households have bought bigger motor boat carrying tourists and fishing on reservoir.

In cultivation of slope soil (dry upland fields), rain water is still the only source. Like other ethnic groups, Tai people have a system of knowledge related to weather. In March (Tai lunar calendar), there are often Xiaoman floods (small flood usually begins around 21 May and ends around 5 June – solar calendar) and annual floods in May (the rainy season). From July to September is still the rainy season, and it is also the time that the heads of paddy grain began to form, so crop will lose if it is drought, without rain. They will Look at the changes of wild grass and trees, the moon and the clouds, hearing the sounds of insects or the wild animals to forecast the weather related to rain. These experiences are expressed though idioms, proverbs, and folk songs. E. g. When the birds "coong cot" sing "khoan pam, phai toc" (cutting, burning), Thai people go to slash – burn preparing new crop.

In the rain season, the Tai people have utilized rainwater to crop. They said that " Pumpkin is planted on a slope soil. Green squash intercrops with cotton. Sugarcane, bananas and other fruit are available. It is delicious to eat, eating to full belly". The method of alternating cultivation is a mixed-intercrop with multistorey that not only utilizes the most of rainwater but also maximizes ability to absorb and retain water. The mixed-intercrop with multistorey is a wise method. On the same upland field, Tai people have mixed – intercropped different species forming multistorey to utilize soil, store water and humus. There are some popular models of mixed – intercrop with multistorey① in upland fields that is: (i) paddy with sesame/taro with peanut with melon/green squash/pumpkin; (ii) maize with bean with green squash / pumpkin; (iii) millet/sticky paddy with sesame with peanuts; (iv) cotton with melon /zucchini; (v) cassava with beans with green squash. Mixed – intercrop is carried out according to the season: Maize is planted in February, then the peanut that intercrops with beans with melon or cucumbers; in March, doing weeding in maize field; in April, doing slash-burn for farming the paddy; in May, harvesting corn and weeding for growth of bean, peanut, sesame; in June, weeding in paddy field and harvesting bean, peanut, sesame, and at the same time continuously cropping maize. The crops in upland field depend on rain. From July to September it is rain season, Tai women are at home to weave to the October, and then they harvest upland paddy in early October. ②

They have got the cultivating techniques on upland field that related to rationally and effectively use of rainwater, such as (i) selective cutting trees, because roots of big old trees limit erosion well and recharge water also; (ii) stacking small humps on the surface of field by utilization of nutrient-rich humus layer preventing runoff (While rains, small humps will prevent speed of runoff. Farmers have figured on, so how rain and runoff will clear humps of nutrient – rich humus after each crop, the surface of field will be covered over with nutrition, limiting washing away of the nutrient – rich humus layer.); (iii) making small rills on the surface of field for drainage (While rains, one part of the runoff over surface is not yet in time seeped in to the soil, and part of this unused water will follow the rills to recharge into soil); (iv) they have farmed by method "poke holes, sow seeds", all seed holes will be covered by humus after rain, and plants will rapidly grow.

Vertical layer of the living space of the Tai community consist of multi-level:

① Highest storey is maize, cotton, cassava, paddy (native varieties), middle storey is beans, sesame, taro, lowest storey is peanut, melon, pumpkin, zucchini (ground cover crop).

② By Tai's farming calendar.

the lowest is the stream and wet-rice field (production zone); in the middle there are house, village and a "well – spring" (a living zone); higher there are upland fields and hunting – gathering zone (production zone) with use of rain water; the highest is sacred space (sacred forest, mountain, spring) – the place of maintenance of water sources. Horizontal layer of the living space consist of multi-zone, house and village in in the central, water flows and a wet – rice field (using spring water) in front of the village, and upland field (using rain water) behind the village. Then beside upland field is a sacred space (sacred forest, mountain, spring). By a way of dividing space, water resource of Tai villages is ensured that the community always has got clean water for life and production, and they use a variety of water sources, and adapt to natural conditions.

Just like the other ethnic groups from the lowland to the highland, the water is always in the mind of Tai ethnic people. All of these water sources are jointly owned by the whole village, and governed by the spirits (natural Gods, the Ghosts, and Ancestors – called the Phi). The spiritual elements have created responsibility of community for water protection and maintenance of well-being living space. Tai's people have got an idiom "Invite the person eating, who will say well. Offer meal to "Phi", the "Phi" will bless", so they have performed many rituals, in which a water as an indispensable element in every rituals of Mueang, tribes, village, lineage, clan, or family... in the worships such Xang khan, as harvest rituals (showing thanks to the gods for a successful crop growing season), rain prayers, worship the ancestors, even in funerals, etc., especially in agricultural rituals related to wet – rice cultivation, such "hach na" (opening of crop); washing rice leaves; "hach pat" (beginning of harvest); cereal ceremony, installing the water wheel, prayers for dam ... or related to the dry – rice cultivating (in upland field) as "hach nam" (opening for the planting season), prayers for filling the hole sowing seeds, prayers for sprouts, prayers for a harvest, the opening the harvest, worship new clearing field...

In the ritual, there must always be thanks for the spirits ("Phi") of land, forests and water. They always sing: "Your Worship Owner of forest, your Worship Owner of mountain. Thanks to your Worship Owner of forest, we have got houses. Thanks to your Worship Owner of spring, we have got water. Thanks to your Owner of land, we have got field. Where are fields, there is rice. We have got houses, rice, and water, thanks to your Worship Owners."

In the Tai's people opinion, land, water, or forest have got souls (spiritual nature). Everything in the world is owned by Gods ("Chau" – owner), and Ghost have watched over. God of water-spring owner was imagined by Dragon (to nguoc), Thai people often have performed worship God of water in August (beginning of rain season), prayers for rain ("loi hang nguoc"), prayers for "timely rains and favourable weather" or prayers for dam.... They have idiom "Dam breaks as father died".

At the same time, they have got many taboos ("cam") that is ingrained in their mind, and along with experienced feeling, has created and raised a belief in blessing or punishment from natural spirits. Only a word "cam" (taboos) can forbid that people don't have to do wrong anything to nature to influence their community, lineages, families or themselves. The beliefs are elements to teach behaviors to nature, and even the beliefs are the root to standardize ethic of individuals and communities that is called "ecological ethic" and "environmental culture" in the exploitation and rational use of natural resources.

Today the belief seems still exist. They are still afraid of natural spirits. In the town and several villages near the town, they often have performed religious practice. The rate of worship or religious practice of whole village performed by community have accounted only for 2% of the total number of villages in Tuong Duong. Conversely, in the remote villages far from the town, community often perform religious practice, and all families will join in.

The group of Mo (worshipper) said that in the past (for long time ago), they had performed annual worships ceremonies (about 4 – 6 times every year), but now they have not performed annual worships ceremonies-they performed once every three or five years, such as Xang khan festival. The households have prayers of health, happiness, good luck two times every month as Viet custom, or they only have performed worship when misfortune has come.

Although, customary law of Tai people in Tuong Duong district related to land, water or forests is not transferred in the form of text or characters, but have been passed down orally only, thus it still has existed in community with the beliefs: (-) do not slash - burn new field at the sacred zone; (-) do not fell sapling or old trees; (-) not hunting in breeding season; (-) do not exploit exhaustively forest. The headman of the village has got important role to conduct customary law, so it is preserved through many generations (Nguyen Ngoc Thanh, 2012) . But the current new regulations laid down that has ignored the previous traditional custom. The current new regulations as a commitment between the authorities and the households with the Management Board of National Park in form of text that do not cultivate in the Park to conservation biodiversity. Current new regulations is "the basic legal framework" and is one of the criteria to consider and recognize a new cultural family.

Conclusions

Scientists have declared that one of the scientific bases on the rationality in the exploitation and use of water resources is the general relationship between protection and increasing value of forest, and when value of forest has increased, then it is a consequence to increase soil nutrients, and change water balance.

(1) Farming technical system (tillage, planting and harvesting time, irrigation, fertilizer ...).

(2) Changing in biological relations through selecting and ditributing varieties of plants for soil quality, or rotational crop and mixed-intercrop with multi-storey to create good growth succession. "Agriculture that uses rotational crops is a fairly complete method, mixed-intercrop with multi-layer is completely right, especially, in tropical regions, where atmospheric rain does not regulate" (Ober G. , Funier F. and others. 1977: 75 - 106); and "It will be very risky, if we will have to stop rotational crop, while the jungle has stopped providing its products, so planting new trees with good resistance and growth, for that, will be more effective than using old forests" (Ellenberg G. and others, 1977: 149 - 169).

(3) Improving vegetation cover (forest development and grass planting for livestock), along with creating an accumulation and maintenance of ecosystems from one generation to the next will lead to the ultimate balance of soil, climate change, water supplying and groundwater protection in both volume and quality (Ellenberg G. and other, 1977: 149 – 169), in which, "there are three ways of exploitation and rational use of forest resources, in which the first way is to increase the value of forest products, then re-distribute forests, making forests accessible and benefit from forest (ownership rights and usufructuary rights), payment of environmental services and other indirect benefits" (Lars Carlson et al., 2006: 57 – 65, William D. Sunderlin et al, 2003: 56 – 70).

(4) Constructing ground reservoirs (natural and artificial), with that the creating a system of canals, irrigation works to regulate water.

(5) Improving water quality by technology and recycling water is one of the above method for exploitation and rational use of water, but it belongs science.

(6) Training local officials is the most common and most important support in developing countries to change the perception of the community (trainer training method), but it belongs to authorities and development project.

(7) The exploiting and rational using aquatic resources is a good way to protect water resources, as plants are ability for creating primary products of aquatic environments (eg. green algae); in the next stage the appearance of organism, which is provided nutrients by green plants, is the second products, with intermediate products that is generated from debris, organic waste and microorganisms. Fish and intermediate animals are the third product that is usually fed by the second product and intermediate product. Each product has a beneficial effect in the water environment, improving the water environment to become better (Perrier Kh., et al., 1977; 107 – 148).

It's clear that the local knowledge of the community can respond to most of the requirements that scientists have proposed above, because evereday they have been and still are doing so since they had been wandering to this land. However, this knowledge system is changing very strongly, deeply differentiating, and being interrupted between generations. The causes are as follows.

Firstly, climate change has changed natural capital. Ecological and biodiversity structure are changed to backward succession by the human destruction of forests, which making the water source more and more scarce in the hot dry season, and affecting the inevitable awareness of groundwater exploition and water storage during the dry season.

Secondly, the government's policy on socio-economic development together with the participation of development projects are the factors that has changes the traditional knowledge on the organization of natural – cultural space, exploitation and use of natural resources, in which policy has changed fundamentally the awareness and behavior of people about land, water and forest resources.

In the process of socio-economic development, the population growth has changed long time stable settlement and more and more reduces the production land area leading to re-distrubution of immigrantion, resettlement, new rural planning, also leading to changing traditional knowledge about living space organization. The organization of living space by the new rural planning and the names of Tai's village is renamed by Viet, which not only has lost the old name , but has lost the cohesion of territorial organization with natural resources (land, water, and forests), because name of places is associated with natural characteristics.

The role of "feeding" of the Government, after openness and integration, (i) in the exploiting water for domestic, such as rural water programs that is implemented from budget, projects, UNICEF, PAM, OXFAM .... (ii) and in the production such as projects on hydropower, irrigation, supplying crop seed and techniques, in the management of water sources ... that the whole have caused to change the way of exploitation and use of water of Tai people in the development context.

Thirdly, the impact of the market economy (economic origin) on people's perceptions of the economic value of natural resources, leads to psychological changes and behaviour towards natural resources, exploitation of natural resources for economic benefits.

Before 1880s, for survival the converting of forests to agriculture is necessary for long time, so certain outcomes are the irrational exploitation and use of resources (including water) making backward succession and unsustainability today. Nowadays, the converting of agriculture to forests by agro-forestry method making advanced succession is the global trend. However, there are some problems: income from forest production is higher than from agriculture; with technology, a risk factor in forest production is lower than food production; especially, labour cost is cheaper ... that trends converting a bushland to the production forest spontaneously, with that, exploiting according to the method of "clear cutting" (without rotation) of Tai people that will be again an irrationality in the exploitation and use of forest ecosystems, certainly, that have followed the outputs of irrationality in the exploitation and use of water resources.

Fourthly, the outcomes of fieldwork show that, many knowledge on water through folk songs, legends, proverb, idiom, etc, is only in memory of few elders or artisans; olders of 50 - 60 years of age remember a fewless, and most youth and children know nothing about folk songs, proverbs, even nothing about Tai's literacy. In daily communication they use 30% of Tai words, 70% Viet words. They are able to join in a religious practice, but can not understand why it performed. They explain simplely that they like to participate and they are pleased to do it.

Fifthly, the loss of natural space will also decrease "belief" in behaviour with the natural environment. Perhaps, it is necessary to reform the practice of traditional beliefs to "environmental culture" and "ecological ethic", together with communication to change awareness of community.

Sixth, although the Government has enacted national law relating to resources (Law of Land, Law of Water, Law of Forest Protection and Development, Law of Biodiversity ...), and many regulations or guidelines are attached, many programs of action were created, with that, the support of international projects, but that is not yet in consonance with context: (i) unsynchronizing regulations or guidelines with terms in the law; (ii) lacking specifics in regulations and terms of law, so difficult to identify objects and violations. This is a special difference between the national law and customary laws, and is also the core that making decision to apply local knowledge on exploitation and use of water, as well as to educate individuals about environmental ethic as in customary law. But customary laws are being lost while new regulations and commitment still are not possible to adjust behavior of individuals in community. Therefore, it is necessary to combine customary law and national law in creating the "environmental culture and ecological ethic" of the community.

Seventh, to preserve and develop the fair value of local knowledge, it may be necessary to propose management methods: (i) while converting food production to livelihoods of forest production still have to ensure food security, even commodity products to increase income of households; (ii) based on that, the conversion to forest ecosystems should be planned to ensure the exploitation and use of resources rationally and sustainably.

Eighth, creating aquaculture livelihoods or ecotourism is implemented in the reservois now, that research team does not comment about , because this exploittaion is implemented on the basis of creating added – value resources and preserving existing resource values. But those activities have to be based on traditional knowledge of ethnic groups, because of scientific value that has been recognized by many aspects: suitable to the ecological conditions of the residence, friendly to the natural environment, is the basis for the ethnic groups to survive and develop and similar to science today. Thus, the community livelihoods have to be creating and the values of the local knowledge system have to be developing, that has to be truly a "community – based on" development.

The final conclusion that the research team wants to propose is: to conserve water needs to use the local knowledge of rotation, inter – cropping and fallow cultivation not only in agricultural production, but also in current forest livelihoods. At the same time, it is not only necessary to change the perception of the community, but need to monitor the use of chemicals in agriculture. Applying inter – cropping in planting mixed – forest with multistorey to utilize land and alternate paddy crop while forest is opening; using rotation in planting and exploiting mixed forest to be not "clear cutting" . Specially, use fallow cultivation to make new advanced succession (planting – semi natural – natural): Land without forests→Forest land allocation program→Agroforestry cultivation (Agri – silviculture) →Final crop→Government have bought a part→Converted function to special forest, that transfers to community – based forest management to construct a cultural space (sacred forest) of community. So, from secondary succession through forever fallow (non – exploiting) will become primary succession (Natural forest).

REFERENCES

1. Berkes, Fikret (2012), *Sacred Ecology*, Third edition, Taylor and Francis Publisher, New York and London.

2. Lars Carlsson, Translator Luong Thu Hang, Editor Vuong Xuan Tinh. (2006). Usufruct rights to land of community: Lessons from problem of community forest in Sweden. *Journal of Anthropology* No. 4 (pp. 63 – 69), No. 5 (pp. 57 – 65).

3. Ellenberg G., Lebren J. (1977). *Natural Vegetation and Methods to Change to Rational Use of Land.* Publisher Progress, Moscow.

4. Pham Hoang Hai, Nguyen Ngoc Khanh (1998), Planning and territorial organization based on landscape research and assessment, *Journal of Earth Sciences*, Vol. 20 (2), pp. 81 – 85.

5. Pham Quang Hoan (2003), Local knowledge of ethnic minorities in Vietnam. *Vietnamese Ethnology of the Twentieth Century and the Early Years of the 21st Century*, Social Sciences Publisher, Hanoi. pp. 83 – 107.

6. Pham Van Hung (2014), *Research on Warning of Risk of Soil Cracking in Nghe Tinh Region*, Report I. Institute of Geology, Vietnam Academy of Science and Technology, Hanoi.

7. Hoang Hung (2005), *Management and Rational Use of Water Resources*, National University Publisher in Ho Chi Minh City, Ho Chi Minh City.

8. Vu Tu Lap (2004), *The Development of Geographical Science in the Twentieth Century*, Education Publisher, Hanoi.

9. Nguyen Thi Phuong Loan (2012), Research on human – ecological approach to assessing the sustainability of shrimp farming development in the coastal area of Nghia Hung district, Nam Dinh province, doctoral thesis of environmental science, Hanoi.

10. Ober G., Funier F., Roozanoov V. (1977). *Land and Maintenance of Fertility, Factors Affecting Land Use.* Publisher Progress, Moscow.

11. Perier Kh. X., Dimitrevxki X., Penman Kh. L., Zextei K., Nemek Đz., Neix R. L.,

(1977), *Issues of Water Reserves: Current and future needs of life*, Publisher Progress, Moscow.

12. Vu Tan Phuong (2006), The value of environment and environmental forest services, *Journal of Agriculture and Rural Development*, No. 15, pp. 7 – 11.

13. Pierre Gourou (2003), *The Peasants of the Tonkinese: Human – Geography Studies*, Translator: Nguyen Khac Dam and others, Editor: Dao The Tuan, Publisher Young, Ho Chi Minh City. (Les paysans du delta tonkinois, Paris, EFEO, 1936.)

14. Nguyen Ngoc Thanh (Editor, 2012), *Local Knowledge of People Living in Pu Mat National Park*, Publisher Social Science, Hanoi.

15. Ha Huy Thanh (editor, 2001), *Issues of Social and Humanity in the Rational Use of Natural Resources and Environmental Protection in Vietnam*, Publisher National Politic, Hanoi.

16. Tissen R, Deprez F. L (2008), *Towards a Spatial Theory of Organizations Creating new organizational forms to improve business performance*, Nyenrode Research Group (NRG), the Netherlands.

17. Doan Doan Tuan et al., (2012), Water demand, suitable irrigation regime for paddy crop by traditional and improved method in the Northern Delta in the period of 2003 – 2009, *Journal of Irrigation Science*, Vietnam Institute of Irrigation Science Research.

18. Xauskin Yu. G. (1981), *Current Economic Geographic Issues in the World*, Publisher Education, Hanoi.

19. William D. Sunderlin, Arild Angel Sen, Sven Wuder. Forest and poverty alleviation. Translator: Đang Minh Ngoc, *Journal of Anthropology*, No. 4 – 2003. pp. 56 – 70 (From Chapter in State of the world's Forests. Rome. pp. 61 – 73).

祈生与驭水：哈尼梯田灌溉社会中的“协商过水”个案研究*

罗　丹**

摘　要：在世界遗产红河哈尼梯田灌溉社会中，祈生（人口再生产）与驭水（水资源支配与管理）两大实践活动，既是多族群共享生态智慧的写照，又是“族群-边界”二元逻辑下集体行动的意义表征。通过开展联合劳动对配置性的灌溉水资源实现控驭，比对权威性资源的予夺，更符合诸梯田农耕族群摆脱生态束缚、实现人口再生产之自然演替及社会发展客观规律的内在需求。来自小型社区哈尼梯田的重要灌溉水系——麻栗寨河的个案表明，在同一纵向水系上占据不同生态位的不同族群，于精神层面通过多族共襄的山神水源祭祀仪式，于制度和技术层面通过协商过水“一致同意”的组织原则，以及传统分水计量器具的保障，实现了对共有水资源的有效管理。实践证明，在共享相同基础资源底数的地方和社群内部相互依赖的行动者，常会通过特殊的制度安排对共有资源实现成功且适度的治理，并将之化约为社会内部结构长期稳定的核心要素之一。

关键词：哈尼梯田　灌溉社会　协商过水

Absrtact: In the world heritage Honghe Hani Terraced Paddy Field irrigation society, praying forlife (population reproduction) and controlling water (water resources control and management) are not only the portrayal of multi-ethnic

---

* 本文系云南大学民族学一流学科建设项目“世界文化遗产哈尼梯田多元水文化与民族交融研究”（2017syl0062）阶段性成果。

** 罗丹，女，哈尼族，云南普洱人，博士，云南省社会科学院民族学研究所助理研究员，云南大学民族学与社会学学院社会学博士后流动站在站博士后。

sharing of ecological wisdom, but also the meaning of collective action under the dual logic of "Ethnic Groups and Boundaries". Compared with the competing for authoritative resources, the implementation of joint labor to control the allocation of irrigation water resources is more in line with the inherent needs of the terraced farming communities to get rid of ecological constraints and achieve the natural succession of population reproduction and the objective laws of social development. A case study from the important irrigation water system of the Hani Terraced Paddy Field irrigation society, the Ma Li Zhai River, shows that different ethnic groups occupying different ecological niche on the same vertical water system can spiritually pass the ritual of mountain and water source sacrifices of multi-ethnic co-ordination, at the institutional and technical levels, adopting the "unanimous agreement" principle of organization to sharing water resources by way of negotiation, in addition, adhere to the technical guarantee of traditional water measurement instruments, to achieve effective management of shared water resources. This study shows that actors who depend on each other to survive in places and communities that share the same base resource often achieve successful and appropriate governance of shared resources through special institutional arrangements, and turn it into one of the core elements of long-term stability in the internal structure of society.

Keywords: Hani Terraced Paddy Field; Irrigation society; Sharing water based on consulting way

近当代被中西学者反复讨论的治水社会,[①] 常与国家集权力量控制下公共行政手段主导的大型水利工程设施相连结，并成为人类社会具有普遍讨论价值的叙事组构。当我们从今天的民族国家疆域体系内去观察那些被标识出来的上古传说中的禹迹（治水活动）分布图，以及以中原王朝国家话

① 魏特夫认为东方社会的形成和发展与治水活动密不可分，出于大规模修建水利工程和有效管理工程的需要，必须建立一个遍及全国至少是遍及全国人口中心的组织，控制这一组织的人致力于行使最高统治权力，从而产生专制君主，这即是东方专制主义。参见〔美〕卡尔·A. 魏特夫《东方专制主义：对于极权力量的比较研究》，徐式谷、奚瑞森、邹如山等译，邹如山校，中国社会科学出版社，1989。

语叙事为中心的历代治水行动轨迹，却不难发现，以西江为界继续向西，尤其到了云岭之南，依旧是小型灌溉社区为主，赛典赤主导的滇中水利疏浚工程[①]固然是通过行政力量主导的“国家在场”行为，但是，更多的碎片化小型灌溉社区依然在中国西南的崇山峻岭中穿插棋布。滇南红河南岸哀牢山脉的哈尼梯田灌溉社会“红河哈尼梯田”，就是由哈尼族、彝族、傣族等民族在长期的生产、生活实践中共同创造的对人类社会具有杰出普遍性价值的世界文化遗产。

哈尼梯田灌溉社会与中国北方的“治水社会”有显著的区别。元代开始，在红河南岸地区由王朝国家任命的“十土司，十五掌寨”分区辖制，这些划片而治并实行松散自治的“夷官”，除了在“官田”里组织佃农局部性地修筑“官沟”以引水灌田外，该地区并未发生由统治者来组织多民族开展大型水利设施建设的活动。中华人民共和国成立之后，国家在完善该区域的水利设施建设方面进行了大量的投入，但也没有开展统一的全域性的大型水利工程建设。因此，哈尼梯田不是一个国家通过集权力量和公共工程实现水资源及地方事务管控的“治水社会”，而是一个有着丰富的自组织体系的“灌溉社会”。[②] 天然的水利资源禀赋和有序的灌溉行动是梯田稻作农耕生计和梯田景观得以存续的重要前提。

哈尼梯田灌溉社会中的多民族自上而下的协商性过水秩序，分别从精神、制度、技术层面得以体现。麻栗寨河水系，自上而下分布着5个梯田农

---

① 元代著名政治家赛典赤·赡思丁（1211～1279），担任云南平章政事（元行省制中的最高行政长官）期间，在滇兴修水利治理河川，贡献卓著。为综合治理今云南省会昆明附近的海口、螳螂川以及保护当时的省会中庆城，赛典赤在任期间主持了盘龙江诸水系治理的工程活动，其治水方略以“泄”为主，综合疏浚治理了今昆明境内的宝象河、马料河、海源河等水系；同时结合“蓄”水备旱策略，通过兴建松华坝水库，以及开凿金汁河、银汁河两条人工河流，组建了蓄水配套灌溉系统。其治水工程的重要成效在于，建成了当时云南最宏大、最科学、最完备的水利灌溉系统，灌溉面积广惠今昆明城郊西北至东北、东南及海口一带重要滨湖（滇池）稻作区。

② 格尔兹在《尼加拉：十九世纪巴厘剧场国家》中将灌溉社会定义为“从一条主干渠引水灌溉的所有梯田。这条作为灌溉社会共同体的财产的水渠引自一条古石坝。如果灌溉社会的规模很大，这条坝也会归全部灌溉社会所有。不过，在通常情况下，它归数个灌溉社会共有，每个灌溉社会都会在建坝中起到重要作用，在过去的很长一段时间内曾经如此，而每个灌溉社会都有一条主渠流经”。他认为“灌溉社会将一帮农民的经济资源——土地、劳力、水、技术方法，和在非常有限程度上的资金设备——组织成卓有成效的生产机器”。参见〔美〕克利福德·格尔兹《尼加拉：十九世纪巴厘剧场国家》，赵炳祥译，上海人民出版社，1999，第81、57页。

耕民族，灌溉梯田面积广，族群、宗教、生态、文化立体分层多元结构显著，在小型灌溉社区哈尼梯田的29条纵向水系中较具典型意义。精神层面上，尽管居住在水系上中下游的不同民族基于各自的经验、特色，在他们各自的物理空间和精神空间内，维系着以族群信仰为特色和边界的传统农耕祈雨仪式。然而在面向相互依存的稻作灌溉（共性生计方式）和再生产（个性种群衍存）的共同诉求时，突破族群、信仰边界，面向“诸水之源”多民族共襄的“神山圣水”集体祭祀仪式，也历时性地实然发生并存续着。就灌溉制度安排和技术结构而言，沿着灌溉水系自上而下“梅花间竹”立体筑居的多民族，往往和他们的近邻结成突破族际和寨际边界的灌溉联盟，通过水利队、管沟人、灌田户等组织，以“自上而下”“上满下流”的基本过水秩序为原点，来组织他们灌溉生活的日常。以利益让渡、共同发展为逻辑的联合灌溉行动，将麻栗寨河水系上的全体成员和他们的配水行动都整合到了“上满下流”分水度量系统中，那些在各自的梯田和灌溉“水路”上进行水资源个体性配置的族群，也因纵向水系的山水相连、田阡互嵌，而需要在联合灌溉行动中遵守经由协商达成一致的共有水资源集体配置秩序。

一　麻栗寨河灌溉水系：一条古老的“生态—族群—文化”线

1. 麻栗寨河灌溉水资源底数

麻栗寨河位于世界文化遗产哈尼梯田核心区，云南省红河州元阳县境内，该水系的主要源头位于元阳县新街镇全福庄村全福庄小寨，也是梯田文化遗产三大景观区之一的坝达景观集群的重要组成部分。麻栗寨河水系上游位于梯田核心区中部，东临大瓦遮梯田，西接牛角寨梯田，主要在新街镇境内。该片区“森林—村寨—梯田—水系”同构的生态系统以及生物多样性体系较完备。其源头最大的支流来自全福庄，左岸和右岸的各个村寨和山涧都有大大小小的水系汇入，水系灌溉着片区内的6000多亩梯田。该水系的水体一直延伸到哀牢山麓河谷坝区的傣族聚居区，为干热河谷傣族寨群提供了重要水源。因汇入的支流众多，且上游接近水源林区的水质较好，该河流上游修建有全福庄水库、麻栗寨水库、安汾寨水库，3个水库以提供集镇生活用水为主，提供灌溉用水为辅。

麻栗寨河的过水区，覆盖新街镇的中高海拔山区和南沙镇的地热河谷区，河段全长21千米，区间过水总面积83.1平方千米，径流面积为200平方千米，年均流量为2.69立方米/秒。除了在水系纵向区域上为各梯田灌溉民族提供重要的灌溉用水，麻栗寨河还是元阳县县府南沙镇的重要饮水水源地。南沙镇傣族聚居区的重要饮用水采水和储水点，位于新街镇壮族村寨计且村，计且村位于麻栗寨河中段，与石头寨（彝族村寨，隶属于南沙镇）隔河相望，距离南沙镇约10千米。计且村城市用水取水点的水源，为麻栗寨河水系上的浅层地下泉水，目前年供水量为130万立方米，为2.21万人提供日常生活用水，其中包括0.21万农村饮用水人口。

2. 麻栗寨河水系上的村寨与民族

麻栗寨河灌溉水系自上而下，连接了除苗族和瑶族之外的全部梯田农耕民族，既是哀牢山腹地山水形变中的一条集水线，又是一条立体而生动的"生态—族群—文化"线。以麻栗寨河水系的流向为参照系，自高地全福庄流向低地南山，水系左岸多为彝族尼苏支系聚居的村寨，如水仆龙、土锅寨、小水井等聚落。而右岸多为哈尼族聚居的村寨，如全福庄、麻栗寨、主鲁、倮铺等聚落。河流和灌渠成为天然物理界线，将不同民族围聚在不同的方位，这与不同民族历史上在梯田灌溉社会中进行空间位移时建村建寨选址的偏好等传统因素相关。

麻栗寨河将梯田灌溉社会中的多民族"梅花间竹"的立体空间分布格局生动呈现，就其纵向灌溉水系的分段族群聚落来看，以石头寨为切割点，河段可分为上游全福庄、土锅寨、麻栗寨，中游芭蕉岭、石头寨、计且村，下游南沙河谷地区的五亩寨三段，不同族群刚好在麻栗寨河水系上呈现立体分层的筑居布局。哈尼族与彝族在海拔相对较高的水系上游毗邻而居。哈尼族依然保持着靠近水源头的居住传统。壮族倾向于选择在海拔持中的水系中游居住，他们主要与族源相同的傣族毗邻而居，有时也会选择与彝族为邻，但少与哈尼族互邻。而在水系汇入江河的低地平坝地区，则是傣族和部分汉族的聚居区，他们更能适应干热河谷炎热少雨、高蒸发量的气候。

二　祈生于自然：麻栗寨河水系上的山神水源分层祭祀仪式

资源（资产）专用性是一个经济学概念，威廉姆森认为资产在不牺牲生产价值的基础上，能够有不同的用途或由不同使用者利用的程度决定了资产专用性的程度。在灌溉社会中，水发挥灌溉功能的资源专用性程度越高，意味着能够被重新配置于其他替代用途（或被替代使用者重新调配使用的程度）就越低，申言之，水对于梯田灌溉社会最主要的功能就是维持稻作农耕生计活动，水对于梯田灌溉社会而言是专用的且有排他性非替代性。纵向灌溉水系上的梯田稻作民族围绕水资源配置活动所形成的“神山圣水”信仰系统，与水资源的专用性密切关联，是诸多民族维持人口再生产，祈生于自然的原初生态观的精神象征。

在麻栗寨河灌溉水系上，因为水资源不可替代的灌溉专用性，立体住居的不同民族群体对自然之水和水源神山都具有敬畏感，水源神山的祭祀礼仪已经成为他们传统农耕生活中的一部分。当然，与空间上的立体分层分布一样，纵向水系上的诸多民族围绕灌溉生活开展的水崇拜和水源神山祭祀仪式也是分段分层的，水系上以民族为边界的多元“神山圣水”分层祭祀仪式迄今生动存续。

1. 水系上游多族共襄的“波玛突”诸水之源山神祭祀仪式

麻栗寨河上游的大部分村落以哈尼族为主，间以部分彝族村寨。水系源头的哈尼族村寨尚存留着“波玛突”[①] 山神水源祭祀仪式，以麻栗寨村的仪式为典型。麻栗寨村委会属于梯田核心区元阳县新街镇，下辖麻栗寨、倮马点、上马点、坝达儿个村民小组，麻栗寨村民小组内部又分为 8 个组，属于纯哈尼族寨，全寨 700 余户。据寨中村民回忆，麻栗寨河上游以哈尼族为主导的最隆重的山神水源集体仪式，要数上马点村附近的“波玛突”仪式。

---

① “波玛突”，哈尼语中“波玛”意指高大的有神灵居住的神山，在本文语境中是指为哈尼梯田提供灌溉水源的哀牢山；“突”指祭祀活动。“波玛突”指一年一度祭祀最高水源神山，祈求风调雨顺、水源不绝、谷粒饱满的集体仪式。

传说有两位神女住在上马点的山头，每年只要给她们献“牺牲”求雨，她们就会给山下居住的人雨水，寨子就会安康，谷子就会饱满。我听我爷爷讲，历史上，整个麻栗寨村包括麻栗寨河水流淌到的傣族、彝族、汉族村寨里的人，都要一起来祭祀上马点山上的水源山——这也是麻栗寨河的水源之一，我们麻栗寨寨脚水田，有上马点的，也有倮马点的，还有坝达的，主鲁寨的。我 1962 年出生，记得我小的时候，什么年份记不清楚了，我们整个村，包括上马点、倮马点和坝达村的哈尼族，一起杀牛，在上马点上方的那个山头做“波玛突”仪式，但是那个时候南沙的傣族没有上来参加，只是听老人传说以前有南沙傣族上山参加祭祀。傣族后来不上山来的原因，听老一辈讲是因为当时交通不便，道路不通，他们顺着麻栗寨河牵猪牵牛上山太不方便，解放前还会在半路上遇到土匪抢钱，而且路途遥远，等到傣族走到山上时，山上的哈尼族已经走到水源山上开始祭祀活动了。所以后来南沙傣族就不怎么上山来了，有一段时间他们光凑钱，人不上来，再后来，解放了，改革开放了，也不流行这些祭祀仪式。近十多年来已经没有这个“波玛突”神山祭祀仪式了，现在就是个别哈尼族寨子自己组织“普础突”[①] 仪式。[②]

随着社会变迁，麻栗寨河上游多民族祭祀山神的集体仪式只是存留在当地少数民族的集体历史记忆中，但是水系上游哈尼族的“波玛突”仪式有中下游的彝族、傣族参与的历史记忆，本身就是一条纵向水系上的多民族基于联合灌溉行动互动往来的象征。仪式能够互动，要基于不同民族在灌溉生活的日常交往中所建构的社会关系网络，例如，哈尼族与彝族、彝族与傣族之间的物质、经济生产资料的传输等，都是区域之间“利益共同体”形成的现实基础。山地和平坝稻作民族都在共同应对来自“自然的限制”的过程中，努力在资源配置方面实现各种社会关系和利益关系的平衡。人与自然、人与人、人与社会，在多元并置的生计空间内不断调适，趋于理

---

① “普础突”：哈尼族村寨内部的成年男子于每年农历四月，在村寨旁的某一片水源神树林里举行的集体祭祀仪式，目的是在庄稼下种之前，祈求风调雨顺，寨子安康，稻谷丰收。

② 材料来源：由笔者 2018 年 1 月 30 日，于元阳县新街镇麻栗寨村委会麻栗寨村四小组访谈村民卢某的田野笔记整理而成。

性平衡。实际上，在维持稻作生计生存需求的共同利益下，在不触及各自社会结构内部集体组织原则的前提下，文化和信仰方面的差异是相对淡化的。

2. 水系中游的彝族山神祭祀仪式

麻栗寨河中游主要聚居着彝族（仆拉支系）、壮族、汉族（通常与彝族杂居）和极少部分的傣族。该水系中游地区以石头寨村委会[①]石头寨村（小组）彝族仆拉支系的山神水源祭祀活动为典型。据较早迁入该区域的彝族仆拉人的迁徙口述史，石头寨村建寨逾200年。石头寨村仆拉人的神山圣水祭祀仪式，虽然没有“诸水之源”麻栗寨那样为多民族所共襄，但其祭祀历史、形式、内容也极为古老而庄重。

据该村寨的彝族民间宗教人士毕摩描述：“祭祀山神的活动，近十几年变化很大，以前非常隆重。我们石头寨的仆拉人，单独献石头寨对面最高的那座山，山名用仆拉话叫作‘石老虎’，上面住着山神保佑着我们有雨水灌溉我们的水田，保佑麻栗寨河水常年不枯竭，保佑寨子安康与仆拉人的发展。以前是三年献一次山。献山的‘牺牲’需要一头黄公牛，包括很多其他祭品。全村每家出一名成年男子参加献山，祭祀完毕，大家就一起分祭品，按全村的家户平均分一点黄牛肉，大家就在山上一起吃，吃不完的可以带回家来。以前是石头寨村的人自己组织，毕摩主持仪式，我父亲、我爷爷都是曾经主持献山的毕摩。现在的祭祀仪式由村小组长组织，大家凑一点钱。这个献山神仪式，主要是我们石头寨村的仆拉人在做，邻近村寨的汉族和其他民族不参加。但是，既然我们仆拉人的毕摩去求了神山，也给山神杀了牺牲（祭品），山神肯定是保佑这个村委会的所有寨子的所有民族，因为我们都是同在一个山头下，共用麻栗寨河水的人。解放前，我们石头寨仆拉人是归南沙的五亩土司（实际上是五亩掌寨）管的，我们被

---

① 石头寨村委会隶属于元阳县南沙镇，世居彝族、汉族，以及一小部分傣族，哈尼梯田灌溉社会中彝族仆拉人主要聚居该村。全村委会共有6个自然村，14个村民小组，总户数900户，总人口3700余人，汉族与彝族在石头寨村委会呈现大杂居、小聚居的格局，其中彝族（仆拉支系）主要聚居于石头寨村，共300余户，1500余人，占全村总人口的35%左右。石头寨村位于麻栗寨河水系的中下游交替地带，上与山地河渠灌区的哈尼族山水田阡相连，下与河谷低地的傣族水系贯通，水田相接。由于地理位置比较靠近南沙河谷地区，石头寨的基础设施和产业经济建设与发展相对较好。在饮水工程方面，1982年有自来水通村委会所在地石头寨村，1994年所有农户通自来水。交通设施方面，2014年公路进村（村小组），一条长达20千米的公路将村委会与南沙镇贯连。农业经济方面，主要种植香蕉和甘蔗作为热带经济作物的农业产业支柱。

称作‘米色颇’，就是彝族人仆拉人的意思。献山的时候，土司和山下面的傣族，山上面的哈尼族（老虎山其实是麻栗寨河水系上游的麻栗寨和主鲁两个哈尼族村寨的山脚）也不来跟我们一起献。不过，据我爷爷讲，上游哈尼族在上马点、倮马点献山的时候，南沙傣族和我们仆拉人，还有石头寨的汉族也一起去参加仪式，但那是我爷爷他们在的时候的事情了，我都70 岁了，我小时候记事开始好像没有上去过上马点献山。解放前，麻栗寨河上的哈尼族、彝族、傣族，都沿着麻栗寨河各自献山献水。”①

石头寨彝族的山神祈雨祭祀仪式，是相对独立的，即仅仅以石头寨彝族仆拉支系为主。由于石头寨仆拉人在麻栗寨河纵向水系上所处的生态位置，他们的集体历史记忆中有关稻作灌溉的联合劳动和多族共襄跨族群、跨地域祭祀山神水源集体仪式的记忆，也最丰富且有层次。毕摩罗某说："至于和山上的哈尼族、山下的傣族的来往，解放前，山上的麻栗寨村、主鲁寨、箐口村的哈尼族会到我们石头寨来打工，就是帮着耕田犁地，那时，大家的土地（梯田）也不像现在这样划分得清楚，有的哈尼族来石头寨一住住了 10 多年，后来解放了，国家开始分田分地了，哈尼族就回去山上种他们自己的田地去了。以前他们在的时候，我们这边的尼苏、仆拉人还有跟他们通婚的，不过仆拉还是跟尼苏嫁娶的多，我们都是一个民族嘛，也有汉族嫁进来我们仆拉、尼苏寨子的，河脚（南沙）那些傣族倒是很少跟我们通婚。从解放前到现在，我们跟山上的哈尼族，对面的土老（壮族）还有南沙的傣族，都是有来有往的，以前是相互帮工，借粮食，换工分等，现在主要是朋友亲戚之间的友好往来关系。"② 事实上，无论是彝族还是哈尼族的稻作农耕礼俗，以及基于灌溉诉求开展的祭祀活动，都是以村寨，或是经由水系地缘联结而突破村寨、族群边界所组成地缘联盟为单位开展。水系地缘联盟内的灌溉秩序、水源山神信仰体系，就是联合劳动着的全体灌溉社会成员的行动逻辑和精神依据。

3. 水系中下游的彝族、傣族、壮族“天生桥”祈雨仪式

到了麻栗寨河水系中游向低地红河河谷热区过渡的地带，以彝族、傣

① 材料由笔者 2018 年 2 月 13 日于元阳县南沙镇石头寨村委会石头寨村，访谈毕摩罗某（来自主持石头寨村祭祀山神仪式的毕摩世家）的田野笔记整理而成。

② 材料由笔者 2018 年 2 月 13 日于元阳县南沙镇石头寨村委会石头寨村，访谈毕摩罗某（来自主持石头寨村祭祀山神仪式的毕摩世家）的田野笔记整理而成。

族、壮族等民族为主穿插杂居，该区域至今沿袭各世居少数民族共同举行的一种集体祭祀仪式，即“天生桥祈雨”[①] 仪式。天生桥祈雨仪式，在南沙傣族地区称作“摩潭”仪式，本身是当地傣族一年中农耕祭祀礼仪的一部分。该仪式有近 300 年的历史，明清时期管理南沙傣族地区的五亩掌寨[②]要求辖境内的各个民族参加“祈雨仪式”，为其属地祈求风调雨顺、丰收和福泽。处在麻栗寨河垂直水系上共用一个山头水源的彝族、哈尼族、汉族等，都会参加该仪式。

当地傣族文化精英杨某在访谈中说：“南沙现在还流行着的天生桥传统祭雨仪式，从明朝五亩掌寨管理这片区域时就开始了，主要是在枯水期（通常是农历二三月份的春旱期）组织辖地内的各民族群众集体到麻栗寨河向南沙河谷转折的地方求雨。解放前，土司组织各个村寨（有石头寨的彝族、计且的壮族，可能还有一部分哈尼族）的头人、长老召集本村寨的人，一起参加仪式。一部分彝族和壮族之所以参加傣族的祭祀仪式，是因为今天元阳县南沙（镇）片区的石头寨（村委会）在历史上就是彝族的聚居区域之一。五亩土司隶属于建水临安府，石头寨又属于五亩土司所管辖的范围之一。天生桥祭雨仪式有近 300 年的历史，明清时期的五亩掌寨请彝族的毕摩主持祭祀，诵祷经文，主要目的是为其属地祈求风调雨顺、丰收和福泽。祭祀仪式结束后在麻栗寨河的天生桥河段进行简单的泼水仪式。我听寨子里的老一辈给我讲，解放前，每年的农历二三月，召勐主陶氏先召集辖地内的各个村寨出钱买祭祀用的活猪，各保长和寨头将活猪抬到天生桥洞口，在洞口宰杀活猪，将收拾干净的猪头献于临时搭建的祭台上，加上猪身上的脏器和猪耳朵、猪尾、猪脖子，再献上酒、白糯米饭和黄糯米饭，鸣响三声土炮，并举火药枪鸣放，石头寨彝族毕摩口念咒语，召勐主陶氏跪拜祈求神灵降雨，各保长、寨长逐一跪拜神灵，并在天生桥洞口与神灵共享祭品，之后所有参加人员在天生桥河洞

---

① 天生桥是麻栗寨河水系中下游（即梯田稻作中高海拔哈尼族、彝族寨群向低海拔傣族寨群聚居区过渡的地方）石头寨山和芭蕉岭山之间自然形成的一道天然溶洞，麻栗寨河从溶洞中间穿过，灌溉南沙坝子和麻栗寨河流域的诸多农田，南沙傣族耕种的大量农田受惠于麻栗寨河水系。

② 五亩掌寨是清代临安府辖区中著名的“十土司和十五掌寨”中的一个，清代临安府辖区主要涉及今哈尼族的大聚居区红河南岸及北岸的部分地区，五亩掌寨为傣族的地方首领，主要统辖今元阳县五亩、五邦、石头寨、排沙等傣族和彝族、壮族先民居住的地区。

里相互泼水，而召勐主陶氏必须被泼得全身湿透，意寓其辖地风调雨顺。[①] 这项祭祀仪式的参加者包括五亩掌寨辖地范围内的傣、彝、壮等共用麻栗寨灌溉河水系的半山及河坝民族。中华人民共和国成立前，祈雨仪式主要由掌寨组织，麻栗寨河水系各村寨各民族群众在传统农业垦殖生计方式中出于对农业灌溉用水的高度依赖和对神灵系统的自然崇拜，积极地参与到仪式过程中。自中华人民共和国成立到20 世纪 60 年代中期以前，各村寨平均凑钱买祭品跟随掌寨陶氏的后人到天生桥举行“摩潭”仪式。随着麻栗寨河水系沿线各传统稻作农耕民族生计方式的现代变迁，天生桥祈雨仪式逐渐演化为一项地方性的民俗活动，并被纳入地方政府建构的南沙傣族“泼水节”节庆活动中去。这种因水资源利用诉求一致而集体祭祀“圣水”源流的仪式，在前工业社会中对麻栗寨河水系中下游的不同稻作农耕族群有着相同的规约作用，仪式所映射的是多族群围绕相同的生计方式，在同一生态下通过协商达成一致的秩序逻辑，这种围绕水资源配置活动所形成的集体行动的寨群互动逻辑，是传统梯田农耕社会中良性寨群互动的典范形式，迄今发挥着积极作用。

三　驭水相生：多民族协商过水秩序及灌溉制度技术安排

稻作和灌溉活动是哈尼梯田农耕族群社会和经济生活的基本形式。在麻栗寨河纵向灌溉水系上立体筑居、梅花间竹、互嵌共生的多民族，在固守族群、文化、信仰边界和跨越边界的资源竞争、互动往来行动中，维系着以共生理念为内涵的生态智慧，基于协商性的集体灌溉实践和利益让渡的制度安排，以及因地制宜、历史相承的古老分水技术，对庞大的灌溉水资源实现适度治理，进而维持了相对稳定的社会结构。

1. 族群边界与族际互动：在守望相助中策略共生

梯田农耕民族因山就势、分层而居的空间结构，在物理和文化空间上具有明确区隔，在日常生产和生活中却又频繁互动，这种既严格又突破的

---

① 材料由笔者 2018 年 4 月 8 日，于元阳县民族中学访谈当地傣族文化精英杨某的田野笔记整理而成。

边界，总结起来就是：梅花间竹，立体共生。麻栗寨河水系上不同民族及寨群，自中间梯田高地地带向两边红河、藤条江河谷而下，散布在一条条纵向河流两侧的分水岭①上，梯田稻作民族善于在相邻两条纵向河流中间凸起又相对平坦的高地上围聚村庄，大大小小的村寨分布在可以提供灌溉用水的大型河渠两侧，一是利于引水灌溉，二是方便排水退水。

纵向水系径流上的多族群对灌溉水资源配置的集体行动，除受自然生态约束外，也要受到持续共生的多元文化的影响，且暗含公共资源配置与族群关系的辩证逻辑。在小型社区哈尼梯田、麻栗寨河的无数条纵向水系上，族群边界和多元文化并置的存续性，也在错综的土地权属、水资源共有关系中无限交缠，构成了丰富多元的和谐图景。

在梯田灌溉社会中，除局部散杂居现象，族群的边界和空间的立体分层清晰呈现。在“森林－村寨－梯田－水系”诸生态要素中，自上而下关联全体稻作灌溉行动者的水资源，自然生成，专用共享，既不能按照村寨的物理边界那样明确切割，也无法按照族群的文化边界那样明确区隔。因而边界明确的族群，往往又被这些共有资源串联起来。以稻作和灌溉为基本生活形式的多族群，必须共同支配和处理那些“你中有我，我中有你”的梯田、水资源权属关系，在此过程中谁都无法“独善其身”而必须开展各种互动往来关系。在哈尼梯田灌溉社会中，选择宜耕的土地，并开展有效灌溉活动，才是梯田精耕农业成型的双重保障。田阡交错的梯田权属关系，以及纵横交织的自上而下星罗密布的河网沟渠系统，进一步夯实了族群间守望相助、密切往来的共生理念和社会实践。

2. 协商过水：灌溉制度安排和秩序逻辑

梯田灌溉社会中，处在以海拔为自然界线的不同生态空间的不同族群，首先分别有一套属于各自文化特征的生态适应策略。其次，他们在纵向灌溉水系上的水资源支配的竞争与合作上，因水田交织互嵌而形成联合灌溉行动并不断地调整着各自的资源占有方式。基于协商一致的过水秩序，一直在探索着各方都满意的配置制度。麻栗寨河水系所串联的多民族，实质是同一纵向灌溉水系上的共有水资源的占用者，而“（公共池塘）资源占用

① 分水岭是指分隔相邻两个流域之间的山岭或高地。分水岭的脊线叫分水线，是相邻流域的界线，一般为分水岭最高点的连线。

者生活的关键事实是，只要继续合用同一个公共池塘资源（即合用同一纵向灌溉水系），他们就处于相互依存的联系中。当采用有限的制度规则来治理和管理公共池塘资源时，这种自然的相互依存并没有消失”。[①] 事实上，为了解决共同面临的水资源配置问题，不同民族根据所占据的生态区位做出的妥协或者说是自身利益的让步、让渡，实质上是指那些与集体灌溉行动相关，但是与族群内部的组织和行动逻辑相关不大或是不相矛盾的内核，基于这种利益让渡所调整出来的是多民族协商一致的灌溉秩序、过水原则。

在哀牢山梯田灌溉社会中，诸如麻栗寨河这样的诸多纵向垂直水系上，不同的梯田农耕民族自上而下立体分层、梅花间竹的互嵌分布状态，意味着水资源的稀缺性，成为影响全体灌溉社会成员之间水资源竞合关系的重要因素。就水资源而言，一旦纵向水系上的灌溉水资源稀缺性开始凸显，水资源竞争关系的负面效应就会出现。当上中下游各族群、寨群间的灌溉社会成员的用水需求不能同时满足时，毗邻水源而居的民族或村寨显然更有优势，这是否就意味着当麻栗寨河水系上的灌溉水资源因季节、年份、气候的原因而达到稀缺的临界，就会引发灌溉社会成员之间的水资源负向竞合——冲突或水利纷争？

就事实而论，无论是从可以查证的历史文献，还是从河段上中下游世居民族的集体历史记忆中来看，麻栗寨水系上都没有出现过族与族、寨与寨之间旷日持久的水利纷争个案，尽管这并不意味着该水系历史上没有出现过灌溉水资源突破稀缺临界的现象，但反映了不同民族依据他们的生态位空间选择，进行着适应环境的策略性调试，也即“人们为了获得与使用资源或者为了及时解决共同面临的问题而扬弃以往的失误，重新调整人际关系”[②] 的过程，这种因生态环境而变革的适应战略在麻栗寨河水系上，尤其是水系的中下游地区得到了验证。自20世纪90年代以来，由于麻栗寨河水系上不断修建水库，历史上专用于灌溉的水源被不断分流出去支撑集镇和城镇的生活用水，水源紧缺问题不断凸显。而另外，随着社会尤其是市场环境的变迁，交通基础设施的不断建设，以及元阳县城搬迁（20世纪90年代初，因地质灾害问题，元阳县城从新街镇搬迁到了南沙镇）的问题，

① 〔美〕埃利诺·奥斯特罗姆：《公共事物的治理之道：集体行动制度的演进》，余逊达、陈旭东译，上海译文出版社，2018，第45页。

② 〔韩〕全京秀：《环境人类学》，崔海洋、杨洋译，科学出版社，2015，第6页。

以石头寨为界，位于麻栗寨河水系中游的石头寨彝族村落、计且壮族村落、南沙镇五亩、五邦等傣族村寨的大量水田被征收为城镇建设用地，不同村寨的不同稻作农耕民族的生计方式也随之改变，人们面对更多的可供选择的发展方式时，总趋向于选择经济回报最优的方式，于是麻栗寨河水系从中游到下游的彝、壮、傣等民族，纷纷选择了将水田改为旱地，种植灌溉需求不是那么大的香蕉、甘蔗等经济作物，这种与现代市场经济和社会发展变迁相适应的生计策略选择，对于麻栗寨河水系中下游的不同民族来讲，只是一种相对较优的选择，但对整个纵向灌溉水系而言，无形中缓解了因水资源变得稀缺而产生的上中下游灌溉社会成员之间的矛盾和隐患。

3. 度量分水：古老的灌溉技术与集体配水行动

在历时近1300年的梯田稻作农耕实践活动中，红河南岸梯田稻作生计空间里的哈尼族、彝族、傣族的先民创造了一系列灌溉水资源分配与管理的技术，并以传统民间机制来维持其技术规范和灌溉秩序。木刻分水和石刻分水作为红河哈尼梯田灌溉系统中千年延续的民间机制，既是一种灌溉分水技术，又是一种灌溉制度，在麻栗寨河水系上也屡见不鲜，成为由一系列村规民约作为制度基础的保障。木刻分水是梯田农耕族群共享水资源的一种制度性习惯，同时也可以理解为民间水规的象征。在四素同构的梯田生态系统中，高山流水自上而下灌溉梯田，影响农耕族群稻作生计，但是水资源又呈季节性和空间分布不均的特征，加之梯田形制与村寨的分布存在一定程度的空间离散性，因此，为保障水资源的均衡分配，避免水利纠纷，在同一条水系灌溉的梯田区域内，农户会根据各级梯田实际灌溉需求（传统上以每份梯田的实际产量来分配该梯田的灌溉用水量），通过集体协商的划定水量，在灌溉干渠的沟头横放一段有大小不等的刻度木头或石条，根据不同水田的用水量将水分流至各块梯田里，盈梯而下，层层放水。

除石刻/木刻分水度量衡器具外，梯田灌溉渠网系统的维系，主要靠从事稻作生计的劳动力通过传统地方性经验知识来维系和保障。在庞大的梯田灌溉水系上，每一条从高山水源自上而下流淌的大型干流以及若干支流所覆盖的梯田和梯田的垦殖者，会通过具体的标准在寨子内部选举出管沟人，管沟人的数量根据一条或数条水沟所灌溉的梯田面积大小而定。被选出的管沟人，要秉承水资源分配公平、公正的基本原则，维持管辖范围内梯田的配水、管水工作。在日常灌溉农事活动里，管沟人负责灌溉沟渠的疏通工作以及区域内小面积受损的水沟或田埂的修复工作等，在枯水期使用分水器具时，管沟人还负责制作并放置分水的“木刻”和“石刻”。管沟人的报酬通常由其所负责的所有沟渠灌溉到的田户，根据自家水田当年粮食的总产量，按照协商好的比例，以稻谷的形式缴付。在现代梯田农耕生产活动中，管沟人的报酬也会通过货币形式来支付。此外，水系上不同族群、寨群之间围绕灌溉水资源配置以及局部水资源纠纷问题，会定期召开集体议事会议，协商解决配水冲突问题。在麻栗寨河水系举行的多族共襄、分层分段的山神水源祭祀活动，除了具有仪式性的象征意义，还实质性承担了“集体议事”解决灌溉水资源资源配置的社会功能。

四 结论

红河南岸哀牢山南段诸如麻栗寨河这样的纵向灌溉水系“上满下流，天然过水”的生态机理，以及当地的土壤、生态、物候结构都为梯田稻作垦殖活动提供了优渥的自然基础。但是，人与自然发生物质和能量交换的关系并不单纯由自然或生态条件所决定，因为人与自然的关系总会在人与人、人与社会关系的变迁中流变，因此整体的梯田农耕社会的社会文化结构也起到了重要作用。这便意味着多民族之间有序、良性的互动，是维系长期稳定、持续发展的社会的必要支撑。当然，因稻作生计高度同质而出现的突破村寨、族群、信仰边界的交往、交流互动和彼此认同，并不意味着梯田灌溉社会就获得了一以贯之的和谐性基础。无论是灌溉有序还是灌溉失序，都始终与可供集体支配和共享的灌溉水资源的充裕性相关。事实上，不同的民族在相邻的空间内各自调整人与自然的关系，并基于灌溉用水和土地等资源集体配置的需求进而促成民族与民族之间的交往与交流，这便意味着不同的群落被整合到了一个连贯的整体性生态系统中，没有一个群体是可以孤立地存在的，因而，协商过水原则必然成为组织多民族联合灌溉行动的基本逻辑。

多民族以灌溉为中心而拓展延续的社会交往活动，是稻作生计空间内实现有序灌溉的具体体现，“由于灌溉的发展改变了人们原有的社会与经济关系，使人们形成了大量的与灌溉相关的社会的、经济关系。例如在灌溉设施的修筑与管理的过程中所形成的合作的规范，灌溉过程中所形成的新的经济关系，例如水的分配、水权、相关的法律制度、管理制度，甚至灌溉的水源地区以及中游、下游之间的社会网络关系，使对水的控制成为社会控制新的力量”。[①] 多民族对共有灌溉水资源的支配与管理，也具有权力竞争的隐喻，然而在多样性并置的哈尼梯田灌溉社会，历史上包括灌溉水资源的配置之争，更多的是配置性资源的控制权之争，而非与权威性资源相关的统治权之争，故不会出现因权力竞争多方之间张力过度而引发大规模的暴力冲突和族群文化兼并的问题。此外，围绕灌溉活动开展交往交流的多民族所共同拥有的经验范畴——也即所达成的“共识域”，往往会成为纾解资源配置权竞争张力的润滑剂。基于这些经验，灌溉社会中的多民族在历史社会互动实践中，面对资源互竞冲突时积极调适与和解，实现利益的让渡及整合，经由协商一致而共构了集体认可的配水秩序，以及灌溉组织原则。

总的来说，在小型灌溉社区的内部，共有资源的“占用者之间进行充分博弈和自由竞争”的想象，固然可以通过连篇累牍的宏大叙述来建构；当社会资本变得重要时，行动者对资源配置方式的选择却未必是全然理性的。资源配置的制度选择，往往是具体社会环境中的市场行为。在特定的社会结构中，对同一地方和社群中相互依赖的行动者而言，个体的行动部分取决于其他行动者的行动，一旦偏离大多数成员共同遵守的集体行动逻辑，就意味着将以失去选择的自由为代价。为了避免成为被牺牲的局部，对共同的文化、规范、传统的服从，才是最优的选项。因此，在哈尼族梯田灌溉社会的水资源配置与制度变迁中，并没有形成必须以一种价值观去凌驾和统御其他文化和价值的历史趋势，也不存在必须牺牲一部分人的生存和发展权利而去服务另一部分人的生存与发展的非此即彼的竞争关系。应该说，不断地“为自己供给新制度来解决（诸如灌溉水资源配置之类的）公共池塘资源问题”，[②] 也是梯田灌溉社会中的联合劳动主体在延续山水林田这些传统公共资源治理规则时，适应制度变迁的一种策略。

---

① 郑晓云：《水文化与水历史探索》，中国社会科学出版社，2015，第 158 页。

② 〔美〕埃利诺·奥斯特罗姆：《公共事物的治理之道：集体行动制度的演进》，余逊达、陈旭东译，上海译文出版社，2018，第 122 页。

海外水历史

罗马帝国的水文明及其政治文化含意

郑晓云*

提　要：在罗马帝国时期不仅修筑了人类历史上最庞大的水利工程，也将水和国家政治、经济、文化紧密联系起来，将水的消费在政治、社会生活、文化艺术等领域发挥到了极致，从而构建起了罗马帝国的水文明。罗马帝国水文明包括修建了人类历史上最大规模以城市供水为代表的水利工程、以水为基础的罗马化生活方式、具有国家文化象征意义的城市水文化景观、相应的水文化理念。罗马的水文明的产生是一种国家力量驱动的结果，反映了罗马帝国鲜明的政治意图，那就是通过水和水利工程建设来达到构筑国家认同、国家权力、国家象征，进而实现国家教化和国家治理的目的。

关键词：水　罗马帝国　水文明　城市　国家治理

Abstract: During the ages of Roman Empire (included Byzantine age), not just a largest hydraulic system in the human history was built, but also the linkages of water and national politics, economy, culture, identity were established, full playing the glory of water in these fields, and accordingly building the water civilization of Roman Empire. Thc water civilization of Roman Empire was consisted with largest scale hydraulic system which was featured with urban water supply, the Roman lifestyle which was based on the water consumption, the urban waterscape which was embodied the meaning of the national cultural symbol, and the related national cultural politic meanings. The water civilization of Roman Empire was a result driven by the national power, and reflected the distinct politic in-

* 郑晓云，湖北大学历史文化学院特聘教授。国际水历史学会前任主席、法国水科学院院士。

tention of building the national identity, power, symbol, etc. and then achieves purposes of civilizing and governing of the empire based on water management.

Keywords: water; Roman Empire; water civilization; city; state governance

在罗马帝国的研究中，关于水控制和管理对罗马帝国兴盛的影响，包括罗马帝国的水文明及其内涵、特征，以及罗马帝国通过水来构建国家认同、巩固领土、实现教化以达到国家治理意图等的研究，目前在国内还是一个近乎空白的领域。然而，不了解罗马帝国的水治理，事实上也就不能透彻理解罗马帝国的兴盛。罗马帝国是一个将水作为神来对待的帝国，帝国的强军、城市化扩展、领土巩固、以“罗马化”为核心的社会教化、国家权力和意识形态的构建等无不与水密切相关。罗马帝国是人类历史上最强大的帝国之一，不仅有广袤的领土、强大的军事力量，也曾经有繁荣的经济、发达的科学技术和文化艺术。然而除此之外，罗马帝国的繁荣还与水有直接的关系，这是人类历史上一个非常典型的现象。在罗马帝国时期，不仅修筑了人类历史上最庞大的水利工程，也将水和国家政治、经济、文化紧密联系起来，将水的消费在政治、社会生活、文化艺术等领域发挥到了极致。无论是在欧洲、非洲北部，还是在中东、小亚细亚，曾经广袤的罗马帝国领土上，到处都可以看到罗马帝国的水利工程，包括了具有典型特征的引水渠、水库、蓄水池、喷泉、浴场、厕所、排水设施等。罗马帝国的水利，尤其是城市水利的兴建，不仅为帝国的强盛提供了强大的资源性支持，同时对罗马帝国巩固其国家权力，实现国家教化，构建认同发挥了重要的作用。水成为罗马帝国国家权力的重要来源，水利及其社会效应，成为罗马帝国挥之不去的光环。在过去的十余年间，笔者先后前往意大利、法国、希腊、葡萄牙等欧洲国家以及埃及、摩洛哥、阿尔及利亚、土耳其等国家对罗马帝国的水利遗存进行了考察，搜集相关的文献资料，与相关专家交谈，对罗马帝国时期的水利和国家文明的关系有了一个初步的了解。本文将通过水来认识罗马帝国兴盛的另一种根基，以及这一人类历史上曾经存在过的规模最大、技术最为复杂的城市为主体的供水系统建设的复杂历史背景及其对国家权力构建、社会教化、国家治理的影响等，以理解罗马帝国是如何通过水来治理国家，构建国家统一的理念、标志和文化纽带。

一　罗马帝国的水文明

罗马帝国是在此之前已存在了近500年的罗马共和国的延续，在公元前27年元老院授予盖乌斯·屋大维“奥古斯都”称号，罗马共和国由此进入帝国时代。公元1453年，奥斯曼帝国苏丹穆罕默德二世率军攻破君士坦丁堡，东罗马帝国（拜占庭帝国）灭亡，罗马帝国存在了一千余年。罗马帝国在全盛时期控制了大约500万平方千米的土地，是世界古代史上国土面积最大的君主制国家之一，同时也是政治、经济、军事、文化、科学最发达的国家之一。

在罗马帝国所创造的辉煌文明中，水利是其中最基础、最重要的构成之一。从公元1世纪开始，罗马帝国修建了人类历史上最庞大的以城市供水为主要特征的水利系统。大规模的水利工程建设一直延续到公元6世纪东罗马帝国时期，此后也还有不断的建设与维护工程。在将水作为一种塑造帝国权力、宣示帝国强盛途径的理念之下，罗马帝国时期修建了大规模的水利，来满足城市、农村的用水，这不仅表现在工程的庞大上，也表现在其对国家治理的深刻影响上。水在罗马帝国的兴盛中刻上了深深的印记，因此，大规模有效的水资源管理是罗马文明的一个主要特征。[①]

罗马帝国的水文明主要包括以下几个方面。

1. 修建了人类历史上最大规模以城市供水为代表的水利工程。这些水利工程的主要特征是修建引水渠进行长距离引水供水，创造了人类历史上最大规模的长距离调水的奇迹。罗马帝国庞大的水利工程，首先是从引水渠开始的。引水渠本身不是罗马帝国的发明，而是希腊文明的遗产，但是这种遗产被罗马帝国发挥到了极致。在欧洲，大部分的土地属于喀斯特地貌，天然的地表河流稀少，在意大利，大部分的城市都是依靠水井及附近的泉水发展起来的，但是这一切并不能满足城市的进一步扩大以及产业的发展，通过引水渠将水从城市之外的泉水或附近的河流、湖泊中引到城市

① Dragoni W.，Cambi C.：Hydraulic Structures in Ancient Rome. 42nd IAH CONGRESS：HYDROGEOLOGY：BACK TO THE FUTURE，Rome，Italy 13th – 18th September 2015. Mid – Week Technical Field Trips，MT1 Field Guide，Wednesday September 16th，2015，p. 1. published by the IAH conference committee.

中，将极大改善城市和农村的供水，因此引水渠成为实现这一目标的重要手段。在公元前4世纪罗马城就已开始修建引水渠，尤其是罗马帝国的繁荣时期，也就是公元50～300年这个时期，罗马帝国修建了大量的引水渠，不仅仅是整个地中海周边，从苏格兰到伊拉克，从高加索山脚下到撒哈拉沙漠，罗马帝国的引水渠无所不在，并且数量十分庞大，仅仅在高卢地区就修建了300多条。目前在欧洲、非洲、亚洲存在的罗马引水渠遗址超过了1600处。这些引水渠工程浩大，有的几十千米，有的长达数百千米。例如西班牙的拉斯梅德拉斯引水渠长达600千米，葡萄牙的特雷斯引水渠长达230千米。引水渠的修建，主要是为了解决城市供水的需要（饮用、沐浴、厕所、生产等），同时也提供农业灌溉、金矿开采等其他产业的用水。引水渠的修建，使城市供水有了极大的增加，促进了城市的繁荣。

引水渠的修建是一项浩大的工程，也是罗马帝国水利工程的标志。修建长距离的引水渠道，必须穿行当地复杂的地貌，尤其是在欧洲广袤的喀斯特地区，这样就需要一系列的配套设施。引水渠一些基本的构成要素，包括引水渠道、跨越山谷河流的桥梁、吸虹管、水库等。在罗马引水渠中，最令人瞩目的莫过于引水渠桥，它是引水渠的象征。今天遍及欧洲的引水渠桥遗址，是人们对罗马引水渠的第一印象，甚至是唯一的印象。引水渠桥事实上已超越了它的实用价值，成为罗马帝国统治的象征，因此被称为“罗马的旗帜”。罗马帝国统治所到之处，都能够看到引水渠桥。引水渠桥是为了引水渠跨越山谷和河流修建的。罗马帝国的引水渠桥一般为三层，地势不高时也有二层。第一二层是桥基，第三层是过水的渠道。大多数渠道只有一条，也有少量的有两条渠道，这主要是为了维修方便。引水渠桥一般高度在20米到50米，长度从数十米到数百米不等，有的长达1000多米。例如在今天仍然可以看到的西班牙塞哥维亚引水渠桥，这一修建于公元1世纪的引水渠桥长达1200米，高35米，共有166个桥桩。引水渠桥完全是石头建筑，基本上是由多孔构成的拱桥，桥孔的多少取决于桥的长度。但是每层的高度却不一样，30米高的桥为三层，但是50米高的同样也是三层，这就使一些桥的桥桩变得十分高，必须要有更高的桥基，使得工程更为复杂浩大。

罗马引水渠最巨大的工程，出现在拜占庭被确立为东罗马帝国首都之后。公元330年，位于博斯普鲁斯海峡边的古城拜占庭被确立为东罗马首都，进入了拜占庭帝国时代。为了满足作为帝国首都的供水需要，东罗马皇帝决定修建新的引水渠。目前在这里仍然可以看到世界上最长的引水渠的很多遗址。在公元4世纪，君士坦丁堡引水渠开始修建，将距离君士坦丁堡100多千米外的泉水通过引水渠引入城市中。这座引水渠工程浩大，沿途修建了89座巨大的引水渠桥。到了公元5世纪，由于水源的不足，这个引水渠不得不延伸到更远的水源地，这样引水渠长度达到了551千米，新建设引水渠桥30座。遍及罗马帝国领土上庞大的引水渠工程，为罗马帝国构建了一个城市化发展的基础资源体系，为罗马帝国实现领土扩张、城市发展、国家治理提供了有力的支撑。

2. 以水为基础的罗马化生活方式。由于大规模引进充裕的水资源，罗马城市建设了各种与水相关的生活、生产、娱乐和景观设施，包括大量的浴场、冲水厕所、花园、城市喷泉、水磨等，极大地提升了城市生活品质和文明程度。这其中最为突出的是修建了人类历史上最大规模的浴场和冲水厕所，使沐浴成为罗马帝国推行国家教化的途径。以沐浴及冲水厕所为代表的卫生生活是罗马生活方式的重要内容。卫生是今天的一个术语，但是罗马人将这种现象看作一种生活方式的提升。大规模的供水首先是让罗马人有了更多的沐浴场所和机会，使罗马沐浴这种文化现象发挥到了极致。随着大规模的引水渠和城市供水设施的建设，大量的沐浴场所也出现在罗马城市中，从首都罗马到其他意大利城市，从英格兰到北非、中亚，罗马浴场遍地开花，无所不在，成为罗马帝国统治的一种重要象征。美国城市史研究大师刘易斯·芒福德写道："罗马对城市卫生和城市形式最典型的贡献，大约就要算浴池了。从有关大型浴池的发展史的记述中，我们甚至可以看出罗马城乃至于罗马帝国本身的简炼历史。"① 出乎今人意料的是，修建宏大罗马引水渠的一个主要目的，就是为了修筑沐浴设施、满足人们沐浴喜好，甚至有的引水渠的修建，仅仅是为大规模的浴场供水。

那么，沐浴对罗马人来说有多重要呢？研究罗马沐浴的著名学者英奇·尼尔森认为，在罗马世界中，沐浴同吃饭、喝酒和欢笑一样重要。即使修建浴场代价昂贵，它们仍是殖民地和新征服的城市首先要建立起来的

① 刘易斯·芒福德：《城市发展史——起源、演变和前景》，宋俊岭等译，中国建筑出版社，2014，第226页。

建筑。城市最重要的是修建最大最奢华的浴场，以此作为城市的骄傲。如果一个人不沐浴，那么他既不是罗马人，也没有被罗马化。沐浴绝对不仅是将身体洗干净，浴场是罗马文化生活的中心。在大浴场中，人们可以从事运动、艺术和文学活动，同时也是社交的中心。沐浴是市民重要的生活内容，尤其是有闲阶层每天必不可少的生活内容，朋友聚会、商谈生意，甚至很多政治和经济、军事决定可能都是在浴场中谈成的。因此，不论是哪一个社会阶层的人，浴场都是人们日常生活中必不可少的一部分。在这种背景下，罗马帝国的统治延伸到哪里，浴场就修建到哪里。

王公贵族的私人住宅都要修建浴场作为社交的场所，同时有钱人和市政部门也会为市民修建公共浴场。这些浴场规模宏大，以至刘易斯·芒福德也感叹道："这些建筑物本身表明了这样一个事实：从建筑学来看，它居于罗马帝国最高成就之列，只有万神殿可与之并称。"① 例如在公元前 1 世纪末修建于罗马城战神广场的新浴场就是免费向市民开放的，因此普通市民也一样有条件享受沐浴，沐浴是一项罗马城市的公共服务。修建于公元 3 世纪初的卡拉卡杨浴场装饰最华丽、最奢侈，里面有绚丽多彩的大理石和马赛克地板，拥有几百座雕塑。这座浴场面积巨大，有 252 根柱子，同时里面还有 4 个冷水池组成的冷水卫生间、2 个温水卫生间、7 个热水池组成的热水卫生间。同时还配备有大型烧热水的锅炉设备、供水和排水系统等，甚至在地下建有一间神庙。据说这个浴场每天可以接待 6000 ~ 8000 人沐浴，只要是罗马公民都有资格在这里支付廉价的费用享受沐浴，维持浴场庞大的开支主要是来自于皇帝和国库。这座公共浴场修建时，每天动用 9000 名工人，花费 5 年时间，在公元 216 年建成。今天在罗马城中仍然可以看见其宏大的废墟，当年罗马城市中沐浴的盛况从中可以窥见一斑。当然，在当时的罗马城市中这样规模的浴场不止一个。到公元 4 世纪，罗马城已经拥有 11 个大型公共浴场、865 个小型浴室。

总之，沐浴成为罗马帝国推行国家教化的重要途径，成为罗马文化一个重要的固化符号，如果说沐浴是一场巨大而神圣的国家仪式的话，那么遍布罗马帝国领土上宏大而难以计数的浴场，为这一场神圣的国家仪式提

---

① 刘易斯·芒福德：《城市发展史——起源、演变和前景》，宋俊岭等译，中国建筑出版社，2014，第 242 页。

供了广阔的舞台。

3. 因水而构建起来的绚丽的城市水文化景观。大规模的城市水资源供给，为罗马帝国城市建设的艺术表达提供了可能，也构建起了一种具有国家符号功能的绚丽城市水景观，使人们能够触摸到水、感受到水的存在和帝国的恩惠、权力。在罗马帝国城市供水系统的建设完成之后，围绕着水呈现了丰富的文化景观现象。在这其中，喷泉是最具有代表性的。英语中的喷泉（FOUNTAIN）一词源于拉丁语，包括了自然的泉水和人工修建的出水建筑物两个方面的含义。它最初是作为人们使用水的末端设施而出现的，随后延伸出了广泛的文化内涵和变异。喷泉可以分为城市供水终端设施和纪念性、象征性、装饰性的建筑物，在欧洲不同地区、不同时期产生了技术与文化上的演变。①

在罗马帝国时期，尤其是以罗马城为代表的中心城市，喷泉已经超越了它作为用水末端设施的基本功能，成为罗马城市的象征，因为它除了作为政府提供的公共产品、政府履行市政公共义务的标志之外，更多地成为装饰性的建筑物，作为一些重大事件纪念性建筑以及城市重要建筑、广场、私人别墅的装饰。在罗马帝国时期喷泉有两个特点：一是罗马帝国大规模的城市供水项目重要组成部分，通过喷泉使得人们能够更便捷地使用水、亲近水，感受到市政公共产品的丰富，从而对罗马帝国统治者和市政当局怀有崇敬感恩之心。因此在罗马帝国时期的城市中，作为公共用水设施的喷泉数量空前。一个典型的例子是建于公元80年的罗马竞技场，由于它可以容纳65000名观众，为了满足观众用水的需要，在这个建筑物中修建了92个喷泉供人们用水，今天仍可以看到这些喷泉。同时在周围还修建了多个冲水厕所。二是大规模纪念性喷泉的修建，是让人们感受到罗马帝国水利工程伟大成就的直观途径，因此它成为罗马城市的重要象征，和浴场、厕所一样，喷泉成为罗马城市的构成元素，也成为罗马帝国城市文化的象征。罗马帝国在被其征服的广袤土地上所建设起来的城市，尤其是纪念性的建筑物，喷泉必不可少。

在罗马帝国的推动下，喷泉成为包含权力、艺术、生存等诸多核心

① Petri S. Juuti, Walter Dragon, Xiao Yun Zheng, et al. Short Global History of Fountains. Water, 2015, 7. pp. 2315 - 2347.

要素的建筑标志，不仅是城市的符号，也是权力的象征，也往往是一个城市的中心。今天，我们仍然可以在很多罗马城市中看到象征城市权力的喷泉。[①] 在一些城邦的战争中，战胜一方往往将战败方的标志性喷泉掠夺到自己的城市中心，甚至是市政厅中安放，作为征服并统治对方的标志。

除了公共喷泉以外，在有钱人的私人府第建筑中，也都普遍建有喷泉。这些喷泉更多地是用于装饰。不论是皇宫还是贵族的别墅，都修建有大量精美的喷泉，有的喷泉甚至有几十上百个喷水口。为了修建喷泉甚至专门修建引水渠供水，将用水的奢侈发挥到了极致。与此同时，在各种和水相关的场所，包括浴场、厕所、喷泉，都会大量修建装饰性的雕塑，尤其是人像雕塑。城市雕塑在水相关的场所往往是最集中、最精美的，罗马战神广场的新浴场拥有雕塑达300多座。用水场所往往都被装饰得美轮美奂，水同样成为罗马城市雕塑艺术繁荣的重要驱动力量。

喷泉是罗马城市必不可少的水设施。公元1世纪，罗马城建成了700个水库、500个喷泉。到了公元4世纪，罗马城已经拥有1352个喷泉，其中很多都是纪念性喷泉。漫步在罗马街头，今天仍然可以看到上千个小型的公共喷泉流淌清澈的饮用水供人们饮用，同时还有大大小小精美的喷泉分布在城市的重要建筑和广场上。正是大规模的喷泉修建，使城市有了水的灵性，包括罗马的其他供水设施，使罗马城市获得了“水皇后”的美称。今天罗马城市内共有近3000个喷泉，2000年来罗马城成为一个人们能够充分享受水生活的水城，这一切都得益于罗马城引水渠的修建。[②] 今天喷泉已经成为世界各地普遍可以看到的公共装饰性的建筑物，给人们带来了水的愉悦。这一方面显示了罗马帝国水文明的辉煌，另一方面也彰显了罗马帝国在构建国家符号过程中的卓越成就，是罗马帝国留给人类的一笔宝贵的文化遗产。

4. 罗马帝国水利所包含的文化理念。罗马帝国大规模的水利工程建设有明确的文化理念支撑，那就是通过水和水利工程建设来达到构筑国家认同、国家权力、国家象征，进而实现国家教化和国家治理的目的，通过水

---

① 一个典型的个案，参阅郑晓云《访水佩鲁贾》，载《江河》2017年第5期。

② Walter Dragoni，Rome's Fountains：Beauty and Public Service from Geology，power and technology. Water Fountainsin the Worldscape. International water History Association. 2012. Finland.

的控制来实现“罗马化”（Romanisation）的政治意图。罗马帝国对水的控制是对先前文明的一种超越，又是现实中罗马帝国显示强盛和力量的新的人间奇迹。因此罗马帝国的水利建设往往超出实际需要，甚至并不考虑当地的水资源状况，更为重要的是构建了一幅作为罗马帝国标志的在人类历史上前所未有的水文化图景。因此罗马帝国水利的修建，“不在于实际需要，更重要的是一种文化态度”。①

由于大规模的显示国家政治意图的水利工程的修建，支撑了罗马文明的成长，也成为罗马文明的组成部分。因此，水不仅是罗马帝国时期的一种生存之源，甚至可以说，没有水的有效供给也就没有伟大的罗马文明。在人类文明历史上，罗马帝国的水文明也是一种巅峰。时至今日，罗马帝国的很多水利技术和长距离引水供水的工程成就仍然没有被后人超越。② 英国学者亚历山大·贝尔在其名著《水的巅峰：文明与世界的水危机》一书中也指出：罗马帝国的水利“其组织程度和技术成就，在人类文明史上只有到了 19 世纪英国工业革命时期才得以再次出现”③。

二　罗马帝国水文明的特征

罗马帝国的水利建设奇迹，有助于我们对罗马水文明的理解。概括而言，罗马帝国的水文明有以下几个方面的特征。

第一，超越前人的大规模水利修建。事实上，罗马帝国时期的水利模式并不是罗马人发明的，包括罗马水利的核心引水渠及喷泉、浴场、冲水厕所等，都是希腊文明的产物，早在公元前 3000 年的克里特岛上已经产生。罗马帝国所创造的奇迹是在继承希腊水文明的基础上将水利的规模发挥到了前所未有的极致。罗马帝国水利的大规模体现在两个方面。一是单个工

① Dragoni W.，Cambi C.：Hydraulic Structures in Ancient Rome. 42nd IAH CONGRESS：HYDROGEOLOGY：BACK TO THE FUTURE，Rome，Italy 13th - 18th September 2015. Mid - Week Technical Field Trips，MT1 Field Guide，Wednesday September 16th，2015，p. 3. Published by the IAH conference committee.

② https：//www. nationalgeographic. com/archaeology - and - history/magazine/2016/11 - 12/roman - aqueducts - engineering - innovation/.

③ Alexander. Bell. Peak Water：Civilisation and the World's Water Crisis . Edinburgh：Luath，2009，p. 47.

程的规模大。罗马帝国的水利以城市长距离引水供水为核心。如前所述，这些引水工程浩大，短的几十千米，长的达到数百千米。其中尤以引水渠桥最具有代表性。例如位于法国南部的加尔（The Pont Du Gard）引水渠桥，是所有罗马引水渠桥中最高的一座。加尔引水渠桥桥高48.8米，底部宽9米，顶部宽3米，总长360米（加两边基础部分），上部桥面长275米，为三层拱桥。第一层拱高22米，第二层拱高20米，第三层拱高6米。从18世纪开始，这里已经成为一个著名的旅游景点，吸引大量的游客，包括很多著名人士前来参观旅游。加尔桥梁的宏大让人在视觉上叹为观止，而人类的力量及其创造物——引水渠桥带给人类的恩惠才真正震撼了访客的心灵，引水渠桥根本性地改变了当地的环境和生活方式。难怪法国伟大的思想家让·雅各·卢梭在1738年造访这一座引水渠桥时被深深震撼："我的脚步走在这些宏大的桥拱上发出的回声，让我浮想联翩，听到了建设者们响亮的声音，我感觉到自己就像一只昆虫落在了广阔的大地上一样，一时间我自己变得那么渺小。感觉到一种莫名的东西让我的灵魂得到升华并大声感叹：我为什么没有生在罗马！"① 在尼姆引水渠逐渐失去它的功能甚至被遗弃后，加尔引水渠桥仍然被完整地保存下来一直到今天，由于其历史重要性和工程壮举，1985年被联合国教科文组织列入世界遗产名录。

二是涉及的范围大。如前所述，罗马帝国的水利伴随着帝国的领土扩张和城市建设在罗马领土四处开花，罗马帝国的统治所达之处，必有水利建设。这样，罗马帝国的水利样式覆盖了地跨欧亚非广袤的土地，这一跨越广大的地域空间的水利奇迹在人类历史上是前所未有的。这种奇迹的产生一方面颠覆了传统的城市供水思维，尤其是将欧洲城市就地取井水、泉水和河水的传统供水方式，改变为长距离调水、大规模供水为主要供水方式。另一方面是改变了广阔地域上的城市供水样式，在罗马帝国领土上的城市都形成了一致的供水模式和相关的水利现象。

第二，实现了超越实际需求的大规模城市供水并驱动了城市水文化变革。引水渠的修建使城市供水有了极大的增加，据测算，在公元3~4世纪

① Rousseau, Jean - Jacques (1998). The Confessions and Correspondence, Including the Letters to Malesherbes. 5. trans. Christopher Kelly. UPNE. p. 214.

罗马帝国的主要城市中，平均每个居民每天拥水量可以达到 200 ~ 500 升，[①] 这甚至超过了今天世界大城市的供水量。最有代表性的是罗马城的供水。罗马城早期通过水井和附近的河流、泉水供水，地表水资源丰富，能够满足城市的需要。但是引水渠的修建为城市的发展注入了巨大的驱动力，罗马城在历史上共修建了 11 条引水渠，这些引水渠从公元前 4 世纪开始修建，一直到公元 1 世纪，先后将近 600 年。引水渠将附近亚平宁山脉山坡地的泉水、湖泊引入城市中，按照罗马城市繁荣时期的 50 万 ~ 100 万人口计算，平均每人每天拥有的水资源量达到 750 ~ 1500 升，远远高于现代城市的人均拥水量。巨大的城市供水量，驱动了罗马城市的社会、经济与文化变革。

在长距离的引水渠修建以后，罗马城市同时也修筑了历史上最复杂庞大的城市水循环系统。在罗马城市中与引水渠工程配套建设了相应的分水设施，通过分水管道将水分布到城市的各个地方，供皇宫、富有的私人住宅、花园、普通居民用水以及公共沐浴、厕所、喷泉等设施使用。同时，罗马城市普遍修建大规模的排水设施，将污水排出城市，或者进入河流，或者用于农田和果树园灌溉。全市供水设施的修建，使罗马帝国的城市因水而发生巨大变化，和水相关的上述设施大量出现在罗马城市中，甚至城市雕塑也作为水景观设施的配套大量出现。在罗马城中，到公元 4 世纪，已经修建了 11 座大型的公共浴场、865 座小型浴场、1352 个喷泉和蓄水池、144 座公共厕所。[②] 东罗马帝国首都君士坦丁堡拥有 8 座公共浴场和 153 座以上的私人浴场。

城市供水的改善也促进了水管理制度的发展，这些制度对于后世的城市水资源管理产生了重要影响。例如在罗马城，引水渠带来的水资源分配有严格的规定，约 17% 的水提供皇家及公共沐浴，39% 供市民使用，44% 为公共用途，包括喷泉、厕所、生产、公众场所的供水等。[③] 在公元 5 世

---

① Dragoni W. , Cambi C. : Hydraulic Structures in Ancient Rome. 42nd IAH CONGRESS: HYDROGEOLOGY: BACK TO THE FUTURE, Rome, Italy 13th - 18th September 2015. Mid - Week Technical Field Trips, MT1 Field Guide, Wednesday September 16th, 2015, p. 1. Published by the IAH conference committee.

② Ward - perkins B. 1985. From Classical Antiquity to the Middle Ages. Urban Public Building in Northern and Central Italy AD 300 - 850. Ox - ford University Press, USA, p 296.

③ Ari J. H, Petri S. Juuti, et al. Water Fountains in the Worldscape. International Water History Association and KEHRAMEDIA INC, 2012, 7. p. 21.

纪，拜占庭帝国通过了很多严格控制、管理水的法律，严格控制水的分配和使用，显示出水对于这座城市的极端重要性。这些法律条款包括了依据房屋的大小使用不同尺寸的供水管，严厉惩罚从引水渠直接窃取水的行为，所有纳税人必须为维护供水系统贡献人力财力等内容。[①]

第三，罗马的水利工程代表了历史性的技术创新水平。水利工程的建设，不论是引水渠还是城市的公共供水系统等，无不代表了那个时代的最高技术水平。尤其是引水渠的修建，包括了引水渠道、地下隧道、吸虹管、引水渠桥、水库等一系列高难度的建设工程，在欧洲 80% 的引水渠道是修在地下的暗渠。水泥的发明和使用，罗马引水工程是最大的受益者。从这些工程建设的细节上，就可以看出其技术水平之高。例如在今天法国南部的尼姆引水渠，这是一条 50 千米长的罗马引水渠，建于公元 40 ~ 60 年，主要为罗马殖民城市尼姆市供水。这一引水渠从位于于泽的泉水引水到尼姆，每天输送 4 万立方米水进入城市，为城市的居民用水、生产以及沐浴、厕所等卫生设施、花园供水。这条 50 千米长的引水渠道，从起点到进入城市的终点，高差仅仅有 12.6 米，工程精度之高令人叹为观止，在当时技术条件下，罗马工程师利用简单的工具创造了一个奇迹。而尼姆引水渠上跨越嘉德河、长达 360 米的加尔引水渠桥建成后，整个桥面两端的水平高差仅仅 2.5 厘米，可以看出其工程的精确度之高。引水桥的修建工程也十分庞大，塞哥维亚引水渠桥使用了两万多块岩石，最大的石块重达 3 吨。加尔引水渠桥修建时用的石块小的一两吨重，最重的达到六吨，数量多达一万多块，今天每一个访客无不惊叹古代人拥有何等的力量能够把这些石块精确地安放到位置上。在施工过程中，使用了大型木制的人力起重机等工具，表明当时的工程技术水平所达到的高度。总之，罗马城市供水设施的修建，代表了罗马帝国时期最发达的土木工程建设水平。

第四，罗马的水文明的产生是一种国家力量驱动的结果。罗马帝国的水利建设，基本上都是属于国家统一意志之下的产物，这不仅体现在水利工程建设作为罗马城市必需的基础建设这一特征上，同样水利工程的投资与组织管理无不是国家意志的体现。罗马帝国的水利工程修建集合了巨大

---

① 〔英〕史蒂文·米森、休·米森：《流动的权力：水如何塑造文明》，北京联合出版公司，2014，第 168 页。

的国家政治、技术、劳动力资源和财富，巨大的水利工程就是这些资源的集合体。事实上在罗马帝国初期所建设的很多城市供水工程，其资金都是源于被占领的领土上所掠夺来的财富。例如在罗马城修建的第二条引水渠，就是利用在公元前280年发动的皮洛士战争中掠夺的财富修建的。修建第三条引水渠使用的是同迦太基和柯林斯战争中掠夺的财富。朱丽娅引水渠和弗戈引水渠的修建经费也是来自战争掠夺所得。包括在高卢地区近300条引水渠，绝大多数也都是用在当地掠夺所得财富修建的。公元52年完工的克劳迪娅引水渠和新阿尼奥引水渠，是用皇帝的私人财产资助修建的，因为这个时候已经没有战争财富可用了。罗马帝国把巨大的战争财富用于修建引水渠，包括罗马皇帝和一些有实力的教会出资，这也反映了城市供水工程在罗马帝国国家治理中的重要性。一些地方的小城市修建引水渠和城市供水设施，也都是由地方税收和一些商人资助的，而地方税收被允许用于建设水利工程，也是国家利益的分割。

最能体现国家政治资源的是军队在水利工程中所扮演的角色。罗马帝国时期最重要的引水渠工程大多数使用军队修建完成。工程的浩大反映了帝国实力的强大，这种强大和军队结合在一起，就更有特殊的内涵。罗马帝国的城市发展和军队的对外征服活动有直接关系，早期的罗马城市往往都是在军队的驻扎营地发展起来的。在罗马军队建立驻扎营地之后，军人家属和为军队服务的人员会迅速增多，随之而形成一个城市。也有很多城市是为伤残军人和他们的家属而修建的。这些城市的修建往往都经过了统一的规划，水资源和水供给是城市建设最基础的考虑。尤其罗马军队是一支十分注重卫生的军队，在罗马军队的军事理念中，具有良好的卫生条件和饮用水的军队，才是一支高效率能战斗的军队。① 军团制度是罗马帝国时期一种重要的社会体制性制度，罗马帝国高度依靠职业化的军团去征服新的领土并且稳固已经归并为罗马帝国的领土。美国政治学家迈克尔·曼也指出了军团制度在罗马帝国权力结构和社会阶层中的重要性，尤其是军团经济在国家治理中有举足轻重的地位。② 因此军队在罗马帝国城市化过程中

---

① Ilkka Syvänne. WATER SUPPLY IN THE LATE ROMAN ARMY. Environmental History of Water, IWA Publishing, 2007. pp. 69 – 72.

② 迈克尔·曼：《社会权力的来源》第一卷，刘北成、李少军译，上海世纪出版集团，2007，第368～371页。

扮演了重要的角色，在和平时期，罗马军队往往是城堡、道路、桥梁等大规模基础工程的建设者。同样在罗马帝国修建水利工程时，军队也扮演着重要的角色。从早期因为军队的驻扎而形成的城市，到后来罗马城市的水利工程扩建，大部分的工程都是由军队完成的。军队是强大的国家资源，也是国家权力的象征。通过军队去修建水利工程有其政治含义，可以显示罗马帝国军队不仅仅在战场上有战无不胜的威武，同时也通过引水渠这种宏伟的工程将军队的威严和力量固化下来。因此引水渠桥不仅显示了它本身的宏伟，还显示了建设它的帝国的强大，尤其是和军事力量结合在一起的时候。

第五，罗马帝国水利工程的修建和罗马水文明的形成，反映了罗马帝国鲜明的政治意图，那就是要通过水利的修建和其所驱动的相关文化现象的形成，去改变国家的样式、实现国家的教化、构建国家的权力，最终实现国家的治理。

三　罗马帝国水利的政治与文化含义

是什么因素驱使罗马帝国在持续千年的过程中去修建遍及帝国广袤领土上大规模的水利工程，实现超越实际需要的供水量呢？事实上这一切都反映了罗马帝国鲜明的政治意图，那就是通过水来塑造国家权力、宣示权力、构建认同、实现领土治理。罗马帝国宏大的水利工程，都是这种政治和文化意图的体现。因此要理解罗马帝国水利工程的修建，就必须深入这些复杂的因素中去，尤其是要深入罗马帝国的权力塑造过程中去。罗马帝国对于水的观念的形成与其复杂的历史文化背景有直接关系。英国著名史前考古学家史蒂文·米森认为，要从整体上概括罗马人对水的态度，必须同时揭示罗马世界的复杂性，将其历史、文化、经济和环境具体结合起来研究才有意义。罗马帝国庞大的水利工程的修建“都是为了满足罗马人的一种渴，这种渴并不一定是为了水，而是为了水可以带来的东西：权力、骄傲和声望”。[①] 古代罗马人对水有着特殊的理念，“人们把水当作神来崇拜，主要用于

① 〔英〕史蒂文·米森、休·米森：《流动的权力：水如何塑造文明》，北京联合出版公司，2014，第149页。

卫生和艺术。水源充足是富华的象征，因此也是权力的体现”。[1]

罗马帝国的水利文明构建，主要包含了两个方面的政治意图。

1. 通过水来体现对先前文明的超越，从而构建一种帝国的文化认同。罗马帝国水理念的来源有着深远的历史文化背景和政治动机。罗马文明是继承了古代希腊文明和伊特鲁里亚文明发展起来的。在公元前3世纪，罗马人开始强大起来，而这个时期其思想与文化是落后的，当罗马人占领希腊化的近东及意大利南部时，其贵族阶层被希腊文化强大的吸引力所深深吸引，甚至成为希腊文化的俘虏。贵族们都热衷于发现、学习、融入、享受希腊文化，这一切对决定罗马文化的历史发展产生了重要的作用。[2] 罗马人崇拜希腊文化，而古代希腊文明则受到了古代埃及文明的影响，希腊的思想家们从古代埃及文明中吸取养分，寻求启发以构建自己的哲学系统，泰勒斯、希罗多德、柏拉图、亚理士多德等希腊古代思想家都曾经对尼罗河的来源、尼罗河与古代埃及文明的形成，尤其是对尼罗河泛滥对埃及文明的影响进行了深入探讨和思考。这些大师对尼罗河的强烈好奇心，是源于这条河流所带来的伟大的文明，甚至有人认为尼罗河和世界上所有河流的起源都不一样，是和世界同时产生的。[3] 因此，除了科学的思考和探索，人们更好奇的是它和文明的关系，围绕着尼罗河在古代希腊产生了大量的神话传说和文学，希腊也保持着对于河神的古老信仰，甚至将这些文化现象传到了后来的西方世界。总之在希腊古代贤哲观念中，尼罗河是一条救世的河流，一条具有让万物再生能力的河流，它培育文明，同时又不像其他河流一样具有破坏力。因此希腊人借用古代埃及的神话去重新构建希腊的古代神话系统。众所周知的是，神话对于古代希腊人的精神世界产生了重要而广泛的影响。那么是什么原因促使希腊的贤哲们要去思考古埃及文明与尼罗河的关系，又是什么原因使罗马的水利与古埃及文明搭上边呢？

在公元前10世纪，甚至更早，古代埃及的尼罗河流域已经通过贸易成为希腊和随后的罗马等地中海地区的粮食供应地。在地中海北岸地区并不

---

① Bono and Boni, Water Suppy of Rome in Antiquity and Today. Environmental Geology, 27 (1996, 126), pp. 126 - 134.

② 〔美〕理查德·E. 苏理文等:《西方文明史》，赵宇烽、赵伯炜译，海南出版社，2009，第161页。

③ Biswas, Asit K, History of Hydrology. American Elsevier Publishing Company, Inc., New York, 1970, p. 27.

生产小麦，那里的小麦及其他粮食要通过贸易从埃及获得，在强大的海上贸易支撑下，这种格局得以形成。埃及成了希腊生计的重要支撑，至少在粮食上离不开埃及。而埃及不仅能产出丰盈的粮食，更有高级的文明存在。虽然人们已认识到埃及文明与尼罗河的关系，但是一种什么样的力量在这其中产生着作用，仍然是人们困惑的，在当时只能将这种困惑托付于神的力量。无论如何，对尼罗河现象的神迷、埃及的高度文明、现实生活中对埃及的粮食依赖，都足以让希腊的贤哲们对埃及产生敬仰与思索。人们不仅从埃及农业文明中去探索自然的规律，更从埃及的文化中吸取养分，这其中非常重要的是对埃及神话的借用来构建希腊的精神世界，使埃及的文化融入了希腊人的精神世界中。①

罗马帝国形成之后，埃及仍然是罗马帝国最主要的粮仓，对罗马帝国的生存至关重要。罗马帝国征服了埃及，将埃及并为自己的一个行省，通过军事力量保障这个粮仓的安全。与此同时，更为复杂的是宗教原因，罗马帝国的一些神的崇拜源自于古代埃及，在罗马城就有崇拜古代埃及神的神庙。既然罗马的文化与希腊文明有渊源关系，那么罗马帝国文明的源头之一就有可能是古代埃及文明，这一点对于强大的、已征服了埃及的罗马帝国来说是不能接受的。在罗马帝国成为埃及的宗主国之后，这一种精神和文化上的微妙联系必须要改变。因此罗马帝国在兴起后做了很多事情，包括将古代埃及人崇拜太阳神的方尖碑从古城底比斯及赫里奥波里斯神庙中运回罗马并重新树立起来，以此宣示罗马帝国在精神上对埃及的战胜。

为了达成超越埃及文明的企图，水成为更重要的因素。如上所述，水是古代埃及文明的源头，在古代埃及文明中，水和文明是一体的，是水创造了古代埃及文明。希腊文化在借用埃及文化时也是从对水的魔力的认识与思考中开始的。而继承了希腊文化，同时也是从有治水大师之称的伊特鲁里亚文明中脱胎而来的罗马人，自然也与埃及人、希腊人一样怀有对水的敬畏。水具有无与伦比的自然力量，同时也是推动文明发展的力量，能够控制水自然也就显示了强大的力量，因此对水的控制最能够显现出对文明源头的超越。罗马帝国通过在现实生活中对水的控制和运用，最能表达

① A. Bell. Peak Water: Civilization and the World's Water Crisis. Luath Press Ltd; 2nd edition, 2012. pp. 28 – 35.

罗马帝国文明对希腊文明的超越。如果创造了一种超越希腊的水文明，那么也就创造了超越希腊文明的奇迹。由此，在对水的控制的意图下修建的宏大的水利工程，是罗马帝国超越其他民族力量的证明和对先前文明的直接挑战。如前所述，罗马帝国所修筑的水利工程的原形并不是罗马的创造，包括引水渠、城市供水系统、喷泉、浴场、冲水厕所等，这些都是在罗马帝国之前一两千年前希腊文明的产物，然而继承希腊文明的罗马帝国要将其发挥到极致，至少在规模上要远远超越希腊文明，创造新的对水控制和工程建设的辉煌，也是人类古代历史上最伟大的水利工程成就。这一点罗马帝国做到了，它超越了古代埃及和希腊。在公元1世纪罗马帝国皇帝克劳狄统治时期被任命为水政官、对罗马城市供水作出了杰出贡献的弗龙蒂努斯说过："我请你，将至关重要的引水渠网络所构成的巨大丰碑和那些无用的金字塔，或者说华丽而无实的希腊旅游名胜做一个比较吧！"① 可见，罗马帝国的水利工程就是当时的金字塔，是文明的丰碑。这也解释了为什么罗马帝国要把水作为神来崇拜的原因。也正因为这样，罗马帝国的水利工程是一种国家的力量，同时作为一种模式在国土进行建设，跟随着罗马帝国军队的开疆拓土遍地开花，使这一帝国旗帜插遍其疆土。罗马帝国通过建设前所未有的庞大的水利工程和对水的狂欢来宣示自己的伟大和文明，借此超越古代埃及的金字塔及其文明。罗马水利工程中的引水渠、引水渠桥、城市供水系统、喷泉、浴场、城市瀑布、冲水厕所、水池，以及这些构成要素中流动着的水，都成为超越过去文明的罗马文明的构成，成为对罗马帝国的认同的要素。因此，对水的发挥，是罗马帝国构建国家认同、获得意识形态权力的一条重要途径，当然也成为罗马帝国文明的重要象征。罗马帝国时期大规模的水利工程彻底改变的不仅仅是居民的生活用水状况，而且是整个帝国的格局，带来了政治、经济和生活方式的巨大变化。因此，大规模的水利，尤其是城市水利成为罗马文明的一个重要特征。②

---

① A. Trevor Hodge, Roman Aqueduct & Water Supply, Bristol Classical Press, London, 2011. p. 1.

② Dragoni W. , Cambi C. (2015): Hydraulic Structures in Ancient Rome. 42nd IAH CONGRESS: HYDROGEOLOGY: BACK TO THE FUTURE, Rome, Italy 13th - 18th September 2015. Mid - Week Technical Field Trips, MT1 Field Guide, Wednesday September 16th, 2015, p. 15. , published by the IAH conference committee.

2. 实现领土治理的意图。这个意图是一种现实的政治意图。罗马帝国有两大特征，一是与之前的欧洲传统权力结构不同，罗马帝国是以一个领土扩张为基础建立起来的国家，是一个领土型帝国。在罗马帝国建立之前，欧洲小国林立，一些大的国家的基础是一些国家或城邦组成的同盟者关系，事实上是同盟者联盟，而非统一的以领土为基础的国家。罗马帝国建立了一个和之前的帝国形式不同的帝国，那就是兼并领土、建立行省为基础的领土控制性国家，它的领土控制达到了当时的人类社会中最高的水准和强度。帝国在各行省派驻官员进行管理，同时派驻军团守卫国土，支持政权的运作。①

二是一个基于城市化的帝国。罗马帝国领土治理的特色在于，在被征服的横跨欧亚非的广袤土地上，推行了有统一元素的城市建设，因此罗马帝国是一个以城市扩张为基础、通过城市建设构建一个统一文化内涵的国家，以实现领土的治理。在罗马帝国的城市中，拥有统一的精神、制度、社会和建筑内涵的符号。从西班牙的大西洋海岸到德国的莱茵河，从苏格兰高地到地中海的非洲北岸，罗马城市具有统一的建筑构成要素：一个商业区、一个广场、一个剧场、一个竞技场、军营及诸多的公共浴场、厕所、喷泉，引水渠。② 罗马帝国城市特有的建筑特征，是罗马帝国的统一标志和统治的象征。不论城市的规模与与模式，都体现出罗马风格。城市建设的理念有其用意，就是通过城市建设把罗马化的贸易、技术、宗教、文化和隐藏在罗马城市化背后的思想观念输出到周边的土著民之中。这种输出分布在帝国的各个方面，有着强大的影响力。城市不仅包括了建设形式，同样也包括了统一的管理制度，一体化的城市模式方便了罗马各级政府行使其管理职能。同时城市还有教育功能，罗马的语言、文化、宗教和技术得到仿效、传播。罗马化的城市有助于帝国维护和平与征税，甚至能将帝国周边的蛮族部落变得文明起来。③

与这些意图相呼应，作为城市生存必不可少的基础设施，引水渠及

---

① 迈克尔·曼：《社会权力的来源》第一卷，刘北成、李少军译，上海世纪出版集团，2007 年第 1 版，第 311 ~ 317 页。

② Bono and Boni, Water Suppy of Rome in Antiquity and Today. Environmental Geology, 27 (1996, 126), pp. 126 - 134.

③ 约翰 - 瓦歇尔：《罗马帝国》，袁波、薄海昆译，青海人民出版社，2010，第 91 页。

供水系统是最基础但是最重要的构成要素。对水的控制是军事斗争之外显示国家控制力量最重要的途径之一，控制了领土上的水资源，也就控制了一个国家最重要的资源，从而最终控制领土。因此罗马帝国统治所及之处，不论当地水资源条件如何，都要修建统一的城市供水系统，这也成为罗马帝国的一个特征，同时也成为罗马帝国重要的国家符号之一。

在罗马帝国领土上以大规模的城市供水为代表的水利工程的修建，不仅仅是作为一种国家符号宣示了罗马帝国的存在，为城市提供的丰富的水资源，甚至远远超过了实际的需求量，也为古罗马帝国在国土上推行制度化的领土控制，实施以城市为中心的国家管理体制、文化、宗教、贸易、税收、军事一体化奠定了基础，城市供水使城市扩张战略成为可能。因此，罗马帝国的国土治理首先从引水为核心的水利工程开始。

3. 通过水来构筑国家权力。美国社会学家迈克尔·曼在其名著《社会权力的来源》中，将权力的来源归结为四个方面的网络构成：意识形态权力、经济权力、军事权力和政治权力。它们各自包含着独特的社会空间组织形式，借助这样的形式，人类能够实现非常广泛的但并未穷尽的众多目标。这四者的重要性在于它们结合了深入的和广泛的权力。事实上在罗马帝国国家治理过程中，这四种权力都有其来源，它们组成的社会权力网络都对罗马帝国的国家治理起到了支撑的作用。罗马帝国有500年共和国历史所积累起来的政治资本，有强大的军事力量，同时也有广袤的土地所带来的财富，这一切成为它除意识形态权力之外的三种权力的来源。在本文的分析过程中，我们更加注重意识形态权力的作用，通过意识形态权力的整合和作用来考察罗马帝国水治理的动力因素。

关于意识形态权力，迈克尔·曼提出其三个来源：一是关于意义的概念范畴，掌握基本知识和意义的社会组织对社会生活是必不可少的。二是规范，即对人们在相互关系中应怎样合乎道德地行事的共识，对于持久的社会合作是必不可少的。一场增进互相信念和集团的集体信念的意识形态运动可能增强它们的集体性权力并且得到比较热情的依附，因此，垄断规范乃是通向权力之路。三是审美或者仪式惯例，一个独特的集团垄断了意义、规范以及审美和仪式惯例，它可能拥有相当广泛和深入的权力。在这些意识形态权力的功能之上，将形成意识形态组织。[①] 意识形态权力的典型是宗教，但是在世俗生活中包括古代希腊文化也是一种意识形态权力的表现。

作为意识形态权力不同的表达方式，包括宗教、伦理、社会规范、社会意识、社会生活方式甚至艺术创造、建筑风格等。美国著名史前史专家费根·布莱恩认为社会权力就是意识形态权力，社会和意识形态权力是可以通过公共或私人仪式、艺术、建筑和文学来表达的公共意识形态。[②]

罗马帝国塑造意识形态权力有其现实的背景。罗马帝国是一个建立在广袤领土上的国家，民族众多，宗教和社会背景差异巨大。在罗马帝国的历史上，长期存在着与其他民族的冲突和矛盾，尤其是所谓蛮族的侵扰，甚至带来对国家安全的巨大威胁。蛮族的问题，一直在罗马帝国历史上纠缠不断。因此，罗马人知道，一个只有军队控制的国家是难以做到长治久安的，国家的整合也必须包括文化的整合。所谓罗马化的推行，就是罗马帝国实现文化整合的重要途径。罗马化的核心之一就是基于水的生活方式和水设施建设。罗马化的推行就是罗马帝国构建国家权力的过程。事实上罗马帝国是构建公共意识形态的大师，在罗马帝国时期，创造了从公共仪式、大众娱乐、文学艺术到生活时尚、公共建筑等一系列罗马文化的符号，包括罗马帝国早期和后期的宗教信仰、科学、艺术、罗马剧场、罗马竞技场、浴室、罗马大道、城市建设的样式、城市供水和排水设施等，对于推动罗马帝国统一的精神文化、生活方式、社会文化直至经济制度等的确立起到了重要的作用。这一切，是罗马帝国在继承了古代埃及和希腊文明、埃特鲁肯斯文明的基础上发扬光大的。对水的控制和利用不仅是罗马帝国构建意识形态权力的重要途径，而且将水的利用在人类社会历史中发挥到了一个极致的阶段。因此，对水在建筑、社会生活、艺术等领域中的发挥只是一种表象，更深刻的原因是通过水来塑造国家的意识形态权力，这一点是迄今为止在罗马帝国历史研究，尤其是罗马帝国的政治史研究中没有被充分注意到的。

罗马帝国时期是一个践行早期西方民主政治时期，其政体深受此前存

① 迈克尔·曼：《社会权力的来源》第一卷，刘北成、李少军译，上海世纪出版集团，2007年第一版，第28～30页。

② Fagan Brian M，World Prehistory：A Brief Introduction. Pearson Education，INC. 2008. p. 189.

在了近500年的罗马共和国的影响，因此在罗马皇帝统治之下的帝国，也构建了一个以罗马公民为主体的社会，政治的运行也同样有相应的民主规则。为民众提供服务是政体存在的理由，是存在于古代罗马的观念性认识。罗马的统治者将城市供水作为一种政治意图，向市民提供免费用水的服务形成了城市管理者和市民之间的契约关系。如果统治者不向市民提供水，那么其权威就失去了法律的基础，水成为社会契约的核心。[①] 罗马的统治者通过向市民提供大量免费的水资源供给，来获得市民的支持以维持罗马帝国政体的合法性和长期存在。也只有向市民提供足够的免费用水，也才能表明罗马统治者对罗马公民身份的承认，而罗马公民阶层的存在是罗马帝国政体的重要支撑。著名的罗马引水渠专家 A. Trevor Hodge 在其名著 *Roman Aqueduct & Water Supply* 一书中写道："来自于真实事实的证据表明，罗马引水渠并不是为了提供饮用水或者卫生而修建的。几乎所有的罗马城市都是依赖于市民家中的水井和蓄水池发展起来的，包括伦敦等城市的早期历史发展也都没有引水渠。总体而言，当引水渠修建以后，唯一的结果就是表现出皇帝或者其市政部门对市民的慷慨，只有这些城市在随后的几十年甚至几个世纪的成长之后，才能显现出它带给这些城市的益处和繁荣。"[②]罗马帝国大规模的水利工程修建，其工程价值在很多地方远远高于实际的需要，其水供给量对于很多城市来说都是极大的多余，但是水利工程必须修建，因此使人们只能得到这样的结论：大量带给罗马城市的水并不是城市生存的必须，本质上是一种文化的态度。[③] 因此大规模的水利工程修建，一方面是为了城市发展的需要，另外一方面是显示罗马帝国行政合法性和行政义务的途径，当然更重要的是显示出罗马帝国统治者和各级城市管理者对市民的慷慨，最终的目的是笼络人心，获得民众的支持。对于罗马帝国这样一个以公民社会为基础的国家来说，这一点是非常重要的。因此罗马帝国企图通过水来构建国家的意识形态权力，夯实执政的基础，这个意图是非

---

① Alexander. Bell. Peak Water: Civilisation and the World's Water Crisis . Edinburgh: Luath, 2009, p. 48.

② A. Trevor Hodge, Roman Aqueduct & Water Supply, Bristol Classical Press, London, 2011. pp. 5 –6.

③ Dragoni W. , Cambi C. : Hydraulic Structures in Ancient Rome. 42nd IAH CONGRESS: HYDROGEOLOGY: BACK TO THE FUTURE, Rome, Italy 13th – 18th September 2015. Mid – Week Technical Field Trips, MT1 Field Guide, Wednesday September 16th, 2015, p. 3. Published by the IAH conference committee.

常鲜明的。

总之，罗马帝国对水的控制事实上是一种复杂的水政治，因为对水的控制和应用是一种国家力量，由国家统一进行布局和经营，以此来达到罗马帝国从精神到现实的国家治理上复杂的意图，通过水来构建国家统一的理念、标志和文化纽带。

宏大的罗马水利的光芒在人类历史的长河中并没有长存至今，而是在随后的岁月中渐渐淡去。三个原因造成了罗马水利工程的衰败：一是罗马帝国国力在随后岁月中的衰落，使需要巨大财力、人力、物力去维护的庞大工程失去了支撑。在罗马帝国后，尽管很多地方仍然在沿用这些水利工程系统，但总体上大多数都渐渐被废弃。二是因为地震破坏而无能力修复。三是战争的破坏。

今天来到罗马市郊区的引水渠公园，人们还能看到多条宏大引水渠的残余，它们仍然让每一个来访者感到震撼，同时也因其而伤感，因为引水渠不仅为城市的富裕繁华提供了养分，更是无数士兵终其一生筑成的丰碑。

四　结论

以城市引水供水为代表的水利工程是古代罗马最伟大的工程之一，也是人类古代历史上最宏大的城市供水工程，不仅表现在工程的浩大和技术的创新上，同时也对人类的社会生活产生了重大影响，因此成为一种公认的人类历史上的文明现象。通过对水的控制和发挥，构建起了一幅人类历史上最广阔的、有统一元素的水景观。

供水工程是罗马帝国的国家行为，属于一种国家力量的驱动，它与其他罗马城市建筑元素一道，成为罗马帝国统治的标志，既是一种政治宣示，也是罗马帝国社会权力的重要来源。它一方面以水的控制与挥霍来显示对以前的文明，尤其是古埃及文明的超越，以让国民拥有对帝国文明的仰视与认同。也让帝国统治疆域内的民众能在享受水供给的好处的同时感受到政治宣示的含意与存在，达到对帝国统治的认同。罗马皇帝曾常常举办大型斗兽或人兽决斗的竞技活动等来笼络民心，但水显然是彰显帝国治理意图最有力量的要素。因此，很多城市引水渠的修建可能源起于沐浴设施和大型园林、喷泉的需要，但是创造一个亲水的环境，让人们能够看到水、触摸水、浸入水，是修建大规模的浴场、喷泉、水神殿等水设施的根本原因。[①] 让人们通过水利去感受罗马帝国的存在、恩惠与强大，是罗马帝国通过治水来构建国家认同、赢得执政合法性的重要理念。

另一方面，大规模的水利设施成为罗马帝国实施统治、实现国家治理的一种重要手段。罗马城市修建如此大规模的引水工程，实现了超越实用需要的供水量，是罗马帝国权力的宣示与通过意识形态权力的扩大来实现国家治理的意图的反映。大规模的水治理达成了罗马帝国国家治理的三个主要目标：领土型国家的构建、以城市扩张为特征的国家控制、推行罗马化而实现国家教化。换言之，没有成功的水治理，罗马帝国国家治理的这些目标是不可能达成的。

水利成为罗马帝国社会权力尤其是意识形态权力的重要来源。迈克尔·曼等学者所描述的罗马帝国的特征和权力来源，包括领土型国家、城市化、精英阶层和军团制度。只不过他们忽略了水在罗马帝国塑造国家的社会权力过程中的关键作用，没有看到水也是罗马帝国社会权力的重要来源和实现国家治理的重要途径。从历史的经历而言，罗马帝国的水利建设无疑是成功的，创造了人类历史上从工程规模、技术创新、政治功效、社会影响最大化的一个理水奇迹。

（本文的压缩改写版以《权力、认同与国家治理：水在罗马帝国兴盛中的角色》为题发表于《社会科学战线》2019 年第 7 期。本文重在阐释罗马帝国的水文明特征，故此原文发表。孟宪范先生在本文的理论提升中给予了实质性的指导，在此特表深切谢意——作者注）

---

① 〔英〕史蒂文·米森、休·米森：《流动的权力：水如何塑造文明》，北京联合出版公司，2014，第 149 页。

殖民地时期南亚水利变迁与农业商业化

李晓霞*

摘　要：在传统南亚农业生产活动中，水资源利用与土地、农业社区具有不可分性。水资源的稀缺性、地理特征和权力结构造就了水利设施的多元性和区域特点。殖民地时期南亚水利建设的主要资金来源是国家公共投资。水利设施建设短期内显著改善了南亚半干旱地区的农业发展环境，增加了农业产出，提高了土地利用率，改变了农产品出口结构，加速了农业商业化进程。从长时间来看，英国人所主持的水利工程数量有限，只是让部分区域受益，主要是那些适宜经济作物地区或有比较优势的地区受益，并未改变南亚农业整体落后的面貌。而水利设施建设作为官僚机构的有机组成部分，加剧了殖民统治对南亚地区农业资源的榨取，是导致南亚农民普遍贫困的原因之一。

关键词：南亚水利　官僚机构　土地利用　农业贸易

Abstract: The utilization of water resources in traditional agriculture was closely related to land ownership and the social structure of village community in South Asia. The war following the decline of Mughal Empire and the conquest of the British had destroyed the social mechanism on maintenance and establishments of irrigation facilities in many regions. Great efforts was made on construction of new irrigation facilities by British India government to combat the famines and meet the developmental requirements of the industrialization process in England from 1860s to 1919. The new irrigation facilities had enhanced the agriculture production and benefited the commercialization of cash crops in South Asia. The management

* 李晓霞，云南省普洱学院人文学院讲师。

of irrigation facilities by the colonial bureaucracy created more tribute from South Asia to Britain, instead of improving the income level of peasants. As a result, South Asia remained one of the most backward agrarian areas and aggravated poverty of peasants.

Keywords: Irrigation facilities; Colonial bureaucracy; land use; Commerical agriculture

英国统治印度既有破坏性的一面，同时也做了一些建设性的工作，这是马克思主义者看待殖民主义双重历史作用的基本观点。在建设性工作方面，经常被人谈及的是英国人建设了南亚铁路网和英国人在南亚修建了一些水利工程。前者曾因被马克思乐观期待（“铁路系统在印度将真正成为现代工业的先驱”①）而为人所知，对后者我国学术界至今研究甚少。近几十年，国外学者对不同时期、不同地区的南亚水利设施的兴建和成效做了大量的研究，已经积累了丰富的文献资料。② 本文拟通过对这些文献材料的梳理和解读，探讨如下问题：英国人为什么要在南亚从事水利工程建设？英国人建设了哪些水利工程？如何评价这些工程的作用及性质？

一　南亚农业与水资源利用的历史背景

南亚是世界上降雨量最丰富的地区之一，但是各区域在时空分布上存

① 马克思、恩格斯：《不列颠在印度统治的未来结果》，《马克思恩格斯选集》第一卷，人民出版社，1972，第73页。

② 最早开展研究的是伊丽莎白·怀特科姆，她分析了殖民地时期大型水利工程的兴建过程、对农业环境的不良后果、官僚机构对赢利性的过度追求倾向，整体评价认为消极作用居多。参见 Elizabeth Whitcomb, “Irrigation”, in Dharma Kumar and Meghand Desai eds., *The Cambridge Economic History of India*, Vol. 2: c. 1757 - c. 1970, Cambridge: Cambridge University Press, 1983, pp. 677 - 737。其次是大卫·卢登，他对泰米尔纳杜地区的水利工程的社会经济效果进行了长期考察，展现了南印度农业水利设施的多种社会力量来源和作用。参见 David Ludden, “Patronage and Irrigation in Tamil Nadu: A Long - time View”, *The Indian Economic History Review*, Vol. XVI, No. 3, 1979, pp. 347 - 365。伊恩·斯通从技术变革的角度分析了恒河流域水利工程兴建过程中的创新之处，以及工程建设对当地的社会经济影响，对水利工程对农业生产效率的提高作用肯定较多。参见 Ian Stone, *Canal Irrigation in British India: Perspectives on Technological Change in a Peasant Economy*, Cambridge: Cambridge University Press, 1984。

在巨大差别。总体来看，沿海多，内陆少；夏季降雨量集中，冬季降雨强度较小。[①] 同时，由于南亚各地蒸发量较大，主要依赖降雨形成的河流也具有鲜明的季节性特征。降雨、地形和河流共同决定了地下水资源的存量和分布。水资源形态是从古至今南亚农业发展的先决条件。

为了减轻水资源对农业发展的限制，中世纪的南亚地区在各地出现了不同类型的水利设施。水利设施的存在、维护、发挥积极作用，往往需要劳动、资金、权力和社会参与。在南亚早期历史中水利设施的区域性和类型参看表1。

表1　南亚的农业区域

农业气候类型	降雨量（毫米/年）	灌溉类别	主要食物	经济作物	地形特点
游牧干旱	<500 <700	水井	谷类、畜产品	棉花	高原、森林
干旱	>500 <800	水井	谷类、豆类	棉花、油料类	高原、平原
干湿混合	>500 <1250	水井、水塘	谷类、水稻	棉花、油料类	平原
湿润	>1000	水塘、水坝	水稻	水稻、园艺类	平原、海岸
热带雨林	>1250	水坝、水渠	水稻、水果类	木材、园艺类	山地、平原

资料来源：David Ludden, "Archaic Formation of Agricultural Knowledge in South India", in Peter Robb eds., *Meaning of Agriculture*, Delhi: Oxford University Press, 1996, p. 67。

水井是大多数北印度地区农业灌溉和日常生活的主要来源。[②]水井根据其容易受破坏的程度至少可以分为两种。坚固的水井，造价较高，分布较少。简易水井，造价低廉，分布较广。在邻近河流的地区地下水位较高容易开凿简易水井，在远离河流的地区则十分困难。在南印度地区，人们在

① 按照降雨量的多少，南亚地区可分为三类，大于50英寸为湿润地区，小于50英寸大于30英寸为半湿润地区，小于30英寸为半干旱地区，参见 Irfan Habib, "The Geographical Background", in Tapan Raychaudhuri eds., *The Cambridge Economic History of India*, Vol Ⅰ: c. 1200 - c. 1750, Cambridge: Cambridge University, 1982, p. 7。还有一种方法根据某地区人均水资源的可得性和社会以及经济发展的对水资源的需求程度，将各地区分为绝对匮乏水资源、相对匮乏水资源、一般匮乏、基本不匮乏四种情况，参见 K. J. Joy and Suhas, Paranjape, "Understanding Water Conflicts in South Asia", *Contemporary Perspectives*, Vol 1, No. 2 (July - December 2007), p. 33。

② Irfan Habib, "The Geographical Background", in Tapan Raychaudhuri eds., *The Cambridge Economic History of India*, Vol 1: c. 1200 - c. 1750, Cambridge University, 1982, pp. 48 - 49.

河流上筑起简易水坝，或通过河塘湖泊以“水库”的形式来灌溉。在英国人接管马德拉斯时期，南印度大小不一的水库（非私人所有）至少有32000个。[①] 除了水井和水坝之外，人们有时还在河流下游地区的平原地带修建引水渠，利用季节性洪水来进行农业耕作。在恒河下游的比哈尔南部地区，地主修建了可长期使用的简易沿河堤坝以便于稻田耕作。在印度河下游的信德地区，也运用季节性洪水的引水渠来种植夏季作物。这些因地制宜的水利设施，存在多种类型的管理方式。

水利设施的规模一般取决于农民、地主或君主的财力。早期水利设施能提供的水资源往往不稳定。水井提供的水源一般只能惠及2英亩左右的土地，用于满足种植市场需要的经济作物的用水需要。水库灌溉面积依赖于河流水位的高低，80%的水库灌溉面积在100英亩以下。水井经常是干旱和半干旱地区的唯一水源。水库和大坝在降雨较为丰富的湿润地区常见。在极端干旱天气发生的时候，年降雨量较多的地区，可以从水库获得备用的水源，如马德拉斯的南部地区。而那些年降雨量稀少的地区，水井会干涸，人们只能放弃土地移居他乡，如西北印度的旁遮普西部地区。水利设施需要长期护理，因此以淘井为业的工匠种姓在北印度很常见。和平时期，富裕农民、地主和君主积极开凿水渠和水井以及修建水坝，以增加收入。当战争和军事冲突不断时，摧毁敌人的水利设施也是一种合理的打击方式。[②] 在战乱最频繁的南亚西北部地区，英国殖民者发现大量村庄和水利设施的遗迹。“废弃的城市、村庄、寺庙、水库、水井、水渠随处可见，这就是过往时代乡村所经历的改变”。[③]

在南亚地区农业发展过程中，水资源利用与土地以及农业社区往往具有不可分性。在印度南部的马德拉斯地区，传统上按照土壤的含水性能来划分等级、缴纳赋税。在需要地主维护水利设施的印度中部比哈尔南部地区，接受水井灌溉的市场化经济作物收取货币地租，不需要灌溉的粮食作物收取实

---

① A. Butterworth, “The District Administration in Madras, 1818 - 1857”, in H. H. Dodwell eds., *The Cambridge History of The British India*, Vol V, *The Indian Empire* 1858 - 1918, Cambridge: Cambridge University Press, 1932, p. 51.

② 大卫·卢登：《南亚农业史》，资谷生译，云南人民出版社，2015，第85页。

③ “*General Report upon the Administration of The Punjab for the Year* 1849 - 50 & 1850 - 51, *Being the Two First Two Year After Annexion*: *With a Supplementary Notice of the Cis and Trans - sutleij Terrritories*”, Lahore: Chronical Press, 1854, p. 3.

物地租。水资源与土地的不可分性是村庄种姓社会内聚力的物质基础。[1] 水利设施的建设和维护需要大量的社会动员和劳动投入，因此水利设施集中在农业和贸易较为发达的村庄，并伴随着一些种姓的农业开垦活动向周边扩散。

19世纪初，东印度公司完全控制了马德拉斯和北印度。由于饥荒肆虐[2]和财政需求，英国人被迫关注当地的农业危机问题。兴建水利设施是解决农业危机和饥荒的主要手段。在此后150多年中，官方机构成为资助、兴建、维护、管理水利设施的主要力量。东印度公司在征服印度和镇压1857年印度民族大起义后背负了巨额的财政压力（见表2），作为直接继承者的英印殖民政府开始重视农业的发展问题。

表2　东印度公司及英属印度债务

单位：英镑

	印度借债	英国借债	总额	利息
1820～1821年	27000000	5700000	33000000	1900000
1856～1857年	45500000	3900000	49400000	2000000
1862～1863年	63800000	31800000	95600000	4300000

资料来源：Harod Cox, " Public Debts of the British Possessions", *The North American Review*, Jan 1, 1902, p. 423。

二　水利设施的公共投资及效果

在东印度公司征服印度的早期活动中，并不存在一个权力集中的中央官僚机构，马德拉斯管区政府和孟加拉管区政府是水利设施修复的主要力量。从19世纪早期到1857年印度民族大起义之前，政府兴建的水利设施主要分布在马德拉斯管区的北部、奥里萨地区、孟加拉管区新兼并的西北省（北印度恒河流域的上游和中游地区）。

① Nirmal Sengupta, "The Indigenous Irrigation Organization in South Bihar", *The Indian Economic History Review*, Vol. XII, No. 2 (1980), pp. 157 - 189.

② 1803年、1812年、1837和1838年，北印度都曾遭遇大规模饥荒。整个19世纪，印度都笼罩在饥荒的影响之下，参看 Iran Habib, *Indian Economy*, 1858 - 1914, New Delhi: Tulika Books, 2006, pp. 81 - 83。

马德拉斯管区的主要水利工程集中于北部地区，包括卡维利河、科隆河上游和下游工程、戈达瓦利河和克里希那河三角洲工程以及帕维亚大坝。这些工程的主要设计者是阿瑟·科顿，[①] 工程的建设力量来自1786年建立的马德拉斯管区军事委员会下属的工程部。工程部曾经几次被改组。有时候工程部是一个独立的部门，建设民用或军用的公路、运河桥梁等各种建筑。有时候工程部被分属于不同的部门。有时候水利设施隶属于田赋管理部门，有时候隶属于军事管理部门，还有时候同时听命于二者。很长一段时间内工程部的名称都是修缮部，后来改成公共工程部，后又改回修缮部。这个机构可以是执行部门，也可以是监管部门，有的时候同时承担执行和监管功能。可见，早期水利设施的建设，在地方政府的各种活动中并没有明确的目标单一的定义，水利设施建设和管理对于军事和田赋部门存在较大的从属性。

卡维利河和科隆河工程始于1836年，该工程可以为大约100万英亩土地提供用水。戈达瓦利河的水坝1846年开始建设，能够为大约50万英亩的土地服务。在改善饥荒的推动下，克里希那河三角洲工程1850年开始投入修建。马德拉斯的水利工程经费都是从当年田赋中支出，1849年，这方面累计支出已经超过800万卢比。[②] 在此过程中，马德拉斯地区改变了田赋征收办法，将土地分为“旱地”和“水浇地”，政府提供水源的水浇地以种植作物的价值来征收赋税。[③] 印度各地的水利工程部门在19世纪70年代初大部分处于亏损状态或者略微营利，只有马德拉斯地区能够实现较为丰厚的利润。[④] 这一结果与当地经济作物种植环境优越有关，经济作物很多是需水量大的作物，例如靛蓝、烟草、棉花、蔬菜等；也与当地运河水量较大、能够从通航中获得收入有关。

---

① 罗梅什·杜特：《英属印度经济史》（下册），三联书店，1965，第298页。杜特对科顿的贡献肯定甚多，但是也有学者认为科顿改变了河流水量分布，使下游原本富裕的坦焦尔县水量减少逐渐贫穷。

② Elizabeth Whitcomb, “Irrigation”, in Dharma Kumar and Meghand Desai eds., *The Economic History of India*, Vol 2: c. 1757 – c. 1970, Cambridge: Cambridge University Press, 1983, p. 684.

③ A. Butterworth, “The District Administration in Madras, 1818 – 1857”, in H. H. Dodwell eds., *The Cambridge History of The British India*, Vol. V, *The Indian Empire* 1858 – 1918, Cambridge: Cambridge University Press, 1932, p. 51.

④ 罗梅什·杜特：《英属印度经济史》（下册），三联书店，1965，第305页。

北印度地区最早修复的水利工程是德里附近的西朱木那河运河、东朱木那河运河以及恒河工程。这些水利工程早在莫卧儿王朝时代已经存在，是为穆斯林王公消遣娱乐或田园或狩猎之用，很少使用坚固的材料，一般依靠废弃的河道或顺河流走向，较少用于农业灌溉。只有旁遮普地区锡克教徒在阿姆利则附近修建的老哈斯利运河可为常年灌溉土地之用。传统工程的特点是大多数只能利用季节性的洪水，很容易被损毁并造成淤积和内涝。

1820 年重新开通西朱木那运河，建设工作由孟加拉军队的工程部门完成。1830 年东朱木那河运河投入使用。此后很多大坝和引水渠作为运河工程的延长和补充逐渐发展起来。早期工程受制于地方政府的财政条件，通常规模较小，大规模的运河建设和重新调整，要到 19 世纪 60 年代资助体系和管理制度发生变革之后才开展起来。

恒河工程是 19 世纪 30 年代西北省规模最大的工程。工程的主要设计者是工程师普罗比 · 考特里。1837 ~ 1838 年的饥荒对这一工程的推动巨大。1839 年，时任奥克兰总督为考特里提供了一笔资金用于调查河间地区[①]的地理状况。政府希望新运河能够为尽可能多的地区提供灌溉，以减轻因饥荒不得不减免赋税带来的财政损失。恒河工程在 1843 年开始建造，1857 年完成，耗资 215 万英镑，是当时南亚地区规模最大的水利工程。[②] 工程的修建大大改善了恒河上游地区的农业发展状况。直到 1854 年，各种公共工程的建设都是由隶属军队的工程部门来执行。对现代化建设十分热心的总督达尔豪西决心改变这种状况。他取消了各管区政府的军事委员会，以一个总工程师代之，同时在加尔各答中央政府内部设立了一个公共工程部以监督地方相关活动。[③] 达尔豪西还提出了筹措建设工程资金的新方法。他

---

① 恒河和朱木那河之间的广阔地区一般称为河间地区。

② Ian Stone，*Canal Irrigation in British India*：*Perspectives on Technological Change in a Peasant Economy*，Cambridge：Cambridge Univerty Press，1984，p. 18.

③ 权力集中的英印政府的出现是非常晚近的现象。未有中央政府之前，英国的殖民统治是地理上隔离的管区统治。三大管区政府在政治上彼此独立，有各自的军队和田赋税收机构和货币体系，征收不同的关税。1773 年，孟买和马德拉斯开始从属于孟加拉的管理，但孟加拉总督只是名义上对后两者有管辖权。1813 年，东印度公司的贸易垄断被英国议会取消标志着工业时代英国对印度的需要和管理开始发生改变。1833 年，英印政府从孟加拉管区中独立出来，并且对孟买和马德拉斯拥有实际的管辖权。1850 年开始，地方政府（管区政府和新兼并的各省政府）逐渐成为英印政府的代理人，英国内阁的印度事务大臣开始总揽英印政府的各种财政事务（包括借款和各种支出）。

认为必要的工程建设和维护费用应该被列为“经常性费用”，以借款的方式来满足，而不必在田赋中支出。他还提出，对于农业改良有帮助的运河建设，每年公共工程部门应分配200万英镑资金。

1857后，水利设施建设的主要决策权开始集中于中央政府。水利设施的修建在19世纪中期更多受到外部因素的推动。

19世纪40年代，英国工业界一直在积极鼓吹自由贸易并期望加大英国制成品对印度的出口，但是直到1857年，英国对印度的出口额度一直排在北欧国家[①]、美国、澳大利亚和加拿大之后。1859年，英国对印度的出口达到1980万英镑，不到当年英国总出口价值的六分之一（当年英国的总出口值为13040万英镑）。[②] 英印殖民政府在各方压力之下，试图借助水利设施建设以推动外贸和印度内部商业的发展。

1866年，总督劳伦斯宣布了新的水利建设政策：水利设施将由英印政府承担，同时通过公共贷款来筹集资金，允许土邦参与水利建设。从1867年开始，水利建设的资金开始得到保障，此后10年间，大约有1500万英镑[③]投入水利建设中。在新政策的推动下，通过印度事务大臣的批准，共有5项水利工程获得资金：希尔欣得运河（位于旁遮普东南部地区，1882年完成），恒河下游运河和阿格拉运河（联合省西部地区，分别在1878年和1877年完成），斯瓦特河下游运河（西北边境省，1885年完成），穆萨运河（孟买管区）。

1867年，新设立的负责协调水利建设部门的总督查斯特雷奇获得任命。他将有权审核各省所有的水利工程经费并为工程建设和管理制定规则。在斯特雷奇治下，水资源的分配开始减少随意性，每个工程均要统筹水资源的分配。所有的新工程都要按照“灌溉第一”原则，以固定的价格给每个农民获得长期、有保证的水资源。水资源的使用，要求更多考虑

---

① 北欧国家包括俄国、瑞典和挪威、丹麦、普鲁士、汉诺威、汉萨城市、荷兰、比利时、法国。

② D. C. M. Platt, Further Objections to an “Imperialism of Free Trade”, 1830 - 1860, *The Economic History Review*, Vol. 26, No. 1 (1973), p. 91.

③ 直到1873年，英镑与卢比的汇率稳定为1∶10，此后卢比大幅下跌，1894年甚至到1∶20，政府取消了卢比的自由铸币，到1900年，使汇率基本稳定在1∶15。每年的借款参照当年利率和汇率来计算。参见 Harod Cox, “The Public Debts of the British Possessions”, *The North American Rewiew*, Jan 1, 1902, pp. 424 - 425。

土地面积，而不是最节省水源。[1] 西北省的恒河工程首先接受这些原则。这一时期形成的一个惯例是，在田赋征收到期以前，政府不能提高水价。

19世纪下半期印度铁路建设兴起，开始与水利设施建设争夺资金使用。铁路建设同样被认为有助于减轻饥荒，被列为公共支出的“生产性工程”范围内，甚至铁路被看做运河的补充。在北印度地区，大部分运河无法提供通航功能。与水利设施相比，同样以借款政策支持的铁路建设更容易得到资金支持。

19世纪下半期频发的饥荒和干旱，使英印中央政府不得不继续回到资助水利设施的立场。1876年和1878年的饥荒使水利设施又获得了新的资金来源。新上任的总督李顿决定每年设立1500万卢比的饥荒救济和保险基金，用于容易受到饥荒的地区建设水利设施，当时在建的工程大都从中获得资金支持。

水利设施与铁路的竞争还引起了英国议会的重视。1879年，英国议会任命了一个特别委员会来审核水利建设资金保障问题。特别委员会的审核结论是继续支持以借款的方式从事水利设施建设，得到资金的水利设施可以从投入使用的第10年开始支付建设费用和借款利息。议会强调这并不是要否认工程的赢利性，或认为赢利性不重要，只是承认在饥荒面前，水利工程在财政方面可以发挥防御性的作用，使政府在饥荒和干旱时减免税收的可能性降低。

水利工程资金得到保证之后，政府资助的各种水利工程有了更大规模的发展。恒河下游工程在1868年开始，1878年完成，与恒河上游工程一起实现水资源合理利用。河间地区（北印度）的水利设施经过不断扩展，在1900年能够覆盖250万英亩土地，在1920年上升到350万英亩，河间地区在20世纪20年代水利设施投资累计接近1000万英镑。[2] 灌溉条件的改善大大增强了北印度地区的农业生产能力（见表3）。

---

① Elizabeth Whitcomb, “Irrigation”, in Dharma Kumar and Meghand Desai eds., *The Economic History of India*, Vol. 2: c. 1757 - c. 1970, Cambridge: Cambridge University Press, 1983, p. 699.

② Ian Stone, *Canal Irrigation in British India: Perspectives on Technological Change in a Peasant Economy*, Cambridge: Cambridge Univerty Press, 1984, p. 29.

表 3 1902～1905 年恒河运河区主要灌溉面积及农作物年均增长率

单位：%

	恒河上游运河	东朱木纳河运河	恒河下游运河	阿格拉运河
小麦	40.1	39.4	40.3	30.2
其他冬季作物	17.5	7.4	25.8	17.2
甘蔗	17.2	21.2	4.0	4.1
稻米	3.8	16.3	3.2	—
棉花	8.9	2.9	8.9	40.9
靛青	2.9	—	3.5	—
大麦	2.6	4.1	4.2	—
其他作物	7.0	8.7	10.1	7.3
总灌溉面积（英亩）	889335	289938	737528	227309

资料来源：Ian Stone，*Canal Irrigation in British India*：*Perspectives on Technological Change in a Peasant Economy*，Cambridge：Cambridge Univerty Press，1984，Appendex 3，p. 352。

19 世纪 80 年代末开始，水利建设投资集中的另一个地区是印度河流域（旁遮普和信德）。旁遮普省这一时期发展最为迅速，1885～1947 年，灌溉面积从不到 300 万英亩扩展到将近 1400 万英亩。① 运河建设的快速扩张与组织移民、土地分配计划、市镇规划、铁路修建等配套措施兼顾，运河的不断延伸和农民持有地的规模增大，使这一地区成为南亚地区农业商业化程度最高的地区之一。

新建水利设施总体上分布在河流水量丰富便于利用的河间地区、西北印度和马德拉斯，在降雨量较少的西印度和中印度地区，灌溉设施仍旧维持原有的基本格局。② 在水利设施的建设过程中，除了自然地理条件和技术水平，土地私有制对水利设施的设计和扩张也产生了限制性影响。一些水利资源丰富的地区，掌握了某些水源的地主及土邦不愿意参与其中，政府往往要做出让步。在中央政府主导大型工程建设的时期，英印政府的决策经常得到英国议会任命的饥荒委员会和灌溉委员会的建议和推动。除了直接建设各种大型工程，英印政府还通过农业部为一些地方利用地下水、发展小型管井灌溉提供资助支持。1900 年后，饥荒极大减少，在政府的统计

① Imran Ali，*The Punjab under Imperialism 1885 - 1947*，Princeton University Press，1988，p. 10.

② 政府曾经通过为地主提供贷款的方式资助当地的水利设施，但是并没有大型工程实现跨流域调水。

中已经很难看到。1919 年的政府改革法案在 1921 年开始生效，教育卫生和农业发展任务被分配给各省。①

20 世纪 20 年代后，水利建设开始向美国学习，注重河流流域的总体治理和多功能开发，不再以农业灌溉为主，而是以发电和服务工业为主。以服务农业为主的水利设施建设高潮在 1921 年结束。水利建设成为各省负责的事务后，英印政府仍旧保留了对需要借款的大型工程的批准权。

对水利设施的公共投资为政府带来了稳定和长期的收益（见表 4）。第一次世界大战前，英印政府建设水利设施的地区，已经遍及包括缅甸在内的所有省份。一位参与水利设施建设的官员认为水利设施有 6 个方面的益处：村庄的产出提高，田赋增加，铁路运费收入增加，民众饥荒减少和痛苦减轻，水利设施的直接利润丰厚，良好的政治效应。②

表 4　灌溉的财政效应 1912 ~ 1913 年度至 1945 ~ 1946 年度

年度	资本支出（卢比）		灌溉面积（英亩）		净利润（%）	
	盈利工程	重大工程	盈利工程	重大工程	盈利工程	重大工程
1912 - 1916	579839535	676027710	15218969	15619661	8.3	4.5
1917 - 1920	598560412	715840834	17007650	17632422	9.0	4.7
1923 - 1927	730837855	1153167211	19106599	22083881	8.5	4.6
1928 - 1932	1001221334	1462375524	21313088	26375762	8.4	4.5
1933 - 1937	1114245641	1462589315	22612454	25882861	7.5	4.3
1938 - 1942	1021484853	1507376095	24391448	28504154	9.3	5.5
1943 - 1945	1039426970	1542139726	26417366	31639838	12.8	7.2

资料来源：Elizabeth Whitcomb，“Irrigation”，in Dharma Kumar and Meghand Desai eds.，*The Economic History of India*，Vol. 2：c. 1757 - c. 1970，Cambridge：Cambridge University Press，1983，p. 729。

水利设施对农业发展的直接影响，体现在改变了土地利用的方式和强度，这一改变在北印度地区最为显著。③ 水利设施发展的另一个重大影响是

① Dhama Kumar，“The Fiscal System”，in Dharma Kumar and Meghand Desai eds.，*The Economic History of India*，Vol. 2：c. 1757 - c. 1970，Cambridge：Cambridge University Press，1983，p. 911.

② John Benton，“Irrigation Works in India”，*The Journal of Royal Society of Arts*，June 13，1913，p. 738.

③ John F. Richards，Edward S. Haynes，James R. Hagen，“Changes in the Land and Human Productivity in Northern India”，*Agricultural History*，Vol. 59，no. 4（Oct. 1985），p. 528.

为农业贸易的结构性转变提供了条件。

三　农业贸易结构的转变

19 世纪前半期，印度农业出口项目主要是生丝、靛青、鸦片和茶叶。这些出口作物多半由种植园经济提供或者由政府垄断专卖控制，对农业经济的整体影响非常有限。农业贸易结构显示印度受到英国工业革命的影响十分有限，对外部经济世界的参与和联系较少（见表 5）。

表 5　印度农产品出口构成及占出口总值的比例（1811～1851 年）

单位：%

	靛青	布匹	生丝	原棉	鸦片	糖	总计
1811 - 1912	18.5	33.0	8.3	4.9	23.8	1.5	90.0
1814 - 1915	20.0	14.3	13.3	8.0	—	3.0	58.6
1828 - 1929	27.0	11.0	10.0	15.0	17.0	4.0	84.0
1834 - 1935	15.0	7.0	8.0	21.0	25.0	2.0	78.0
1839 - 1940	26.0	5.0	7.0	20.0	10.0	7.0	75.0
1850 - 1951	10.9	3.7	3.8	19.1	30.1	10.0	77.6

资料来源：K. N. Chaudhuri, "Foreign Trade and Balance of Payment (1757 - 1947)", in Dharma Kumar and Meghand Desai eds., *The Cambridge Economic History of India*, Vol. 2: c. 1757 - c. 1970, Cambridge: Cambridge University Press, 1983, p. 842。

19 世纪下半期，印度农业出口项目转变为大宗原材料产品和谷物，包括黄麻及黄麻制品、棉花及棉织品、各种粮食作物及蔗糖。棉花和粮食作物出口都是在加强农业经济基础之后发展起来的。棉花是印度农业适应世界经济体系最有代表性的例子。1850 年之前，印度棉花主要出口中国，作为鸦片贸易的补充。美国内战使英国对印度棉花需要大增，这一市场刺激当时虽然只是短期效应，但是印度棉花很快在欧洲大陆市场占据一席之地。出于价格和棉纺织技术的实际，欧洲大陆比英国的纺织厂更乐意使用印度棉花。印度出口到英国的棉花大约一半转运到了欧洲大陆。1900 年后，孟买成为日本棉纺织厂的主要原料来源。[①] 印度黄麻业受益于全世界海运业

① B. R. Tomlinson, *The Economy of Modern India*, Cambridge: Cambridge University Press, 1993, p. 53.

的发达。南亚的谷物出口主要是稻米和小麦，前者主要来自缅甸，后者来自印度西北部的旁遮普地区。废除谷物法之后，英国小麦市场开放，海外供应增加，最初主要来自美国和俄国。20世纪初，印度小麦开始在英国占据一席之地。1903～1904年度，旁遮普省出口英国的小麦占到了当年该地区总产量的37%，高达1136447吨[①]（见表6）。19世纪下半期及20世纪前半期印度农业农产品出口的结构转变说明，印度农业已经成为世界经济体系的一个重要组成部分，并且与英国、欧洲、日本的工业化进程存在紧密的联系。

表6　印度农业出口及占总出口的份额（1860～1936）

单位：%

年份	原棉	棉制品	靛青	粮食	生麻	麻制品	毛皮	鸦片	油料作物	茶叶
1860～1861	22.3	2.4	5.7	10.2	1.2	1.1	2.0	30.9	5.4	0.5
1870～1871	35.2	2.5	5.8	8.1	4.7	0.6	3.7	19.5	6.4	2.1
1880～1881	17.8	4.2	4.8	17.1	5.2	1.5	5.0	18.2	8.6	4.2
1890～1891	16.5	9.5	3.1	19.5	7.6	2.5	4.7	9.2	9.3	5.5
1900～1901	9.4	6.4	2.0	13.1	10.1	7.3	10.7	8.8	8.3	9.0
1910～1911	17.2	6.0	0.2	18.4	7.4	8.1	6.2	6.1	12.0	5.9
1920～1921	17.4	7.6	—	10.7	6.8	22.1	3.5	—	7.0	5.1
1930～1931	21.0	1.6	—	13.5	5.8	14.5	5.3	—	8.1	10.7
1935～1936	21.0	1.3	—	—	8.5	14.5	—	—	—	12.3

资料来源：K. N. Chaudhuri, "Foreign Trade and Balance of Payment (1757 - 1947)", in Dharma Kumar and Meghand Desai eds., *The Cambridge Economic History of India*, Vol. 2: c. 1757 - c. 1970, Cambridge: Cambridge University Press, 1983, p. 844。

综上所述，印度水利设施建设是殖民当局恢复农业秩序、使南亚农业与外部经济世界建立联系的媒介，也是部分地区农业商业化和农业发展的技术前提。从水利设施的修建过程来看，无论是地方政府还是英印政府都受制于资金和权力的限制，将农业的赢利性置于可持续性之上。从水利设施的管理方式来看，殖民当局在田赋之外又开辟了稳定且具持续性的收入

① H. Calvert, *The Wealth and Welfare of the Punjab*, Lahore: Civil and Military Gazetter Press, 1922, p. 156.

来源。这一过程中水利设施的管理方式加强了殖民当局对农业的榨取能力，也增强了殖民统治基础。对殖民统治而言重要的是“法律”“秩序”“公正”，最后才是“重视穷人”。[①] 对于重建水资源与农业发展的关系而言，这是一场代价昂贵的试验。

① James Willson, “The Punjab”, *The Journal of Royal Society of Arts*, December 24, 1909, p. 139.

西班牙埃赛克亚灌溉遗产：一个水文明缩影的考察

郑晓云，Martinez－Sanmartin（西班牙）*

摘　要：本文实地考察了西班牙瓦伦西亚及其周边地区现存的埃赛克亚灌溉系统。结合三个城乡和瓦伦西亚水法庭的实例，考察了这一古老灌溉系统的历史和现状，揭示了这个古老灌溉系统在当地自然环境改良过程中所起到的积极作用，尤其是在干旱沙漠地区治理过程中所发挥的重要作用。同时也通过瓦伦西亚水法庭考察了这个灌溉系统的管理机制。通过对技术和制度两个方面的考察，并结合当地的历史发展过程，揭示了这个灌溉系统的特征及其可持续价值。对于我们理解当地的环境治理，尤其是欧洲干旱沙漠治理的历史和现状有较高的价值，同时也有助于我们理解水在人类文明传承传播中所扮演的重要角色。

关键词：埃赛克亚　灌溉　干旱　遗产　西班牙

Abstract: Based on the field work, this article investigated the subsistent Acequia irrigation system in Valencia, Spain. With three cases of the urban and rural areas, the history and current situation of the Acequia, and its active action in the process of the improvement of the local environment, especially its role in the local drought management are investigated. Simultaneously, the institutional mechanism of irrigation management was also investigated by visit of Valencia Water Tribunal. Accordingly, based on the aspects of technological and institutional visits, this article revealed the features and sustainable values of Acequia in Va-

* 郑晓云，湖北大学历史文化学院特聘教授。Martinez－Sanmartin，前任国际水历史学会主席、法国水科学院院士、西班牙加泰罗尼亚自治政府文化遗产监管局研究员。

lencia. It is valuable for us to understand the local environmental improvement by water management, especially the history and current situation of drought management in Europe.

Keywords: Acequia; Irrigation; Drought; Heritage; Spain

在西班牙地中海海岸地区，存在着一种典型的古老农业灌溉系统：埃赛克亚（Acequia）。[①] 埃赛克亚灌溉系统是一种主要通过筑坝拦截河水，修建坝后引水渠将河水引到生活和农业灌溉区，辅之以一套完整的管理制度的水利系统。埃赛克亚灌溉系统最早起源于中亚地区，后来由阿拉伯人传入伊比利亚半岛，对伊比利亚半岛的农业生产发展起到了关键的作用。在16世纪以后，埃赛克亚灌溉系统再由西班牙人传入北、南美洲的一些国家。埃赛克亚穿越文明和时空，对人类历史发展产生了重要的影响。难能可贵的是这一古老的灌溉系统今天仍然发挥着作用，无论在西班牙还是在墨西哥北部、东北部和美国的西部，都还能寻觅到它的踪迹，尤其是在西班牙地中海岸的瓦伦西亚地区，埃赛克亚今天仍然在滋养着当地的自然和社会。为了理解这个灌溉系统的历史背景、作用及其管理制度，笔者在2018年前往西班牙瓦伦西亚地区进行了10天的实地考察。

一　波特瑞斯市（Potries）：埃赛克亚的缩影

波特瑞斯市距离瓦伦西亚市区约70千米，是一个有古老农业灌溉传统的城市。城市规模不大，干净而幽静，具有西班牙典型小城镇的建筑风格。

波特瑞斯市现存的引水灌溉系统即埃赛克亚灌溉系统，建于公元8～13世纪阿拉伯人统治当地时期，使当地的农业灌溉得到了较大的提升。今天这个灌溉系统仍然保留着13世纪以来的原有风貌，并且仍然在运作。这里的引水渠在距离城市约2千米处，人们在赛皮斯河上修建了拦水坝。这是一个石头修建的滚水大坝，从靠近城市的一侧修建了引水渠口，将大坝拦截的水通过引水渠引到城市和农田中，成为当地最重要的生活与生产性水资

① Acequia一词源于阿拉伯语，是水沟渠的意思。但acequia并非泛指水渠，而有特定的意思，仅指在西班牙伊比利亚半岛上的阿拉伯时期以后的灌溉系统及与此相关的美洲西班牙人居住区的灌溉系统。

源。这条引水渠称为瑞依埃引水渠，由于它在当地的重要性，在历史上曾被命名为“阿尔科伊皇家引水渠”（Royal Acequia of Alcoi）。

这条引水渠最著名的是它的分水系统。在引水渠进入平地以后，人们在河流上建立了第一个分水设施卡萨－佛斯卡（Casa Fosca）分水站。从卡萨－佛斯卡分水站出来的水被分为两条支渠。为了公平分配水资源，人们在主渠上面建设了一座石头圆拱形顶的建筑，类似一座房子，使分水的设施保持封闭状态（见图1）。从石头房子的窗口，可以看到里面在渠道上建有一排石质的水闸门，每个闸门高约50厘米，宽约30厘米，一共有48道门，将水分为48行，人们可以开闭这些闸门，这样就可以根据需要控制水的流量，让水按照人们议定的流量被分到外面的两条水渠中。修建石头房子把分水器封闭起来的目的，就是为了不让人们随意改变水的流量。

图1　水渠上的分水设施

过去管理分水设施有严格的规定。人们不能随意进入分水站调节水量。在今天的市政厅大厅里可以看到一道外面包上铁皮的大木门，上面安了5把锁。这一道木门就是一个分水站的大门，每一把锁的钥匙由灌溉渠中不同灌区农户的代表掌握。这意味着这条引水渠下游一共分为5个灌溉区，每个灌区掌握一把钥匙，只有当5个灌区的代表同时在场，分水房的门才能被打开，并且可以调节水流量，这样做是为了保证水量分配的公平，以保障水能够到达灌区的每一块农田。这道大门作为当地水资源管理的一个重要文物得到妥善保存，是历史上人们科学公正管理水资源的重要实证。同时，当地的农民组成了相关的协会，处置水权争议，协调水资源的分配，维护水利设施。通过制定相关的规则，明确用水人的权利和义务、数量等。

另外一座分水站是建在其中一条支渠上的卡萨－克拉那分水站（Casa Clara）（见图 2）。这一座分水站初建于 14 世纪，在 1511 年被重建。这一分水站上面建有 4 道石质的围墙将里面的分水口包围住，没有顶，目的只在于让分水口处于封装状态。围墙长 10 米、宽 24 米，只留下两个小孔可以观察内部。渠道中的水通过两个孔进入分水站，由于分水站较宽，水流面也相应变宽，水流缓慢地通过分水站中的石头水闸门，被分为 48 行。水流出分水站之后，除了分出几条小支流流入附近的农地之外，再被分成两条大的水渠，分别流向两个下游的城镇刚地亚（Gandia）与欧利瓦（Oliva），这是分水站建有高大围墙的原因，主要还是保障水流分配的公平，不被人随意调节分水量。这座分水站的门上有两把锁，分别由两个城镇的代表持有两把钥匙，只有他们同时在场的时候才能打开门，调节里面水的分配量。最终，一条引水渠经历了上百次的公平分配，将水引入每一块田地中，这就是它的奇妙之处。

图 2　分水站内景

二　埃尔切市（Elche）：埃赛克亚与沙漠绿洲的变迁

埃尔切市位于干旱沙漠地区，地表是山地，除了河谷地带以外树木稀少，都是沙漠岩石地貌。然而当人们跨越山丘到达这座城市边缘的时候，就可以看到沙漠山丘环抱中是一片广阔的平原绿洲，在平原中有茂盛的棕榈树林，城市和农田都掩映在棕榈树林之中，呈现出了一种沙漠绿洲的典型景观。这实际上是一个人们在历史上改造沙漠所形成的人工奇迹，埃尔切椰枣园也在2000 年被列入了联合国教科文组织世界遗产名录。

由于伊比利亚半岛属于地中海气候，冬天温暖，夏天酷热，水资源的获得主要是靠降雨。这里夏天不是炎热干旱就是可能遭受暴雨洪灾，因此在当地沙漠地带中的降雨条件下是不可能确保农业生产获得丰收的，这就需要修建灌溉系统进行引水灌溉，确保农业生产能够有正常的灌溉用水。当地最大的河流维那罗波河的水量仅仅能够维持河道的存在，并且是咸水。

图 3　沙漠绿洲埃尔切

公元 8 世纪阿拉伯人和柏柏人到达这个地区以后，他们开始修建新的水利灌溉系统，这个系统集合了其传统的历史智慧、经验和知识，同时也吸收了其他民族最好的水利技术，从而融合创造了适应当地的水利灌溉系统。

这个水利系统集合了美索不达米亚、埃及、希腊、罗马、印度和阿拉伯人的文化，因此更加显现其创新性。同时也引种了很多耐旱、耐盐的植物进行种植，如椰枣、石榴、苜蓿等。到了公元10世纪和11世纪，灌溉系统得到了大规模的发展，并且改变了当地整个农业灌溉的面貌，甚至是自然景观，在沙漠中建起了一个绿洲（见图3）。

在公元13世纪初，今天西班牙人的先民战胜阿拉伯人开始统治这一地区，但是他们并没有摧毁此地宏大并且实用的灌溉系统，而是将这些灌溉系统较好地继承下来，仍然保持着阿拉伯人的水利灌溉模式，并加以扩大，继续支撑着后世的农业社会发展。

阿拉伯人在公元10世纪左右修建的拦水坝今天仍然存在。在茂密的树林遮掩之下的水坝历经近千年，今天仍然可以看到清澈的河水慢慢流过石坝（见图4）。这个水坝是一个滚水坝，长约20米，完全用石条筑成，石坝抬高了河流的水位，让侧面的引水渠将水引到渠道之中，然后流向河谷平原。这个水坝虽然不大，但是千年来为当地的沙漠绿洲默默做出了不可磨灭的奉献，在其他大坝修建以前，这是涵养埃尔切沙漠绿洲的主要水源，因此除了实用价值以外，还具有宝贵的历史和文化价值。

图4　公元10世纪阿拉伯人修建的水坝

从进入城市的跨河大桥向上游行走大约4千米，就可以看到一个巨大的水库，这个水库的形成是大坝建设的结果。顺着水库边沿行走，水库四周都是茂密的树林，在水库的水源地带还形成了较大的湿地，成为干旱沙漠中的一个亮丽的景观。来到水库的出水处，就可以看到这座潘塔诺大坝（Dam Pantano de Elche）（见图5）。大坝宽约200米、高50米。大坝的建设非常独特，不是直的坝体，而是两道大坝形成一个底部对着河流下游的扇型，其中一半的坝体是直接建在河道中的一块巨大的岩石上，对内成圆拱形，另外一面大坝则是直的。大坝是滚水坝，河水从大坝两侧坝顶上翻滚而下，再从岩石上流下来，成为一道令人叹为观止的美妙景观，据说这也是世界上最美的大坝之一。大坝的侧面就是这个城市主要的引水渠，将水引到平原干旱河谷中，浇灌农田，哺养城市。由于这一座大坝的修建，当地引水渠引导水量较过去翻了几番，这就使得河谷洲的绿洲获得了更大面积的灌溉，这也是西班牙人在继承了当年阿拉伯人的水利遗产之后的拓展。总之，今天来到埃尔切地区，所看到的已经不再是沙漠山丘，而是被大面积的椰枣树林为主的树木覆盖的绿洲。不仅城市掩映在椰枣树林中，四周的农田也被树木所包围，一条条灌溉渠道穿行其中，农作物得以生长，成为一个人工创造的伊甸园（见图6）。

图5　潘塔诺大坝

图6　绿洲中的水渠

三　古老的农村生活用水设施

除了农业灌溉以外，埃赛克亚引水渠设施也提供了人们的生活用水，生活用水设施也同样充满着智慧，成为在欧洲大陆上具有阿拉伯特征的水利景观。

在奥尔莫斯市（Aras de los Olmos）遗留有阿拉伯时代的水利文化遗产，包括灌溉系统和社会生活用水设施，其中较早的生活用水设施建于16世纪。完整的日用生活水设施，包括出水的喷泉、供人们取饮用水和牲畜饮水、日常洗涤等多种设施。总的建筑使用原则是顺序用水，喷泉中流出的水首先进入第一个池子供人们取饮用水，水流进第二个池子让牲口饮水，随后进入一个大的洗衣房之后，有个大的池子供人们洗衣服，最后的水流进水沟用于灌溉农田（见图7）。

这个用水设施的第一部分，是一个传统希腊式的喷泉建筑，墙面上有泉水流出的出口，下面是一个水池。泉水在通过喷泉建筑之后，流进了一个四五米长的水槽，这个地方过去是骡马饮水的地方。随后，建有一个30平方米左右的洗衣房。洗衣房是开放的，中间有一个供人们洗衣服的水池，泉水被吸虹设施吸进中间的水池中，水池的四边有40厘米左右宽的台边，

图7 中世纪遗留下的农村用水设施

供人们在上面搓揉衣服。历经数百年，今天这个水设施仍然流出清澈的泉水，流经不同的用水段建筑物，最后进入长达数千米的水沟用于灌溉农田。每天到村中的水池取水、洗衣服的最多的是妇女，这个场所也是人们社交的场所。男人们只有下午才会带着牲口去饮水。洗衣服最繁忙的时间是每周的星期一，因为这一天人们会把星期天换下来的衣物和家庭用品拿来洗涤。这种传统一直沿袭到20世纪六七十年代，由于城市供水系统的改进而使用管道供水，才使这个设施渐渐淡出人们的生活。但是由于在家庭里较大的生活用品，例如床上的床垫不方便使用洗衣机，有一些妇女至今仍然来到这里洗涤大件的物品。这是一个典型的民间生活用水设施，这种用水的设施在当地普遍存在，使人们的生活用水更加科学、规范，成为人们生活中重要的组成部分。

四　瓦伦西亚水法庭与灌溉管理

瓦伦西亚的水法庭是世界上最古老的法庭，也是保障埃赛克亚灌溉系统得到正常运行的行政机制。它最初建立于公元960年前后，而正式成立则是在公元1238年，以征服了瓦伦西亚王国的阿拉伯统治者豪西一世颁布成立水法庭的法令为标志。法令要求水法庭将阿拉伯人的水管理制度在当地建立起来并延续下去，因此这个水法庭的职能和它的管理方式，与阿拉伯人到达伊比利亚半岛以后推行的埃赛克亚灌溉系统是相一致的，它维护了这个系统的正常运作。水法庭的职能就是保障当地的水资源在农田中公平分配，以及引水渠道的正常运作。水法庭每个星期四中午12点开庭一次，当场解决有关水资源和农田灌溉的争执（见图8）。

图8　瓦伦西亚水法庭

水法庭的建立与当地的自然和社会经济发展是一致的，它适应了瓦伦西亚周边灌溉平原（西班牙语称为Huerta）、农田和果园的需要和这些农地所有权的状况。瓦伦西亚的气候非常干旱，虽然当地靠近地中海，但是每年平均降雨量只有400～500毫米，尤其是夏天干旱少雨。因此，对于农业生产来说，水利灌溉就显得非常重要。瓦伦西亚冲积平原主要是由图利亚河（River Turia）形成，但是在阿拉伯人到来之前，图利亚河水资源的利用非常有限。在阿拉伯人到来之前的公元2世纪，罗马人就已经来到这里开拓农业，并且也修建了大型的引水渠等设施，但是由于受到水资源条件的限制，主要的农业生产区域限制在当地潟湖地区的沼泽地和一部分河流湿地，在其他地方的农业发展非常有限。公元10世纪阿拉伯人到达这个地区之后，除了带来了新的社会组织方式以外，最重要的就是带来了先进的水利技术——埃赛克亚水利灌溉技术。通过这个灌溉系统，从图利亚河修建引水渠引水，建立起一个覆盖广阔的引水沟渠网络，健全了相应的水管理制度和管理组织，使当地的农业灌溉得到了较大的改进，从而也使得有灌溉条件的农地面积得到扩大，促进了农业生产。目前在瓦伦西亚主要有 8 条引水渠，将图利亚河的水输送到了每一块农田。在河流两岸的引水渠之间，相互有很多支渠将临近的引水渠连接起来，形成一个复杂的沟渠网络，以保证每一块农田都能够得到灌溉。这 8 条引水渠的灌溉区域在瓦伦西亚市的半径 15 千米左右，灌溉面积约为 13000 公顷。

到了公元 14 世纪，由于引水渠的大量修建，使得瓦伦西亚平原的农田面积迅速扩大，尤其是过去靠近海边的低洼地区开辟了很多新的农田，在潟湖周围很多被遗弃的沼泽农地也重新被开发为农田，这一时期瓦伦西亚冲积平原农田面积增加了 20% 。但是从 15 世纪一直到 18 世纪，这里大多数的耕地属于教会和贵族。一直到 19 世纪早期，经历了一系列的社会变革之后，这里的大多数农田才慢慢变成了小农户和新兴资产阶级的财产，人们通过各种方式购买了当地的土地而成为业主。尤其是到了 20 世纪中叶，这里形成了一个非常有趣的现象，土地大多数成为零散的小农户的财产，农民们都有自己的土地，80% 的农地中独立产权单位面积都不超过 1/3 公顷，也就是说总农地的 80% 是由每一块产权面积不超过 1/3 公顷的零散的土地构成的，其他 10% 的独立产权农地产权面积超过 1/2 公顷的土地很少，土地被分成了非常碎片化的产权单位，从而形成了非常复杂的土地产权关系。

为了保障农业生产，水是其中的关键因素，甚至是决定一块土地能否耕种和销售价值的决定性因素，没有水一块农田就没有价值。因此在当时，买卖土地甚至不是以土地的面积为基准的，而是以水权为基准的，买卖一块土地实际上就是买卖这块土地上的水权，农田是以灌溉权来出售的。因此这种土地分散的权属关系更加剧了水资源分配的复杂性，要使水能够到达每一块土地，就需要每一个土地产权者通力合作，遵守规则。水资源管理的目的，就是要使水资源能够得到公平的分配，能够灌溉每一块农田。

水法庭的产生，正是为了适应水资源分配的要求，保障水资源能够得到公平有效的分配。水法庭有两重职能：一是司法职能，二是行政职能。

司法职能负责水权纠纷的判决，处置判决有关水资源的案件，而行政职能负责水资源的管理工作，包括水资源状况的检查、灌溉网络的维护、收缴费用等。

水法庭由 8 名法官组成。这 8 名法官分别来自于 8 条引水渠（见图 9）。每一条引水渠都有自己的管理组织，由农户选择出一个行政性的管理协会，这个协会负责协调本引水渠的日常事务，包括水资源的分配、水沟渠的维护、缴纳费用等。每一条引水渠的管理协会都会选出一个会长，这个会长必须满足三个条件，一是他必须是使用水资源的农户，拥有自己的土地；二是他必须自己务农，而不能是土地出租者；三是他拥有的土地在当地是面积较大的，能够满足自己的生存需要。当然，这其中很重要的因素，就是他必须拥有较大的水权，同时为人公道，有一定的文化，能够代表大家说话办事。会长任职年限根据不同引水渠协会的规则要求不同，每一届 2～3 年，可以连选连任。一条引水渠协会的会长，就当然成为水法庭八位法官之一，除了日常的引水渠管理职责以外，在水法庭担任法官是他更重要的职责。

图 9　水法庭外的喷泉，8 个少女雕像代表了 8 条引水渠

五　结论与启示

通过对瓦伦西亚地区埃塞克亚灌溉系统的考察，我们可以看到这种灌溉技术自传入伊比利亚半岛一千多年来，在当地获得了不断改进和发展，对于当地的环境改良和经济发展起到了重要的作用。这一灌溉系统的源头来自于中亚，但是在伊比利亚半岛能够生根，取代原有的罗马帝国灌溉系统而获得发展，就在于其切合了当地的自然条件，通过河流引水，建设大规模的细小水沟渠，满足了农地灌溉的需要。同时与灌溉配套的管理制度的健全，使灌溉系统能够长期有效运行。这个灌溉系统在当地起到了两个方面的重要效应：一是有效地改善了当地的自然环境。对于瓦伦西亚周边的干旱沙漠地区来说，有效的灌溉改变了自然环境，把干旱沙漠变成了一个绿洲。时至今日，埃塞克亚灌溉系统仍然是当地应对干旱和沙漠化的重要基础。对于瓦伦西亚中部的沼泽地区来说，它有效地减轻了历史上的洪涝问题，通过沟渠建设将沼泽地区的水加以合理利用或排入潟湖。二是有效改善了当地农业生产环境，使农业获得了发展，这一地区的干旱沙漠和沼泽变成了西班牙重要的农业丰产区。这两方面的功能，对今天的瓦伦西亚地区仍然十分重要。

从这一个案的考察中我们可以获得以下几点启示。第一，瓦伦西亚地方灌溉发展的历史证明，成功的灌溉发展对于改造当地的自然环境，创造有利的人居条件非常重要，同时对于地方社会、经济、文化的发展也同样起到了重要的促进作用。类似的案例在世界各地虽然都可以找到，但是瓦伦西亚埃塞克亚灌溉系统堪称典范，因为它不仅是多种文明相结合的产物，同时也产生了巨大的影响。在16世纪西班牙人殖民美洲时，将这个灌溉系统的技术和制度移植到了美洲干旱半干旱沙漠地区，成为当地西班牙人生存的重要基础。时至今日，这种灌溉系统在中南美洲仍然大量存在，同时也被传到了菲律宾。从这个实例中，我们可以理解水利在地方文明发展进程中所扮演的重要角色。

第二，从埃塞克亚灌溉系统中我们也可以看到，技术和制度是车之两轮，拥有先进的技术，更需要有科学有效的管理制度相配合。埃塞克亚灌溉系统，正是完美结合了制度和技术两个方面。当地的社会组织构建基本上都是基于灌溉系统，完善的管理组织和制度保障了引水沟渠的有效运行，在这个过程中，农民对于水渠的制度制定与管理维护有充分的参与。参与性的管理成为埃塞克亚灌溉系统核心的制度基础，做到了水资源管理的公正、透明。因此，基层水利的建设，制度不可缺失。

第三，埃塞克亚灌溉系统是一种可持续的水利灌溉系统，在今天仍然具有不可忽略的价值。埃塞克亚灌溉系统利用自然引力驱动整个系统的灌溉并运行了一千多年，今天虽然当地城市供水及现代农业灌溉技术已经获得了发展，但埃塞克亚灌溉系统低成本和可持续性，在当地的社会生活和经济发展中仍然起着重要的作用。因此现代的水利发展不应该取代传统水利工程，今天仍然应该正视传统水利工程的价值。只要有良好的制度存在，传统的灌溉系统仍然有长期存在的价值。

水信仰

明清云南龙王庙信仰和地域分布

江　燕*

摘　要：龙王庙是历史上官府祭祀及民众遇旱祈雨的地方，香火往往十分鼎盛，是重要非物质文化遗产。本文拟从现存明清云南通志所记龙王庙史料文献入手，梳理明清时期云南龙王庙分布概况，探寻古代云南先民如何依托山川河流地域优势所形成的以龙王庙祠祀活动为中心的自然观、生态观、民俗观、文化观，以及民心相通、多民族和谐共处的社会价值观，为水历史文明发展变迁及水文化遗产的保护传承，提供新的文献依据。

关键词：明清时期　龙王庙　信仰

Abstract: The Dragon - king shrines, where both the Chinese officials and the commoners prayed for rain during drought, were highly revered religious venues, and constitute important cultural heritages at current time. Based on both Ming dynasty and Qing dynasty's historical documents on Yunnan's Dragon - king shrines, this article learns about the Dragon - king shrines' geographic distribution in Yunnan, and explores how Yunnan's natural surroundings had shaped the Yunnan forefathers' views on nature, ecology, cultures, inter - ethnic harmony centered around Dragon - king shrine worship. This article offers new materials for studying the development of water - civilization and for the water - cultural heritages' preservation.

Keywords: Ming and Qing Dynasties; Dragon - king Temple; belief

---

* 江燕，云南省社科院宗教研究所研究员。

一 云南龙王庙的信仰

大宗伯，周官名，春官之长，职掌祭祀、典礼等事。《周礼·春官·宗伯第三》对大宗伯之职作了详细叙述。

> 掌建邦之天神人鬼地示之礼，以佐王建保邦国，以吉礼事邦国之鬼神，以禋祀祀昊天上帝，以实柴祀日月星辰，以槱燎祀司中、司命、飌师、雨师，以血祭祭社稷五祀五岳，以貍沈祭山林川泽，以疈辜祭四方百物。

中国是农耕社会，每年农历五月，多地正是夏潦水涨的季节，为祈求大水不将水稻淹没，每年的这个时候都要祭神，也就慢慢形成了与水有关的很多节日和祠祀活动。中国古代以农历三月上旬的第一个巳日为“上巳”，旧俗以此日在水边洗濯污垢，祭祀祖先，叫作“祓禊”“修禊”。魏晋以后，上巳节固定在三月三日。历史上，云南曲靖陆凉州曾多次遭遇大水，明清文献记载不下 15 次，甚至因大水为害不得不迁城，“永乐四年丙戌(1406 年)，大水由西北淹城，建城方经八年而水患屡侵，故议迁今城。永乐六年戊子（1408 年），迁城今址，以石递年修筑，经二十余年工始毕”。[①]

明洪武元年（1368 年），朱元璋下令天下郡县皆置山川坛，“三年(1370 年)，革前代岳渎封号，惟以山川本名称其神。六年（1373 年），礼部议祭风云雷雨及境内山川城隍，共为一坛。春秋二仲上巳日祭，各郡县同。嘉靖九年（1530 年），奉制更神之序，曰云雨风雷”。[②] 自此全国由礼部议祭风云雷雨及境内山川城隍，春秋二仲上巳日祭，各郡县同。《祠祀志》设“云雨风雷山川坛”，记载地方官吏定期率绅众致祭之礼。朝廷最高统治者颁布命令，中央部门亲自管理，各级地方官吏依例遵循，从而形成一整套礼敬自然、尊崇山水的政府主导、群众广泛参与的隆重盛大的祭祀

① （清）沈生遴纂修：乾隆《陆凉州志》卷五《杂志·祲祥》，陆良县地方志办公室据乾隆十七年（1752 年）石印本校注，云南人民出版社，2014，第 313 页。

② （明）刘文征撰：天启《滇志》卷十六《祠祀志·祀典·云南府》，古永继点校，云南教育出版社，1991，第 543 页。

活动。清朝因之，通省府属各州县皆与府同。光绪《云南通志》卷八十八《祠祀志一・典祀一》明确记载云南建坛，当在明洪武十四年（1381 年）既入版图后，称“风云雷雨”，嘉庆十八年（1813 年），改称“云雨风雷”。

山有仙则名，水有龙则灵，历史上龙王庙都是官府祭祀及民众遇旱祈雨的地方，香火十分鼎盛。中国远古有禹王舍家治水，民间有龙王崇拜，都成为华夏世界的非物质文化遗产。据史载，龙王庙源于唐宋，初称五龙庙、龙神庙，唐玄宗开元二年（714 年），诏祠龙池，右拾遗蔡孚献《龙池篇》。又诏置坛及祠堂，每仲春将祭则奏之。宋京城东，旧有五龙祠，因唐礼行具祀，用中祀礼。又城西南隅有九龙堂，赐名普济堂。宋徽宗大观四年（1110 年），诏封英灵顺济龙王为灵顺昭应安济王。是年八月诏，天下五龙神皆封王爵：青龙神封广仁王，赤龙神封嘉泽王，黄龙神封孚应王，白龙神封义济王，黑龙神封灵泽王。[1] 从此，龙神庙又称龙王庙。

《大清会典》对龙王庙祭祀在时间、仪式、祭品方面有明确规制，亦使地方龙神祠祭祀有了参照标准。

> 雍正二年（1724 年），敕封四海龙王之神，东曰显仁、南曰昭明、西曰正恒、北曰崇礼。遣官赍送香帛，地方官致祭。五年（1727 年），分送各直省龙王神象，建庙奉祀。乾隆二十四年（1759 年），贵州巡抚周人骥请定外省龙神祠祭祀日期。经礼部议复，照在京致祭龙神祠，于春秋仲月辰日致祭。祭品、仪注悉照永定河神庙之制，先期斋戒一日，不理刑名。用帛一、爵三、簠簋各二、笾豆各十、羊一、豕一。行三跪九叩礼。《祝文》：维　年　月　日，具官某，谨以牲、帛、醴齐、粢盛庶品之仪，致祭于龙王之神曰：惟神德洋寰海，泽润苍生。允襄水土之平，经流顺轨；广济泉源之用，膏雨及时。绩奏安澜，占大川之利涉；功资育物，欣庶类之蕃昌。仰藉神庥，宜隆报享；谨遵祀典，恪按良辰；敬布几筵，肃陈牲币。尚飨！[2]

龙王或在天，或在渊，福善祸恶，莫测其妙，士民无不崇重。敬水就

① 《文献通考》（影印文渊阁四库全书本）卷九十《郊社考・杂祠淫祠》。

② （清）陈奇典修，刘慥纂：乾隆《永北府志》卷十五《祠祀・龙王庙》，乾隆三十年（1765 年）刻本，第 47 页。

要保护水环境，畏水则要通过宗教祭祀等途径来达到与自然的沟通。云南嵩明民间将此节称为三月头龙节，即农历三月第一个属龙的日子所举办的节日。水民间信仰，是云南水文化重要组成部分，也是云南传统文化的重要组成部分。云南历史上有蒙氏之先女子沙壹触龙生九子的神话，最早见于东汉杨终《哀牢传》，惜已佚。现存记载最早的是东晋常璩《华阳国志·南中志》。

> 永昌郡，古哀牢国。哀牢，山名也。其先有一妇人，名曰沙壶，依哀牢山下居，以捕鱼自给。忽于水中触一沈木，遂感而有娠。度十月，产子男十人。后沈木化为龙，出谓沙壶曰：若为我生子，今在乎？而九子惊走，惟一小子不能去，倍（古通“背”）龙坐。龙就而舐之。沙壶与言语，以龙与倍坐，因名曰元隆，犹汉言倍坐也。沙壶将元隆居龙山下。元隆长大，才武。后九兄曰：元隆能与龙言，而黠有智，天所贵也。共推以为王。时哀牢山下，复有一夫一妇产十女，元隆兄弟妻之。由是始有人民。[①]

永昌府城另有九隆山、九隆池。池之上，则有龙王庙，永乐三年（1405年）明佥事刘寅撰记。

明大理李元阳将此传说载入《怪异》名曰“浮木感娠”。

> 九隆氏之先有蒙迦独者，一云低牟苴，阿育王第三子骠苴低之子也。分土于永昌，其妻摩梨羌，名沙壹，世居哀牢山下。蒙迦独尝捕鱼，死哀牢山水中，不获尸。沙壹往哭于此，见一木浮而来，妇坐其上，甚安。明日往视之，触木如故，遂尝浣絮其上，若有感，因妊，产十子。一日，往池边，忽浮木化为龙，语曰：若为我生子，今悉何在？众子惊走，惟季子不能去，背龙而坐，龙因舐其背。其母鸟语，谓背为九，谓坐为隆，遂名曰九隆。其十子：一曰眉附罗，二曰牟苴兼，三曰牟苴诺，四曰牟苴酬，五曰牟苴笃，六曰牟苴托，七曰牟苴林，八曰牟苴颂，九曰牟苴闪，十即九隆也。九隆长而黠智，尝有天乐奏、凤凰栖、五色花开之祥，众遂推为酋长。时哀牢山下有奴波息者生十女，九隆兄弟娶之，

---

① （晋）常璩著，任乃强校注《华阳国志校补图注》，上海古籍出版社，2007，第284页。

厥后种类蔓延，各相分据溪谷，是为六诏之始也。[①]

为安放龙神祇，云南各地建有很多祠庙，以供信徒膜拜，而记述其兴造之缘由、经过、捐资者的金石碑刻众多，反映了一定历史时期当地的经济、文化发展水平。据《云南金石目略初稿》[②] 题录，可知楚雄黑盐井龙王祠原有康熙三十三年（1694 年）提举王策撰、岁贡杨璿书《七局村龙神祠碑》拓片，惜未访得。今存有武康臣撰、施光灿书，道光十七年（1837 年）立《重修七局村龙神祠碑记》，碑现存楚雄黑井中学，高 69 厘米，宽 96 厘米，楷书直行。重修碑文记述了黑井西北有七局山，山顶有龙潭，碧水一泓，灌田千顷，原建七局龙祠一所，内祀龙王，“其形九首，或曰即所谓九头金介如意大自在龙王也。左女像，亦九首，或曰龙女也，右有神，青面赤目，或曰蟹神也，兴云沛雨，泽被一方，相传为井主龙”。此龙神祠始建于元代，旧有修建碑铭，历年既久，剥落摧残，明宣德初膺“九头金盖如意大自在龙王”封号，春秋礼祀，凡有祈祷，其应如响。弘治六年（1493 年），淫雨连霄，围垣倾摧，太和人赵信、洪斌等募卤民金帛重修。道光十七年（1837 年），西江进士刘石生又倡修，使龙之灵有以安其宅。

民以食为天，田以水为利。“圣人治于世也，其枢在水”。作为人的生命之源、生存之本，社会的生产之基、生活之要，水在治国理政中有着不可替代的重要作用和影响，历代水患与人类文明的兴起、王朝命运息息相关，紧密相连。我国河流名称，多具有含义，如黄河、红河则以水色；怒江、盘江则因水势；金沙江、珠江则由水产。云南是全国水资源最为丰富的省份之一，但 2009 年遭受的持续干旱，对人民生产生活造成的巨大损失，使我们对当前所面临的水危机有了更清醒认识。清代孙髯翁“天下第一长联”《大观楼长联》描述的“汉习楼船、唐标铁柱、宋挥玉斧、元跨革囊”云南重大历史事件，与江河山水都密不可分。特别是云南六大水系中有四条为跨境河流，分别是独龙江 - 伊洛瓦底江、怒江 - 萨尔温江、澜沧江 - 湄公河、元江 - 红河，它们将云南同南亚东南亚国家连接为命运共同体，

① （明）李元阳纂：万历《云南通志》卷十七《杂志·怪异》，刘景毛、江燕等校注，中国文联出版社，2013，第 1536 页。

② （民国）李根源编，李希泌校《云南金石目略初稿》卷三，苏州葑门曲石精庐，1935，第 10 页。

“山脉变幻难定，必以水为断”,[①] 历史上云南府州厅县划分及与邻国边界，多以江河为界，明确江河流域所属，在国家安全和边疆防线中有着重要的历史参考价值和现实指导意义。由此应运而生的云南龙王庙祠祀活动普遍而广泛，就不足为奇。

二　云南龙王庙地域分布

“滇处天末，声教所讫，薄海皆同，圣天子崇德报功，特隆其礼。今取例得官为致祭者为一类，曰《典祀》，即以见俎豆馨香，义各有当，司其事者，莫不恭虔以蕲致其诚敬焉。”[②] “故志《祀典》，而以《群祀》[③] 系之，所以广恭敬也。”[④]《礼经》所载，释奠于先圣先师及山川社稷、五祀八蜡之祭，皆《祀典》之正。古代大祀、中祀以下列在祀典的祭祀，为群祀。民间习俗相沿立为庙祀的，为俗祀。明清云南通志及各府州县志《祠祀志》，对祭祀对象、名称、等级、责任人等都有明确规定：“祀事之掌于礼部，职诸有司者既汇为祀典，缀诸祠祀之首矣。其有民间习俗相沿立为庙祀者，醵钱祭酺，合乎古人二十五家置社之意，春祈秋报，亦例所不禁。滇俗旧尚鬼神，四时恒多祭赛，今综而纪之，俾各有所考云。”[⑤]

从史载可知，明清时期，云南龙王庙信仰广泛分布于全省各地，设有龙神祠、海神祠、龙王庙、神泉庙等名，如澜沧江滨有“黑水神祠”，以有风涛覆溺之患，建祠以祀江神；大理洱海有“洱水神祠”，以祷雨防旱。其中以龙王庙分布最广，数量最多，目的就是祈求风调雨顺，禳灾除旱。“楚郡城内外，有龙神祠三，皆列《祀典》。”[⑥] “有为民间俗尚相沿立之庙祀者，

① （清）赵元祚：《滇南山水纲目》卷上《滇山纲目》，民国三年（1914年）云南丛书本，云南图书馆藏板，第2页。

② （清）阮元等修，王崧等纂：道光《云南通志稿》卷八十八《祠祀志一之一·典祀》，道光十五年刻本，第1页。

③ 群祀，古代大祀、中祀以下列在祀典的祭祀。

④ 万历《云南通志》卷十二《祠祀志第八》，第1044页。

⑤ （清）岑毓英等续修：光绪《云南通志》卷九十一《祠祀志二之一·俗祀上》，光绪二十年刻本，第1页。

⑥ 陈璜：《重修碧霞井龙神祠记》，辑录自苏鸣鹤修，陈璜纂：嘉庆《楚雄县志》卷9《艺文志中·古文》，《中国地方志集成·云南府县志辑59》据嘉庆二十三年（1818年）刻本影印，第21页。

表 1　明代云南通志中记载的龙王庙

正德《云南志》		万历《云南通志》			天启《滇志》		
	祠庙		祀典	群祀		祀典	群祀
云南府	龙王庙，在滇池西海口，主祀水神。不知始创年月，弘治十六年巡抚右副都御史陈金重修。	云南府		龙王庙有二：一在大小河浪里海口，主祀水神，弘治间巡抚都御史陈金重修；一在滇池西海口。	云南府		白龙庙，在府治南菜海子，其庙，村落处处有之，龙以雨自随，多伤禾稼，农家祀而禳之。 龙王庙，在府城西南罗汉山下，其神曰灵伏仇夷滇河圣帝，其在各州县者甚多，唯呈贡黑、白二龙祠最称灵应，每三月上辰日，有司致祭。
大理府	洱水龙神庙在洱河西滨，蒙氏时建。邓川、浪穹俱有。	大理府	海口龙神庙，在府城南三十里。岁太和县春祭，赵州秋祭。	安龙庙，在府城西南隅。初建城时，惟西南角随筑随圮，父老谓宜安龙，遂立庙，自是城不复圮。 神宝泉庙，在府城南五里，其地出三泉，灌溉田畴，古昔立庙祀其龙神。嘉靖间，庙灾，泉亦闭，民白其事于官，重立庙，明年，泉复出。 上关龙王庙，在府城北六十里龙首关。	大理府	海口龙王庙，在府南三十里，岁太和县春祭，赵州秋祭。	安龙庙，在府城西南隅，初建城时，筑至此辄圮，父老谓有龙在焉，因为立庙，自是城不复圮。 上关龙王庙，在府北六十里龙首关。

续表

正德《云南志》		万历《云南通志》			天启《滇志》		
	祠庙		祀典	群祀		祀典	群祀
大理府	洱水龙神庙在洱河西滨，蒙氏时建。邓川、浪穹俱有。	大理府	海口龙神庙，在府城南三十里。岁太和县春祭，赵州秋祭。	喜洲龙王庙，在府城北五十里何矣城村，与府东洱水神祠同出。按《白古通》谓：点苍山脚插入洱河最深长者，唯城东一支与喜洲一支。南支之神，其形金鱼戴金钱；北支之神，其形玉螺。二物见则为祥。 龙王庙有二：一在赵州治东八里，一在浪穹县北十里许宁海之滨。有修撰杨慎《诗①》："峰头才见一泓幽，沙尾惊看四岸浮。流水罗纹堪并色，嘉陵石黛迥添愁。秦源欲问桃花渡，楚望浑迷杜若洲。亦有沧浪旧歌曲，晚来乘兴上扁舟。" 东龙庙，在州治东十里，唐邓赕诏所建水神祠也，非惟资灌溉，而祈祷亦应，州之春祈诣焉。	大理府	海口龙王庙，在府南三十里，岁太和县春祭，赵州秋祭。	喜洲龙王庙，在府城北五十里何矣城村，与府东洱水神祠同建。 龙王庙有三：一在赵州治东八里，一在浪穹县治北十里许宁海之滨，一在五井司左，各井皆有。 东龙庙，在州治东十里，唐邓睑诏所建水神祠也，水资灌溉，祈祷亦应，州之春祈诣焉。

① 此诗，《升庵集》卷二十六题作"泛浪穹海子"。

续表

正德《云南志》		万历《云南通志》			天启《滇志》		
	祠庙		祀典	群祀		祀典	群祀
临安府	龙王庙二处：一在城西北板桥铺，曰龙泉甸，岁旱祷之即雨，每岁三月，府卫官致祭；一在府东南甸尾铺。	临安府		龙王庙，在州吕公山。	临安府	白龙潭龙王庙，在府西北十二里，兵备蒋宗鲁置灵泉观，岁春仲，卫官祭。	龙王庙　有二：一在州吕公山，一在新平县南三百武。 白龙祠　在县治南。
楚雄府	无	楚雄府	紫溪龙王庙，在府城西一十五里，岁季春祭。		楚雄府	紫溪龙王庙，在府西二十五里，岁季春祭。	
澂江府	龙王庙有三：一在西浦泉，一在北坡泉，一在海口铺。	澂江府	西浦龙泉神庙，一名西磬龙泉庙，在蟠龙冈麓，岁春三月上辰日，本府致祭。 东浦龙泉神庙，一名北波龙泉庙，在府治东缺摩山麓，岁三月上巳日，本府致祭。 龙王庙，在路南州，有二，一在州东十二里黑龙泉，一在东北十五里白龙泉，岁三月致祭。		澂江府	西浦龙泉神庙，一名西磬龙泉庙，在蟠龙冈麓。 东浦龙泉神庙，一名北波龙泉庙，在缺摩山麓。岁三月辰巳日本府致祭。 路南州龙王庙二：一在州东黑龙泉，一在州东北白龙泉。岁三月本州致祭。	

续表

正德《云南志》		万历《云南通志》			天启《滇志》		
	祠庙		祀典	群祀		祀典	群祀
蒙化府	龙王庙，在府城东东山下，上有龙潭，有灌溉之利，每年四月中有司致祭，旱则祷之。	蒙化府		龙王庙，在东山麓锦溪上流，知府左文臣重修，祷雨辄应，岁以五月致祭。	蒙化府	龙王庙，在东山麓锦溪上流，知府左文臣重修。岁五月致祭，每旱祷焉。	
景东府	无	景东府	无		景东府		龙王庙，在府北一里。
广南府	无	广南府	无		广南府	无	
广西府	无	广西府	无		广西府	无	
镇沅府	无	镇沅府	无		镇沅府	无	
永宁府	无	永宁府	无		永宁府		龙王庙，在府治。
顺宁府	无	顺宁府	无		顺宁府	无	
曲靖军民府	无	曲靖府	无		曲靖府	龙王庙，在府西南五里，岁春季，府县卫所俱祭。沾益州亦有。	
姚安军民府	无	姚安府		龙王庙有三：一在穴石溯，一在白石的，一在大康郎。	姚安府		龙王庙有三：一在大石溯，一在白石的，一在大康郎。

续表

正德《云南志》		万历《云南通志》			天启《滇志》		
	祠庙		祀典	群祀		祀典	群祀
鹤庆军民府	龙王庙有二：一在府治西五里，即西龙潭；一在府治西北十里，即北龙潭。永乐十一年土官知府高兴重建，郡人凡有旱涝，必往祷焉。	鹤庆府	西龙潭祠，在府治西，其下又有龙宝、黑龙、白龙、吸钟诸潭龙祠，本府以七月九日俱咐祭。	白龙王庙，在州治西一里，正统间建。	鹤庆府	西龙潭祠，在府城西，其下又有龙宝、黑龙、白龙、吸钟诸潭龙祠，本府以七月九日祭。	
武定军民府	无	武定府	无		武定府	无	
寻甸军民府	无	寻甸府			寻甸府	无	
丽江军民府	无	丽江府	无		丽江府	无	
元江军民府	无	元江府	无		元江府	无	
北胜州	无	北胜州		在州治内。	北胜州		龙王庙，在州治五里。
新化州	无	新化州	无		新化州		
者乐甸长官司	无		无				
澜沧卫军民指挥使司	无						
金齿军民指挥使司	龙王祠有二：一在城西龙泉门外，一在城西北一十五里，其下有泉，灌田甚广。	永昌府		龙王庙有二：一在府城龙泉门外；一在郎义村北一里，腾越州亦有。	永昌府		龙王庙有二：一在州吕公山，一在新平县南三百武。 白龙祠，在县治南。

续表

正德《云南志》		万历《云南通志》			天启《滇志》		
	祠庙		祀典	群祀		祀典	群祀
腾冲军民指挥使司	无						
车里军民宣慰使司	无	者乐甸长官司	无				
木邦军民宣慰使司	无	五井盐课提举司	龙王庙，在司治左，各井皆有。				
孟密安抚司	无	黑井盐课提举司	龙王庙　在黑井山上，岁春秋二祭。				
孟养军民宣慰使司	无						
缅甸军民宣慰使司	无						
八百大甸军民宣慰使司	无						
老挝军民宣慰使司	无						
孟定府	无						
孟艮府	无						
南甸宣抚司	无						
干崖宣抚司	无						

续表

正德《云南志》		万历《云南通志》			天启《滇志》		
	祠庙		祀典	群祀		祀典	群祀
陇川宣抚司	无						
威远州	无						
湾甸州	无						
镇康州	无						
大候州	无						
钮兀长官司	无						
芒市长官司	无						
车里靖安宣慰使司	无						
八寨长官司	无						
孟琏长官司	无						
瓦甸长官司	无						
茶山长官司	无						
麻里长官司	无						
摩沙勒长官司	无						
大古剌宣慰使司	无						
底马撒宣慰使司	无						
合计	12 个	28 个			31 个		

其庙曰……黑龙，乾隆五十八年（1793年），知府郭柱建于九龙池旁。”[①]“白龙庙，在府治南菜海子，其庙村落处处有之，龙以雨自随，多伤禾稼，农家祀而禳之。”[②]

从明清现存云南通志记载看，明初全省各地供奉的龙王庙（祠、神）不多，正德《云南志·祠祀志》有12尊，万历《云南通志·祠祀志》28尊，天启《滇志·祠祀志》31尊（见表1）。

表2 清代云南通志及民国《新纂云南通志》中记载的龙王庙（尊）

康熙《云南通志》	雍正《云南通志》	道光《云南通志稿》	光绪《云南通志》	《新纂云南通志》
22	42	145	170	168

由此可见，云南龙王庙正式入《祀典》于明初，清道光、光绪年间最盛，民国相承，呈现信仰范围广、信众多，及佛、道文化与当地少数民族原始宗教相互影响、互为渗透等特点，既是当地执政者政绩考核的风向标，又满足了广大民众虔诚信仰、隆重祭祀的精神追求，也成为当地最具特色的民间活动之一。尤其是在湖泉密布的滇池、江河险峻的澜沧江、攸关一地饮水灌溉的丽江象山、蒙氏发源地大理，及盛产井盐的黑井、白井、琅井等地，龙王庙信仰最广，建造数量最多。“龙王庙，一在府城西南罗汉山下；一在府城东白龙潭；一在府城北黑龙潭；一在昆阳州北海门村牛舌洲上，明洪武末勅封‘惠济龙王’；一在嵩明州西十五里，嵩境田亩，全资各处龙泉灌溉，惟此龙泉利润更溥，明知州余化龙详请以季春辰日致祭，若知州弗与祭，辄多亢旸。”[③]后来，随着新文化运动及破四旧之风，新修省志及地州县志已不专列《祠祀志》，龙王庙文献记载逐渐散失。

设立“风云雷雨山川坛”“龙王庙”目的，都是妥神安民，警醒官吏内修，祈盼风调雨顺，更多的是彰显地方官员的执政能力、环保意识和服务大局。《春秋》有灾必书，盖示恐惧修省之深意。旧方志首及《天文

---

① （清）戴絅孙纂修：道光《昆明县志》卷四《祠祀志·俗祀》，《中国地方志集成·云南府县志辑②》，南京凤凰出版社、上海书店、巴蜀书社，2009年3月据光绪二十七年刻本影印，第20~25页。

② （明）刘文征纂修：天启《滇志》卷十六《祠祀志第九·群祀·云南府》，古永继校点，云南教育出版社，1991，第543页。

③ （清）鄂尔泰修，靖道谟纂：雍正《云南通志》卷十五《祠祀志·云南府·群祀》，清乾隆元年（1737年）刻本，第4页。

志》，多述祥异、气候。云南历史上出于对大自然的敬畏之心，每逢风雨失调，久旱不雨，或久雨不止时，民众都要到龙王庙烧香祈愿，以求龙王治水，风调雨顺。大涝大旱之年，官吏甚至带头赤足前往，或跪地而行，或禁食多日，以示祈祷虔诚，留下大量祈雨告文，如明杨士云撰《祷雨文》，明云南巡抚顾应祥撰《告海口龙王祠文》，沈懋价《山川社稷风云雷雨之神》《东山箐殊夷龙王》《菖蒲潭龙王》，清朱若功《太华山龙王庙祈雨题匾》，清王昶《祭山川风雨神文》。甚至一人多篇，如清周钺先后撰《祭赤龙溪文》《祷雨告龙王文》《又祷雨告龙王文》《告赤龙溪文》《又告赤龙溪文》《祭境内山川龙王之神》《再祷雨》《又再祷雨》《谢雨文》《求晴文》等。

对于像母亲河滇池附近影响大、信众多的龙王庙，还曾受到朝廷敕封。如龙神祠，在省城西门内菜海子旁（即九龙池），“雍正六年（1728 年），奉旨勅封‘福滇益农龙王’，内府造像辇送至滇，建祠以时致祭，月吉瞻礼”。[①] 安宁龙王庙，旧在州治西，今移建于城东河岸，与盐井相向，“雍正二年（1724 年），奉旨敕封灵源普泽龙王，春秋致祭”。[②] 海口龙王庙，在省城北海门村牛舌洲上，“明洪武末建，敕封‘总督惠济龙王’，康熙三十一年（1692 年），总督范承勋、巡抚王继文捐修”。[③]“龙王庙，旧《云南通志》：在城西南十里，每岁季春辰日，有司致祭，郡有水旱必祷。《南宁县採访》：嘉庆二年（1797 年），黔苗不法，巡抚江蘭驻曲靖，时旱诣祠，祷祈雨降，是岁大熟，事闻，奉旨勅封‘巡抚龙王’。”[④]

有一地多达数个龙王庙的，如大理赵州有 10 尊：“汉邑村龙王庙，《赵州志》：在城东八里，蒙代时建，水出庙左。庙前有紫薇树，大数围。又有冬青一本，青紫交荣。”“西冲小黑龙庙，《赵州志》：在城西云台山界。”“治水龙王庙，《赵州志》：在德胜驿西，明正德间建。”“九头龙庙，《赵州志》：在东晋湖边地，名九龙吐水，明崇祯二年（1629 年），生员何显宗请祀”“赤子龙王庙，《赵州志》：在城西三里，旧有庙圮，康熙四十七年（1708 年），郡绅郑荣重建，前有萃爽楼。”“三子龙庙，《赵州志》：在定西

① 道光《云南通志稿》卷八十八《祠祀志一之一·典祀一·云南府·昆明县》，第 7 页。
② 道光《云南通志稿》卷八十八《祠祀志一·典祀一·云南府·安宁州》，第 33 页。
③ 道光《云南通志稿》卷八十八《祠祀志一·典祀一·云南府·昆阳州》，第 35 页。
④ 道光《云南通志稿》卷八十九《祠祀志一·典祀二·曲靖府·南宁县》，第 36 页。

岭。”“大庄龙王庙，《大理府志》：在大庄界，庙前有池，涌泉如珠。”“圣御龙王庙，《赵州志》：在弥渡东门。”“九股龙王庙，《赵州志》：在弥渡东山九龙箐口。”“光耀龙王庙，《赵州志》：在上达村东山下。”①

有具体交待所祀水神名称的。如：“龙神祠，《邓川州志》：在下山口，主瀰苴河之神。”②“青龙庙，《邓川州志》：在鱼潭坡，祀洱水神。”③“龙神祠，在城西北四里土官箐，清乾隆三十三年（1768 年），知县陈崑捐建，祀洪本泉神。”④

对于建庙时间古老、对当地民众生产生活影响大的龙王庙，留下大量碑记诗作。主要有明永乐三年（1405 年）佥事刘寅撰《永昌龙王庙记》、明按察胡僖撰《苏髻龙王祠记》，清康熙二年（1663 年）黑盐井廪膳生员李尔白撰《黑井龙王灵赡碑记》、康熙四十四年（1705 年）黑盐井提举司沈懋价撰《重修东井龙王祠记》、康熙四十七年（1708 年）年郡绅郑荣撰《重建赤子龙王庙碑记》、雍正三年（1725 年）东川知府崔乃镛撰《创建龙王庙碑记》、乾隆二十年（1755 年）东川知府义宁撰《九灵龙王庙记》、清朱若功《太华山龙王庙祈雨题匾》等。

海口龙王庙，在滇池西海口，主祀水神，始创年月不详，弘治十六年（1503 年），巡抚右副都御史陈金重修。⑤明崇祯十一年（1638 年）十月二十五日清晨，大旅行家徐霞客从茶埠墩出发，沿螳螂川南岸前往海门村，见龙王堂以一洲之势峙其上。此龙王堂，明洪武末曾勅封“总督惠济龙王”。庙中碑额甚多，“皆（成）化、（弘）治以后，抚按相度水利，开浚海口免于泛滥，以成濒海诸良田者，故巡方者以此为首务”。⑥

玉河，位于丽江城西北二里，源出象山麓，泉眼数处，汇流成河，南流入鹤庆，为漾工江，附近城郭田亩，咸资灌溉。乾隆元年、二年（1736 年、1737 年）连续河源水竭，知府管学宣借此事，主张修建龙王庙，让当

① 光绪《云南通志》卷九十一《祠祀志二·俗祀一·大理府·赵州》，第 17 页。
② 光绪《云南通志》卷八十九《祠祀志一·典祀二·大理府·邓川州》，第 7 页。
③ 光绪《云南通志》卷九十一《祠祀志二·俗祀一·大理府·邓川州》，第 20 页。
④《新纂云南通志》卷一百十一《祠祀考三·典祀三·元江直隶州·新平县》，民国三十八年（1949 年）铅印本，第 35 页。
⑤ 参见正德《云南志》卷二《云南府·祠庙》，第 22 页。
⑥（明）徐弘祖：《徐霞客游记·滇游日记四》增订本，朱惠荣校注，云南人民出版社，1999，第 845 页。

地民众知晓礼敬自然、祠祀有序、保护水源之重要性，“自今以往，官若民其一秉于礼，洗心必净，澡身必洁，治家治事，清本澄源，勿淫以污，此则守者勤民祠神之本意乎”！①

遍布云南城乡村寨的“龙王庙”祀祠活动，丰富多样。“黑龙潭，《嵩明州志》：在城西三十里邵甸里龙潭营。谨案：盘龙江发源于此，雨旸不时，祷之甚应。明沐国公与巡按祷雨其祠，雨即降。康熙五十三年（1714年），盐道金启复祈雨，三至其地，捐金修庙，二潭连环，每季春辰日，邵川阖境祀之。”② 中甸青龙潭，在城东山脚下，“顺山发源，其水清澈，冬温夏凉，潭深堤长，涵濡于境内之田亩，能避青霜。曲水流觞，如玉带之环城，金钩之锁路，潆洄流入西山之草湖焉。咸丰二年（1852年），守备马霄汉建立龙王庙于潭上，四时晴雨，文武各官，俱到此祈祷拈香，龙神无不灵应焉。”③ “龙王庙，在府城西南罗汉山下，其神曰灵伏仇夷滇河圣帝，其在各州县者甚多，唯呈贡黑、白二龙祠最称灵应，每三月上辰日，有司致祭。”④ “龙王庙有二：一在府治西五里即西龙潭，一在府治西北十里即北龙潭。永乐十一年（1413年）土知府高兴重建，郡人凡有旱涝，必往祷焉。”⑤

云南又是少数民族聚居区，藏族、纳西族、哈尼族、傣族、布朗族、基诺族、佤族等流传下来大量关于水的传说、宗教信仰和对水的祭祀仪式，有供奉原始宗教的山神、水神（龙王）、风电雷雨神，有的设庙祭祀，有的立碑警世。西双版纳一带有井塔，即在水井上建塔形小屋以保护水源，“普济众生”。巍山县有《巍宝朝阳洞玄极宫新置常住水磨碑记》，称“永支水磨，为香灯之举”，水资源的循环管理，成为当地佛僧寺院的主要经济来源之一。源于少数民族语言保留下来的水名、风俗习惯、祭祀活动、约信盟

① 《新建玉河龙王庙碑记》，引自乾隆《丽江府志略》（1991年丽江纳西族自治县县志编纂委员会办公室据乾隆八年木刻本翻印，丽江纳西族自治县史志丛书之一）下卷《艺文略·记》第268页。

② 道光《云南通志稿》卷九十一《祠祀志二之一·俗祀一·云南府·嵩明州》，第11页。

③ 《青龙潭记》，转录自吴自修校，张翼夔纂：光绪《新修中甸厅志》卷中《山川志》，《中国地方志集成·云南府县志辑82》，南京凤凰出版社，2009年3月据钞本影印，第500页。

④ 天启《滇志》卷十六《祠祀志·群祀·云南府》，第549页。

⑤ 正德《云南志》卷十《鹤庆军民府·祠庙》，《天一阁藏明代方志选刊续编》，上海书店据明正德刻本影印，第9页。

誓等，也丰富了云南水文化内涵，“托诺河，在城西南二百五十里，下流入府境，夷谓松曰托，沙石曰诺，以河畔有松树、沙石，故名”。[①] “蕴古泉，在城南八十里，一名甕古，夷语谓泉为甕，谓涌为古，其水清澈，可鉴毛发。”[②]

敬畏山水的自然生态观，丰富了云南各民族宗教文化，形成了多元多层次的云南宗教文化特色。尤其元明清时期，随着大量内地移民的迁入，儒道释文化也随之融入云南各民族地区，与云南原始宗教和地方民族文化相融合，形成独具云南地域性和民族性的宗教文化特色，对当地生产生活和文化教育产生不同程度的影响，成为中华优秀传统文化中不可分割的一部分。

结束语

综上所述，为使优秀传统文化更好地彰显其生命力，一定要保护和传承好老祖宗留下来的珍贵文化遗产，尊重水历史和水文化遗产，发挥其在当代的水管理、水环境建设和水教育中的积极引导功能。保护为主，抢救第一，合理利用，加强管理。建议尽快完善龙王庙水文化遗迹的摸底调查、建档立卡。有条件的地方恢复“龙王庙”祭祀等民俗民间文化节日，增强各级政府及当地民众的生态环境保护意识。通过对以“龙王庙”为代表的水历史遗迹的普查、登记、整理、研究、宣传，丰富主题公园建设，修建水文化保护遗址，开展保护环境、节约用水等宣传教育活动。通过群众喜闻乐见的民俗民间文化活动，唤醒深藏在广大人民群众心底的乡愁情结，掀起一场爱国爱乡的文化遗迹保护和启迪民智的宣传教育热潮。进一步拓展水历史文明的研究视角，丰富研究内容，提升文化自信，推进云南多民族和谐团结的文化繁荣兴盛，更好地适应人民日益增长的美好生活需求，促进公民素质和文明程度达到新高度。

---

① 雍正《云南通志》卷三《山川·昭通府·镇雄州》，第35页。

② 雍正《云南通志》卷三《山川·顺宁府》，第56页。

近三十年来龙王庙文化研究综述*

张　敏**

摘　要： 龙王庙文化是中国传统文化重要的组成部分之一。其起源、发展、盛衰与水旱灾害密切相关，体现着中华文明天地人关系的变迁，并具有浓厚的地域色彩。近年来，学术界加强龙文化研究，对龙文化的历史传承、内容和特征等方面进行了深入的论述。关于龙王信仰与龙王庙历史渊源等问题，则多从地域和文学领域展开研究。对以龙求雨习俗的研究取得了比较丰硕的成果，学者们注意到不同的地理环境、人文氛围孕育出不同的信仰内容与仪式活动。

关键词： 龙王庙　传统文化

Abstract: Dragon - king Temple culture is an important part of Chinese traditional culture. Its origin, development and ups and downs are closely related to floods and droughts, reflecting the changes of the relationship between heaven, earth and man in Chinese civilization, and has a strong regional color. In recent years, the academic community has strengthened the research on dragon culture, and made a deep discussion on the historical inheritance, content and characteristics of dragon culture. As for the relationship between the belief of the Dragon - king and the historical origin of the temple of the Dragon King, many studies have been carried out in the field of region and literature. The research on the custom of praying for rain by dragon has achieved fruitful results. Scholars have noticed that different geographical environment and cultural atmosphere breed different belief

---

* 本研究为2018年度湖北省教育厅人文社会科学研究项目“湖北龙王庙文化研究”的阶段性成果。

** 张敏，博士，湖北大学历史文化学院副教授。

contents and ritual activities.

Keywords: Dragon - king Temple; Traditional Culture

中国传统以农业立国，水利是农业的命脉。在生产力不发达、科技不昌明的条件下，人们在兴修水利的同时，逐渐兴起了对主管兴云降雨的龙神的信仰，并为之修立庙宇，进行祭祀。龙王庙的分布十分广泛，千百年来，全国各地大都建有规模不等的龙王庙。作为传统文化重要的组成部分之一，龙王庙文化的起源、发展、兴衰都与水旱灾害密切相关，体现着华夏文明天、地、人关系的变迁与演进。同时，龙王庙文化还具有浓厚的地域色彩，不同的地理环境、人文氛围孕育出不同的信仰内容与仪式活动。

近代中国学者对龙王庙文化的学术研究，最早可追溯到顾颉刚先生对龙王庙会之研究，以及闻一多和茅盾等先生对中国神话传说中的龙之研究。但由于种种主客观条件的限制，当时的学者对龙王庙文化还无力进行深入的研究。中华人民共和国成立以后，由于众所周知的原因，在一段时间内大陆学术界受“左”的思想的影响，学术研究有了许多禁区，龙王庙文化研究遭到冷落。这种状况直到改革开放以后才得到改观，但与龙王庙文化的重要性相比，相关学术研究还显得很薄弱，无论是研究的深度还是广度都不尽如人意，并存在许多研究的空白，仍然有待于学者们进一步的深入发掘和探索。

一　龙文化整体研究

自7000多年前的新石器时代直至今天，龙，几乎贯穿了这一漫长而复杂的文化发展历程，并在宗教、政治、文学、艺术等各个领域充当着重要角色。这种现象在人类发展史上是罕见的。龙不仅在中华文化中处处可见，而且还远传到东亚、南亚各国。中国是龙的故乡。龙那神奇怪异的特性及其在中国文化中的重要地位，引起了古今中外众多学者的极大关注。

龙王庙文化属于龙文化研究的一部分。而龙作为中华民族象征，关于龙文化研究的成果十分丰硕。近年来，学者们分别从考古学、文献学、历史学、民俗学和文化人类学等视角探讨了龙文化起源、形成及发展的历史。

多数学者认为，中华龙文化肇始于原始部落的图腾崇拜，发展于宗教信仰的多元刻画，分化为帝王象征与民间崇拜，并最终升华为中华民族的文化符号。如刘志雄与杨静荣合著的《龙与中国文化》指出，龙最典型的特征之一就是其身体各部具有不同动物的特征。[①] 陈授祥则认为："与龙有关的文化现象堪称是中华民族文化的缩影。龙所展示的独特形态，蕴藏着中华文明中最奇妙、最有趣的华彩；龙所表述的观念，牵连着中华文化中最隐秘、最曲折的精萃。姑且不论近世流传的'龙的传人''龙族文化'等称谓确切与否，仅就龙的造型历史来看，亦足以展示一种民族文化在数千年发展中特有的足迹。"[②]

王宇信指出，作为中华民族象征的"龙"是与中国古代文明形成的进程密切相关的。[③] 古史传说时代的"五帝"们，不但与龙有千丝万缕的联系，而且为华夏民族的形成与融合、发展做出了贡献。历史所形成的矢志不移地追求精神、诚信厚德、移风易俗和追求社会和谐的"龙德"，既是华夏民族的精神，也是炎黄文化的精髓。

王大有对几十种龙凤图形的起源变迁及其所表现的民族心理和审美意识进行了综合的研究，提出了中华龙凤文化同源一祖说。[④]

梁东兴、杨玉荣讨论了中华龙文化的主要内容。他们指出，中华龙文化是中华民族的伟大创造，在数千年的历史发展中，是维系中华民族团结奋进的精神纽带，蕴涵着极其丰富的内容。中华龙的创造，反映了先民们的和谐心理。中华龙的神性表现为：能通天入地，使天人交流；能司雨排涝，使天人和谐；能显灵示异，使天人合一。龙是中华各民族走向融合的共根认同；是中华各民族发祥和文化肇端的象征；是中华各民族维护团结统一的民族魂。[⑤]

此外，庞进《龙的习俗》（陕西人民出版社，1988 年）和《呼风唤雨八千年——中国龙文化探秘》（四川教育出版社，1998 年）、鲁谆《龙文化与民族精神》（上海人民出版社，2000 年）、何新《龙：神话与真相》（上

---

① 刘志雄、杨静荣：《龙与中国文化》，人民出版社，1992。

② 陈授祥：《中国的龙》，漓江出版社，1988。

③ 王宇信：《炎帝、黄帝与中国龙——兼谈中国龙的"龙德"与炎黄文化的和谐精神》，《殷都学刊》2008 年第 1 期。

④ 王大有：《龙凤文化源流》，北京工艺美术出版社，1988。

⑤ 梁东兴、杨玉荣：《中华龙文化中的和谐意蕴》，《中华文化论坛》2012 年第 2 期。

海人民出版社，2000 年)、吉成名《中国崇龙习俗》（天津古籍出版社，2002 年)、朱乃诚《中华龙起源和形成》（三联书店，2009 年)、王笠荃《中华龙文化的起源和演变》（气象出版社，2010 年)、王树强和冯大建《龙文：中国龙文化研究》(南开大学出版社，2012 年）等研究专著分别对龙文化的历史传承、内容和特征等方面进行了深入的述论，是近年来龙文化研究的代表作。

二　龙王信仰与龙王庙历史渊源的研究

我国古代的龙王信仰是印度佛教文化与中国传统文化的融合生成物。在宗教、社会与文化的合力作用下，龙王信仰逐渐发展成为一种具有全民性、实践性的民俗信仰，在社会生产和生活中发挥着重要的作用。同时，龙王信仰也是龙王庙文化在意识形态方面的基础，推动了龙王庙文化的发展。

学者们一般从地域入手对龙王信仰进行研究，如苑利撰写了关于华北龙王的系列研究论文，包括《华北地区龙王传说研究》(《民族艺术》2002 年第 1 期)、《华北地区龙王庙配祀神祇考略》(《西北民族研究》2002 年第 2 期)、《华北地区龙王庙主神龙王考》(《西北民族学院学报》2002 年第 4 期)、《从龙王信仰看研究民间信仰的学术价值与意义》(《青海民族学院学报》2004 年第 1 期）等。他认为，龙王信仰是依托一定的文本加以传承的。支撑着华北地区龙王信仰的文本载体主要包括讲述龙王世家及其相关信仰的民间传说和使人信以为真的个人经历故事；记录历史上龙王显灵、祷雨获应的碑文，记录庙宇兴建、修缮过程的纪念碑文，具有民间法规性质的警示性碑文以及具有记录功德性质的功德碑；祈雨仪式中使用的易懂易记、琅琅上口的民间祈雨谣、道家祈雨经以及官办祈雨仪式上吟诵的祈雨文等。这些文本类型从不同角度阐释并巩固着民间传承的龙王信仰，为我们研究中国华北地区龙王信仰，提供了大量翔实而可信的文本资料。

崔云胜对始建于西夏的张掖黑河龙王庙进行了详细的考察。他认为，黑河龙王庙经过漫长的历史岁月，和黑河流域民众的生产生活发生了密切的关系，承载着许多历史信息，诸如当地的民族、信仰、行政机关、农业生产信息等。比如立于下龙王庙的西夏皇帝李仁孝敕谕黑河诸神碑，记载西夏皇帝李仁孝曾亲临黑河桥，躬祭龙神等诸神以祈求“水患永息，桥道久长”，体现出西夏统治者对农业生产的高度重视；同时也反映出当地经常发生的是水灾而不是旱灾。这和后世明清时期水源紧张、旱灾频发的情况形成了鲜明的对比。①

涂德深与杨志超梳理了武汉龙王庙的历史。他们指出，该庙始建于明朝洪武年间，位于长江与汉水汇合处。清乾隆四年（1739 年）在龙王庙的旁边修建了码头。民国时期改建为花园和图书馆，是汉口最繁华的商埠之一。②

王鹏龙等《明清时期雁北地区的龙王信仰与民俗活动》（《山西大同大学学报》2011 年第 6 期）、申丹莉《潞城市东邑村龙王庙及迎神赛社考》（《文物世界》2008 年第 2 期）、田探《陕南地区民间信仰特征——以陕西城固龙王庙村为例》（《华夏文化》2010 年第 1 期）分别对山西大同和潞城、陕西城固等地的龙王庙与龙王信仰进行了历史文化方面的考察。

从文学领域对龙王信仰及龙王庙文化进行研究的成果亦不断涌现，如黄贤指出，魏晋隋唐之前，龙的文学形象比较单一。龙王、龙女形象在中国文学中始现于唐代小说，单就龙女故事而言，其主题多为“龙女报恩”及“煮海降龙”等模式。至元代，出现了两部著名的龙女题材戏——杂剧《洞庭湖柳毅传书》和《沙门岛张生煮海》。在剧中，龙女与书生相互爱悦、终成眷属，主题由报恩、煮海等模式向婚恋主题转变。剧中的龙女一跃而为故事演述的主角，作品用大量的唱词、对话、动作等细致地刻画出龙女的形象，龙女对自由爱情的追求贯穿了整部戏剧的始终，而有情人终成眷属的大团圆结局则表现了对这种自主精神的肯定。③

刘守华比较了古代中国和印度在龙女报恩故事方面的差异。该文指出，印度故事中的龙女，属形体丑陋、地位卑贱的畜类，虽有某些神通，龙宫中也有许多珍宝，她们在人类面前常自惭形秽，把人间男子对她们的爱怜追求，视为“降尊就卑”，在男人面前俯首贴耳，显然是印度种姓制度下贱民阶层贫困苦难生活的象征。而在中国的龙文化中，龙女不仅有崇高的地

① 崔云胜：《西夏建张掖龙王庙史迹考述》，《西夏学》2011 年第 7 辑。
② 涂德深、杨志超：《武汉龙王庙的变迁》，《湖北文史资料》2002 年第 3 期。
③ 黄贤：《元杂剧龙女形象研究》，首都师范大学硕士学位论文，2008。

位，而且有优美的心灵和巨大的能耐。[①]

沈梅丽认为，龙王信仰的文化意义主要体现在生存哲学和宗教史两个层面上。[②] 从人的生存哲学层面上来看，历代小说中的龙宫信仰故事所包含的入龙宫与龙女成婚、从龙宫得宝以及得道成仙等情节，表现出古人对个体生存状态的关注始终贯穿于历代小说中，这种关注主要落在期望较高的生活品质的保障，如婚姻美满、物质富裕、身体健康无疾以及博取功名等方面。从宗教交流史来看，龙王信仰故事从一个侧面反映出道教对佛教的主动吸纳过程，如《柳毅传》篇中洞庭龙王与太阳道士是处于水火“灵用不同，玄化各异”的对立状态，之后小说则出现了龙王慕道、化道、学道的情节。又如龙女形象从唐代护珠龙女形象到明清道教女仙形象的历史演变，这种情况与历史佛道互相融合的发展过程是一致的。

三 以龙求雨习俗的研究

以龙求雨习俗是指人们以龙为崇拜对象而求雨的习俗，主要包括求雨巫术与祭龙求雨。张强系统梳理了中国古代以龙求雨风俗的变迁，他指出由于社会进步、统治阶级推崇、人们的功利心理等因素，以及受佛教传入影响，中国以龙求雨习俗发生了很多变化：龙形道具变化多样，由蚌朔龙发展为土龙、草龙、画龙，甚至与龙相似的蜥蜴、壁虎也成为旱时人们祭拜的对象。人们认为舞龙容易感应真龙，带来雨水。于是，人们舞龙求雨。后来，人们把龙当作神灵。于是，形成了祀龙求雨习俗。在此过程中，龙升格为王，龙王庙遍布全国各地。为避免旱灾发生，人们还进行前期感情投资。于是，形成了农历二月二日、五月二十日祀龙神的节俗。以龙求雨习俗变迁呈现出多样化、祭祀化、娱乐化等特点。[③]

学者们对以龙求雨习俗进行了断代研究，并取得一批有分量的研究成果。如崔华和牛耕指出，作为水旱神的形象的女魃、风伯、雨师、雷公、河伯、长虹、应龙及月神女娲等众神灵被刻于汉代画像石上，是古人祈求“风调雨顺”民俗意识的形象化。反映龙神画像在全国各地出土的画像石、

---

① 刘守华：《中印龙女报恩故事之比较》，《中国比较文学》1999 年第 3 期。

② 沈梅丽：《古代小说与龙王信仰研究》，上海师范大学硕士学位论文，2005。

③ 张强：《中国以龙求雨习俗变迁研究》，湘潭大学硕士学位论文，2008。

砖、壁画及帛画中极为常见，多数是以神仙境界中的祥瑞之物而出现的。不过，也有一些龙应是以雨神的身份而存在的。如河南南阳英庄汉画像石墓及王庄汉画像石墓墓顶天文画像中的龙形象。①

张健彬《唐代的祈雨习俗》（《民俗研究》2001 年第 4 期）一文指出，唐代普遍存在着祈雨习俗，政府对于祈雨有着明确规定。在祈雨仪式中，龙是一个重要角色。许多祈雨对象事实上都是想象中龙的出没地点，有时甚至直接以龙神为祈祷对象。

王利华根据大量地方文献记载和现代民俗学者的实地调查，对唐宋以来江南地区与农业直接相关的种种巫术和禁忌，诸如农事占验、祈雨、祈晴、除虫禳灾等巫术事象进行较系统的清理。② 江南农业巫术的内容、实施时间等是与当地农业生产内容、农事季节安排以及诸多农业生产实际需要特别是战胜自然灾害的心理需要密切联系在一起的。“物类感应”“万物有灵”等虚妄信仰是种种农业巫术赖以存在的共同观念基础，然而这些虔妄的观念强调事物之间的相互感应关系，相信万事万物俱有灵性，并相信人可以通过法术能动地利用事物的灵性及其相互之间的感应关系来达到课晴卜雨、禳祸消灾从而获得农业丰收的目的，中国传统自然观、认知方式、行为方式等诸多方面的文化特质在此得到充分体现。

刘黎明认为，宋代民间向龙祈雨的事例很多，体现了巫术的感应律和接触律。③ 所谓感应律，就是认为通过一定的模仿行为能达到某种预期的结果，以改变客观事物。所谓接触律，就是认为两种事物发生接触时彼此能对对方施加一种影响，从而改变和控制对方。两个相互隔离的事物间之所以能够相互影响，中间似乎存在着某种极其有力量的媒介物，这种媒介物在中国古典文献中有时表达为“气”。这种“气论”是宋代民间求雨巫术的重要特征。

区域研究方面，林涓认为，江南地区虽属平原水乡泽国，但是由于季风气候的缘故，降水变率大，往往旱涝不常，因此旱期祈雨，在江南水乡也很普遍。④ 江南地区的祈雨一般选择在龙王庙、观音庙、城隍庙以及其他

① 崔华、牛耕：《从汉画中的水旱神画像看我国汉代的祈雨风俗》，《中原文物》1996 年第 3 期。
② 王利华：《唐宋以来江南地区的农业巫术述论》，《中国农史》1996 年第 4 期。
③ 刘黎明：《宋代民间求雨巫术》，《西南民族学院学报》2002 年第 12 期。
④ 林涓：《祈雨习俗及其地域差异——以传统社会后期的江南地区为中心》，《中国历史地理论丛》2003 年第 1 期。

神灵和已故乡贤名宦的祠庙中进行。江南有共同的祈雨对象，但区域内部这种祈雨却呈现了多样化，有其各自的特色和主要的侧重对象，并且在地域分布上也有明显的差异。可以认为，江南地区祈雨神灵的分布特点和地区差异完全是受地理环境影响的结果。

滕占能《慈溪的龙王庙及求雨活动》（《中国民间文化》1992年第1期）、安德明《天水求雨习俗》（《民俗研究》1996年第4期）和《农事禳灾：一种特殊的农事信仰活动》（《民俗研究》1997年第1期）、胡炳章《从“鞭石”到祭龙——土家族求雨巫俗的历史变迁》（《中南民族学院学报》1997年第2期）、陈勤建《越地祈雨中的“龙圣”崇信析论》（《华东师范大学学报》2000年第3期）、苑利《晒龙王祈雨仪式研究》（《民间文化》2001年第1期）、李英《舞龙运动的历史回顾与展望》（《解放军体育学院学报》2004年第2期）等论文则对其他地区的以龙求雨习俗进行了研究。

综上所述，关于中国龙文化的整体研究已经取得相当的进展，但系统性地对中国龙王庙文化进行探讨的成果数量却还不多。究其原因，一方面是学界对于龙王庙文化研究的重要性还没有提到应有的高度，对龙王庙文化的概念及内涵的理解还存在着一些争议；另外一方面也是相关领域的研究头绪众多，微观研究成果较多，而能够全面、系统地考察龙王庙文化及其当代价值的研究论著则比较鲜见。因此，学术界有必要对龙王庙文化进行更加系统、深入的研究。

今后研究的重点应该是结合历史文献和田野调查，系统考察全国各地龙王庙的分布与演化，探索不同地区与不同时期龙王庙文化中意识形态因素的异同。同时，我们应该采用跨学科综合研究方法，阐释中国龙王庙文化发展的民族性与地域性特点，使人们对这一重要文化现象有一个全面的认识，并从中揭示人地关系发展的一些规律，从而为当代中国文化建设提供有益的历史借鉴和智力支持。

水情势

应对水危机大众传媒不可缺位

——一个高级记者的水故事与思考

任维东*

摘　要：水问题今天已演变成一个重要的社会问题。新闻媒体具有强大的社会动员力、影响力与号召力。必须高度重视运用与发挥大众传媒在应对水问题、水危机方面的作用。本文通过一个新闻人的亲身感受认为，在互联网时代更应借助覆盖面广大、影响力深远、高效便捷的新闻媒体，实现对社会大众有关水问题的知识普及和水情警示教育。同时，新闻媒体应主动担当，加大对水问题、水危机报道的力度。

关键词：水危机　大众传媒　水科学

Abstract: The water problem has evolved to be a visible social problem in present age. Utilization and play the role of mass media to dealing with water problems should be attached more attention since the mass media with powerful social mobilization force and influence. Depended on personal long news experience, this paper gives some reviews and suggestions about how to use the mass media to dealing with the water crisis. It concluds that in the time of internet, we should pay more effort to use the news media that with large coverage, deep influence and high efficiency, to achieve to the education of water knowledge, water crisis and water situations. At same time, the mass media should take the initiative to strengthen the report about the water issues and the crisis.

Keywords: Water crisis; Mass media; Water issues

---

* 任维东，光明日报云南记者站站长。

城市水资源匮乏，农村饮用水不清洁，众多的江河湖污染，频发的洪涝灾害，饮用不洁水致病……这一系列的水问题，已成为全中国乃至全世界一个人人都不能回避、事关我们大家生命安全的全球化危机。

新闻媒体和媒体人，面对如此严重的社会问题，是袖手旁观，还是应该做些什么？

现在请允许我用 2 个故事来表达我对此问题的一些个人看法。

第一个是一位资深记者与“两湖一河”的故事。早在 1989 年 6 月，一个不满 30 岁的小伙子，人生第一次当记者，就有幸进入了中国第一大报——人民日报，被报社派驻云南省开展新闻报道工作。云南省地处中国西南，面积达 39.4 万平方千米，与缅甸、老挝、越南接壤，省内拥有众多的大江大河与高原湖泊。很快，他在工作中便遇到了一个后来举世瞩目的重大水污染问题，那就是昆明市的滇池污染。

当时中国的改革开放已经进行了十多年。在经济的快速发展中，中国各地普遍都不同程度地出现了环境污染的问题，特别是水的污染问题。这一点，地处边疆的云南省虽然其发展的步伐比内地和沿海要滞后许多，但也未能幸免。

滇池，位于昆明城的西南，紧邻人口稠密的城区和村镇，是云南省最大的淡水湖泊，占地面积达 330 平方千米，流域面积为 2920 平方千米，属于长江上游干流金沙江支流普渡河水系。早在一千多年前，它就孕育催生了古滇国的文明，今天又是昆明市数百万市民生产和生活的最重要水源。然而在经济社会快速发展过程中，由于从一开始就缺乏保护意识，滇池水的污染问题越来越突出，部分污染严重的水域发黑并发出了阵阵臭味。

那个时候，大家对生态环境保护重要性的认识，比起今天来还相去甚远，许多人对环境污染问题都不以为然，不少地方考虑最多的是如何快速、超常规发展，有的甚至不惜以破坏、污染环境来实现经济利益的最大化。各地都在努力追求的是高 GDP 指标，而往往很少考虑如何保护生态、保护包括水资源在内的自然环境。

由于工农业生产急剧扩张以及人口快速增长带来的一系列问题，加上长期污染的积累，从 20 世纪 90 年代起，被誉为高原明珠的滇池几次爆发了蓝藻，污染在加剧。面对日趋严重的污染，如果再不及时采取措施治理保护，被誉为昆明人民“母亲湖”的滇池势必毁于一旦。当时，云南各方对是否就此进行新闻报道的意见是很不统一的。云南的一些地方政府官员并不同意甚至是反对媒体进行报道，因为怕影响经济发展的速度，也担心因此而影响他们在仕途上的晋升。到底应不应该报、要不要报？经过一番激烈的思想斗争，这位年轻的记者决定顶住压力，为了云南人民的利益，为了昆明人民的利益，为了保护滇池，应该对这个问题进行报道，以引起中央政府和云南省及各级地方政府的重视并及时采取措施加以治理。

于是，这位年轻记者便写了《滇池已遭严重污染部分池水变黑发臭》一稿，文章特别列举了当时 168 名昆明市人大代表，在昆明市第九届人大三次会议上提出的《关于滇池治理问题的质询案》，强烈呼吁治理滇池污染。这引起了时任国务院副总理邹家华的重视，他对此报道做了重要批示，从此拉开了从中央到云南省、昆明市重拳治理滇池污染的序幕，使得滇池治污被纳入了国家大江大河大湖污染治理的重点规划。“九五”以来，国务院连续 4 个五年计划都将滇池纳入国家“三河三湖”重点污染治理项目。有关部门的统计数据表明，仅“十一五”期间，滇池治理完成投资 171.77 亿元，是“九五”“十五”总投资的 3.6 倍；2018 年，昆明市共实施了 67 个滇池保护治理项目，滇池治理完成投资 23.4 亿元。经国家环保部门考核，通过连续多年的治理保护，滇池水质由持续了 20 多年的劣 V 类改善为 2016 年全湖 V 类，2018 年持续好转为 IV 类，其污染恶化的势头得到了有力遏制，有了明显好转。

说到这儿，我想各位都已经猜到了，那个年轻的记者就是我。这里，再自我介绍一下，我 1989 年 6 月从中国社科院研究生院硕士毕业后，就进入人民日报社当记者，这期间被派驻到云南记者站工作，一直干到 2003 年 3 月。2003 年 3 月以后，我调到了光明日报社工作，又被光明日报社派驻到云南记者站任站长，一直到现在。

应该说，从 1993 年起，也就是我当记者的第 4 个年头起，我便一直跟踪关注着滇池污染的治理，继续采写了多篇滇池治理保护的报道。比如，2011 年 8 月我在《光明日报》发表了通讯《滇池治理初现曙光》，2012 年 11 月采写了《滇池综合治理六大工程取得积极进展》，2019 年 2 月 1 日又在《光明日报》发表了关于滇池保护志愿者的长篇通讯《“市民河长”让昆明大众成为滇池卫士》。

与此同时，我把对水问题的关注，又扩大到了云南省其他高原湖泊上，比如说洱海。洱海位于云南省大理苍山脚下，也是我这些年特别关注、重点加以报道的另一个著名的高原湖泊，因为，我担心它成为第二个被严重污染的“滇池”。近十年来，我每年都要去大理几次，每年都要写上至少一篇关于洱海治理的报道。为了解洱海污染与治理的情况，我专门到洱海的源头洱源县的弥苴河、永安江、罗时江与茈碧湖考察，深入洱海周边的双廊、凤仪、喜洲、银桥、挖色、才村、龙下登、南五里桥等众多村镇，跟着农村污水收集车和垃圾清运车到污水处理站、垃圾处理站体验，忍着刺鼻的臭味看污水和垃圾如何处理。所写有关洱海保护治理的报道中有一些产生了比较大的社会影响。比如我在 2017 年 4 月写了关于洱海治理的评论《保护洱海，重在斩断私利链条》，在文章中明确说，“不惜代价保护好洱海是全体大理人民、云南人民乃至全国人民、世界人民的最大‘公利’；为了个人利益、小团体利益、部门利益、企业利益等，不管以任何冠冕堂皇的理由对洱海进行掠夺式开发与攫取，都是‘私利’”“当前洱海保护治理已经无路可退。为了洱海的清澈秀美以及周边居民的美好生活，必须坚决斩断借洱海谋取私利的利益链”，在《光明日报》、光明网、《光明日报》的微信公号发表，也为国内众多媒体网站转发，引发了当时社会舆论的热议，有力推动了大理州政府当时正在推行的“洱海保护七大行动”。

2019 年 1 月 25 日，《光明日报》的“光明调查”版发表了我与另外 2 位合作者撰写的调查报告《云南大理：谱写洱海保护治理新篇章》，在《光明日报》用一整版的篇幅，对大理探索的“全域治理，系统修复，综合整治，绿色发展，全民参与”的洱海保护治理新模式进行了比较全面的调查总结，并明确指出了治理中存在的洱海流域水环境承载力有限、生态退化、自我修复功能弱、项目资金缺口大、资金筹措难等主要问题，全文长达 7000 字，也受到社会普遍的关注，为人民网、新华网、搜狐、网易、中工网、中国领导网等国内众多权威网站转发，反响很好。

我对水问题的关注并不局限于滇池、洱海，也密切关注云南省的抚仙湖、异龙湖、泸沽湖和澜沧江、怒江、金沙江。还利用各种机会在国内其他地方了解水问题，实地察看了西藏的羊卓雍湖、纳木错湖，青海省的青海湖，上海的黄浦江、苏州河，杭州的西湖，成都锦江，重庆嘉陵江，以及黄河、京杭大运河等。

在关注中国水问题的同时，我还把目光投向了国外的海与河。我实地考察过朝鲜的大同江水电站、澳大利亚的大堡礁、缅甸的伊洛瓦底江，去俄罗斯看过涅瓦河、黑海等。尤其关注了湄公河。

湄公河被誉为“东方的多瑙河”，在中国境内叫澜沧江，从云南西双版纳州勐腊县关累港出境后被称作湄公河。这条纵贯中、缅、老、泰、柬、越 6 国的澜沧江 - 湄公河是亚洲一条非常重要的国际河流。

而澜沧江 - 湄公河次区域，地处东南亚、南亚和中国西南 3 个经济圈的结合部，拥有 220 多万平方千米的土地和 2.3 亿多人口。该流域内拥有丰富的水能、矿产、生物、旅游资源，充满着巨大的投资与贸易机会，其中一些地方还是尚未开发的处女地。因而，国际社会十分看好这一区域。

对湄公河，我前后进行了 3 次考察。第一次是 1993 年 10 月，我专门从澜沧江云南段的思茅港乘坐“公主”号，沿澜沧江—湄公河顺流而下，到缅甸、老挝、泰国考察湄公河，每天吃住都在船上，历时约半个月，回来时人已经变得又黑又瘦。

2002 年 10 月，我与一批新闻媒体朋友，应云南省西双版纳傣族自治州邀请，乘坐国际旅游大巴，从景洪市出发，经勐腊县的磨憨口岸出境，从陆路进入老挝，第二次来到位于湄公河畔的老挝古都、世界文化遗产琅勃拉邦，对当地与中国云南省开展经贸往来及湄公河沿岸的风俗民情做了调查。

为了实地看看湄公河的入海口，2003 年春节期间，我与几个朋友放弃了与家人团聚良机，自费专门到柬埔寨、越南考察湄公河，最后一直深入湄公河的一个重要入海口——越南的美托市。我于 2004 年把那些年的考察感受及沿途拍摄的照片汇集出版了一本书《探访东方大河》。

这期间，我利用工作上的便利，先后几次参加了有关澜沧江 - 湄公河流域合作与开发的重要国际会议。一次是 1996 年 8 月 30 日在昆明举行的亚洲开发银行次区域经济合作第六届部长会议，来自湄公河流域的中国、缅甸、老挝、泰国、柬埔寨、越南 6 国及亚行、联合国开发计划署等的高级官员参加，时任国务院副总理姜春云出席了开幕式。2002 年 12 月 16 日，由中国国际贸易促进会、云南省政府与东盟工商会联合举办的第二届中国—东盟商务理事会暨中国—东盟商务合作论坛在昆明举行，时任国务院总理朱镕基代表中国政府向大会发来了贺信。

2005 年，大湄公河次区域经济合作第二次领导人会议在昆明召开。时任国务院总理温家宝到会讲话，高度评价了次区域合作以往所取得的丰硕成果，他说："大湄公河次区域国家地缘相邻，文化相通，政治关系良好，民间往来密切，都处在发展的重要阶段，开展互利合作既有共同需要，也有许多有利条件。次区域合作机制启动以来，我们加强在交通、能源、电信、贸易、投资、旅游、环境、人力资源、农业等领域合作，卓有成效地实施了100多个合作项目，建成了一批标志性工程，促进了各国经济和社会发展，使成千上万的人口特别是贫困人口从中受益，也对维护地区和世界和平作出了积极贡献。"

上述3次事关澜沧江－湄公河流域国家合作的重要国际会议，我作为记者都有幸亲临现场参加。

通过对湄公河的考察及多次参加有关澜沧江－湄公河次区域合作的国际会议，我对这条东方大河的历史、现状有了直观且深入的了解，充分感受到了流域内相关6国为共同开发保护所付出的努力，也看到了这里虽然拥有巨大的开发潜力，但同时存在着贫困、污染、盗伐、毒品走私及发展极度不平衡等诸多问题，进一步加深了对澜沧江－湄公河的认识和了解。

现在，我高兴地看到，经由这条国际著名河流联系起来的6国合作又有了新突破。

澜湄合作是首个由流域6国共同创建的新型次区域合作机制，是共商共建"一带一路"的重要平台。在中国的积极倡导下，2016年3月正式启动的澜沧江－湄公河合作是中国与周边国家开展次区域合作最具成效的机制之一。近年来，在中方的积极推动和相关各国的共同努力下，澜湄合作建立了领导人会议、外长会议、高官会议、优先领域联合工作组会议等四个层次机制，形成了"高效务实、项目为本、民生优先"的合作模式，如今又将"3+5合作框架"发展为"3+5+X合作框架"，以"澜湄效率"和"澜湄速度"引起世人瞩目，取得了超出预期的成效。专家认为，在逆全球化、贸易保护主义、孤立主义等势力抬头的背景下，澜湄合作"风景这边独好"，成为次区域合作和国际流域治理的典范。

2018年1月10日，国务院总理李克强在柬埔寨首都金边的和平大厦出席澜沧江－湄公河合作第二次领导人会议并发表讲话。他指出："澜湄6国地缘相近、人缘相亲、文缘相通。澜沧江－湄公河就像一条天然的'彩练'，把我们紧紧联系在一起。2016年春天，我们在三亚举行首次领导人会议，全面启动澜湄合作进程。两年来，我们心往一处想、劲往一处使，推动澜湄合作一步一个脚印从倡议变成现实，首次领导人会议确定的早期收获项目绝大部分已完成或取得实质进展，形成了‘领导人引领、全方位覆盖、各部门参与’的澜湄格局，创造了‘天天有进展、月月有成果、年年上台阶’的澜湄速度，培育了‘平等相待、真诚互助、亲如一家’的澜湄文化。”

在这次讲话中，李克强总理提出今后6国加强合作的第一条建议就是关于水的。他说：“第一，做好水资源合作。水是生命之源、生产之基、生态之要。澜沧江－湄公河流域水资源充沛，足以支撑流域经济社会发展。关键是要相互信任、相互理解、相互支持，加强上下游协作，照顾彼此关切，统筹处理好经济发展和生态保护的关系。中国已连续15年向有关国家提供澜沧江汛期水文数据。澜沧江水电梯级开发不消耗水量，还可实现‘调丰补枯’，有效帮助下游国家防洪抗旱。我们要着眼于水资源可持续利用，制定‘水资源合作五年行动计划’，加强旱涝灾害应急管理，开展水资源和气候变化影响等联合研究，改进水质监测系统。中方建议充分发挥澜湄水资源合作中心作用，办好水资源合作论坛，加强政策对话、信息交流、技术合作，打造共建共享的水资源合作平台。澜湄合作因水而生，也必将因水而兴。”

值得关注的是，李克强总理还在讲话中明确提出了“澜湄国家命运共同体”的概念。他重申：“中方愿与湄公河国家一道，全面梳理总结澜湄合作的进展，在新的起点上谋划好合作未来，打造澜湄流域经济发展带，建设澜湄国家命运共同体，为本地区和平与发展注入强劲动力。”

据初步统计，2017年中国同5国贸易总额达2200亿美元，同比增长16%。中国累计对5国各类投资超过420亿美元，2017年投资额增长20%以上。自首次领导人会议以来中国与5国新增航线330多条，2017年人员往来约3000万人次。中国已成为柬埔寨、缅甸、泰国、越南第一大贸易伙伴，是老挝第二大贸易伙伴。无疑，澜湄合作已是本地区最具活力、最富成果的合作机制之一，将为地区经济社会发展提供更有力的支撑和更广阔的舞台。

无疑，澜沧江－湄公河流域的6国人民和国际社会的有识之士，都为澜沧江－湄公河这些年所创造的新的文明成果而感到高兴。

我初步梳理了一下，到目前，我在《人民日报》、《光明日报》（包括所属的光明网、光明日报微博、光明日报微信、光明日报手机客户端）发表的有关水问题的各种新闻报道文章已经超过了 100 篇，图片超过了 1000 幅。其中有若干篇引起了中国国家领导人和云南省领导人的高度重视，对推动相关问题的解决起了明显促进作用。比如 1997 年 7 月 12 日，我在《人民日报》上发表了《蓝色的忧思——对昆明水危机的反思》，在文章中，我直言不讳地指出作为一个严重缺水的大城市，“缺水已经危及昆明市的生存与发展”，分析了在“取水、用水、管水”三个环节存在的体制矛盾与认识偏差，提出要开源节流与保护并举。巧的是，此文发表的当天，又受到了正在昆明市考察、时任国务院副总理李岚清的关注。近年来，云南省委书记、省长对我有关洱海保护中出现的资金匮乏、困难重重的相关报道也做出了重要批示。由此，可真切感受新闻报道的力量与重要作用。

我要讲的第二个故事就是和水问题专家郑晓云教授的故事。我和郑晓云教授是好朋友。在水问题方面他是专家，在新闻报道方面我是专家，这些年我们两个在相互交往中取长补短，相互学习，结下了很深的友谊。郑教授有什么新的文章、有什么新的理论观点，他会主动提供给我，这样就使我对他的学术上的研究成果和进展有一个及时的了解，也便于我帮助他做新闻报道工作。比如说 2019 年 4 月 13 日发表在《光明日报》我对郑晓云教授的专访《社会科学不可缺位水问题研究》，就是我们两个一起喝茶交流、主动沟通的结果，文章在《光明日报》发表以后，在各界引起了比较大的反响，光明网、搜狐、中国社会科学网、东方新闻、长江水利网等都做了转发。《光明日报》的微博也同时对这篇文章做了转发，仅仅在微博上阅读此文的就有 7 万多人。

湖北大学历史文化学院党委书记、教授刘明达说：“解决水问题不单单是个技术活。这篇文章向我们揭示了水不仅是人类及其他生物繁衍生存的基本条件，也是人们生活不可替代的重要资源，是生态环境中最活跃、影响最广泛的因素。”浙江水利水电学院教授、水文化首席专家闫彦说，看了《光明日报》对湖北大学教授、法国水科学院院士郑晓云就“社会科学不可缺位水问题研究”的访谈，我多年从事水文化与水资源研究，对此文有着深刻的感触和体会。中国在快速发展过程中遇到的水问题，迫切需要从水利学、社会学、经济学、管理学、文化学、历史学等学科加以研究，特别需要中国的社会学家共同来探讨，做出“中国水智慧”答案，更需要我们从水科学、水战略、水管理、水文化等多维角度去创新与实践。

著名的民族人类学者、云南大学教授尹绍亭先生一针见血地评论说：“看了《光明日报》记者任维东先生采访郑晓云教授的文章《社会科学不可缺位水问题研究》，深有感触。该访谈的振聋发聩之处，是一针见血地指出了社科界对我国面临的严重的水问题、水安全反应迟钝、应对散漫的状况，同时指出了解决问题的有效途径。有学者曾尖锐批评，我国社科研究产出垃圾太多。原因何在？缺乏人文、民族和国家关怀，无疑是重要原因之一。有鉴于此，我希望社科界的同人们好好看看这篇采访。看看采访者是如何敏锐选择对象和提出问题；看看被采访者是怎么关注现实重大问题，怎么依据深厚专业背景融合多学科知识并站在国际学术视野的高度研究问题。”

需要说明的是，虽然这些年来，我采写了一些有关水问题的新闻报道，但我并不是专职报道水问题的记者。报社给我在云南的报道任务，涉及一个省里社会生活的方方面面，如工业、农业、政治、经济、教育、生态等等。尽管如此，我这些年对水问题的关注一直持续。长期对水危机的采写报道，使我学习了许多关于水的知识，认识也不断提高，充分认识到了水问题的重要性，这也促使我更加重视对水问题的采写报道。

通过对我这26年有关水问题报道的回顾梳理，就新闻媒体今后如何进一步向社会和大众传播报道好水问题，让更多的人关爱水资源、水环境，我又有了以下一些新的思考。

第一，要充分认识到新闻舆论在应对水问题方面不可缺失的重要作用。众所周知，古今中外，舆论历来都是影响社会发展的重要力量。以中国为例，在当今移动互联网为王的时代，传统的报纸、广播、电视等新闻媒介仍然在社会生活里扮演重要角色，新兴的微博、微信、手机客户端、短视频等媒体传播手段异军突起，依托互联网，它们无论是在传播信息，促进人际沟通，还是在营造舆论等方面都发挥着越来越重要的作用。

以目前我工作单位光明日报社为例，《光明日报》是一份有着70年办报历史的全国综合性大报。目前，我们光明日报社，除了纸质《光明日报》与光明网，还办有光明日报微博、光明日报微信、光明日报手机客户端，同时在著名的新媒体平台今日头条、百度等都开设了自己的官方账号。2019年3月全国“两会”期间，仅半个多月时间里，《光明日报》推出的文章、有声漫画、视频、直播、图解、动画、VR 全景、图片等全媒体产品累计浏览量达 3.2 亿次。其巨大的社会影响力及作用非简单的数字统计所能衡量。

因此，作为大众传播的重要手段和表现形式，新闻舆论对一个国家、对全社会乃至全球一体化下的国际社会都具有强大的社会动员力、影响力与号召力。既然新闻媒体的作用如此之大，我们就必须高度重视运用与发挥大众传媒在应对水问题、水危机方面的作用，而不是忽视它。必须承认，无论是水问题研究学界还是新闻界，在这方面所做的工作还很不够。

第二，新闻媒体应当主动担当，加大对水问题、水危机报道的力度。当前，中国正在大力推进生态文明建设，水文明作为生态文明中极为重要的组成部分，理应受到社会各界的高度重视。毋庸讳言，水问题日渐严重，水危机愈演愈烈，而大众的应对无论是从认识到行动都很不足。另外，从中国的现实来看，新闻媒体对水问题的关注和报道，会影响到从中央政府、省级政府乃至地州市县乡各级政府的决策，为他们提供决策咨询参考，并且对各级政府部门、相关企业、个人对水环境的不友好行为进行舆论监督批评，促使相关问题的解决。如前所说，新闻媒体的社会影响力、动员力及号召力是非常巨大的，尤其在中国这样一个社会主义国家里，政府主办主管的新闻媒体常常担负指导推进相关工作的重任。纵观中国国内许多传媒机构，如《人民日报》、新华社、《光明日报》、《经济日报》、中央电视台等主流媒体，这些年对中国各地水问题、水污染、水危机等都做了大量的报道，对促进相关水问题的解决都起了很好而且显著的作用。这方面，新闻媒体还任重道远。

第三，新闻媒体对社会大众在水问题知识普及和水情状况教育方面可以实现“多快好省”。有关资料显示：我国是一个干旱缺水严重的国家，人均淡水资源仅为世界平均水平的 1/4，是全球人均水资源最贫乏的国家之一。全国人均可利用水资源量仅为 900 立方米，并且分布极不均衡。20 世纪末，全国 600 多座城市中有 400 多个城市存在供水不足问题，其中比较严重的缺水城市达 110 个，全国城市每年缺水 60 亿立方米，每年因缺水造成经济损失约 2000 亿元。遗憾的是，如果行走街头，随便找一个普通的中国人问一下中国的基本水情状况，应该说，大多数人回答不出来。除了极少数水问题研究者和水务工作者，许多国人对这样一个极为严重的中国水形势并不知晓。

在中国这样一个国土面积广袤、地区发展严重不平衡的国家，许多人由于所在地域的不同、受教育程度的不同、学习专业的不同，对日趋严重的水问题、水危机并不了解，或所知甚少，很难真正认识到其危害性，自然也就不会重视。这或许是因为，虽然水是人类的生命之源，十分重要，但又看起来非常普通，似乎是随处可见、唾手可得，大多数人都被表象所迷惑，很少有人能认识到水问题的严重性。这就是严峻的现实。而借助覆盖面广大、影响力深远、高效便捷的新闻媒体，可以“多快好省”实现对社会大众水问题知识普及、水情警示教育。因为水的问题，在今天，不再单纯是一个自然的问题，它的社会属性日益凸显，并越来越多地演变成一个广泛而严重的社会问题。既然是社会问题，就需要全社会的重视、关注，大家一起协力来解决，而不是只靠研究关注水问题的某一小部分学者、教授或者是新闻媒体。在这方面，云南省大理市借助国家级新闻媒体、省州市级媒体和互联网等多种手段，在全体市民包括学校的少年儿童中，大力宣传报道洱海污染的危害及保护的重要性，倡导“洱海清，大理兴”“保护洱海人人有责”，做到了家喻户晓，收到了很好的效果。

第四，新闻媒体应当注重培养水问题、水危机报道方面的专门人才，从而提高相关报道的水平。根据我的观察，从中国大众传媒现状看，无论是国家级媒体、省级媒体，还是地市级媒体乃至近几年快速兴起的各类新媒体，目前基本上都没有专注于水问题报道与研究的专业部门与专业记者。几乎所有报道水问题的记者都是水问题的非专业人士，属于临时应急，人员不固定，相关知识缺乏，今天需要了就仓促上阵应付，导致对水问题的报道缺乏深度与持久性，所写有关水问题的报道其专业水准也不高。

无论是新闻界还是研究水问题的学术界，对如何运用新媒体搞好对水问题的新闻报道、促进更好地应对严重的水危机，目前均缺乏专门且深入的研究与思考。这也导致众多媒体在开展水问题报道时基本上处于没有科学指导、引导的低水平应付状态，也没有很好地适应新媒体这一传播形态的改变，未能更好地发挥大众传媒应有的作用。因此，时代与现实呼唤更多的新闻媒体及媒体人士持续关注、报道及研究水问题。

第五，新闻媒体应当高度重视并进一步借助新媒体，搞好水问题、水危机的报道。

当前，互联网已经在深刻改变着人类社会，传统的大众传播形态因此也发生了重大的改变。报纸、广播、电视、杂志等传统传播方式受到了互联网，尤其是移动互联网的强烈冲击，越来越多的人特别是年轻人，主要是通过互联网来获取各种信息而不再依靠传统传播媒介。

根据 2018 年中国互联网协会发布的《中国互联网发展报告 2018》，截至 2017 年底，中国网民规模达 7.72 亿，其中手机网民规模达 7.53 亿，移动互联网的快速发展带动了网民规模的增长，2017 年手机上网人群占比由 2016 年的 95.1% 提升至 97.5%，手机已经成为最主要的移动上网设备。截至 2017 年底，10～39 岁的网民群体占整体网民的 73%，其中 20～29 岁的网民占比最高，达 30%。此外，2017 年中国网络新闻用户规模达 6.47 亿人，网民覆盖率为 83.8%，用户规模保持稳定增长。

这也是为什么在今天的中国，以微信、今日头条、抖音、微博等为代表的新媒体蓬勃发展的主要原因之一。

面对大众传播方式的剧烈变化，无论是新闻界还是相关学界，都必须重视研究应对之策，适应新形势，充分并善于应用新媒体平台做好水问题的新闻报道，以大众喜闻乐见、通俗易懂的方式，使广大的移动互联网用户受到相关水情教育，认识水危机，关爱水环境，人人都能为水问题的解决贡献一份力量。这应该是我们努力的方向。

第六，新闻界应当重视并加强与水问题研究学界之间相互的交流沟通。这样可以及时了解获取有关水问题研究的进展情况并向社会大众加以传播，提高媒体对水问题的专业知识素养，提高相关新闻报道的专业水准。目前看，双方间偶尔的交流大多限于几次研讨会，缺乏专门而定期的沟通机制，许多水问题学者多数只是埋头于自己的研究，不太注重或很少主动与新闻记者交朋友，也不善于运用大众传媒把自己的学术成果让大众认知。作为媒体人，为了做好水报道，理应主动和水问题专家学者交朋友。

同时，还应探索与国际新闻媒体加强对跨国跨界的国际海江河湖的合作报道。

针对上述存在的这些问题，需要水科学研究界与新闻界共同来重视并努力开展研究，寻求更好的解决之道，为全人类的水安全做出应有的贡献。

非洲水治理的探索历程

张　瑾*

摘　要： 非洲水资源稀缺和珍贵，并不是由于地理上的缺水，而主要是由分布不均、开发不足、供水效率和水治理能力极其低下造成的。非洲的水问题是非洲历史的一面镜子，尽管非洲有着悠久的水文明，历经殖民水政策洗礼，都希望借助国家力量进行资源再分配，却因为资金和人力等多重原因，水治理能力较差，不得不倚重外国和国际组织的水治理援助。从非洲水治理的探索历程看，在国际、洲际、国家等多层面，非洲各国、非洲国际组织都进行了水治理探索。其特点是多领域、多参与者共同参与治理，水治理的结果不可预测性较高，传统文化习俗影响力较多。尽管非洲国家整体能力提升是非洲水治理的必要前提，但在全球化时代，如何尊重传统，发挥民众的自发力量，审时度势协同治理，是当下非洲水治理必须思考的问题。

关键词： 非洲　水资源　水问题　水治理

Abstract: The scarcity and preciousness of water resources in Africa is not due to geographical water scarcity, but to uneven distribution, inadequate development, water supply efficiency and extremely low water management capacity. The water problem in Africa is a mirror of African history. Although Africa has a long history of water civilization and has been baptized by colonial water policy, when African nationals got their independence, they hope to redistribute water resources. However, due to multiple reasons such as limited capital and poor manpower, mediocre water governance, African water management has to rely on water governance assistance from foreign and international organizations. From the

* 张瑾，上海师范大学非洲研究院副教授，主要研究非洲问题和中非关系。

perspective of exploration process of water management in Africa, African water management has its own characters as: multi - faceted combined with the international, intercontinental, and national actors; have water management exploration mainly carried out synergism by African countries and African international organizations. The water management results mainly unpredictable and easily influence of traditional cultural practices. Although necessary prerequisite for water governance in Africa is the overall capacity improvement of African countries, in the era of globalization, how to respect the tradition, give play to the spontaneous power of the people, are core issues that must be considered in current water governance in Africa.

Keywords: African; Water resources; Water issues; Water management

一 非洲水资源概况

水资源包括经人类控制并直接可供灌溉、发电、给水、航运、养殖等用途的地表水和地下水，以及江河、湖泊、井、泉、潮汐、港湾和养殖水域等，是发展国民经济不可缺少的重要自然资源。然而，水资源在世界各地分布不均，很多地方的水需求与水供给存在很大缺口。近年来，有许多研究发现地球的淡水资源正在耗竭。虽然超过70%的陆地表面由水组成，共计3.4万亿~4.6万亿立方米，但是淡水只占其中不到3%。这些淡水资源中，74%保存于冰川和极地冰雪，其他25%保存在土壤中，除非消耗地下水，否则不能被使用。这样，只有不到1%的地球淡水来满足所有人类、动植物所需。有学者进而推论，根据最近20年来的发展，2050年左右，淡水的需求将超过供给能力，尤其是那些降水稀少地区，将根据需要来计划供水。

非洲拥有较为丰富的水资源，[①] 占世界水资源的比例约为9%，约为4050立方米/年。但非洲水资源在季节分配上多寡不定，地区分布也不均衡。非洲70%以上的水资源集中在中部和西部非洲，北部和苏丹-萨赫勒地区只占总量的5.5%。非洲水资源的不均分配也造成了不同区域、国家各自不同的水资源需求。总的来看，非洲超过40%的人口生活在贫瘠、半贫

① 但这并不为人所知，笔者给学生上“非洲水资源研究”课程之前，都会给学生做非洲水资源的印象问卷，五年以来得到最多的关键词是“缺水”和“污浊”。

瘠和半干旱半潮湿地区，8 亿非洲人口中有 3 亿处于缺水环境中。[①] 非洲人均可用水资源量不仅远低于全球平均水平，而且仍在下降。

由于水资源开发不足，非洲水资源的供水率、利用率和水治理能力极其低下。非洲大陆只有 38% 的水资源被用于农业供水和工业用水，可耕地中只有 5% 有灌溉。[②]与此同时，非洲各国供水和用水需求之间的差距还在不断扩大，人民生活水平的提高和消费方式的改变，使水需求日益增长。但由于农业、采矿和工业的竞争性需求以及水质恶化，非洲总体的供水量正在下降。近 3 年来，以南非开普敦为首的地区遭遇了历史性的干旱，其水库容量只相当于平时的 20% 。[③]由是，各国纷纷转向使用战略储备资源的地下水，但过度开采和未经处理的污水排放等问题，已经威胁到地下水源。[④]

作为发展中国家最集中的大陆，非洲是世界上经济发展水平最低的一个洲，其水资源的供水率、利用率和水治理能力极其低下。非洲大陆只有 38% 的水资源用于农业、工业和日常生活，可耕地中只有 5% 左右得到灌溉，[⑤]只有 44% 的城市人口和 24% 的农村人口拥有足够的水处理设施。更严重的是，非洲总体水供应量呈下降之势，人均可用水资源量远低于全球平均水平且不断下降。[⑥] 非洲各国用水供需矛盾日益突出，人民生活水平的提高和消费方式的改变，造成用水量大增。农业、采矿和工业的竞争性需求，更致使水质恶化。因此，非洲水资源的总体形势每况愈下。20 世纪 80 年代，在联合国“国际饮用水供应与卫生十年”（International Drinking Water

---

① “Water in Africa”, UN – system – wide support to AU/NEPAD, 2006.

② Matt McGrath “Huge´water resource exists under Africa”, Journal Environmental Research Letters, 2012. https: //www. bbc. com/news/science – environment – 17775211.

③ Evan Lubofsky . “A massive freshwater reservoir at the bottom of the ocean could solve Cape Town's drought – but it's going untapped”, https: //www. theverge. com/2018/2/15/17012678/cape – town – drought – water – solution. 2018 – 2 – 15.

④ World Bank, 2012. A Primer on Energy Efficiency for Municipal Water and Wastewater Utilities. Technical Report No. 1. Washington, DC, Energy Sector Management Assistance Program, The World Bank.

⑤ 根据 IWMI/AU/NEPAD/USAID 等的统计数据，灌溉一般在 3% ~7% 。参见 Ian Kunwenda, Barbara van Koppen, Mampiti Matete, and Luxon Nhamo “Trends and Outlook: Agricultural Water Management in Southern Africa”, Technical Report, October 2015; Matt McGrath “Huge' water resource exists under Africa,” https: //www. bbc. com/news/science – environment – 17775211。

⑥ The Water Project, “WATER AND HUNGER, Improving Sustainability in Rural Africa,” https: //thewaterproject. org/why – water/hunger.

Supply and Sanitation Decade：1981－90）的倡议下，非洲不少国家铺设了自来水管网，建设了一批供水卫生设施。但由于发展过缓，大多数国家政府财政吃紧，后续投入极为有限。随着城市人口急剧增长，[①]很多国家目前使用的还是20世纪八九十年代的供水设备，且由于疏于维护而渗漏严重，即使在非洲最发达的国家南非，仍有36%的水费是因为漏水损失而无法收取的。其他国家的水浪费更是无法统计。[②]

水卫生条件不足是非洲地区霍乱、伤寒等各种传染病和热带疾病不定时流行的主要原因。根据世界卫生组织和联合国儿童基金会等方面的报道，在全球近8亿缺乏水处理的人口中，一半以上居住在非洲，其中在撒哈拉以南非洲的人口数达6.95亿，3.19亿人无法获得清洁饮用水。[③]多数人仍使用河流、湖泊为载体的地表水，[④]每小时有115人死于恶劣环境或个人卫生及受污染水源引发的各种疾病。[⑤]据世界卫生组织测算，每投入1美元用于水和卫生设施，经济回报在3～34美元。[⑥]但是，这些投入对于积贫积弱的非洲国家来说可谓望洋兴叹。

二　非洲水治理的探索历程

水治理是在治理理论[⑦]视域下，对水资源合理使用和管理产生的政治、

---

① 从1960年的大约2.85亿增加到今天的近13亿，非洲的城市用水和废水管理也面临着新的挑战。预计到2050年，非洲总人口预计将突破25亿，其中55%生活在城市环境中。

② 东京和金边的这一比例只有3.7%和8%。参见“´No drop´Water Conservation Report”，http：//www.gcx.co.za/no－drop－water－conservation－report/。

③ 其中的16%人口缺乏改善的卫生条件，36%的人缺乏洗手用的肥皂。World Health Organization“Key Facts from 2015 JMP Report，”http：//www.who.int/water_sanitation_health/publications/JMP－2015－keyfacts－en－rev.pdf?ua＝1；World Health Organization，“WHO in the African Region，”http：//www.afro.who.int/en/clusters－a－programmes/hpr/protection－of－the－human－environment/programme－components/index.php?

④ WHO/UNICEF Joint Monitoring Programme for Water Supply and Sanitation“2015 Report and MDG Assessment，”http：//www.wssinfo.org/.

⑤ 联合国：“生命之水十年”，http：//www.un.org/zh/waterforlifedecade/.（上网日期：2018年8月2日）。

⑥ World Health Organization，“Evaluation of the Costs and benefits of water and sanitation improvements at the global level”，http：//www.who.int/water_sanitation_health/wsh0404.pdf.

⑦ 治理理论（governance theory）作为国际社会科学领域重要的跨学科理论思潮，是对国家（政府）、市场失灵的反思以及全球合作共治、新地区主义等现实的回应，也是对传统公共管理和政权理念的冲击。治理理论将市场、社会组织等多元主体的作用予以（转下页注）

社会、经济和行政影响进行综合考量，寻求解决路径的探索。

（一）国际组织倡导非洲水治理

非洲水资源的分散性、跨国性、气候年际变化明显，单靠非洲国家自身没有能力应对所有的危机，国际组织往往会加入非洲水资源的协调和管理进程中，这不仅是国际组织的诉求，也是非洲水资源治理所需。因此，非洲水治理通常与非洲的政治发展、非洲的千年发展目标、非洲减贫发展计划等项目紧密相连，这些项目都旨在通过强化水资源管理的机构、机制、能力建设和行业目标，以水资源能力发展作为主要抓手，提供私有领域参与公共事务中的便利。

作为最大的国际协调机构，联合国主导推动了一系列关于非洲水的改善方案。希望通过全球治理的逻辑体系，为政府和利益相关者搭建平台，使国家与社会、经济与生态协同，从而促进可持续发展，满足世界上 20 亿需要改善水质的人口需求。2010 年，联合国在“千年发展目标”中专门提出将提升安全用水的人口比例作为基本人权的实现手段。

针对世界各国不同的水发展能力，联合国于 2007 年推出了“水机制十年能力发展方案”，把关于非洲水资源的会议基本都设立在非洲本土召开。① 从非洲具体的实施效果来看，非洲的水治理水平有所提升。2015 年，城市 80% 的区域改良水从 1990 年的 26% 上升到 2010 年的 38%，农村 80% 以上

(接上页注⑦)凸显，对于国家和社会孰为中心的论辩，使“治理”（governance）在地方（local）、社会（society）、次国家（sub - national）、国家（national）、次/区域（sub/regional）、全球（global）等诸多层次，显示出不同的含义，甚至变成可以映射任何事物的“流行词汇”。对治理的一般定义仍存在争议，不同愿景的人倾向于不同的界定方式。但最常被引用的治理定义之一是：“在一个国家的事务管理中行使政治，经济和行政权力。治理包括复杂机制，过程和制度，通过治理，公民和团体可以明确各自利益，调解分歧，行使其合法权利和义务。”

① 包括：新闻工作者培训内容（2009 年，埃及开罗），针对农业用水效率而开发的水作物软件的应用培训（2009 年 7 月非洲布基纳法索瓦加杜吉，2010 年 3 月南非布隆方丹），中东和北非区域政策制定者的培训内容（2009 年 10 ~ 12 月的三个研讨会）、为水资源管理者开办的区域性应用水损失减少研讨会（2010 年 1 月，摩洛哥拉巴特），以及在塞内加尔首都达喀尔举办的第一届 G - WADI 网络研讨会的协作工作（2010 年 4 月），2010 年 3 月，乌干达首都坎帕拉水能力建设讨论会，2011 年 3 月，开普敦针对非洲水资源损失减少举办活动，继之 2012 年又在摩洛哥和南非就“农业废水的安全使用”项目，举办了区域性研讨会。

区域的改良水从1990年的5%上升到2010年的10%。已获取改良水源的人数增加了20%，共4.27亿人在千年发展目标期间获得了改良饮用水源。但非洲仍是发展最滞后的区域，仍有3.19亿人无法使用改良水，改良水覆盖率低于50%的3个国家（安哥拉、赤道几内亚与巴布亚新几内亚）中，非洲国家占2国。[①]

目前，参与非洲水资源治理的国际机构除了联合国等重要的全球性组织外，还包括以下几家：世界银行国家政策和体制评估机构，非洲开发银行国家政策和体制评估，世界银行的世界治理指标，透明国际的腐败感知指数，失败国家指数，和平基金，千年挑战公司国家记分和易卜拉欣非洲治理指数等。这些机构都通过不同的项目参与非洲各国的水资源治理，并通过不同的体系在一定程度上促进了非洲水资源的发展。

（二）非洲各国的自身努力

非洲有潜力满足当前和未来就业需求的行业，大多依赖水资源或相关行业，比如社会服务、农业、渔业和水产养殖、零售和酒店业、制造业、建筑业、自然资源开采（包括采矿业）和能源生产（包括石油和天然气的水力，地热）等，所有这些部门都在不同程度上需要保障水资源的可获得性和可靠性。可是，由于发展阶段和产业能力所限，非洲各国目前尚不完全具备应对自然危机的能力，一旦遇到气候变化和降雨变化，主要生产部门就很容易受到影响，继而影响到大多数非洲国家的整体经济。一些产业和部门的用水不当，可能促成短期就业，但对宏观和长远的水资源供应会造成负面影响，并危及其他产业，从而影响到国家的发展大局。以加纳为例，2011年加纳首次生产石油时，经济增长了14%，但到2015年增长率只有3.9%。尽管值得深究的原因很多，其中基础设施，尤其是基本的水和能源基础设施无法满足国家快速增长的经济需要，严重掣肘未来发展。加纳主要依靠伏尔塔河的阿克苏博水力发电大坝供电，近年来，由于降雨量减少，自然流量受限，水电站仅能在半数时间进行运作，且需要24小时关闭一次，无力支撑经济发展和生活需要的电力。[②]

---

① WHO Library Cataloguing - in - Publication Data, Progress on Sanitation and Drinking Water - 2015 update and MDG assessment. NLM classification: WA 670.

② *The United Nations World Water Development Report* 2016: *Water and Jobs*. Paris: UNESCO. 2016.

非洲各国普遍认识到水问题的重要性，并采取了一系列治理行动予以规范，再加上建设必要的水供应设施来做到用水的配套。[①] 20 世纪 90 年代以来，多个非洲国家都制定了相应的水法规范形式，包括莫桑比克、乌干达、津巴布韦、布基纳法索、斯威士兰、肯尼亚、坦桑尼亚、赞比亚、加纳和南非等。另外，多个国家也以国际项目作为抓手，推进国内相关事务的同时发展。比如，埃塞俄比亚制定环境法规，同时以“水、卫生和健康（WASH）”项目作为关键抓手，从政府的战略和协议出发，将社会发展进一步拓展到卫生服务推广等领域。

非洲多个国家的水务部门通过政策框架，确定了一系列高级别宣言、决议和行动纲领，旨在发展和利用非洲大陆的水资源促进社会经济发展、区域一体化。其中包括《非洲水愿景 2025》及其《行动框架》（2000 年）[②]、非洲联盟水与农业特别首脑会议及《苏尔特宣言》（2004 年）、《非盟沙姆沙伊赫——水和卫生宣言》（2008 年）和《2063 议程》（2014 年）。[③]

然而，由于大多数非洲国家的国债负担沉重，经济发展水平低下，加之缺乏管理水资源的财政与管理能力、环境管理方面的法律与政策不平衡、缺乏专职办公人员等，非洲在改善水资源管理上面临着巨大困难。由于公共资金有限，非洲国家各行业对资金的争夺十分激烈，每个行业都试图说明自身是带动国家发展的关键部门。但各国对于合理吸收利用现有资源的能力却不足。水资源、环境卫生和个人卫生项目的资金不足，超过 80% 的国家在完成既定全国环境卫生及饮用水工作上已大幅落后，大多数非洲国家难以实现在水资源、环境卫生和个人卫生方面所做出的承诺。更严重的

① 参见 Kaufmann, D., A. Kraay, and M. Mastruzzi.（2004）.“Governance Matters”, Washington, DC: World Bank; World Bank（2006）“Handbook for Evaluating Infrastructure Regulatory Systems”, Washington, DC。

② UNECA/AU/AfDB, 2000.

③ 非盟《2063 议程》渴望建立一个经济包容性增长和可持续发展为基础的繁荣非洲。认为应对水资源进行公平和可持续的使用和管理，以促进社会经济发展、区域合作，并呼吁其他国家：通过投资于他们的健康、教育以获得技术、机会和资本，改善青年失业和就业不足状况，支持青年成为非洲复兴的驱动者。通过在所有学校、学院和大学建立非盟俱乐部，鼓励年轻人之间的交流和倡导泛非主义。确保加快非洲大陆招生、课程、标准的统一，并提高高等教育的标准，争取在 2025 年促进非洲青年和人才在跨越大陆的流动性。

是，尽管多方努力，撒哈拉以南非洲水环境卫生的覆盖率仍只有30%，即自1990年来仅增长了4%。[①] 加之持续不断增长的人口数量，尤其是贫穷国家或者城市贫民区的人口增长更加迅速，非洲水资源退化趋势正在加快。即使经济发展有先天禀赋的一些国家，也因为水资源管理滞后，拉慢了经济发展的速度和效率。

2000年左右，非洲多国在世界银行、非洲经委会、非洲发展银行带动下，加入《非洲水前景》所提出的每5年提升5%的水资源潜力的计划，以适应农业、水电、工业、旅游和交通在国家层面的目标。2005年，非洲多国加入联合国主导的“生命之水十年行动”（International Decade for Action “Water for life，2005－2015”），以响应联合国提出的千年发展目标。多年努力后，非洲水环境的提升呈现出明显的区域差别。仅在获取水资源领域方面，北非和撒哈拉以南非洲就有很大区别。北非的覆盖率达到92%，很快即可实现千年发展目标中提出的94%的目标。但撒哈拉以南非洲只有61%水资源覆盖率，离千年发展目标75%的区域目标还很遥远。从撒哈拉以南非洲35个国家（占该地区人口的84%）的数据分析，显示了最贫穷和最富有的农村和城市人口之间的差异。90%以上的城市富人使用改良水源，超过60%使用自来水。在农村地区，只有60%的家庭拥有自来水，约一半人口没有任何一种改良水。[②]

2011年非洲各国在水资源、环境卫生和个人卫生项目方面再次做出承诺，同意增加拨款，并增强领导力与协调力。大多数国家还设立了透明的“水、卫生和健康（WASH）”项目规定的目标，并提供了相应的政策支持与监管措施。多个非洲国家联合通过了《2025年非洲水远景》，旨在以水资源为抓手，推动非洲发展与非洲团结的新型合作关系。

（三）水、流域协同与综合管理：新型非洲集体解决机制探索

撒哈拉以南非洲地区大约75%的区域都位于53个跨境国际河流流域内，加之非洲国家面临着普遍的贫困和粮食不安全状况，几乎所有国家都

---

① WHO Library Cataloguing－in－Publication Data, Progress on Sanitation and Drinking Water－2015 update and MDG assessment. NLM classification：WA 670.

② http：//www. un. org/zh/waterforlifedecade/africa. shtml.

缺乏相应的人力、经济和制度能力来有效、可持续地开发、管理水资源，进行水治理。通过合作治理水资源，是非洲各国的不二选择。

通过对赞比西河流域多个部门的研究表明，在没有外部投资的情况下，流域合作仍可使企业能源产量增加 23%。① 跨国、跨区域政策协调从 20 世纪 80 年代起就受到非洲各国的重视，创建了不少跨界合作的体制和法律框架，在推动非洲水资源开发中越来越扮演重要角色。如水资源综合管理（IWRM）②、赞比西河流域管理局、南部非洲发展共同体议定书、沃尔特河管理局和尼罗河流域委员会等。

1994 年，肯尼亚、坦桑尼亚和乌干达签订了《维多利亚湖三方环境管理规划筹备协定》，1995 年在此基础上建立了一个基金项目，其中心主要是渔业管理、污染控制、杂草入侵控制和流域地区的利用管理。1995 年，南部非洲发展共同体通过了《关于共享河流系统的议定书》，确立了利益一致和密切合作的原则。1999 年颁布的“尼罗河流域草案”是一个在尼罗河流经的 10 个国家之间实施的联合项目，其目的是确保可持续资源的开发、安全、协作和经济联合。2012 年，非洲设立了基础设施发展项目，其中优先行动计划在 2020 年前将启动 51 个不同领域的短期项目，旨在推进非洲的基础设施建设，跟进全球经济增长步伐。另外，位于世界最高发电潜力的刚果河流域的英加水电站，③ 似乎显示了非洲可能通过大坝产生的水能和电力分配，来满足非洲多个地区的需求的可能性。尽管仍需要进行详细的生态环境评估，仍需要协调各国合作的政治意愿，探索建立多边共赢体制框架，但以协作方式，为所有参与者提供最佳解决方案，或许是解决非洲水问题的一个最好抓手。

---

① World Bank，http：//www.worldbank.org/en/news/feature/2015/09/10/collaborative - management - of - the - zambezi - river - basin - ensures - greater - economic resilience.

② 水资源综合管理（IWRM）的概念首先于 1992 年在都柏林和里约热内卢召开的水与环境国际会议上提出，是旨在帮助各国按照成本 - 效益较优和可持续的方法尽力处理水问题的一种过程，概念提出以来已得到不断改进。基本定义为：是以公平的、不损害重要生态系统的可持续性的方式促进水、土及相关资源的协调开发和管理从而使经济和社会财富最大化的过程。

③ 英加水电站，又称英加水坝、英加大型水电枢纽，是位于刚果河上的重要水利设施，设计总装机容量 44000 兆瓦。工程建设共分六期，其中第三期工程预计于 2020 年建成，全部建成后将成为世界第一大水电站。工程自 1972 年开工以来，一直存在环境和生态可持续问题的争议，还值得进一步研究。

三　非洲水治理的特点

1. 多领域、多参与者合作治理

由于水资源与各行业、领域有相关性和联动性，非洲水治理往往与卫生与健康防疫、人权（尤其是妇女权益等）领域密切合作，以满足各个领域的改善需求。非洲水治理中涉及多方参与者的信息、技术、数据和专业性，自然就存在不对称，因此，在处理一个问题中，不同的参与者往往有不同的价值偏向和政策选择，为非洲的水治理带来了不同的发展维度争议。非洲的水资源治理需要与不同领域的参与者协调合作，这不仅受限于国际政治体系因素，是非洲政府需要面对的难题，也涉及非洲各国内部公私部门的权力分享与争夺，对非洲整个社会的发展进程的影响都很大。长远来看，非洲水治理究竟由谁主导，也是非洲如何在全球化浪潮中发展的关键问题，需要非洲各国加以理性对待。

2. 水治理的结果不可预测性较高

可靠的数据对政策决策、监测和评估结果提供至关重要的信息，非洲进行有效的水治理，首要的条件就是掌握非洲水资源的数据和特点。但非洲国家经费有限，绘图、监测和调研能力不足。许多国家虽然已经建立了WASH监测框架，但大多数报告的数据不一致，最后还是依赖于国际组织提供的数据，削弱了非洲水资源数据评估和结果分析的严谨性。即使援助国家和组织有比较周密的水治理计划，但非洲国家水治理的执行能力差。WTO的一份报告发现，只有三分之一的受访非洲国家正在实施、资助和定期审查国家WASH计划。在大多数非洲国家，监测不一致导致了严重的决策差距。[①]即使是确定供水系统[②]和卫生系统的具体方位，也往往受制于各方利益角逐，这些都为非洲水治理结果带来了较大不确定性。

3. 非洲水文化和水习俗的潜在影响

非洲的传统生计，都是以土地和水作为基础的，水文化在非洲的发展中有非常重要的作用。尼罗河流域居民通过观测尼罗河水文区分季节

---

① “UN Reveals Major Gaps in Water and Sanitation, Especially in Rural Areas”, https：//www. qualityassurancemag. com/article/un - water - sanitation - gaps/ 2014 - 12 - 2.

② 也称为出水点、水井和水窖。

进行农业生产，根据传统水文化知识准确地预测尼罗河泛滥时间，再将每年尼罗河定时泛滥留下的肥沃污泥用于耕作，留下璀璨的尼罗河文明。至今，非洲社区中仍以水井作为活动中心地带，取水、洗澡、钓鱼等都在这里进行，这里也是非洲妇女和儿童之间互动最多的场合。非洲其他涉水区域通常也都有较明确的宗教仪轨和维护规则。对非洲本土社会而言，进行非洲水治理不仅有非洲基础设施等硬件的改善，也必须包括对所在区域水文化、水技术、水本土知识等作为非洲农业家庭劳动分工的因素考察。

4. 中国作为新兴参与者的角色值得期待

2015 年 3 月 3 日，作为南南合作的典范，联合国环境规划署 - 中国 - 非洲“水行动”合作项目报告于第 15 届非洲环境部长会议期间发布。该项目报告重点突出了各项目在流域管理、雨水蓄积、饮用水处理、污水处理、干旱农业和防治沙漠化方面的成果，尤其关注能力建设与合作模式的经验总结。据此项目报告，有约 1000 名非洲技术人员、管理人员和农民从培训班、研讨班、实地考察和奖学金研究生项目中获益。[①] 2016 年前半年南部非洲干旱，包括中国在内的很多国家前往非洲为当地开凿水井，并与此同时，进行了简单的水处理装备配置。中国通过“一带一路”倡议，在基础设施、医药、卫生、技术、教育等多个领域与非洲展开切实的合作，成为未来非洲水治理可以期待的积极力量。

四　结语

尽管非洲有着悠久的水文明，非洲各国也投入了一定的力量进行水利治理，但因为资金和人力等多重原因所限，效果较差，不得不倚重外国和国际组织的水治理援助。非洲水问题折射了非洲对自身水资源掌控随着时代旁落的变迁历程，是非洲进入全球治理体系而无力进行其他选择的表现，是非洲整体历史命运的客观写照。

非洲水治理关乎未来各个行业和领域发展，是非洲发展的基本问题之

---

① 联合国环境规划署 - 中国 - 非洲“水行动”项目报告发布，2015 - 3 - 5，转引自 http://www.tanpaifang.com/zhengcefagui/2015/030542827.html，2015 - 3 - 5。

一。由于非洲水治理与非洲的政治、经济和社会联系紧密，是检验非洲能否联合自强的关键领域，因此，促进非洲各国整体能力的提升，是更好地进行非洲水治理的必要前提。在当前的形势下，尽管非洲水治理需要更多全球范围的援助，但以非洲各国及民众为主体来应对和解决非洲水问题，以促进长期、可持续发展，仍是解决非洲水问题的基本路径。

《水历史与水文明研究》集刊征稿启事

由水利部宣传教育中心、湖北大学中国长江文化研究院、水历史与水文明研究所共同主办、湖北大学特聘教授郑晓云主编的《水历史与水文明研究》(The Journal of Water History and Water Civilization Studies)是一本年度连续出版的学术刊物，由社会科学文献出版社出版。本刊以中文文稿为主，每期将刊登3~5篇英文文稿，海内外同时发行。集刊将通过成熟的相关学术网络渠道在国际学术界进行交流，欢迎投稿。

本刊的办刊目的是刊发中国和国际学者关于水的历史文化研究的最新研究论文，包括对中国和国外的水历史和水文明理论探讨、个案研究和水生态文明研究方面的最新研究成果。本集刊的出版将为这个领域的学术成果发表和交流搭建平台，从而将推动学科领域的发展，尤其是将推动中外的水历史文化交流，共同应对当代的水危机，服务于生态文明建设。本刊欢迎基于历史学、人类学、社会学、文化学等学科以及社会科学与自然科学交叉对水的历史与发展问题的研究成果。

本集刊初步设定的栏目有：1. 水历史与水文明理论研究；2. 水与中华文明；3. 海外水历史文明研究；4. 历史上的水利与社会；5. 水与生态文明研究；6. 水历史的田野考察。

《水历史与水文明研究》是学术研究刊物，只接受原创性学术研究论文和报告。中文稿件字数不超过15000字。所有投稿都将通过评审专家的匿名评审决定是否采用，投稿者应当认同这一规则。

投寄到以下邮件地址：zhengxy68@163.com、hxqsh@163.com。请注明投稿。

图书在版编目（CIP）数据

水历史与水文明研究. 第1辑 / 郑晓云主编. -- 北京：社会科学文献出版社，2021.1
ISBN 978 -7 -5201 -6957 -8

Ⅰ. ①水… Ⅱ. ①郑… Ⅲ. ①水 - 文化研究 - 中国 ②水 - 文化研究 - 世界 Ⅳ. ①K928.4 ②K918.4

中国版本图书馆CIP数据核字（2020）第133291号

水历史与水文明研究（第1辑）

主　　编 / 郑晓云

出 版 人 / 王利民
责任编辑 / 徐永清　张建中

出　　版 / 社会科学文献出版社 · 政法传媒分社（010）59367156
　　地址：北京市北三环中路甲29号院华龙大厦　邮编：100029
　　网址：www.ssap.com.cn
发　　行 / 市场营销中心（010）59367081　59367083
印　　装 / 三河市龙林印务有限公司

规　　格 / 开　本：787mm × 1092mm　1/16
　　印　张：18.25　字　数：302千字
版　　次 / 2021年1月第1版　2021年1月第1次印刷
书　　号 / ISBN 978 -7 -5201 -6957 -8
定　　价 / 78.00元

本书如有印装质量问题，请与读者服务中心（010 -59367028）联系